Dictionary of Latin American Cultural Studies

UNIVERSITY PRESS OF FLORIDA

Florida A&M University, Tallahassee
Florida Atlantic University, Boca Raton
Florida Gulf Coast University, Ft. Myers
Florida International University, Miami
Florida State University, Tallahassee
New College of Florida, Sarasota
University of Central Florida, Orlando
University of Florida, Gainesville
University of North Florida, Jacksonville
University of South Florida, Tampa
University of West Florida, Pensacola

Dictionary of Latin American Cultural Studies

EDITED BY

ROBERT MCKEE IRWIN

AND MÓNICA SZURMUK

University Press of Florida

Gainesville · Tallahassee · Tampa · Boca Raton

Pensacola · Orlando · Miami · Jacksonville · Ft. Myers · Sarasota

Printed in the United States of America on acid-free paper

First cloth printing, 2012
First paperback printing, 2014

Diccionario de estudios culturales latinoamericanos. English
Dictionary of Latin American cultural studies / edited by Robert McKee Irwin, Mónica Szurmuk.
p. cm.
Summary: "A reference work containing 54 entries defining and explaining generally accepted cultural studies terms as well as those specific to the study of Latin American culture"— Provided by publisher.
Includes bibliographical references and index.
ISBN 978-0-8130-3758-5 (cloth: acid-free paper)
ISBN 978-0-8130-6087-3 (pbk.)
1. Latin America—Civilization—Dictionaries. 2. Latin America—Intellectual life—Dictionaries. 3. Culture—Dictionaries. I. Irwin, Robert McKee, 1962- II. Szurmuk, Mónica. III. Title.
F1408.3.D5513 2012
980.003—dc23
2011037513

The University Press of Florida is the scholarly publishing agency for the State University System of Florida, comprising Florida A&M University, Florida Atlantic University, Florida Gulf Coast University, Florida International University, Florida State University, New College of Florida, University of Central Florida, University of Florida, University of North Florida, University of South Florida, and University of West Florida.

University Press of Florida
15 Northwest 15th Street
Gainesville, FL 32611-2079
http://www.upf.com

Contents

Acknowledgments

We are grateful to our Spanish language publishers Siglo XXI and the Instituto Mora, along with institutional sponsors UC-MEXUS, for helping us get this project off the ground. We are also indebted to the Instituto Mora and Chancellor's Fellowship funding from the University of California, Davis, along with the patient efforts of the volume's authors, for making possible the translations to English and the minor revisions made to the original Spanish-language text. Formal feedback from Ignacio Sánchez Prado and Ana del Sarto, as well as more informal comments from Néstor García Canclini and Benjamín Juárez Echenique, helped us to rethink various details regarding the project's constitution. Logistically, we would have been lost without the help of Ruth Halvey, Julia Morales, Isabel Porras, Ana Rodas, and especially Karl Zoller, who helped with details regarding proofreading, copyediting, and reconciliation of bibliographies, and Jinni Prudhan, who aided with final proofreading and indexing. Special thanks are also due to Amy Gorelick of the University Press of Florida for her patient and wise editorial guidance and to Ann Marlowe for her meticulous copyediting.

Introduction

ROBERT MCKEE IRWIN AND MÓNICA SZURMUK

As with any exercise in taxonomy, this dictionary is an attempt to codify, unify, and put in order. The coordinators of this project seek to infuse life into this taxonomy via a portrait of a moment in the history of Latin American cultural studies. This dictionary took shape long distance, transnationally, and with the collaboration of scholars from diverse disciplines, living and working all across the American hemisphere. The enthusiasm with which authors from different countries, disciplines, generations, and work situations signed on to our project is reflected in the richness and diversity of the entries they authored. This edition, it should be noted, is a translation from the original Spanish-language edition, published in 2009 in Mexico City by Siglo XXI and Instituto Mora. Most of the definitions have been made more concise, and six new entries have been added: Anthropophagy, Audience, Digital Culture, Ethics, Tropicália, and Violence. We hope that these additions help to make this volume more representative of the work being carried out under the rubric of cultural studies among Latin Americans and Latin Americanist scholars.

The term "cultural studies" is used to refer to a broad range of interdisciplinary research methodologies, and in this dictionary that concerns itself specifically with the multifaceted project known as Latin American cultural studies, that breadth is evident. The fifty-four definitions of key terms here offered—forty-eight of them from the original Spanish edition, and the six new ones—arise from within a range of intellectual paradigms that we consider fundamental for those interested in the field.

This is the first English-language dictionary specifically targeted to specialists in Latin American cultural studies. Other cultural studies references that have been published in English have limited themselves to an Anglophone context—usually Britain, the United States, Australia, Canada—and have been ignorant of Latin American intellectual production and debates. Several of the terms included in this dictionary ("lettered city," "transculturation") have genealogies that are very specifically Latin American, while other more universal terms ("subalternism," "memory") have established significant trajectories in Latin Americanist contexts. In selecting terms to include in this project, we have privileged those that are of consequence in the field of Latin American cultural studies, and that function as important references for cultural studies scholars working on the region. Terms that, although important, did not seem to cross disciplinary boundaries with much flexibility, or did not come up frequently within debates in the field, are omitted. In general, each entry consists of a summary of the term's meanings and uses within cultural studies in general, a discussion of its particular significance and applications in Latin American cultural studies, and finally a list of basic readings on the topic. We have also included a general bibliography, which can be used as a reference resource for the field.

The emphasis in the entries is on the genealogy of the terms as well as their influence on the praxis of cultural studies in the context of Latin America. We are particularly interested in highlighting the trajectory of Latin American cultural studies along with its political (left-wing, anti-hegemonic) and transformative potential—an interest that in fact is long established in Latin American cultural criticism. The other fundamental characteristic of Latin American cultural studies is its special interest in traditionally marginalized cultures (or subcultures), including those of subaltern groups or of communities that have suffered discrimination due to prejudices of race, gender, sexual preference, and so forth, and its focus on every kind of cultural expression from the most refined elite forms to the most banal genres of mass culture, along with all categories of popular cultural expression.

In this introduction, we will present a brief overview of the field, noting its genealogies and describing its current state both in Latin America and in the Anglophone academy, especially that of the United States, where activity in Latin American cultural studies has assumed such a prominent status in worldwide markets of ideas that U.S.-based Latin Americanists have been accused of appropriating the role of arbiters of the field (Richard).

Genealogies

Cultural studies emerged as an interdisciplinary field in the Anglophone world in the 1950s and 1960s as part of a movement to democratize the academy's treatment of culture. In Latin America, the use of the concept of "cultural studies" is much more recent. Although this Latin American strain is informed by the British tradition, it also builds on another, autochthonous tradition, that of the Latin American essay of the nineteenth and twentieth centuries (note that our view of this genealogy closely follows that of Sarto, Ríos, and Trigo; for a selection of key texts, see Zea). An important objective of this dictionary is to review the range of themes and issues that make up what might be called, as an umbrella term, Latin American cultural studies at the beginning of the twenty-first century.

Cultural studies asserts itself as a diverse, interdisciplinary, and political field of academic inquiry and critique. In Latin America the field's political roots can be traced to the traditional Marxism of the 1930s, which took on institutional form with the Cuban revolution of 1959 and subsequent revolutionary movements in the 1960s and 1970s. These movements created a continental narrative that imagined Latin America as a whole, and that made one of its central concerns the relationship between culture and political destinies. The mark of culture—most especially literature—on Latin America's revolutionary movements is substantial. Although other cultural products did not achieve the same international visibility as Latin America's literary Boom, and Mexican *muralismo*, this link between revolutionary politics and artistic production is also evident in dramatic works, popular music, film, and other areas of the arts of the era. Debates on the relationship between literature and revolution, such as that arising from the Padilla case of 1971, interpellated intellectuals and artists throughout the continent to define themselves in both intellectual and political terms.

The genealogy of Latin American cultural studies is multiple. One might think of its formation as a process of constant retroalignment among different groups from civil society, modes of popular culture, cultural institutions, nation-states, and currents of continental and international thought. Some key moments in the development of Latin American cultural studies are:

- the tradition of the Latin American essay of the nineteenth and twentieth centuries
- the Latin American reception of texts of the Frankfurt School, the Birmingham Center for Contemporary Cultural Studies, French poststructuralism, and Italian Marxism (especially the works of Antonio Gramsci)
- the horizontal (South-South) relationship with intellectual developments and projects from other geographic areas, such as subaltern studies and postcolonial studies
- the development of a Latin American cultural studies agenda in the United States, where cultural studies took cues from social movements of identity politics: feminism, Chicano and African

American civil rights movements, gay and lesbian activism, all of which played important roles in the incorporation of critical theory and a general questioning of canons and epistemologies into academic debates, as well as from the participation of Latin American academics who came to work in U.S. universities

Rather than discussing the ins and outs of this genealogy, which we have outlined elsewhere (Szurmuk and Irwin, "Presentación" 11–19; see also Sarto, Ríos, and Trigo), we will focus our attention on where it has led.

Latin American Cultural Studies in Its Institutionalization

Cultural Studies entered into critical debate among Latin American critics and Latin Americanists working abroad in the 1980s and 1990s, a period of some major cultural, political, and intellectual shifts that seemed to draw attentions to the inadequacies of the prevailing paradigms of disciplinary inquiry. This period saw the fall of oppressive military dictatorships, truces in many countries that had been rife with guerrilla warfare for decades, the advent of neoliberalism as a major trend in economic policy, the rise of the global narcotics trade, and a surge in migrations and displacements of people. As an interdisciplinary endeavor with many different theoretical practices, it is fair to say that most Latin American intellectuals in the humanities and qualitative social sciences came into dialogue (or actively refused to come into dialogue) with some configuration of cultural studies by the end of the millennium—although many key figures affiliated with cultural studies had been translated and read widely in the region for many years (Stuart Hall, Fredric Jameson, Edward Said). Some of the key participants in these debates spoke from Latin America (Raúl Antelo, Santiago Castro Gómez, Néstor García Canclini, Alejandro Grimson, Ricardo Kaliman, Jesús Martín Barbero, Daniel Mato, Renato Ortiz, Aníbal Quijano, Rossana Reguillo, Nelly Richard, Beatriz Sarlo, José Manuel Valenzuela Arce), while others, some born and/or trained in Latin America, some not, spoke from metropolitan centers abroad, mostly in the United States (Arturo Arias, John Beverley, Sara Castro-Klarén, Román de la Campa, Jean Franco, Francine Masiello, Walter Mignolo, Sylvia Molloy, Mabel Moraña, Alberto Moreiras, Mary Louise Pratt, Ileana Rodríguez, Doris Sommer, George Yúdice) (see, for example, *Revista Iberoamericana* nos. 193 and 203). The large presence of Latin American intellectuals in the U.S. academy, in particular, and the intersections of their interests with debates on multiculturalism, democratization of culture, neoliberal politics, and minority cultures sparked lively debates that encouraged a diverse corpus of cultural studies. These debates took place with an ever changing cast of players, but with many clear protagonists (including all those mentioned above) on conference panels at the Latin American Studies Association congresses, at specialized conferences and symposiums in both North and South America, in special issues of journals, in anthologies from such publishers as the Instituto Internacional de Literatura Iberoamericana in Pittsburgh or the independent Cuarto Propio in Chile, through collaborative research projects, and in monographs authored by these same scholars in which they cited, disputed, concurred with, questioned, or reformulated the ideas of their interlocutors. While almost everyone agreed on the idea of fomenting a focus on culture broadly defined, dialogue and collaboration across disciplinary boundaries, politicized academic inquiry, antielitist cultural criticism, theoretically informed analysis, and challenges to cultural and political hierarchies of all kinds—that is, what could be said to be the defining tenets of cultural studies—very often these debates were about cultural studies itself and whether this critical paradigm, imported as it was from England and trendy as it had become in the U.S. academy, was an appropriate one for Latin America.

By the new millennium, these debates were leaving institutional traces as the field of cultural studies began to consolidate itself in Latin America and among Latin Americanists. However, the institutionalization of the field has been quite uneven and in many ways quite haphazard. As a number of the scholars who set the stage are reaching the tail end of their careers, a new generation, often trained by those scholars, are entering into positions within the academy from which they are capable of following up and applying key conclusions drawn from the debates of the 1990s to their own institutional spaces, through curriculum change, the foundation of programs, formation of professional networks and associations, and interventions into academic journals and book publishing. Yet despite its sometimes rapid and highly visible institutionalization, in many spaces cultural studies remains at the margins or, worse, an embattled concept, condemned by disciplinary purists.

In Latin America there has been a proliferation of new graduate programs in cultural studies, including doctorates at Universidad Andina Simón Bolívar in Quito and Universidad de Costa Rica in San José and master's degree programs at many more universities in such countries as Peru, Chile, Argentina, and Mexico. Bogotá alone now has three graduate programs in cultural studies at some of Colombia's most prestigious universities, Universidad Nacional de Colombia, Pontificia Universidad Javeriana, and Universidad de los Andes. Many of these institutions founded their cultural studies graduate programs as part of a process of expanding graduate education in general; fields defined in interdisciplinary terms are particularly attractive to administrators who lack funds to open programs in every discipline and see cultural studies as a way to bring in students with backgrounds in multiple areas of the humanities and social sciences. However, in many places—particularly in large institutions that already have well-established graduate programs—cultural studies has been unable to make inroads (see Szurmuk and Irwin, "Los estudios culturales"). In countries like Argentina, much of whose academy is structured through *cátedras*, pedagogical and research units have centered around a handful of institutionally powerful senior professors. Cultural studies enters those spaces, defined in traditional disciplinary terms (literature, communications, anthropology), only when one of these senior professors permits it, and then only within the limits of that professor's own *cátedra*. Likewise, strong disciplinary programs at universities like the Universidad Nacional Autónoma de México or the Pontificia Universidad Católica de Chile are well known for stubbornly resisting change and jealously defending territory.

Meanwhile in the United States, which served for the most part as the conduit for the arrival of cultural studies to Latin America, and where cultural studies—sometimes in a watered-down (read: "apolitical") form—has been booming for years as a field within academic publishing, the presence of degree programs is rare. The few programs that have been established at such institutions as Claremont Graduate University, George Mason University, Bowling Green State University, and the University of Hawaii have been popular with students but have not made sufficient impact to encourage the establishment of new programs in the U.S. academy. While some such programs, including those at the University of Pittsburgh and the University of California, Davis, have welcomed Latin Americanists, much cultural studies work in the United States has been U.S.-focused. Latin Americanists most often earn their Ph.D.s in a traditional discipline and then find jobs in that discipline. While many would locate their work, including both research and teaching, under the rubric of cultural studies, few are formally trained in cultural studies or have any affiliation with a cultural studies program.

The typical location of cultural studies in the United States, as well as in many Latin American universities, is within traditional disciplines, especially literature (Spanish, Portuguese, or occasionally Comparative Literature in the United States: see Irwin and Szurmuk), anthropology, communications, sociology, history, film studies, or art history. Disciplinary programs increasingly tolerate cultural studies work, and sometimes even seek it out, as it tends to better reflect contemporary interests and intellectual preoccupations of students—meaning higher enrollments for departments. All disciplines mentioned above have indeed been transformed in one way or another by cultural studies. Once-rigid curricula in, for example, literary analysis and canons, or regional histories and methodologies of historiography, have become more flexible to allow for more interdisciplinary, less elitist, or more diverse perspectives; still, the incorporation of cultural studies—its genealogies, its theories, its methodologies and practices, its approaches to interdisciplinarity, fundamental elements of a cultural studies curriculum in dedicated programs—is never realized in a cohesive, organized manner. Complaints that cultural studies in the United States exhibits poor scholarship have sometimes been justified, although the issue for many practitioners is that they have had to improvise training; they are encouraged to engage in cultural studies work because it sells, it attracts students, and it makes sense for the treatment of many contemporary phenomena, but they must devise their own formation in the theories and methodologies to carry out cultural-studies-oriented projects.

So, while research and pedagogy affiliated with or strongly influenced by the intellectual project of cultural studies appear to be ubiquitous in both the Latin American academy and in Latin Americanist academic spaces in the United States, the new generation of cultural studies practitioners, with only a few exceptions nearly all located in Latin America, has failed to accommodate its paradigms in a rigorous and undiluted form within the institutional spaces in which they work.

On the other hand, while some journals associated with early debates in the field, such as the Argentine *Punto de Vista* or Chile's *Revista de Crítica Cultural*, have run their course, newer interdisciplinary journals such as Colombia's *Tabula Rasa* and *Nómadas*, Venezuela's *Estudios*, the Chilean *Bifurcaciones*, Brazil's *Fênix*, Mexico's *Estudios Fronterizos*, Ecuador's *Comentario Internacional*, *Intercambio* in Costa Rica, and *Anclajes* in Argentina have taken on the politicized interdisciplinary perspective of cultural studies, as have U.S.-based journals such as *Revista Iberoamericana*, *Istmo*,

A Contracorriente, *Chasqui*, and *Ciberletras*—along with, of course, Britain's venerable but bizarrely monolingual *Journal of Latin American Cultural Studies*.

Likewise, monographs and anthologies that fall clearly under the rubric of Latin American cultural studies continue to be published throughout the hemisphere. The recent publication of edited anthologies including Ana del Sarto, Alicia Ríos, and Abril Trigo's *Latin American Cultural Studies Reader*, Stephen Hart and Richard Young's *Contemporary Latin American Cultural Studies*, Danny Anderson and Jill Kuhnheim's *Cultural Studies in the Curriculum: Teaching Latin America*, and Sara Castro-Klarén's *A Companion to Latin American Literature and Culture*, along with Mabel Moraña's *Nuevas perspectivas desde/sobre América Latina: El desafío de los estudios culturales*, Catherine Walsh's *Estudios culturales latinoamericanos: Retos desde y sobre la región andina*, Daniel Mato's *Cultura, política y sociedad: Perspectivas latinoamericanas*, Ignacio Sánchez Prado's *América Latina: Giro óptico*, Santiago Castro Gómez and Eduardo Mendieta's *Teorías sin disciplina: Latinoamericanismo, poscolonialidad y globalización en debate*, José Manuel Valenzuela Arce's *Los estudios culturales en México*, and our own *Diccionario de estudios culturales latinoamericanos*, along with countless more specialized anthologies and monographs on such topics as postcolonialism, alterity, cultural consumption, memory, violence, cultural diversity, new media, cultural participation, performance, and deterritorializations, have served to consolidate the field as a category of knowledge production without laying solid foundations for its long-term self-preservation.

In universities where cultural studies programs have attained their own institutional space, they often encounter resentment among traditional disciplines that must compete with them for scarce resources, and jealousy of cultural studies' popularity among students, many of whom enroll in programs without knowing exactly what cultural studies is about, but eager to engage in studies that are not rigidly limited by what they may see as outdated or arbitrary disciplinary boundaries, and that seem to be more relevant that disciplinary paradigms for addressing contemporary social, political, and cultural issues. In universities where the field has accommodated itself within traditional disciplines, cultural studies scholars often coexist with their discipline-bound colleagues in a fragile state of truce in which the discipline allows cultural studies space as it happily absorbs its students, but tacitly prohibits cultural studies from establishing a coherent curricular presence.

It is also interesting to note the tenuous relationship of what we are calling Latin American cultural studies (cultural studies realized from or about Latin America) with larger constructions of cultural studies as a field or discipline. In the United States, Latin Americanists' participation in the Cultural Studies Association, the field's national professional organization, has been minimal; indeed, among the fifteen current senior officers and members of the organization's executive committee, there is one Latin Americanist. On the global level, Latin Americans and Latin Americanists have also been mostly marginal players at the International Association for Cultural Studies. For example, the organization's 2010 biannual conference in Hong Kong featured, among its ten key speakers, multiple participants from the Asia Pacific region, Europe, and the United States, but only one, Catherine Walsh of the Universidad Andina Simón Bolívar in Quito, from Latin America, while its current governing board includes five European representatives, four each from Asia and North America, and two each from Australia/New Zealand, Africa, and Latin America (Eduardo Restrepo of Pontificia Universidad Javeriana in Bogotá and Rosario Radakovich of Universidad de la República in Montevideo).

Our interpretation of Latin America's marginal status in these professional cultural studies organizations is that Latin American cultural studies, while sharing part of its critical genealogy, methodologies and practices, and key areas of inquiry with cultural studies as it is practiced elsewhere in the world, is distinct enough to be considered as its own paradigm. The preeminence of English as the lingua franca of cultural studies has also limited the impact of Latin American cultural studies in the professional cultural studies associations. Clearly the most important venues for presenting work in Latin American cultural studies have been the Latin American Studies Association's congresses, which bring together Latin Americanists from throughout the Americas (although the organization has been accused of being U.S.-centric), implying that scholars working in Latin American cultural studies find more productive dialogue with sociologists, literary critics, political scientists, historians, film scholars, anthropologists, or even economists specialized in Latin America than with cultural studies scholars who have little or no interest in Latin America. This segregationist pattern both reflects and reinforces existing hierarchies of knowledge production in global markets of ideas.

In addition, an argument might be made that cultural studies in Latin America has insisted much more than in the United States on retaining the project's political vocation. The doctorate in Latin American cultural studies at the Universidad Andina Simón Bolívar in Ecuador, considered by many the model program for the region, indeed aims "to build new critical communities of thought, interpretation, *and intervention*" in a "space of encounter between disciplines and intellectual, *political* and ethical projects" (Walsh, "Shifting" 233, emphasis ours). A recent symposium featuring key players in cultural studies in Latin America, including participants from Ecuador, Brazil, Argentina, Mexico, Colombia, Peru, and Costa Rica, titled "Estudios Culturales en las Américas: Compromiso, Colaboración, Transformación" (http://estudiosculturales.ucdavis.edu/people/), debated strategies for ensuring collaborations between cultural studies scholars and political and social movements even as the field becomes more deeply entrenched in institutional academic structures in Latin America (see *Tabula Rasa* 12).

This dictionary is a tool for both research and pedagogy in Latin American cultural studies, and a consultation source for other (non–Latin Americanist) cultural studies scholars interested in learning from the contributions of Latin Americanists to the field. We hope that its publication will help to more firmly establish the field within the Anglophone academy, and to strengthen the position of Latin American cultural studies in global contexts.

Suggested Reading

Anderson, Danny J., and Jill S. Kuhnheim, eds. *Cultural Studies in the Curriculum: Teaching Latin America*. New York: Modern Language Association, 2003.

Castro Gómez, Santiago, and Eduardo Mendieta, eds. *Teorías sin disciplina: Latinoamericanismo, poscolonialidad y globalización en debate*. Mexico City: Miguel Ángel Porrúa, 1998. www.ensayistas.org/critica/teoria/castro/.

Castro-Klaren, Sara, ed. *A Companion to Latin American Literature and Culture*. Malden, Mass.: Blackwell, 2008.

Hart, Stephen, and Richard Young, eds. *Contemporary Latin American Cultural Studies*. London: Hodder Arnold, 2003.

Irwin, Robert McKee, and Mónica Szurmuk. "Cultural Studies and the Field of 'Spanish' in the US Academy." *A Contracorriente* 6, no. 3 (2009): 36–60.

Mato, Daniel, ed. *Cultura, política y sociedad: Perspectivas latinoamericanas*. Buenos Aires: CLACSO, 2005. http://bibliotecavirtual.clacso.org.ar/ar/libros/grupos/mato/cultura.htm.

Moraña, Mabel, ed. *Nuevas perspectivas desde/sobre América Latina: El desafío de los estudios culturales*. Pittsburgh, Pa.: Instituto Internacional de Literatura Iberoamericana, 2002.

Richard, Nelly. "Globalización académica, estudios culturales y crítica latinoamericana." In Mato, *Estudios latinoamericanos*, 455–70.

Sánchez Prado, Ignacio M., ed. *América Latina: Giro óptico*. Puebla, Mexico: Universidad de las Américas/Gobierno del Estado de Puebla, 2006.

Sarto, Ana del, Alicia Ríos, and Abril Trigo, eds. *The Latin American Cultural Studies Reader*. Durham, N.C.: Duke University Press, 2004.

Szurmuk, Mónica, and Robert McKee Irwin, eds. *Diccionario de estudios culturales latinoamericanos*. Mexico City: Siglo XXI/Instituto Mora, 2009.

———. "Los estudios culturales en programas de postgrado en América Latina: Propuestas pedagógicas y metodológicas." *Tabula Rasa* 10 (2009): 49–75.

———. "Presentación." In Szurmuk and Irwin, *Diccionario*, 9–42.

Valenzuela Arce, José Manuel, ed. *Los estudios culturales en México*. Mexico City: Fondo de Cultura Económica, 2003.

Walsh, Catherine, ed. *Estudios culturales latinoamericanos: Retos desde y sobre la región andina*. Quito: Universidad Andina Simón Bolívar/Abya Yala, 2003.

———. "Shifting the Geopolitics of Critical Knowledge: Decolonial Thought and Cultural Studies 'Others' in the Andes." *Cultural Studies* 21, no. 2 (2007): 224–39.

Zea, Leopoldo, ed. *Fuentes de la cultura latinoamericana*. 3 vols. Mexico City: Fondo de Cultura Económica, 1993.

Aesthetics

KATE JENCKES AND PATRICK DOVE

"Aesthetics" comes from the Greek word *aisthanumai*, which refers to sense perception. The term was recuperated in the eighteenth century by German philosophers to designate a theory of perception that related especially to the beautiful and the frightening; subsequently, the term came to be associated with artistic experience (perception, intuition, and representation). One of the most influential texts on aesthetic theory is Friedrich Schiller's *On the Aesthetic Education of Man* (1794), which proposes an ideal connection between the individual and the state mediated through aesthetic experience. For Schiller, aesthetic experience is capable of uniting the spheres of the sensible and the rational, and the particular and the universal, in such a way as to resist the growing fragmentation of the human condition in the modern era. Schiller's ideas about aesthetic education were appropriated in nineteenth-century liberalism by influential Spanish American intellectuals such as Esteban Echeverría, and had strong repercussions in several instances in the twentieth century in which art and culture were considered pillars of the nation-state.

In Latin America, aesthetic questions lay at the heart of educated criollos' search for a national or regional identity that would not be a mere imitation of European culture. Efforts to found an autochthonous artistic culture increased at the end of the nineteenth century and in the first decades of the twentieth century with movements such as *modernismo* and *vanguardismo*, which in spite of their strong European influences represented attempts to establish an artistic style that would be properly Latin American. The desire to identify new origins of Latin American culture is also evident in the cultural populism developed after the Mexican revolution by figures such as José Vasconcelos and Diego Rivera. The flurry of narratives produced in the middle of the twentieth century, known as the Boom, could be said to constitute a kind of synthesis of these different movements, by weaving together original and unique representations of some of the varied currents of Latin American culture and history. While proponents of such literary and artistic movements endeavored to create forms of expression that would be specifically Latin American, their critics argued that they ended up ignoring, excluding, or appropriating the heterogeneous experiences of the Americas in order to create cultural objects whose intended audience was in Europe or the Eurocentric metropolitan centers of the Americas.

This is an explicit tendency in one of the foundational texts of modern Latin American aesthetics, *Ariel* (1900), by the Uruguayan José Enrique Rodó. In this essay, the author exhorts the "youth of America" to embark on a new stage of Latin American history, starting from an aesthetic education that would establish the basis of social and political values in relation to a notion of art as ideal representation. This ideal is rooted in elements of German philosophy that attribute to art the qualities of being universal, reasonable, disinterested, and spiritual. Rodó contrasts this ideal, embodied by the character Ariel in Shakespeare's *The Tempest*, with the materialism, personal interest, and irrationality of the character Caliban. Rodó employs this opposition to justify an antidemocratic hierarchy in which the social and cultural elites of Latin America would have hegemony over the poor and illiterate; furthermore, he advocates the spiritual superiority of Latin Americans over North Americans, who, according to him, lack cultural and artistic sensibility.

Such an opposition between culture and materialism turned out not to be sustainable in twentieth-century Latin America, where heterogeneous social and historical forces tended to interrupt attempts to establish universal notions of culture. *Ariel* represents an extreme view that was mostly left behind by the main literary and artistic movements of the twentieth century, which readily incorporated any number of "material" elements that Rodó would have found distasteful: for example, representations of technology, mass culture, ruptured language, and mixes of cultures and discourses. Nevertheless, many works that attempted to represent the heterogeneous forces of the Americas ended up appropriating them and neutralizing their difference with respect to hegemonic structures.

The second half of the twentieth century witnessed renewed attempts to define Latin American culture beyond the purely artistic endeavors of the preceding years. A paradigmatic expression of this redefinition appears in the essay "Calibán" (1971) by the Cuban writer Roberto Fernández Retamar, in which the author explicitly rejects the hierarchy posited by Rodó and suggests that the symbol that best corresponds to the experience of Latin America is exemplified not in Ariel but in Caliban. In *The Tempest*, Caliban is a slave who chooses not to follow the master's commands, as Ariel does, but instead rebels, using the language the master has taught him in order to curse him. Fernández Retamar suggests that this portrait represents the true cultural heritage of the continent, and he lists political and cultural figures from Rubén Darío to Che Guevara who contributed to a cultural politics of rebellion, hewn from the tools of the European and North American "masters." The figure of Caliban evokes a material reality that dominant powers cannot idealize or eliminate.

If hopes of creating forms of culture and politics that would reflect material realities and lived experiences of Latin America strengthened after the 1950s, the following decades saw brutal suppressions of such possibilities. As a result of the civil wars in Central America, the repression of popular protests in Mexico, and the rise of brutal military regimes in many South American countries, artists, writers, and intellectuals throughout Latin America were forced to question their roles and their place in the world. These intellectuals felt compelled to seek new forms of representation and new spaces of thought and creation, given that traditional structures were being eliminated or appropriated by official discourse. These new forms included mass media, such as cinema and popular music, as well as media more traditionally associated with art and literature. Film, it was felt, promised to change perceptions and expand consciousness to places beyond the reach of metropolitan intellectuals. Popular music, both folkloric and rock, combined political denunciation with poetic lyrics and rhythm and melody. Visual art was radicalized, leaving the protected enclaves of the museum or gallery and bursting into public spaces with sculptures made from the detritus of modern life, or in performance pieces that were designed to shock and confuse the norms and distinctions that ordered national imaginaries.

Elena Poniatowska, Carlos Monsiváis, Nelly Richard, and Beatriz Sarlo are some of the most prominent figures to produce texts that function as both analytical and cultural interventions during these years. Their works effectively changed the direction of aesthetic thought and production in Latin America by integrating elements from a variety of genres, including chronicles, journalism, fiction, sociology, psychoanalysis, political activism, and visual arts. Furthermore, they have played important roles in the formation of public opinion on cultural production and on sociopolitical events in their own countries and in Latin America as a whole, and made significant contributions to the field of cultural criticism on an international level.

In Mexico, Elena Poniatowska and Carlos Monsiváis recuperated the chronicle as a means of denouncing the simultaneous repression of popular sectors and the privatization of the state in Mexico following the turbulence of 1968. Poniatowska's *La noche de Tlatelolco* (1971) represents the first such use of this form. The book is a montage that incorporates different materials and media, including interviews with participants of the student movements who were repressed by the Mexican army, as well as with government officials responsible for organizing the repression.

In his own unique manner, Monsiváis also tends to employ the structure of montage to denounce corruption and incompetence of the Mexican state in relation to natural disasters and the forces of late capitalism, and as a way of vindicating minor triumphs of the oppressed. A noteworthy example is *Entrada libre: Crónicas de una sociedad que se organiza* (1987), a collection of essayistic chronicles that address a series of social ruptures characterized by a state that abandoned its role of reconciling social conflicts. The chronicles aim, through a "polycentric and performative" mode of writing (Kraniauskas xiii), to mark the emergence of new conjunctures within the temporalities of late capitalism.

Since the 1980s, Nelly Richard has developed a distinctive essayistic and editorial style in her own publications as well as in her role as founder and editor of the influential (but now defunct) journal *Revista de Crítica Cultural*. Focusing on Chile during and after the Pinochet dictatorship, her work explores the capacity of artistic and literary productions to resist and subvert power. Although ideologically aligned with the left, Richard has stressed repeatedly how certain forms of artistic, literary, and critical representation provide an important alterative to traditional leftist political and academic discourses, which tend to reproduce the hierarchies and totalizing schemes of the structures they aim to critique. Influenced by Michel Foucault, Roland Barthes, and the Argentine journals *Contorno* and *Punto de vista*, among other sources, Richard has promoted a form of essayistic writing that combines observations about art, society, popular culture, urban space, and gender, and that stresses micropolitics and fragments alongside major political and social events.

In Argentina, Beatriz Sarlo developed a critical style that bears its own distinguishing characteristics. Both as editor of the journal *Punto de vista* and in her own writing, Sarlo has sought to probe the historical and material bases of Argentine cultural production, interrogating both the conception of cultural autonomy and the instrumentality of art presumed by political "commitment." Influenced by English cultural materialism and French sociology, among other sources, her work has sought to demythologize a homogeneous notion of Argentine culture, focusing on social and historical margins, and on the cultural and experiential paradoxes of late capitalism.

While the critical forms advanced by these writers have a great deal in common with cultural studies, they have expressed their differences with cultural studies as practiced in North American academic circles since the 1990s. Richard, for example, acknowledges the importance of the Latin American cultural studies movement in its attempt to decentralize the notion of culture from its monumental and hegemonic form, by increasing the visibility of the multiple manifestations of culture in a given society, and by underscoring underlying tensions between culture and ideology, history, aesthetics, economics, politics, and social inscription. Nevertheless, she has criticized the enthusiasm with which North American academics adopted cultural studies as a way of bypassing Latin American intellectual discourse in order to get at a cultural-material "truth" of Latin Americanness. She urges critics to focus on the singular aspects of culture and experience in Latin America, concentrating on the form or style of those singularities, which are capable of resisting capture by the normative and totalizing discourse characteristic of academic investigations. For her part, Sarlo shares Richard's suspicions vis-à-vis the implicit marginalization of Latin America in metropolitan cultural studies, but the solution she proposes is different. Basing herself on a particular interpretation of the Frankfurt School, Sarlo rejects mass media as revealing texts about culture and society, and demands a return to a critical discourse based on aesthetic value and national literary traditions, in spite of the apparent normativity and conservatism that such a gesture would provoke.

The ideas expressed by Richard and Sarlo about cultural studies point to a significant tension between cultural production and criticism and the category of the aesthetic, a tension that has been largely forgotten in the turn to cultural studies over the past few decades. The change of focus in the study of culture from traditional institutions of art and literature to popular or mass culture does not guarantee that the new focus will be able to maintain critical distance from aesthetic and culturalist ideologies that served as the basis of older forms of criticism. To the extent that cultural studies reproduces a concept of culture as plenitude or as depository of social values, it will continue to be either too aestheticist or not aesthetic enough. The future of cultural studies depends on how it responds to an internal tension that has marked and divided it since its inception: on one hand, a desire to critique aesthetic ideology and its complicity with structures of domination and normativity, and on the other, a search to affirm materiality—even within language—as a necessary condition for any relation between subject and world.

Suggested Reading

Franco, Jean. *The Decline and Fall of the Lettered City: Latin America in the Cold War*. Cambridge, Mass.: Harvard University Press, 2002.

González Stephan, Beatriz, ed. *Cultura y tercer mundo*. Caracas: Nueva Sociedad, 1996.

Herlinghaus, Hermann, and Monika Walters, eds. *Posmodernidad en la periferia: Enfoques latinoamericanos de la nueva teoría cultural*. Berlin: Langer, 1994.

Kraniauskas, John. "Critical Closeness: The Chronicle-Essays of Carlos Monsiváis." In *Mexican Postcards*, by Carlos Monsiváis, ix–xxii. London: Verso, 1997.

Monsiváis, Carlos. *Entrada libre: Crónicas de la sociedad que se organiza*. Mexico City: Era, 1987.

———. *Mexican Postcards*. Translated and introduced by John Kraniauskas. London: Verso, 1997.

Ramírez, Mari Carmen, and Héctor Olea. *Inverted Utopias: Avant-garde in Latin America*. New Haven, Conn.: Yale University Press, 2004.

Richard, Nelly, ed. "La crítica: revistas literarias, académicas y culturales." Special issue, *Revista de Crítica Cultural*, no. 31 (2005).

Sarlo, Beatriz. "El relativismo absoluto o cómo el mercado y la sociología reflexionan sobre la estética." *Punto de Vista*, no. 48 (1994): 27–31.

Alterity

SILVANA RABINOVICH (TRANSLATED BY EDUARDO RABASA)

The temptation to define the concept of Otherness has been a constant of Western thought. Such aim can be read as the confession of a certain chimeric impulse that is found among the sharpest pens of the history of philosophy (the pretension to identify Otherness through the language of Sameness is revealed as a—perhaps irresistible—chimera). From the German trenches of the First World War, the Jewish-German philosopher Franz Rosenzweig asserted that the expression "everything is" has been, since Thales of Miletus, the repetitive philosophical gesture that tried to reduce Otherness to Sameness, "from Jonia to Jena." The verb "to be," since the meaning that Parmenides—for whom being is identity—assigned to it, works as an identification device that seeks to suppress difference. What has been so far stated here is a warning to dissuade those who seek in this entry a definition of Otherness. What follows here are some notes that allude to echoes of alterity in certain contemporary thinkers, with an emphasis on the meaning they acquire in Latin America, especially in Mexico and in Guatemala.

The term "other"—*otro*—is multifaceted: it can function as an adjective, a pronoun, a noun; it alludes both to temporality and to an indefinite quality. It indicates repetition and difference, a repetition that differs both in the temporary and in the ontological senses. Among the philosophers who saw a problem in the recurrent attempt to reduce Otherness to Sameness, Friedrich Nietzsche criticized the zeal to subordinate the alterity of singularity in concepts; Jacques Derrida suggested the radical difference on which every conceptual building is installed; Emmanuel Levinas insisted on the Other as a constituent of the subject, precisely so as to never forget the "other," the fellow human. These are only some philosophers who named the Other without attempting to define it, but in the twentieth century, especially since the traumatic experiences of both world wars, there are many more thinkers who share this gesture. For instance, psychoanalysis transformed the identity of the Cartesian subject until it tore it apart. From a dialogical perspective, Mikhail Bakhtin answered "I am too" to Descartes' "I think therefore I am," and Eugen Rosenstock-Huessy "bent the neck" of the Cartesian saying to the point of uttering "respondeo etsi mutabor" (I answer even when I change). In sum, the matter of the fellow man in its alterity is revealed as an imperative in the field of intersubjective relationships and, in the face of this demand that questions the subject's autonomy, the answer to the other's interpellation is displayed as heteronomous ethics. With this transformation of meaning that moves toward heteronomy, the problem resides no more in the limits of the cognoscible (it is no longer about knowing or acknowledging otherness) and it is now about responsibility toward the other. Human are survivors; to speak means to testify in the name of the other.

Emmanuel Levinas (1906–1995) is the philosopher who is most immediately associated with alterity. Born in Lithuania, Levinas was Jewish by descent and French by choice. In *Totality and Infinity* (1961) Levinas defines heteronomous ethics as *prima philosophia*, and takes the other as its starting point. The other is defined in reference to the biblical figures of the poor, the widow, the orphan, and the foreigner. Icons of vulnerability and fault. However, this biblical tetrad is not used to define alterity, but rather to evoke a responsible subjectivity toward the other since time immemorial. Such heteronomous responsibility does not come from the will of the responsible subject, but is instead constitutive of subjectivity. Thus the term "subject"—*sujet*—must be understood as past participle, linked to the "other" by language and time.

Enrique Dussel, an Argentinean philosopher who works in Mexico, translated the heteronomous ethics to the Latin American Philosophy of Liberation. His ethics is heavily indebted to the restlessness brought on by an early reading of *Totality and Infinity.* In *Ética de la liberación*, Dussel draws from Levinas to approximate that "other" inspired in the biblical tetrad to Latin America. Dussel, however, sees alterity as strongly lodged within exclusion. He claims that these "others" are euphemistically called "minorities," even if they are a majority of the population, a name possibly owed to their being considered "minors" in the sense of *infans*. This resonates in the Zapatista Movement's claim of being an ornamental object, a colorful decoration forgotten in a corner of society—but never a human being.

Doris Sommer rereads Dussel's project in *Proceed with Caution When Engaged by Minority Writing in the Americas*, privileging Dussel's interpretation of Levinas and neglecting to see that in Levinas's heteronomous ethics, the "other" still has a voice. Notwithstanding, if the Levinasian "Saying" (in the heteronomous notion of language developed in *Totality*) is displayed as listening to the other, this presumes at least that the other has a voice and words; therefore, this reading of the heteronomous ethics of Levinas through Dussel is problematic.

Levinas's heteronomous ethics does not attempt to become programmatic politics, but when it questions the concept of autonomy, it does become political thought. In Western cultures the obsession with the "other" adopted many forms, which can be summed up in the somewhat parodic question "Why is the other an Other and instead not another I?" In political terms, this translates as war, conquest, colonization, and, when it becomes untenable, as genocide (Todorov).

Poetry has grappled with the issue of otherness. In Rimbaud's words "*Je est un autre*" the object rules over the grammatical subject; the subject becomes a hostage to the object. The grammatical hierarchy is altered, the subject can no longer be distinguished from the object; this poetic expression results in the emergence of the intersubjective within subjectivity itself. The copulative verb loses the reductive meaning of alterity. Rimbaud managed to go further than the social movements' slogan "We are all . . . the other" (" . . . Jews and Germans," said youth and workers during the French protests of May 1968 upon the discrimination suffered by the student leader Daniel Cohn-Bendit; " . . . Marcos," said the Mexicans—others would have preferred to hear "Indians"; "Jews" was the performative word uttered by the Danish government when facing the Third Reich's demand of discriminating "their" Jews with the yellow star).

The first person plural remains obsessed with the autonomous subject. According to Carlos Lenkersdorf, in the Tojolabal language it is possible to say "uno (de nosotros) cometimos un crimen"—"one of us committed a crime"—with an emphasis on "us" and an implication that "we" are responsible. This alludes, as the anthropologist shows, to a conception of the subject that considers the Other within the first person "I" under the mark of responsibility. The Mayas embody the heteronomous ethics: they claim to be in constant contact with the dead, to carry the dead "under their skin."

In a similar vein, Walter Benjamin situates the historian as an heir who is responsible for the injustices of the past. The responsibility toward the dead is unavoidable, and the different voices of alterity agree on this. In this way, his second thesis of the philosophy of history states that not even the dead are out of the grasp of the enemy. In post-civil-war Guatemala in the 1990s, the Maya-Quiché heirs to the disappeared experienced this as a claim for justice.

In philosophical terms there is a resonance of Levinas's heteronomy that states, not that I have a son, but that I am him, as long as we understand the verb "to be" under the sign of plurality, contrary to its univocal meaning. Jorge Luis Borges writes in the poem "Al hijo": "It was not I who begot you. I was the dead" and, later on, in a distant echo of Rimbaud, "I too am those others" (245). Another River Plate area poet, Antonio Porchia, puts it in an aphoristic form, questioning knowledge, which is always an act of faith, even of credulity, in favor of his commitment to life and its future, writing in one of his *Voces*, "If I had thought that the other was the same, my life wouldn't have had any extension." Here, "life" and "extension" are synonyms.

On the occasion of the fifth centenary of the European discovery of America, Roger Bartra wrote a memorable book in which alterity is read both from the point of view of sameness and of otherness. The eloquent title, *El salvaje en el espejo* (*Wild Men in the Looking Glass*), suggests an unexpected reflection that goes full circle around European civilization through the invention of its savage. In his brilliant investigation, the Mexican anthropologist claims he was witnessing the very creation of the notion of the Other:

> The Western obsession with the Other, as an inner experience and as a form of autodefinition, has veiled the presence of other voices, or, put another way, *the Other has concealed the other.* My hope is that, within the scope of Western man's understanding of the mythical nature of the European wild man, he shall be able to confront the history of the third millennium, lessening or even avoiding predictable or unpredictable misfortunes by finally coming to terms with the fact that he might have existed otherwise with less suffering than man suffers today for having abandoned so many alternative paths, paths occasionally evoked in the melancholic voice of the poet or the curiosity of the eccentric scholar. The European wild man reminds us that we might have been something else. (208)

It is alarming to verify that "the Other has concealed the other," that is, that the speculation that seeks to establish the limit between the Same and the Other conceals injustice and even (in a slight variation of Porchia's aphorism) becomes murderous. The border between the Same and the Other is guarded by the illusion of pure identity, enclosed by the "inner experience" in its zeal to define the I. "Inner experience," ignorant of the prefix "ex" that stresses its heteronomous ethics, takes on an empiricist form that reduces the Other to sameness, thus eclipsing the political possibilities of alterity. This overlapping of civilization and savagery drawn by Bartra warns us against the madness of purity—which arrived in America with the conquest in the sixteenth century and which became the cruel sign of the twentieth century. What becomes evident through a careful reading of the texts surveyed in this entry is that sameness as the origin of identity is engendered by the alterity it excludes.

Suggested Reading

Bakhtin, M. M. *The Dialogic Imagination*. Translated by Caryl Emerson and Michael Holquist. Austin: University of Texas Press, 1981.

Bartra, Roger. *El salvaje en el espejo*. Mexico City: UNAM/Era, 1992. Translated by Carl T. Berrisford as *Wild Men in the Looking Glass: The Mythic Origins of European Otherness* (Ann Arbor: University of Michigan Press, 1994).

Benjamin, Walter. *Angelus Novus*. Berlin: Suhrkamp, 1988.

Derrida, Jacques. *Margins of Philosophy*. Translated by Alan Bass. Chicago: University of Chicago Press, 1982.

Dussel, Enrique. *Philosophy of Liberation*. Translated by Aquilina Martinez and Christine Morkovsky. New York: Orbis, 1985.

Ejército Zapatista de Liberación Nacional. "Al Congreso Nacional Indígena: El dolor nos une y nos hace uno." http://palabra.ezln.org.mx/comunicados/2001/2001_03_04.htm.

Lenkersdorf, Carlos. "El mundo del nosotros." In *Lecciones de Extranjería*, edited by Esther Cohen and Ana María Martínez de la Escalera, 147–53. Mexico City: Siglo XXI, 2002.

Levinas, Emmanuel. *Totality and Infinity: An Essay on Exteriority*. Translated by Alphonso Lingis. Pittsburgh, Pa.: Duquesne University Press, 1969.

Nietzsche, Friedrich. "On Truth and Lying in an Extra-Moral Sense." In *Literary Theory: An Anthology*, edited by Julie Rivkin and Michael Ryan, 2nd ed., 262–65. London: Blackwell, 2004.

Rosenstock-Huessy, Eugen. *The Origin of Speech*. Norwich, Vt.: Argo, 1981.

Rosenzweig, Franz. *The Star of Redemption*. Translated by William W. Hallo. New York: Holt, Rinehart, and Winston, 1971.

Sommer, Doris. *Proceed with Caution When Engaged by Minority Writing in the Americas*. Cambridge, Mass.: Harvard University Press, 1999.

Todorov, Tzvetan. *On Human Diversity: Nationalism, Racism, and Exoticism in French Thought*. Translated by Catherine Porter. Cambridge, Mass.: Harvard University Press, 1993.

Anthropophagy

CARLOS JÁUREGUI

Cannibalism, as a trope that sustains the very distinction between savagery and civilization, is a cornerstone of colonialism. However, from the European visions of a savage New World to the (post)colonial and postmodern narratives of contemporary cultural production, the metaphor of cannibalism has been not just a paradigm of otherness but also a trope of self-recognition, a model for the incorporation of difference, and a central concept in the definition of Latin American identities.

The Brazilian modernist anthropophagy movement, elaborated in the late 1920s by Oswald de Andrade (1890–1954) and others in the *Revista de Antropofagia* (1928–1929) and its iconic "Manifesto antropófago" (1928), is a central reference in literary and cultural studies. Canonized as an *avant la lettre* Latin American cultural theory on consumption and a counter-colonial discourse, anthropophagy has become an obligatory genealogical foundation for contemporary academic debates on hybridity and postcolonialism. However, anthropophagy was not an academic movement, a theory of identity formation through consumption, or a social emancipation program. It was a heterogeneous and often contradictory aesthetic venture. As Antônio Cândido indicated in 1970: "It is difficult to say what exactly anthropophagy is, since Oswald never formulated it, although he left enough elements to see some virtual principles under the aphorisms" (84–85, translation ours). So rather than being the only original Brazilian philosophy (A. de Campos), "the most original meta-cultural theory ever produced in Latin America to the present day" (Viveiros de Castro 25, translation ours), a Latin American translation theory (Barbosa and Whyler), or even a counter-colonial proposal (Santiago; Vieira; Cocco), anthropophagy has become these things and more as it has been appropriated, resignified, and transformed; paradoxically consumed and devoured.

The relation of 1928–29 anthropophagy to consumption is less theoretical than symbolic and historical. As Andrade himself recognized, Brazilian modernism originated in the mentality created by São Paulo's industrialist push for an export-oriented capitalism. At the end of the nineteenth century, São Paulo initiated an accelerated process of modernization and urban development based on government-protected coffee exports (Fausto).

Between 1890 and 1920, the population of São Paulo increased from some 65,000 to 580,000 and the city gained a modern face: buildings, electricity, phones, trains, public transportation, automobiles, and social unrest. The development of a labor-intensive industrialization was accompanied by immigration, the growth of an urban proletariat, and an exaggerated enthusiasm for industrial development, all of which occurred within a still predominantly agricultural economy. This enthusiasm for progress had its aesthetic complement in the formation of small groups of cosmopolitan intellectuals, consumers of modern cultural artifacts of Europe and North America. They imagined Brazil to be on the verge of modernity, yet they were confronted with the reality of a country still treading in the waters of underdevelopment. The emblematic Semana de Arte Moderna in 1922 is often cited as the beginning moment of Brazilian modernism, although such origins could be traced to the 1917 debate over Anita Malfatti's expressionist paintings, or even to the controversial reception of futurism in 1910s. The Semana tried to offer a modernizing shock therapy to local literature and arts with a series of events, concerts, exhibits, conferences, and recitals sponsored by millionaires of the coffee economy, such as Paulo Prado. Brazil exported coffee and other raw materials and imported the latest trends of European culture, including futurism, dadaism, cubism, modern architecture, and psychoanalysis, together with expensive cars, fashions, and technological wonders (not to mention cheap labor).

A frantic modernist marathon of events, publications, and conspicuous consumption sought to produce an *aesthetic modernity* by—as Andrade indicated in his earlier "Manifesto de Poesía Pau Brasil" (1924)—synchronizing the outdated neoclassicist clock of national literature and arts trapped by academicism and traditional cultural institutions. Modernization presented both an economic challenge and a cultural dilemma for a lettered elite within an overwhelmingly illiterate society. How to be modern without surrendering one's Brazilian cultural specificity? The definition of national culture was, as throughout Latin America, divided between *cosmopolitanism* and several forms of *localism* marked by nationalistic or regional cultural anxieties. Pau-Brasil had tried to mediate between these two extremes. Assuming the name of the dye-producing brazilwood of early colonial exports, modernists claimed to have "rediscovered Brazil." Baroque architecture, religious festivities, and other local "anachronisms" represented a sort of raw material to be processed by national modern art, using the cosmopolitan aesthetic tools of cubism, cinematographic language, and so on. Pau-Brazilian modernism was supposed to transform the timeless national "native originality" and "innocence" into global cultural commodities: primitivist-yet-modern "poetry for exportation." For Andrade the problem was how to "be regional and pure *in our time*," reconciling localism with modernity, against the problematic archaism of academia and the arts. Like Martín Barbero or García Canclini today, Andrade conceived Latin American modernity as a heterogeneous ensemble of the primitive and the modern: favelas, tacky colors, carnival, shamans, and tropical laziness together with futurist references to airplanes, skyscrapers, and electric turbines. Anticipating anthropophagy, Andrade declared: "Just Brazilians in our own times. . . . Everything digested." Thus, Brazilian modernists embraced a modernity produced by cultural consumption, first of European symbolic goods and then of the vernacular national culture reprocessed with cosmopolitan techniques. Before being a "cannibal," the modernist artist was indeed a cultural consumer with his taste split between the cultural signifiers of Western modernity and those of the local color, with no choice but to embrace the "double and present base" of Brazilian modernity.

Yet modernist cultural consumption was still regarded as a passive stance toward foreign cultural influence. The "digestion" of European suits, books, theories, and high art did not look very Brazilian to many traditionalists, even with the "local spice" of Pau Brasil's master trope. The Recife Group of Gilberto Freyre and José Lins do Rego exalted Luso-African culture and cuisine, rejecting "foreign preserves, Swiss pharmaceuticals, and U.S. novelties" in their "Manifesto regionalista" of 1926. A movement in 1926–29 even called itself Verde-Amarelismo from the green and yellow of the national flag. For Andrade this kind of uber-nationalism basically advocated "the closing of the ports."

As a conceptual character, the *cannibal* evoked imaginary indigenous "origins" for Brazil, inverting the negative connotations of the colonial stereotype and rendering a very "Brazilian" consumer of the foreign. Anthropophagy appears as yet another modernist attempt to offer a symbolic answer to the questions and anxieties posed by both cultural influence and the asynchrony of Brazilian modernity. Not surprisingly, anthropophagy has been seen as a "misplaced idea" and a triumphalist aesthetic interpretation of Brazilian *underdevelopment* (Schwarz, *Misplaced Ideas*; R. Ortiz, *A moderna cultura*).

Anthropophagy had at least two historic moments during Andrade's life, first in 1928–29 as a collective modernist movement around the *Revista* (in turn divided into two distinct periods), and later in the 1950s when Andrade revisited his modernist utopian roots. Cultural studies usually refers to the first moment, and primarily to Andrade's "Manifesto." This text is usually read with a preconceived formula for its interpretation, so the few aphorisms quoted from it serve the purpose of confirming that anthropophagy "proposed" the creative consumption of European *cultural capital* in the tropics in order to produce a national culture beyond the anxieties of influence. Little of the "Manifesto" supports this interpretation; most of its 52 paragraphs instead refer to other matters such as utopian visions of the sexual freedom of the indigenous, the oppressive role of reason and science, the allegedly reactionary nature of Catholicism, the outdated postures of Brazilian romanticism, and the injustices of capitalism. The "Manifesto antropófago" also brings futurist images of technology (including television!) together with triumphal visions of Brazilian "primitiveness." The text is diffuse and fragmented rather than cohesive; even visually its paragraphs are separated by long typographical lines (regrettably suppressed in most editions). Many of the aphorisms simply resist interpretation, such as "A alegria é a prova dos nove," found twice in the "Manifesto" and translated into English by Adriano Pedrosa and Veronica Cordeiro as "Happiness is the proof of the pudding" (538–39) and more literally by Leslie Bary as "Joy is the proof of nine" (43)—sentences that do not make much sense, but at least render the surrealist effect of the original. Critics often quote the "Manifesto" as an essay, referring to what "it says" as if it were a systemic proposal instead of a collection of surrealist phrases that work against rational argumentation to produce a sense of *ostranenie*, disrupting habitual perceptions of familiar things: romantic *indianismo*, José de Alencar, cannibalism, Luso-Brasilian historiography, the authority of academia, monogamy. The "Manifesto antropófago" is largely aimed to free thought from the imprisonment of grammar, philosophical speculation, and logic, and to produce *affects* and *percepts* rather than *concepts* (Deleuze). This does not mean that these aphorisms lack ideas but that they playfully explore the poetic dimensions of those ideas, inviting the reader to contrast divergent signifiers: "printed psychology," "grammar," "science," "canned consciousness," "objectified and cadaverized ideas," "hypotheses," and "speculative tedium" are juxtaposed to "prelogical mentality," "instincts," personal experiences, "surrealist language," sensuality, and magic. The "Manifesto antropófago" favors contradictory sentences and antirationalism: "long life and death to all hypotheses" or "Let's get rid of ideas." Incidentally, this is the "posture" found in the 1928 painting *Abaporu* (Man-eater), a birthday gift from Tarsila do Amaral to Andrade that inspired Andrade's *Antropofagia*. *Abaporu* depicts a sensualist cannibal thinker, a naked savage with a voluminous body and a minuscule head in the same position as the famous 1882 sculpture *Le Penseur* by Auguste Rodin.

Anthropophagy was a collective movement. Besides Andrade, there were Tarsila do Amaral, Oswaldo Costa, Raúl Bopp, Mário de Andrade, Antônio de Alcântara Machado, and many others, each with his own notion of anthropophagy. They used the cannibal trope to make ethnological speculations about sexual freedom, monogamy, and happiness, to ridicule romantic images of the indigenous, to embrace Nietzsche's Epicureanism and critique of Christianity, to discuss Tupinamba's language, and so on. Cultural consumption was just one part of a wide semantic spectrum. It was not even "proposed" in the "Manifesto," but rather in other articles and interviews. Yet because of its relevance to contemporary debates, cultural consumption became the canonical definition of anthropophagy (Jáuregui, *Canibalia*).

The end of anthropophagy coincides with the economic crisis triggered by the 1929 stock market crash, the ruin of São Paulo's coffee bourgeoisie, and the rise of Getúlio Vargas to power in 1930. International capitalism devoured modernist fortunes and optimism, together with anthropophagy's answers to the dilemma of modernization. Vargas's national populist Estado Novo (New State) defined the nation using an ideology of miscegenation, reediting a fascist-like image of the Tupi Indian, and pushing mega-modernizing industrialist policies. Andrade, like many other modernists, became Marxist and abjured anthropophagy (although his writings maintained a modernist ethos).

In the 1950s, after leaving the Communist Party, Andrade alone revisited modernist anthropophagy in various monographs in which he imagined the "synthesis" of natural and civilized man in a techno-industrial utopia where machines and technological advances would liberate humanity for creative leisure, love, and happiness and where metaphysical fears, authoritarian patriarchy, and the state would be replaced with the Pindorama matriarchy. Andrade's utopia expressed both disenchantment with the Communist Party and Marxism, uncritical Browderism, and an exaggerated optimism about post-WWII industrialization. Unlike the modernist movement, this *theoretical anthropophagy* was not a collective enterprise. Furthermore, its academic style sharply differs from the fragmentation, irrationalism, and the anarchic discursive nature of the first anthropophagy.

In the 1960s, after Andrade's death, anthropophagy attracted renewed interest due to two circumstances: first, the 1967 premiere of Andrade's

O rei da vela (1933) by the Group of Celso Martinez Corrêa, which ridiculed Brazil's underdeveloped industry and criticized the national bourgeoisie's alliance with international capitalism, and second, the success of the musical and cultural movement Tropicália that took from anthropophagy its irony toward hardcore nationalism, and its formula for creative appropriation—now of rock-and-roll and 1960s avant-garde counterculture (Perrone; Dunn). In the 1970s and 1980s the highly influential works of Augusto and Haroldo de Campos on the *Revista* and Andrade's poetry framed the contemporary reception of anthropophagy as a poetic and theoretical proposal equivalent to transculturation and cultural appropriation (a modernist antecedent of cultural studies paradoxically anchored in the fine-arts and literary realms). Since then, the "anthropophagic paradigm," as Chamberlain calls it, became a recurrent preoccupation of cultural and literary critics who linked Andrade's writings with postmodern and postcolonial debates. Anthropophagy's conflicted desire for modernity turned into a critique of modernity, colonial reason, and even androcentric culture. Andrade's references to matriarchy and pre-logic mentality, for example, have been read as psycholinguistic denunciations of the Law of the Father that anticipate Kristeva's theorizations (Vinkler) and as a challenge to the Socratic and patriarchal reason that structure modern Western subjectivity (Castro-Klarén). The anthropophagic matriarchy certainly had an emancipatory horizon (abolition of property, monogamy, and the state), but the subject of that liberation remained masculine. The mother occupied the problematic place of alterity: savage nature, primitive other, pre-logic mind, and so on. The same could be said of anthropophagy's carnivalesque use of the indigenous as an image associated with sexual freedom, unconscious creativity, and happiness; a cultural fetish derived from romantic ethnographic images rather than a reappraisal of ancestral heritage for a counter-colonial project (Rodríguez-Núñez), an "anticolonial" theory (Santiago; Viveiros de Castro), or an attempt "at freeing Brazilian culture from mental colonialism" (Vieira). Nor was the modernist adoption of the cannibal sign an artistic echo in solidarity with the social and political struggles of indigenous and Afro-descendent populations (Ferreira de Almeida). Given anthropophagy's specific cultural practices (within the agenda of an aesthetic revolution promoted by a cosmopolitan bourgeoisie) and its disconnect from any social movement or actual decolonization effort (particularly the labor movement and indigenous resistance toward modernization), the characterization of this movement as postcolonial seems unsubstantiated. Today, of course, anthropophagy's importance lies beyond its historical and ideological contextualization: it is an ethno-poetic model that has become a "malleable foundational discourse" (Prado Bellei) for contemporary cultural theory as attested by the dissimilar interpretations of its significance by Haroldo de Campos, Roberto Schwarz, Silviano Santiago, and Renato Ortiz, among others. Anthropophagy's fertile legacy can also be seen in a large corpus of literature (from the de Campos brothers to João Ubaldo Ribeiro, Antônio Torres, Glauco Ortolano, and Marcos Azevedo), popular music (from Tropicália and Caetano Veloso to Adriana Calcanhoto or Daniela Mercury), and cinema (from Nélson Pereira dos Santos to Luiz Alberto Pereira). Even highly institutionalized cultural events such as the 24th Bienal de São Paulo in 1998 use anthropophagy, provoking some critics such as Coelho Netto to express some exhaustion vis-à-vis the anthropophagic "monomania" of this foundational myth in Brazilian contemporary culture.

Suggested Reading

Boaventura, Maria Eugenia. *A vanguarda antropofágic*. São Paulo: Ática, 1985.

Campos, Augusto de. "Revistas Re-vistas: Os antropófagos." Introduction to *Revista de antropofagia: Reedição da revista literaria publicada em São Paulo*, 1–13. São Paulo: Abril, 1975.

Campos, Haroldo de. "Da razão antropofágica: A Europa sob o signo de devoração." *Colóquio/Letras* 62 (1981): 10–25.

Jáuregui, Carlos A. *Canibalia: Canibalismo, calibanismo, antropofagia cultural y consumo en América Latina*. Madrid: Iberoamericana; Frankfurt-am-Main: Vervuert, 2008.

Nunes, Benedito. "A antropofagia ao alcance de todos." In *A utopía antropofágica*, by Oswald de Andrade, 5–39. São Paulo: Globo, 1990.

Prado Bellei, Sérgio Luiz. "Brazilian Anthropophagy Revisited." In *Cannibalism and the Colonial World*, edited by Francis Barker, Peter Hulme, and Margaret Iversen, 87–109. Cambridge: Cambridge University Press, 1998.

Santiago, Silviano. *Uma literatura nos trôpicos: Ensaios sobre dependência cultural*. São Paulo: Perspectiva, 1978.

Schwarz, Roberto. *Misplaced Ideas: Essays on Brazilian Culture*. London: Verso, 1992.

Audience

ANA WORTMAN (TRANSLATED BY RUTH HALVEY)

Throughout the twentieth century, audience research on radio, film, and television aimed to analyze the construction of social meaning by looking at the impact of these emerging cultural industries. Such research was done from within the dominant sociological models of the 1940s and 1950s, such as functionalism, whose goal was to analyze the effect of messages on behavior, taking for granted a unidirectional framework, in which media exercised an influence on audiences, but not vice versa. In this context, the studies conducted by Paul Lazarsfeld are of particular note. Although Lazarsfeld's perspective appeared to conform to the theories of the day, he recognized that the impact of the media was not direct, but rather mediated by the environments of individuals, their neighborhoods, their political identities, their opinion leaders.

In the 1960s and 1970s, in alignment with the academic and political climate of the times, many audience studies were permeated by Marxist perspectives as well as the ideologies underlying dependency theory. Researchers analyzed the ideological character of messages (Dorfman and Mattelart), with "manipulation" being a key concept, borrowed from early culture-industry critiques of the Frankfurt School. In this framework, cultural analysis tended toward one of two extremes: a focus on elite culture (in the traditions of literary criticism, art history) or an interest in traditions, particularly of "premodern" groups (in the tradition of anthropology). The new focus on popular media, cultural industries, and their audiences developed in conjunction with trends toward creation and stabilization of democracy and, later, with debates on social and cultural equality/inequality that emerged in the more recent era of neoliberalism.

In the 1980s, research on the reception of communication processes assumed a largely cultural focus. At this point the concept of cultural consumption appeared in the Latin American context where scholars advanced an interdisciplinary perspective in order to examine the link between subjects and artistic and media offerings. This research developed as part of a general reflection on cultural politics. These areas of research proved extremely productive because they articulated a series of questions from a point of view that is theoretical as well as methodological and empirical. This new outlook arose along with the renewal and modernization that occurred in the social sciences, as part of a political agenda put in place in Latin American countries at a time when many countries were transitioning to democracy after years of military dictatorship.

Thus scholarship interrogated the political character of media production while considering the micro-quotidian aspects of media consumption; at the same time Latin America saw a timid recomposition of cultural, intellectual, and artistic fields in terms of producers, media outlets, and publics, all of which had been profoundly shaken not only by the tragic experiences of the dictatorships but also by the heightened ideological tensions of the era (Sarlo; Landi).

The notion of culture in Latin America required a rethinking of theoretical and methodological perspectives regarding relationships of power, and social relationships in general. We know from Gramsci and subsequent rereadings (such as those of British cultural studies) that hegemony cannot merely be imposed. As owners of the means of production and circulation, the bourgeoisie play a decisive role in the material and ideological organization of social life, which they can use to efficiently exert their own hegemony. Nevertheless, the bourgeois media not only must construct their products and messages in ways that directly benefit their own sector but must also, from the moment of production, include "reciprocal benefits"—that is, cultural aspects that would make these products useful and meaningful to the majority. Thus, García Canclini *(Los nuevos espectadores)* affirms that questions such as whether tango and rock are hegemonic or subaltern are poorly formulated: tango and rock cannot be ascribed to one group or another solely on the basis of their cultural origin and content. Rather, it is necessary to examine their uses and relationships to mechanisms of power in a given context.

Consequently, the new research agenda of the 1980s created models that privilege the analysis of consumption. In effect, consumption deals with the social processes of the appropriation of products—and therefore class struggles over issues relating to distribution of wealth and social planning. In this sense, consumption is much more than a repertoire of attitudes and tastes catalogued by functionalist surveys of market and opinion, or an area where the productive process is realized. Rather it is a key concept to explain everyday life and to help us understand the habits that organize the behavior of different social sectors, their mechanisms of adherence to hegemonic culture or group difference, of subordination or resistance.

Even if, as we have seen, the concept of cultural consumption arises out of a particular historical context, scholars soon began to use it to rethink earlier historical moments. Several key texts of Latin American cultural studies follow this paradigm. In *El imperio de los sentimientos*, Beatriz Sarlo takes inspiration from Raymond Williams in analyzing the structure of emergent feeling of a society in formation. Analyzing the sale of *folletines*, inexpensive pamphlet-like publications with a circulation often reaching 100,000 or 200,000, she considers Argentinean society between 1910 and 1920. Since it is not possible to interview each one of the readers of *folletines*, she reconstructs their profile based on the texts that interested them. Her critical study presents the issue of cultural consumption's meanings in relation to anxieties about the impact of a popular and massively consumed genre vis-à-vis the elite institution of literature, focusing especially on the forms this consumption took.

It is not only in literary-cultural criticism that we can find contributions to these concepts. Research in the field of communications has generated lines of investigation into audiences, and practices that add to the reflection on cultural consumption. The work of Jesús Martín Barbero has been key, for example, in proposing the concept of "mediations" to "perceive communication from a quite different perspective, from its 'other' side, namely reception. This revealed to us the resistances and varied ways people appropriate media content according to manner of use" (2). Carlos Monsiváis, for his part, re-focused film criticism on audiences; in a study of "golden age" Mexican cinema, he noted with his characteristic irony that "all the people came and did not fit onto the screen" (49).

The prevailing optimism of the 1980s motivated people to go out into public spaces where they engaged in both political participation and cultural consumption. However, at the same time people opted more and more frequently to consume media within the home; it soon became evident that, although practices were multiple, media in the home was more relevant than previously imagined. Oscar Landi carried out research on this phenomenon in *Públicos y consumos culturales en la ciudad de Buenos Aires*. This line of interrogation gave rise to a new subfield that examined the relationship of subjects with technology, echoing and updating Walter Benjamin's reflection on art in the age of mechanical reproduction. Mediations both in production and consumption resignify the cultural, artistic, and intellectual fields.

Between the 1980s and 1990s, in addition to large urban studies such as Landi's, other studies addressed cultural consumption in medium-sized cities such as Córdoba, Santa Fe, Paraná, Mar del Plata, and Mendoza, all in Argentina. This research confirmed that inhabitants of those cities were especially receptive to the incorporation of new technologies, such as cable TV and video, in the home. By providing access to cultural goods and services previously concentrated in the city of Buenos Aires, social practices were transformed. Additionally, researchers recorded a notable decrease in cultural consumption in public environments, evidenced by the reduction in attendance at cinemas, theaters, concerts, and the like. These interdisciplinary investigations bring together fragmentary data from varied sources, such as consultants, cultural magazines, and media associations, whose dissemination was often belated and limited (Terrero).

What factors have brought about the reduction of audiences in movie theaters? U.S. studies (Tasker) could often be extrapolated to Latin America, documenting the growth of home-delivery culture, transformations of cities into megacities, and growing suburbanization as the determinant causes of a decrease in cultural consumption in public spaces. British sociologists such as Morley and Silverstone effectively analyzed the emergence and increasing presence of television in the daily life of middle-class families, relating this phenomenon to the growing privatization of society in Thatcher-era Britain and the omnipresence of consumerism.

Some Mexico-based research continues in this direction. The transformation of the city into the megacity, the suburbanization of the middle classes, and the so-called home delivery of culture have been major factors in bringing about the decrease of the public in movie theaters, a hypothesis guiding Néstor García Canclini in *Consumers and Citizens*. García Canclini alludes to the creation of a city that tends to deurbanization; Mexico's case is emblematic, given its exponential growth over the last fifty years. Moreover, he refers to the emergence of newer practices of cultural consumption, such as those related to cable TV and video rental, that regenerate social bonds that had been weakened by the big city. Even if the practice of going to the movies has diminished, as it has in Mexico, the movie industry is renewed through practices of consumption of new technologies. However, the same does not occur with public cultural life. This is noted in research on cultural consumption carried out by Landi and others. Here we can see the conjunction of these two processes: the increase of television consumption, which coexists with a permanent desire for people to go out into public spaces, just not necessarily into movie theaters.

The film viewer has changed over the last decades. In investigating how cinephiles and videophiles form their knowledge of film, surveys reveal that the majority of those who go to movie theaters as well as of those who watch videos cannot name the directors of the films they watch. In movie theaters almost the entire audience leaves before the credits run.

Guillermo Sunkel's reader *El consumo cultural en América Latina* is representative of the formation of this field of study in Latin America. More recently, a CLACSO working group, "Cultural Consumption, Markets, Politics, and Practices," has begun presenting and publishing work on the theme on various new (and older) media and contexts of consumption. Lately the topic of consumption has also been taken up by anthropologists

(Leitão et al). A very recent publication on the topic titled *Buscando señal: Lecturas sobre nuevos hábitos de consumo cultural* (Barbieri) brings consumption studies to bear on various contemporary technological innovations, including the rise of mobile devices in everyday life.

Suggested Reading

Barbieri, Mariano, ed. *Buscando señal: Lecturas sobre nuevos hábitos de consumo cultural.* Córdoba, Argentina: CCEC, 2009.

Bourdieu, Pierre. *Distinction: A Social Critique of the Judgment of Taste.* Translated by Richard Nice. Cambridge, Mass.: Harvard University Press, 1984.

Dorfman, Ariel, and Armand Mattelart. *How to Read Donald Duck: Imperialist Ideology in the Disney Comic.* Translated by David Kunzle. New York: International General, 1975.

García Canclini, Néstor, ed. *El consumo cultural en México.* Mexico City: Consejo Nacional para la Cultura y las Artes, 1993.

———, ed. *Los nuevos espectadores de cine: Cine, televisión y video en México.* Mexico City: Consejo Nacional para la Cultura y las Artes, 1994.

Grimson, Alejandro, and Mirta Varela. *Audiencias, cultura y poder: Estudios sobre la televisión.* Buenos Aires: EUDEBA, 1999.

Karol, Jorge, and Susana Finquelievich. *El impacto de las nuevas tecnologías en la vida cotidiana.* Buenos Aires: Biblioteca del Centro Editor de América Latina, 1990.

Landi, Oscar. "Cultura y política en la transición a la democracia." *Nueva Sociedad* 10–11 (July–August 1984): 65–78.

Landi, Oscar, Ariana Vacchieri, and Luis Alberto Quevedo. *Públicos y consumos culturales en la ciudad de Buenos Aires.* Buenos Aires: Documentos CEDES, 1990.

Lazarsfeld, Paul. "Los medios de difusión y las masas." In *Historia y elementos de sociología del conocimiento,* edited by I. L. Horowitz, 2: 171–81. Buenos Aires: EUDEBA, 1964.

Leitão, Débora Krischke, Diana Nogueira de Oliveira Lima, and Rosana Pinheiro Machado. *Antropologia e consumo: Diálogos entre Brasil e Argentina.* Porto Alegre: AGE, 2006.

Martín Barbero, Jesús. *Communication, Culture and Hegemony: From the Media to Mediations.* Translated by Elizabeth Fox and Robert A. White. London: Sage, 1993.

Monsiváis, Carlos, and Carlos Bonfil. *A través del espejo: El cine mexicano y su público.* Mexico City: El Milagro/Instituto Mexicano de Cinematografía, 1994.

Sarlo, Beatriz. *El imperio de los sentimientos: Narraciones de circulación periódica en la Argentina, 1917–1927.* Buenos Aires: Catálogos, 1985.

Silverstone, Roger. "The Suburbanisation of the Public Sphere." In *Television and Everyday Life,* 52–77. New York: Routledge, 1994.

Sunkel, Guillermo, ed. *El consumo cultural en América Latina: Construcción teórica y líneas de investigación.* 2nd ed. Bogotá: Andrés Bello, 2006.

Tasker, Yvonne. "Approaches to the New Hollywood." In *Cultural Studies and Communications,* edited by James Curran, David Morley, and Valerie Walkerdine, 213–28. London: Hodder Arnold, 1996.

Terrero, Patricia. "Técnica y cultura urbana." In *La mirada oblicua: Estudios culturales y democracia,* edited by Silvia Delfino, 129–37. Buenos Aires: La Marca, 1993.

Wortman, Ana. *Construcción imaginaria de la desigualdad social.* Buenos Aires: CLACSO-ASDI, 2007.

———, ed. *Pensar las clases medias: Consumos culturales y estilos de vida urbanos en la Argentina de los noventa.* Buenos Aires: La Crujía, 2003.

Body

GABRIEL GIORGI

Cultural studies approaches the question of the body as both a historical construction and a field of political disputes; to a great extent, it offers *critical narrations on the political historicity of the body.* Unlike traditional inquiries and approaches that have assumed an ahistorical body as the ground of subjectivities and as the target of power, a body anterior and exterior to social and cultural determinations, cultural studies presumes the body as a result and effect of historical and political technologies, a stance that persistently problematizes any clear-cut distinction between the "social" and the "natural," the "biological" and the "political." Cultural studies thus reckons with the entrance of the body into history, through which diverse terrains—sexuality, nutrition, race and reproduction, health and social performativity, to name a few—can be read historically with regard to mechanisms of power and political technologies that operate as lines of transformation and rearticulations of meanings and behaviors. The body becomes, thus, a terminal site of historical and social processes, and as such it becomes a privileged site of inquiry in cultural studies.

To problematize the historical and political construction of bodies, however, is to leave us with neither a singular nor a standardizing methodological foundation. Perhaps one of the most evident methodological distinctions among the different ways of approaching the question of the body can be posed between those that emphasize discursive and semiotics practices that represent and, in a social and cultural dimension, "constitute" the body as a signifier, and those that highlight the material transformations of bodies as they are inscribed in social technologies and political *dispositifs.* In the first approach, the focus falls upon the intersection of the body as a terrain of discursive inscriptions that constantly reshape its place, its visibility, and its relations to the social order. Racialized, sexualized, or gendered identities, for instance, can be approached along these lines in terms of cultural and political productions of meaning whose significations and configurations are constantly transformed. The body is captured within these discursive configurations whose ability to signify depends upon their determinative potency, their political and symbolic force. However, the body is never reducible to its discursive orderings: it also emerges as an interruption to, and displacement of, the discursive economies that describe and prescribe corporeal needs, desires, and potentialities; it appears as a disruptive force within classificatory and disciplinary orders, hegemonic languages, even common sense. Thus relations between body and discourse take place under the sign of a radical ambivalence in which the body is constituted by the languages that "speak" it and at the same time exceed it, inscribing an opacity that cannot be captured by semiotic practices. Butler's critical trajectory is anchored/invested in the cultural and symbolic dimension—that is, in the universe of discourse, languages, and codes that represent the body in its multiple dimensions and allow it signification. The influence of Lacanian psychoanalysis, especially Slavoj Žižek's readings of popular culture and its political significations, has incited a great deal of critical work conjugated around the gap between the insistence of desire and the institution of meaning.

Other approaches to the question of the historical and political status of the body, closer to the Foucauldian tradition and its developments around biopolitics, aim at placing more centrally the interactions and exchanges between the biological and the discursive. Health, reproduction, pleasure, nutrition, sexuality, all demonstrate specific historicities in which discursive practices are shown in their relation to nondiscursive practices. The threshold between bodies and words, between discourses and organisms, comes to the fore, exposing the opening of the body, and of life itself, to its own historicity and indeterminacy. At stake are not only the ways we represent and signify the body but also the ways in which it becomes a terrain of disciplining and capitalization as well as experimentation, subjectivation, and reinvention. Practices regarding racial purity, gender identity—as in the transvestite, transsexual, and intersex bodies—or the more recent biologization of social and political identities under the impulse of new biomedical knowledges highlight this new status of bodily life in the cultural and the political imagination. The question of the post-human, the a-human, and the post-organic—the very limits between the human and the "living others"—comes to the fore, as the body expands its possibilities and as traditional understandings of its recognizability are being radically altered.

Above and beyond its unique juncture between natural and cultural histories, between the social and the biological, and between life and politics, the body foregrounds tensions, displacements, and ambivalences that are reducible to neither a "constructivist" nor a "biologistic" perspective. The body inevitably reveals a zone of exchange and transformation for which both essentialism and cultural relativism remain inadequate. We might venture that the problem of the body delineates a frontier for cultural studies; as investigations around it grapple with its historic, cultural, and political mutations, they are obliged to confront the domain of the cultural with medical discourses and practices, with the rising vocabularies of "bioeconomy," with biological and genetic experimentation, and more. The body becomes, in this sense, a site of multiple intersections between discourses and technologies that are irreducible to a traditional understanding of the cultural. It is this fast-changing place of the body that cultural studies faces as an epistemological challenge and a disciplinary problem: it is located, so to speak, at the very limit of the cultural.

Within Latin American cultural studies, the body as object and instrument of critique plays a central role in diverse fields of research. The following themes might organize some of the principal concerns with regard to cultural and social inscriptions of the body in Latin America:

1) *Coloniality and the Body*: The body has been a protagonist of the ways in which cultural imagination represented and signified the colonial violence that forced the (Latin) American subjection to Western domination. The colonial subject is, above all, a subjected body, and this capturing of the body within the complex set of colonial relations shapes, in decisive ways, its place in colonial and postcolonial cultures. From the "savage" as pure embodiment—in a way: a "pure" bodily life—to the "barbarian" and the different figures that, throughout the twentieth century, incarnated Latin American distance from the Western "norm," the body has been a principal terrain where colonial relations are made visible and, therefore, where they are fought.
2) *Gender and Sexuality*: The historicity of the body is particularly relevant where gender and sexuality become visible as technological and practical effects. In Latin America, studies of gender and sexuality have gained greater importance in recent decades, and now constitute a prolific field of critical inquiry and historical

revision. They illuminate operations for those whose bodily social inscription would otherwise have no place without a clear assignment of gender or sexual identity within the universe of codified sexual practices—that is to say, without a fixation upon normative masculine and feminine relationships. In this field, discussions around Catholic and colonial legacies have joined debates regarding modern disciplinary mechanisms of the nation-state and the neoliberal market, producing analyses regarding political and cultural constructions with respect to heteronormativity and queer alterity. In this vein, certain hegemonic constructions of collective identity—national, regional, ethnic, political, for example—are constituted through the evacuation of certain possibilities of gender performance and sexual practices that often, for normative culture, appear intolerable or impossible.

3) *Mestizaje*: Another key trajectory with regard to the body and cultural studies is *mestizaje* and the ways it has been identified with Latin-Americanness. The uses of *mestizaje* in reflections upon Latin American cultures are traversed by tensions between rhetorics of racial democracy that celebrate mixture and hybridization as a particularly Latin American resolution to racial difference and conflict, and the converse: *mestizaje* as a strategy of securing the hierarchies and racial disaggregations initiated during European colonial expansion. The racialization of Latin American bodies passes (perhaps inevitably) through the rubric of *mestizaje*, a foundational condition for the inscription and politics of race and other narratives that engage sexual and cultural reproduction.

The interdisciplinary nature of cultural studies of the body sheds light not only on blind spots of contemporary critical languages, but also on experimentations and transformations that claim new vocabularies. Debates and research are unfolding on the status of the body in relation to new thresholds of biotechnologies, new modes of capitalization of life; to shifting limits between the natural and the technological; to the understanding of the living as a "passive" object of economic and/or political investment, or, on the contrary, as the instance of a potentiality that cannot be governed. Through these themes and discussions, the question of the historical, political, cultural, and aesthetic resonance of the body's potentialities shows the directions for cultural studies' new challenges.

Suggested Reading

Balderston, Daniel, and Donna J. Guy, eds. *Sex and Sexuality in Latin America*. New York: New York University Press, 1997.

Butler, Judith. *Bodies That Matter: On the Discursive Limits of "Sex."* New York: Routledge, 1993.

Deleuze, Gilles. *The Logic of Sense*. Translated by Mark Lester with Charles Stivale. New York: Columbia University Press, 1990.

Esposito, Roberto. *Bios: Biopolitics and Philosophy*. Translated by Timothy Campbell. Minneapolis: University of Minnesota Press, 2008.

Foucault, Michel. *Abnormal*. Translated by Graham Burchell. New York: Picador, 2003.

Franco, Jean. *Plotting Women: Gender and Representation in Mexico*. New York: Columbia University Press, 1989.

Graham, Richard, ed. *The Idea of Race in Latin America, 1870–1940*. Austin: University of Texas Press, 1990.

Lamas, Marta. *Cuerpo: Diferencia sexual y género*. Mexico City: Taurus, 2002.

Masiello, Francine. *Between Civilization and Barbarism: Women, Nation and Literary Culture in Modern Argentina*. Lincoln: University of Nebraska Press, 1992.

Nancy, Jean-Luc. *Corpus*. Translated by Richard A. Rand. New York: Fordham University Press, 2008.

Nouzeilles, Gabriela. *Ficciones somáticas: Naturalismo, nacionalismo y políticas médicas del cuerpo: Argentina, 1880–1910*. Rosario, Argentina: Beatriz Viterbo, 2000.

Rose, Nikolas. *The Politics of Life Itself: Biomedicine, Power, and Subjectivity in the Twenty-first Century*. Princeton, N.J.: Princeton University Press, 2006.

Silverblatt, Irene. *Modern Inquisitions: Peru and the Colonial Origins of the Civilized World*. Durham, N.C.: Duke University Press, 2004.

Stoler, Ann Laura. *Race and the Education of Desire: Foucault's "History of Sexuality" and the Colonial Order of Things*. Durham, N.C.: Duke University Press, 1995.

Border

MARISA BELAUSTEGUIGOITIA (TRANSLATED BY ISABEL PORRAS)

The revision and re-elaboration of the concept of "border" in Latin American and Anglophone critical theory in the last two decades is one of the foundational operations of cultural studies. Cultural studies has theorized "the border" beyond its geographic or geopolitical character to inscribe it as a pedagogical device, tied to the production and administration of knowledges and practices that cultivate notions of citizenship inscribed in democratic regimes.

The pedagogical nature of "borders" of knowledge (how they are produced and transmitted) in turn generates geocultural epistemologies that disarticulate difference and asymmetry. The meeting point between critical pedagogy and epistemological rupture is foundational in cultural studies. In other words, cultural studies offers a new method for administering and producing knowledge whose essential function is disciplinary and geocultural border crossing. This pedagogy of crossing and overflow, and of the transgression of disciplinary boundaries has contributed to a redesign of Latin America that privileges a critical return to the regional and local as well as a proposal of transnational or intercultural citizenships.

What counts as "knowledge" and who produces it in an asymmetrical global context? How can we negotiate access to and preservation of "other" knowledges, practices, and experiences that adjoin hegemonic and universalist structures? What borders must dissolve, what boundaries should we construct, and what limits should we draw in order to produce a circulation of knowledge and experience that takes into account discourses and projects "from below"? From which discursive limits, with which transnational boundaries, through which material thresholds and reappropriation of our history can we approach the development of an inclusive and intercultural citizenship in Latin America?

Borders render (in)visible that which can adjoin, oppose, and hide. The epistemological and critical function of borders comes from the act of making transparent the effects of the exercising of power and resistance. The crossing and tracing of borders as an alternative delimitation of new transnational collectives and its consequent revision of identities makes evident the maps and geographies that spring from resistance, struggle, and representation "from below" for an economically and socially just and equal society. With the topological expression "from below," we join Appadurai, Anzaldúa, Mohanty, Moraña, Alarcón, García Canclini, and other critics of globalization in searching for a citizenship that does not eliminate differences, or specificities of groups and communities.

The analysis of the term "border" that these scholars propose refers to the act of making inequities, resistances, and negotiations, be they hidden or explicit, visible to power. It also highlights particular acts of demarcation, asymmetries or junctures between pedagogic hegemonic practices and those that propose some deviation or rupture. Deviations or ruptures are products of the encounter between the demands and necessities of survival and representation tied to: identity, pedagogical practices, and hegemonic spaces and languages.

The concepts of space and identity have been appropriated by cultural studies with the goal of highlighting the migration triggered by transfigurations to flows of capital, discourses, media, and politics of representation that are particular to Latin America, and that continuously reconfigure its geocultural and imaginary borders.

The overlap proposed by cultural studies between disciplines, between territorialized and deterritorialized spaces such as memory and desire, would not be fully understood without the crossings proposed by transnational feminism, Latin American feminist literary criticism, and the social movements and citizens studied and impelled by feminism—in other words, without the active friction of concepts of identity, space, and pedagogy introduced by gender studies.

The critical interventions of cultural studies place it at the border with gender studies. Stuart Hall expands Gramsci's concept of hegemony to encompass not only to class relations but also gender, race, subalternity, and the role of pleasure as elements to consider in analyses of power relations. Gayatri Spivak has highlighted the limits of representing subalternity within the violent epistemologies of the West. Mabel Moraña has pondered the ties between the state and the production of knowledge by intellectuals from the perspective of gender in Latin America. Many Latin American and Latin Americanist intellectuals, such as Nelly Richard, Ileana Rodríguez, Mary Louise Pratt, Doris Sommer, Margo Glantz, Beatriz Sarlo, Francine Masiello, Mónica Szurmuk, and Jean Franco, have pointed out those borders that women and their otherness must cross and reinvent in order to make sense of the limits of language and hegemonic pedagogies, with the objective of proposing alternative canons, citizenships integral to partial subjects, and politics of translation and mediation that might make possible a Latin American culture not fundamentally based on the production of elites. These scholars have asked themselves: How can we subvert language in order to show the boundaries of female or "other" experiences? How can we appropriate a narrative that represents the experiences, the silences, and the unnamable of women and otherness? What kinds of identities and which narratives are mobilizing diasporic Latin American identities? What border crossings and what new languages must be generated to represent and listen to these experiences? Which marginal spaces of enunciation must we attend to? And the ultimate question: Where have we been looking?

One of the most important tasks of both these fields is to address the escape and overflow of female and/or subaltern subjects from national and disciplinary boundaries. John Beverley points to the impossibility of containing Latin American knowledge within these boundaries, whether disciplinary or territorial. As a result, both gender and cultural studies privilege the concepts of transdisciplinary scholarship and of deterritorialized spaces. The destabilization of geographic and disciplinary borders via transdisciplinary scholarship and deterritorialization allows for studies of the limits of established disciplines and the ways in which these limits trap the voiceless and bodyless subaltern subject, as well as the constraint and control exerted by nations on their identities. In this way, transdisciplinarity and transnationality are two concepts strategically derived from the crossing and overflow of geographic and disciplinary boundaries. The production of cultural representations by U.S. Chicanas, the negotiations of survival and citizenship by Puerto Ricans in New York, and the outsider status of Peruvian migrant children in the Argentine school system are three examples of the reinscription of alterity in the interstitial territories of disciplines and nations.

Transnationality, transdisciplinarity, and transexuality constitute categories that are situated at the frontiers of disciplinary boundaries as well as *beyond* hegemonic concepts such as the sovereign state and the male/female gender binary. "Trans-" draws its strength from *beyond* metanarratives tied to monolithic, gendered and disciplinary identities.

Arjun Appadurai highlights the speedy movement of people, capital, and ideas toward disjunction and deterritorialization as destabilizing forces of the contemporary order that give strength to the concept of transnationality. As a result, the dispute between the concept of "place," the politics of (territorialized) "places," and the force of movement (politics of deterritorialization) comes into play.

Some questions arise: How can we think of resistance, identity, and knowledge from the limits of nation, gender, and discipline? What new role do nations and territories play when faced with deterritorialized and diasporic movements?

The concept of limit elaborated by Julio Ramos is particularly relevant here because, if sovereignty and national discourse render difference invisible, the modern construction of nation based on citizenship can be reclaimed from within its limits and be forced to respond to both migrant groups and local communities from within their mutated languages.

The discussion develops in a scenario that delimits the frontiers from which the Latin American subject thinks and is thought. Walter Mignolo pinpoints the problem in the localization and demarcation of the "place" from which we think Latin America and Latin Americans are constructed by others. The concept of "border thinking," based on the work of Chicana scholar Gloria Anzaldúa, is critical here. This concept emphasizes a pedagogy of marginality, limits and interstice in the face of a dominant administration of knowledge. Border thinking implies thinking the nation from its borders, from its most fragile zones, those that begin to devise politics of inclusion and cultural diversity.

In her text *Borderlands/La Frontera: The New Mestiza*, Gloria Anzaldúa specifies which borders must be removed, which must be crossed, which bridges to construct, which linguistic territories must be appropriated, and which identities must be reclaimed in order to generate forms of coexistence and representations specific to the metaphoric and literal border between the United States and Mexico. Anzaldúa's goal in this text is to increase the discourse, materiality, and reasons for generating inclusive, intercultural, transnational, and multiethnic or multicultural citizenships.

In this search for bridges and borders, Norma Alarcón's scholarship proposes an epistemological rupture that seeks to make visible what constitutes "knowledge" and who produces it. Alarcón affirms that Chicana writers are not characters in search of an author, but women attempting to get rid of their authors. Alarcón offers a border pedagogy that reappropriates modern European authors (Derrida, Lacan, Freud, and Foucault) by applying them to the context of extreme racial, sexual, and gender inequality and the necessities of minorities, in this case Chicanas. Her pedagogy of appropriation of voice and knowledge (self-produced as well as dominant) by the other is radical. The structures of domination and the pedagogical repercussions of the assimilation, appropriation, or questioning of knowledge take a different form when we consider what Mary Louise Pratt deems *contact zones*. These zones are defined as spaces of traffic, interchange, and the construction of cultural representations densely traversed by conditions of coercion, racial inequity, and deep conflict. Pratt proposes that, in addition to the contact among people, groups, merchandise, and ideas, contact zones are marked by the instabilities and asymmetries corresponding to the sexual, class, racial, and national positions of contact.

José Manuel Valenzuela Arce analyzes structures of domination and the forms of knowledge that can impose themselves or survive within these structures through his theoretical investigations of popular culture. Valenzuela understands the popular as a relational dimension with collective orders, which is constituted as the site of social interaction that is the expression and reproduction of social, economic, and symbolic asymmetries.

He seeks to establish forms of representation that connect the borderlands with the popular, with particular focus on Mexico's northern border. He explores the popular in conjunction with the feminine, with poverty, Norteño music (*banda* and electronic), the North American Free Trade Agreement, new religions and cults, social movements and their effects as devices of transgression, and disciplining and the way in which this phenomenon generates discourses of power. Valenzuela establishes the borderlands as coterminous territory densely permeated by economic, spiritual, artistic, and market interactions. In this way he returns to the local as well: ways of life, consumption habits, symbols and values, social movements, and autonomous and artistic expressions.

One of the fundamental questions that mark these critical pedagogies is: How can we rearticulate "other" knowledges beyond the codes implied by dominant languages, disciplines, and epistemological structures of domination? In other words, how can we think beyond domination? From where, with which language, which body? The answer is clear: from the borderlands, from the limits of national discourses of gender, race, and class; from the spaces between disciplines, between nations, between imaginaries, between languages. The interstitial zone is located beyond the regimes that compromise the mobility and fluidity of disciplines, territories, and imaginaries of the embodied and discursive representations of alterity.

Chicanas, transborder women par excellence, have developed a situated knowledge, a historico-political localization in body and language, from which to think and be thought. Gloria Anzaldúa constructs this "place," in the borderlands between Mexico and the United States, as an emotional, geographic, linguistic, material and imaginary border. Her text *Borderlands/La Frontera* sparked intense debates within the U.S. academy and brought about the revision of canons that had left out critical reflections of the concepts of nation, space, and identity proposed by excluded subjects. Other Chicanas—Norma Alarcón, Chela Sandoval, Cherríe Moraga, Ana Castillo, Norma Cantú, Sandra Cisneros, Lucha Corpi, Helena Viramontes, and Emma Pérez, among other border women—have sought to structure languages that speak to the particular experience of crossing and inhabiting one of the world's largest, most unfathomable, and most traveled borders. *Border Women: Writing from La Frontera* by Debra Castillo and Socorro Tabuenca maps the tensions, themes, and differential politics of women writers from both sides of the borderlands.

Chicanas have developed a pedagogical understanding of transdisciplinarity and a subversive representation of transnational female experiences.

Their constant pedagogical mission to teach, write, and translate and their way of inhabiting these borderlands have led them to theorize and narrate marginal experience through the notion of *oppositional thinking* elaborated by Chela Sandoval and further employed by Chandra Mohanty, Donna Haraway, Ernesto Laclau, and Chantal Mouffe. Cultural studies has returned to these tensions and questions and made them its own. From these bodies and languages the field analyzes globalization encroached upon by imagined communities: by migrant Mexicans, Caribbeans, and Latin Americans in the United States with a focus on the forms of vernacular and local knowledge that globalization dis/articulates and the knowledge of globalization that its scholarship makes possible (transnational coalitions and networks).

Feminist Latin American, Caribbean, and Chicana literary criticisms constitute transborder bonds that need to be strengthened. These criticisms have worked through notions of identity, space, and pedagogy in order to represent the body and language of alterity beyond national sovereignty, gender binaries, and dominant pedagogies through transdisciplinarity, transsexuality, and transnationality, thereby materializing the operations that give sense and possibility to the recognition and representation of alterity by means of reinventing geographic, disciplinary, and gender borders. These transborder pedagogies allow us to link south-south, from below, from the interstices of Peru and Argentina to the U.S.-Mexico border. Caribbean scholar Yolanda Martínez San Miguel's work in *Caribe Two Ways: Cultura de la migración en el Caribe insular hispánico* highlights the cultural strategies (visual, narrative and discursive) of the identity negotiations of Dominicans in Puerto Rico and Puerto Ricans in New York.

These feminist scholars have forged new alliances between Latin, Latin American, and Caribbean pedagogies. We should read them back to back in order to understand the new spaces, identities, and forms of administration of knowledge of our mobile, diasporic, and local experiences that are gestating from the deepest North to Patagonia.

Efforts to decipher and impel forms of collaboration between border-crossing pedagogies and dissent in the reconfiguration of Latin America are of fundamental importance today, especially in present times when borders are being reinforced for poor or persecuted migrants but relaxed for capital or for pedagogical exchanges between hegemonic cultures. It is imperative that we reinforce scholarship that contemplates "from below" the crossings and limits that the voices, demands, and subversions of dissent propose, to guarantee their survival and well-being.

Suggested Reading

Anzaldúa, Gloria. *Borderlands/La Frontera: The New Mestiza*. San Francisco: Aunt Lute Books, 1987.

Appadurai, Arjun, ed. *Globalization*. Durham, N.C.: Duke University Press, 2001.

González, Patricia Elena, and Eliana Ortega, eds. *La sartén por el mango: Encuentro entre escritoras latinoamericanas*. Santo Domingo: Huracán, 1985.

Martínez San Miguel, Yolanda. *Caribe Two Ways: Cultura de la migración en el Caribe insular hispánico*. San Juan: Callejón, 2003.

Mohanty, Chandra Talpade. *Feminism Without Borders: Decolonizing Theory, Practicing Solidarity*. Durham, N.C.: Duke University Press, 2003.

Moraga, Cherríe, and Gloria Anzaldúa, eds. *This Bridge Called My Back*. Watertown, Mass.: Persephone, 1981.

Moraña, Mabel, and María Rosa Olivera Williams, eds. *El salto de Minerva: Intelectuales, género y estado en América Latina*. Madrid: Iberoamericana/Vervuert, 2005.

Poblete, Juan, ed. *Critical Latin American and Latino Studies*. Minneapolis: University of Minnesota Press, 2003.

Ramos, Julio. *Paradojas de la letra*. Caracas: eXcultura, 1996.

Rodríguez, Ileana, ed. *Convergencia de tiempos: Estudios subalternos/contextos latinoamericanos estado, cultura, subalternidad*. Amsterdam: Rodopi, 2001.

Valenzuela Arce, José Manuel. *Nuestros piensos: Culturas populares en la frontera México–Estados Unidos*. Mexico City: Consejo Nacional para la Cultura y las Artes, 1998.

Canon

ANA ROSA DOMENELLA AND LUZELENA GUTIÉRREZ DE VELASCO

At present, terms like "canon" and "canonical" are employed as conciliatory concepts referring to a space that institutionalizes, or to a conglomerate list that attempts to establish certain norms or values in a cultural field. But the term also refers to the behavior and action of individuals or institutions. In England, the "secular canon" is related to the formation and transformation of the Christian canons; according to the *Encyclopaedia Britannica*, these are understood as "bodies of rules and regulations" that in some way guide the conduct of the individuals and institutions of certain churches. In the *Dictionary of the Spanish Royal Academy* the term "canon," from the Greek word *kanōn*, is associated with a rule or a precept like Catholic Church dogma, a catalogue of sacred texts, or a part of the Mass (the "Te igitur"). In the formulations of philosophers like John Stuart Mill and Immanuel Kant, the term "canon" is associated with a regulatory principle, and therefore with a concept of invariability. Inasmuch as this restrictive sense of the word is relaxed, it is possible to consider the canon as something in between constancy and alterability.

The term was originally used not only in the context of religion but also in music to refer to a composition in which two or more voices chime in at different times to repeat or imitate the prior verse. Its meaning has gradually broadened to the point that it has now become what Harold Bloom calls "a choice among texts struggling with one another for survival, whether you interpret this choice as being made by dominant social groups, institutions of education, traditions of criticism, or by late-coming authors who feel themselves chosen by particular ancestral figures" (19).

In literary studies, the concept of "canon" refers to a list of masterworks and sometimes to a list of authors, giving pause as to its composition with regard to value and value judgments in the literary field. Therefore, as Raquel Gutiérrez Estupiñán notes, since its appearance in the fourth century b.c., the canon "has had a notable influence on literary and cultural criticism" (32, translation ours) and operates on a principle of selection.

Canon, Tradition, and Norm

For the Russian formalists, in dialogue with the authors and schools of the artistic avant-gardes, the value of literature resided in its "novelty and originality"; thus the canonical procedures were eliminated in a quest for the renovation of traditional elements and stereotypes. In the same vein, Jan Mukařovský views the problem in a historical framework that overcomes the immanentist analysis; he proposes that the artistic work oscillates between the past and future state of the aesthetic norm. If we perceive it from a present moment, we note the "tension between the past norm and its transgression, which in turn is destined to become a component of the future norm" (quoted in Volek 156, translation ours).

T. S. Eliot argues that tradition "cannot be inherited, and if you want it, you must obtain it by great labour." He goes on to say: "The existing order is complete before the new work arrives," and judgments are made by comparison; nevertheless, one "must be quite aware . . . that art never improves, but that the material of art is never quite the same" (21, 23). For other scholars, the problem is related to the specific nature of the literary field, as a space of tensions, attractions, and rejections. From Susana Cella's point of view, "the idea of canon can be addressed by expressing opposite or synonymous relations" with terms like "tradition, classic, margin and center" (8, translation ours).

If the word "canon" is related to the word "marginality" in the sense of being complementary and, at the same time, subordinate, according to Noé Jitrik, "the canonical would be all that is regular, established, accepted as the guarantee of a system," while "marginality" is what turns away "voluntarily," not because "it doesn't accept or doesn't understand the canonical demand." It is also important to take into account that the canon is "something less and something more than tradition, which subordinates itself to an ordering aspect . . . ; with respect to the marginal, tradition is, rather, a structure of behaviors that reappears under certain conditions" (19, 27, translation ours).

Nicolás Rosa, on the other hand, argues that, in the framework of the discussion about the supposed "crisis of the Humanities" along with the "crisis of theory," the "authors' canon" becomes a "critics' canon" (73, translation ours). An example would be the polemic in United States universities between Harold Bloom and those who defend cultural studies.

The process of the inclusion and exclusion of women from the canon was radically transformed in the 1970s with the contributions of theoreticians like Elaine Showalter, who emphasized the revitalization of "women's literary tradition." Showalter insisted on the need "to understand how men's writing has resisted the acknowledgment of female precursors" (204). The canon was remodeled in consequence of the influence of gender theory on the evaluation of texts, and works were introduced that had been slighted because of the predominance of androcentric culture.

Canons in Latin America

If the canon consists of "the selection of representative works of a certain ideology in a particular time and space" (Pozuelo and Aradra, translation ours), each era and geographical territory produces its own canon in accordance with the principles related to national problems, taste, political interests, and official cultural strategies or those of a particular group.

We can reconsider the unique literary milestones, between tradition and rupture, in the light of the political independence of our countries in the nineteenth century. Distancing ourselves from European domination in our Latin American sphere meant that Latin American writers looked toward a past that had been rejected, as in the case of indigenous cultures of origin. In this effort, certain texts that had been marginalized by the hegemonic colonial order, such as the poetry of Nezahualcóyotl or *Los comentarios reales* of the Inca Garcilaso de la Vega, were recovered; new themes were introduced and non-Hispanic European models were adopted, all of which propitiated an anti-Spanish position among romantic writers who, in turn, were often politicians and military men. In the terrain of language and particularly the "national languages," as Jorge Luis Borges would say, the first American grammar book was written by the Venezuelan poet and statesman Andrés Bello and published in Chile in 1847.

The forging of the literary canons of the young American nations fluctuated toward that other, older Latin American canon. In constant tension and dialogue with the European canons, the Utopía de América was proposed: "Latin American literature is defined as the expression of a culture whose quest involves the work of the historian and the critic" (Zanetti 87, translation ours). At the beginning of the twentieth century the "American libraries," collections of canonical works, made their appearance. The Biblioteca Americana collection published in Mexico and the Biblioteca Ayacucho collection published in Venezuela organized a meticulous archive of Latin American canonical literature.

The absence of a kind of supranational academy to guide the readers of the new generations led to a focus on national and regional discussions, as was the case with the debate over the originality and pertinence of the *gauchesca* literature of Río de la Plata, whose study became a "treatise on the fatherland," opposed to migratory flows and multicultural tendencies.

Few literary works crossed national borders during the height of the popularity of the new Latin American novel in the 1960s. Notable cases are the delay of two centuries in the recognition of the work of Sor Juana Inés de la Cruz, due to a generalized rejection of the baroque aesthetic, and the muted homage in 1967 to Rubén Darío on the hundredth anniversary of his birth. On the other hand, the revered writers of the so-called Boom of the Latin American novel are all white, male, educated people from "the lettered city." The opposition between a cosmopolitan canon and a regional one or between a canon based on European models and a neo-indigenist one could be analyzed by looking at the reluctance of José María Arguedas to accept the work of Alejo Carpentier or Julio Cortázar. In the next generation, the discussion centered on the pertinence of writers like Manuel Puig, who incorporated into his novels material that was considered subliterature, material from the popular culture. This discussion led to considering the problem of the canon in relation to the expansion of the literary corpus. At the same time, in the sixties, a narrative emerged in South American countries over dictatorships and exile, which demanded new paths into analysis in order to approach the "unspeakable" and "ominous" nature of institutionalized violence. In the eighties, voices from the margins of the society were heard (writing by women and sexual and ethnic minorities), which had repercussions on literature and literary criticism in most Latin American countries. This was also true of reader preference for historical novels at the end of the twentieth century, impelled by editorial policies that offered national and international prizes with publicity campaigns based on marketing strategies. The academic criticism that had incorporated structuralist methods and immanent interpretations of literary texts in the sixties and the beginning of the seventies was shaken by the explosion in gender studies (for example, in feminist literary criticism as well as lesbian-gay and queer studies) and, in the last decades of the twentieth century, cultural and postcolonial studies. Canonical authors and texts were reinterpreted from these new theoretical and critical perspectives. Such was the case with the reinterpretation of the love and social poetry of Sor Juana Inés de la Cruz and with the ambiguous figure—virile yet maternal, mestiza yet criolla—of Nobel Prize winner Gabriela Mistral, considered the "teacher of America" but also the "national mother" of Chile.

As an example of diverse groups opening up the canon, we can offer our own experience as members of the Taller de Teoría y Crítica Diana Morán of Coyoacán, which has, since 1984, practiced the precepts of Hélène Cixous promoting women's writing. Various stages can be defined in the development of this research collective, which coincide with the rise of feminist literary criticism in other latitudes: (1) recognizing and revealing misogyny in literary practice; (2) rescuing literary "mothers" and "grandmothers," resulting in the critical anthology of Mexican women writers born in the nineteenth century, *Las voces olvidadas* (Domenella and Pasternac), and the discussion between the center and the margins of society in the two volumes of *Mujer y literatura mexicana y chicana: Culturas en contacto* (López y Malagamba); (3) the reformulation of the conceptual bases and theoretical suppositions that have ruled "phallogocentric" criticism (Derrida) or domestic "macho-criticism"; this new challenge has led to the publication of feminist criticism, as seen in *Escribir la infancia* (Pasternac et al.) dealing with Mexican narrative women writers, and in *De pesares y alegrías* (Gutiérrez de Velasco et al.) on Latin American and Caribbean women writers; and lastly, (4) the incorporation of studies on masculinity. In an effort to approach a multiple, trans-generic subjectivity (Nelly Richard, *Masculino/femenino*), two volumes have been published, titled *Escrituras en contraste*, dedicated to female/male literary pairs in Mexico (Castro Ricalde et al.) and in the Americas (Martínez Zalce et al.). At the present time, the Taller Diana Morán is working on a new project on five women writers, titled *Desbordando el canon.*

The Canon and Cultural Studies

The most radical critic of the canon questions not only its content but also the hegemonic, elitist nature of literature itself. As John Guillory points out, the debates on literary canon reflect a crisis in literature more as a form of cultural capital than as a medium of artistic representation or expression. In this sense, it is an institution to which access (of production, consumption, and study) is determined by a system of exclusion based on differences in social class.

The notion of literature in Latin America is inseparable from the concept of the "lettered city" of Ángel Rama. As John Beverley indicates, literature is a colonial institution that was introduced into the Americas by colonizers and was indispensable for the foundation of national cultural autonomy, and as such has been almost exclusively the property of the ruling classes. Beverley, upon recognizing both the new cultural hegemony of the mass media, which has the ability to reach broader, more diverse social sectors than literature does, and the importance of seeking academic strategies to encompass subaltern cultures that are not looking for access to the institutions of the "lettered city," adopts an anti-literature posture, which ultimately implies an affiliation with the criticism of the cultural studies project.

Suggested Reading

Beverley, John. *Against Literature.* Minneapolis: University of Minnesota Press, 1993.

Bloom, Harold. *The Western Canon: The Books and School of the Ages.* New York: Harcourt Brace, 1994.

Cella, Susana, ed. *Dominios de la literatura: Acerca del canon.* Buenos Aires: Losada, 1998.

Eliot, T. S. *Selected Essays.* 3rd ed. London: Faber, 1972.

Guillory, John. *Cultural Capital: The Problem of Literary Canon Formation.* Chicago: University of Chicago Press, 1993.

Gutiérrez Estupiñán, Raquel. *Una introducción a la teoría literaria.* Puebla, Mexico: Benemérita Universidad Autónoma de Puebla, 2004.

Mignolo, Walter. "Entre el canon y el corpus." *Nuevo Texto Crítico* 7, nos. 14–15 (1995): 23–36.

Pozuelo Yvancos, José María, and Rosa María Aradra Sánchez. *Teoría del canon y literatura española.* Madrid: Cátedra, 2000.

Rama, Ángel. *La ciudad letrada.* Hanover, N.H.: Ediciones del Norte, 1984.

———. *The Lettered City.* Translated by John Charles Chasteen. Durham, N.C.: Duke University Press, 1996.

Rosa, Nicolás. "Liturgias y profanaciones." In Cella, *Dominios de la literatura,* 59–83.

Sánchez Prado, Ignacio M. *El canon y sus formas: La reinvención de Harold Bloom y sus lecturas hispanoamericanas.* Puebla, Mexico: Secretaría de Cultura, Gobierno del Estado de Puebla, 2002.

Showalter, Elaine. "Feminist Criticism in the Wilderness." *Critical Inquiry* 8, no. 2 (Winter 1981): 179–205.

Volek, Emil, ed. *Signo, función y valor: Estética y semiótica del arte de Jan Mukarovsky.* Translated by Jarmila Jandová. Bogotá: Plaza y Janés/Universidad Nacional de Colombia–Universidad de los Andes, 2000.

Zanetti, Susana. "Algunas consideraciones sobre el canon literario latinoamericano." In Cella, *Dominios de la literatura,* 87–105.

Communications Media

JESÚS MARTÍN BARBERO

(TRANSLATED BY HÉCTOR FERNÁNDEZ L'HOESTE)

To think of communications media in Latin America has become a task of anthropological dimensions, because what comes into play is not only displacements of capital and technological innovations but also deep transformations in the everyday cultures of the majorities: changes that mobilize fragmenting and dehistoricizing imaginaries while at the same time bringing to the surface unfathomable strata of collective memory. These are changes that bring us face to face with an accelerated deterritorialization of cultural boundaries and disconcerting hybridizations in identities. The proposals, models, and cultural offerings of mass media increasingly mold the daily culture of most of the population—not just in cities but also in the countryside. And as scandalous as it might sound to us, it is already a fact that the masses in Latin America join modernity not by way of the book but through the formats and genres of the cultural industries of radio, film, and television. This is a transformation of collective sensibility that, precisely because it takes place not through lettered but through audiovisual cultures, raises some disconcerting challenges. To begin with, there is the challenge that the majority of the population appropriates modernity without relinquishing its oral culture, transforming it into a secondary orality—that is, set to the grammar of the devices and syntax of radio, film, and television. The challenge that this cultural transformation implies renders populist as well as enlightened modes of analysis and assessment obsolete; we cannot keep condemning a sensitivity that defies our notions of culture and modernity, and from which the modes of observing and reading, of imagining and loving, of perceiving and expressing identity are being transformed. This is the strategic scenario in which the relations between communications and culture are currently located: that of the destructuring of communities and the fragmentation of experience, that of the loss of autonomy of culture and the mixing of traditions, that of the emergence of new cultures that defy educational systems incapable of taking charge of the meaning and cultural relevance of mass media, inasmuch as cultural policies are mostly reduced to conserving and condemning.

The Media in the Transformations of the Latin American Cultural Field

Neither twentieth-century politics nor culture is thinkable without the molding that communications media have exercised. From the very idea of modernity that supported the project of the construction of modern nations in the 1930s, there was already an articulation of an economic movement—national economies started to belong to the international market—into a political project: to form nations through the creation of a culture, an identity, and a national sentiment. But this project was possible only through communication between urban masses and the state. The media, and radio in particular, became the voices of the interpellation that, from the state, transformed the masses into a people and the people into a nation. The populist leaders discovered in the radio the means of a new form of communication and the materialization of a new political discourse, which would break with the rhetoric of sermons as well as with speech, a new discourse that had in radio a fundamental mediation with "popular" language, with its capability to reelaborate orality and certain forms of the colloquial expressiveness that link the territorial with the discursive: the transition from expressive-symbolic rationality to the informative-instrumental rationality that organizes modernity.

On the other hand, modernization also represents an organization of the national market in which communication devices and technology play a key role: the highways and railroads, the telegraph, radio, and telephone—because making a country is more than enabling a region's production to reach other regions, or to get to port for exporting; it is also a political and cultural project: forging nations through the creation of a culture and a national sentiment.

To the social visibility of the masses—expressed in the pressure of their demands for work, education, health, and entertainment—the state responds by nationalizing them: making them into social subjects based upon the idea of *nation*, since they are the new content of the idea of *people* in which these new subjects who portrays national character recognize themselves. Therein lies the decisive role played by mass media in the communication between leaders and popular masses: becoming the voice of interpellation that transformed the masses into people and the people into nation—interpellation that came from the state but that was effective only to the extent that the masses recognized in it some of their basic demands and the presence of some of their forms of expression. In the resemantization of these demands and the recognition of expressions that came from the popular world, the action of media entailed creating the osmotic space to configure the popular discourse of the masses, one in which the masses recognized and transformed themselves, were aroused and appeased.

The cultural sense of communications media then alludes to the appearance on the social scene of a new sense of the popular that emerges with urban cultures. Leaving behind the signification of "the popular" as a space for the primitive and the uncivilized, it comes to mean, according to José Luis Romero's pioneering and accurate expression, "alluvial folklore": that of tango, film, and soccer, the earliest hybridization of the national and the foreign, of popular pathos and middle-class obsession with mobility, of what comes from the slum and the underworld with what comes from manners and respect for forms. "Alluvial" designates, in a Latin fashion, what Anglos have called "massive," which is, at the same time, what masses provide—their demands that what had previously been a privilege of minorities in terms of environment or education, of health or entertainment, be a right of anyone and everyone—and what media provide: radio, making possible the transition from still-majority rural cultures to the new urban culture without completely abandoning certain traits of its oral nature, and film, creating nation through dramatization, disrupting customs to the point that what had for a long time been equated with tasteless vulgarity became a configurative element of "national idiosyncrasy." And both media contributed decisively to the gestation of a powerful Latin American imagery, composed of musical genres and rhythms like the tango, bolero, and ranchera, and cinema icons like María Félix, Libertad Lamarque, and Cantinflas.

The modernity that our countries currently incarnate is not only different but, to a large extent, contrary. Communications media are one of the most powerful agents of devaluing the national and erasing the Latin American, because what media bring into play is a contradictory movement of globalization and fragmentation of culture, and also of internationalization and revitalization of the local. The press as well as the radio and, in an accelerated fashion, television are today the most interested parties in distinguishing cultures by region or age, while at the same time connecting them to the rhythms and imagery of what is global. On the other hand, the presence in the world's audiovisual space of companies like Mexico's Televisa or Brazil's Redeglobo occurs for the most part at the price of molding the image of these peoples into audiences that are increasingly neutral, less distinguishable. The demands of the model imposed by globalization orient those changes. These are demands that become evident in the privatizing reordering of national television systems throughout the world. But the expansion in the number of channels, the diversification and growth of cable television and satellite connections have increased the amount of programming, fueling an intense demand for shows that has opened the market, as never before, to Latin American production, and from which the soap opera in particular has benefited, producing small gaps in U.S. television hegemony and in the division of the world into a North identified with productive countries and a South with countries that only consume. However, we are witnessing the success of the market experience in commercializing cultural difference to renovate worn-out narratives, connecting them to other sensibilities whose vitality is resemanticized in favor of a culture of indifference.

The contradictions that run through and support Latin America's globalized integration lead decisively to the questioning of the impact of audiovisual industries in these processes, since these industries operate in the strategic field of images that these people make of themselves and through which they make themselves recognizable to others.

Communications, Social Sciences, and Cultural Studies

From its beginning in the early 1970s, and especially since the mid-1980s, the field of communications studies in Latin America has found itself torn between two issues: the technological drive—the "technological fact" with its modernizing, developmentalist reasoning—and the cultural one, the question of memory and identities in their struggle to survive and reconstitute themselves through resistance and reappropriation. The uncertainty, the theoretical-political hesitation of these studies, has little to do with the ambiguity that comes with a mixed knowledge of two logics: that of *knowledge* regulated by laws of accumulation and compatibility, and that of *awareness* of differences and cultural citizenships—because what the communications/culture relationship in Latin America brings into play is the very plot of modernity and cultural discontinuities, of anachronisms and utopias that support and resist, assimilate and confront mass communications in our lands.

The profound changes in the configuration of communications studies came not only, nor mainly, from an inner evolution, but from a general movement in the social sciences. The questioning of *instrumental reasoning* did not pertain only to a model of information, but rather revealed the view of doctrinaire Marxist ideologism as an epistemological and political horizon. On the other hand, the transnational question overwhelmed the matter of imperialism in practice and theory, forcing a revised thinking about a new layout of actors, contradictions, and conflicts. The displacements necessary for a conceptual and methodological remaking of the field of communications came from the sphere of social movements and new cultural dynamics, opening research to the transformations of social experience.

There is then a new mode of relation with, and from, the social disciplines, not exempt from mistrust and misunderstandings, but defined more by appropriations than by thematic recurrences or methodological borrowings. From communications studies there is work on processes and dimensions, which incorporate historical, anthropological, aesthetic questions and knowledge, while at the same time history, sociology, anthropology, and political science deal with media and the ways in which culture industries operate. Examples are the work on the history of popular cultures in Buenos Aires, or the history of the transformations experienced by black music in Brazil leading to its legitimization as national music, urban and mass produced; in anthropology, the research on the changes in the production system and the symbolic economy of Mexican handicrafts, or on the rituals of carnival, religion, and body culture in Brazil; in sociology, studies on cultural consumption and on the cultural and communicational story line of politics.

Still, more decisive than the explicit thematization of communication processes or media in the social science disciplines is the overcoming of the tendency to ascribe communications studies to a discipline, and the growing consciousness of its transdisciplinary order. Within this new perspective, cultural industry and mass communications are the name of the new processes for the production and circulation of culture, which correspond not only to technological innovations but to new forms of sensibility and to new types of enjoyment and appropriation, which have, more than an origin, their most decisive common narrative in the new forms of sociability with which people confront symbolic heterogeneity and urban uncontainability.

It is through new forms of coming together and excluding, of recognizing and failing to recognize oneself that what takes place in and through media and new information technologies eventually gains social depth and cognitive relevance. For it is thus that media have come to constitute the public sphere—that is, to mediate in the production of a new imaginary, which in some way integrates the heartrending urban experience of citizens, be it through the substitution of street dramatization with television sensationalization of the rituals of politics, or dematerializing culture and freeing it of its historical sense through technologies that, like videos and games, propose discontinuity as the dominant perceptive habit.

Transdisciplinarity in communications studies does not mean, therefore, the dissolution of its objects into those of social disciplines, but the construction of articulations—mediation and intertextualities—that make for its specificity. That which today neither information theory nor semiotics can aspire to—despite being founding disciplines—as demonstrated by advanced research in Europe and the United States, and which, viewed from Latin America, represents an increasing convergence with cultural studies, makes possible the overcoming of a binary reasoning that prevented thinking of relations and conflicts between cultural industries and popular cultures, beyond the seamlessly interconnecting idealisms of difference, defined as external matters or resistance.

Despite all the misunderstandings and distortions brought about recently by the interpenetration of cultural and communications studies, such an encounter corresponds to the strategic junction that currently forms culture and communications—because for the plurality of world cultures to be taken into account politically, it is essential for the diversity of identities to be narrated, recounted. And it should be so in every one of their languages, as well as in the multimedia language that currently traverses them through the dual movement of translations—from oral to written language, to the audiovisual, to the hypertextual—and hybridizations: that is, of an interculturality in which the dynamics of the economy and world culture mobilize not just the heterogeneity of groups and their readaptation to global pressures, but also the coexistence within a common society of varied codes and stories, in this way unsettling the experience of identity we had until today.

It has been necessary to let go of heavy ideological and theoretical burdens to make possible the analysis of the culture industry as a matrix of disorganization and reorganization of social experience, in an intersection with deterritorializations and relocations that carry through the social migrations and cultural fragmentations of urban life. An experience that reorganizes the field of tensions between tradition and innovation, between great art and the cultures of the people and the mass media, something that can no longer be analyzed from the central categories of modernity—progress/reaction, avant-garde/kitsch—since they do not correspond to the new sensibilities. A revised approach is required because "identity" has recently come to imply two diametrically different dimensions. Until only recently, to mention identity was to speak of roots, of deep tradition, of territory, and of a long period, a symbolically dense memory. That and only that made up identity. But to speak of identity today also implies—unless we wish to condemn it to the limbo of a tradition disconnected from the perceptive and expressive mutations of the present—talk of networks and flows, of migrations and mobilities, of instantaneousness and lack of anchoring. English anthropologists have expressed this new identity through the splendid image of moving roots or, even better, of roots in motion. For much of the binary and essentialist imaginary that still permeates anthropology, sociology, and even history, this metaphor will be unacceptable, yet within it there is a glimpse into some of the most prolifically disconcerting realities of the world we inhabit—for, as a Catalan anthropologist stated, "without roots, it is not possible to live, but too many roots will not allow you to walk."

Suggested Reading

Ford, Aníbal. *Navegaciones: Comunicación, cultura y crisis*. Buenos Aires: Amorrortu, 1994.

García Canclini, Néstor, ed. *Cultura y comunicación en la ciudad de México*. 2 vols. Mexico City: Grijalbo, 1998.

Hopenhayn, Martín. *Ni apocalípticos ni integrados*. Santiago, Chile: Fondo de Cultura Económica, 1994.

Martín Barbero, Jesús. *Communication, Culture, and Hegemony: From the Media to Mediations*. Translated by Elizabeth Fox and Robert A. White. London: Sage, 1993.

Piccini, Mabel. *La imagen del tejedor: Lenguajes y políticas de comunicación*. Mexico City: Gustavo Gili, 1987.

Reguillo, Rossana. *En la calle otra vez: Las bandas: Identidad urbana y usos de la comunicación*. Guadalajara, Mexico: Iteso, 1991.
Sodré, Muniz. *A verdade seduzida: Por um conceito de cultura no Brasil*. Rio de Janeiro: Codecrí, 1983.

Cultural Critique

MICHAEL J. LAZZARA (TRANSLATED BY ERIK LARSON AND JONATHAN DETTMAN)

Broadly, the label "cultural critique" seems to encompass a series of concerns linked to a desire for social change and the perfecting of the human subject, including (but not limited to) the role of intellectuals in society, the functioning of power and institutions, the place of the subaltern, the relationship between center and periphery, high and popular culture, the nature of social practices, and a questioning of the concept of the canon. In order to analyze these problems rigorously, cultural critique employs a wide range of methodologies—among them textual analysis, surveys, interviews, and historical investigation—and advocates for an escape from the rigid compartmentalization of academic disciplines (Preminger and Brogan 262).

A source of tension that has historically divided practitioners of cultural critique concerns the separation between "elitist" and "nonelitist" views of culture. Early perspectives such as that of Matthew Arnold (*Culture and Anarchy*, 1869) privilege poetry and art (in the Neoplatonic sense) as higher forms for fomenting social change and the dissemination of values. In contrast, a thinker like Theodor Adorno ("Cultural Criticism and Society," 1951) positions the intellectual *within* culture, not above it, and assigns him the task of finding an escape route from criticism's potential complicity with ideology or totalizing meaning ("negative dialectics"). Faced with the "transcendent critics" who think that both their own positionality and that of the art objects they analyze exist in a sphere independent from society and its norms—a mode of thinking that for Adorno constitutes a flawed, elitist ideology—the practitioners of "immanent critique" recognize that both they and the cultural objects they discuss are simultaneously part of and a reflection of the social sphere that produces them. For Adorno, the challenge of *Kulturkritik* is to achieve, to the degree possible, a standpoint that is at once inside and outside culture. In a more radical gesture toward the democratization and amplification of the notion of culture, Raymond Williams (*Culture and Society*, 1958) suspends the division between high and low, arguing that "culture" is found in spheres as varied as the workplace, politics, and daily life. Along with Richard Hoggart, another of the "founding fathers" of British cultural studies and a member of the English New Left of the 1950s and 1960s, Williams challenges the cultural elitism of the university institution and strives to forge solidarity networks with the working and popular classes.

In Latin America, cultural critique seems to be born of an impulse to establish Latin American particularities, to interrogate the North-South axis, to conceive of one's own identity without borrowing theories from foreign contexts, and to measure distances between the metropolis and the so-called Third World. Without ever establishing itself as an institutional practice, Latin American cultural critique, broadly defined, emanates from heterogeneous spaces and intellectual traditions, mainly from leftist writers and intellectuals interested in promoting nationalist, progressive, or anti-imperialist politics (D'Allemand). It is rooted in diverse and noncontemporaneous authors like Martí, Sarmiento, Bello, Mariátegui, Rama, Cornejo Polar, García Canclini, Martín Barbero, and Sarlo. And, in that sense, it seems feasible to argue that Latin American cultural critique long predates the institutionalization of British and American cultural studies (Yúdice, "Contrapunteo").

Given the breadth of the term and its varied intellectual paths, I prefer to focus here on a recent tendency of cultural critique, that of Nelly Richard—a tendency that is situated in the Chilean context and that, in recent years, has established an intense dialogue with cultural studies. My purpose is to explore the origins of Richard's cultural critique and specify its differences and continuities with cultural studies as it is practiced in the Anglo-Saxon world. Finally, I will consider various critiques and self-critiques of Richardean thought.

Nelly Richard and Cultural Critique *from* Latin America

Nelly Richard stands out currently as one of the most important public intellectuals and as the founder of a critical practice that, by way of contrast with cultural studies, calls itself "cultural critique" (*crítica cultural*). Born in France, Richard studied modern literature at the Sorbonne and moved to Chile in 1970, where she lived, intensely, the experience of Salvador Allende's Popular Unity government (1970–73). Her critical work emerged during the convulsive years of Pinochet's dictatorship (1973–90) and served to foreground an important group of neo-avant-garde artists, designated by Richard as the Escena de Avanzada, whose works sought to interrogate, via a fragmentary, partial, and oblique aesthetic, the grammars of hegemonic, dictatorial power.

Since the beginning of the transition to democracy in 1990, Richard has continued to research the connections among art, politics, culture, and theory, particularly in reference to the problematics of memory, neoliberalism, globalization, identity, democratization, and gender. Within this critical trajectory, her work maintains a constant focus on the margins, interstices, and edges of cultural expression, venturing that those "residual" sites are the most suitable places from which to question both totalitarian discourse and the macronarrative constructs of the present (Richard, *Cultural Residues* 3). With her *Revista de Crítica Cultural*, founded at the beginning of the postdictatorial period, Richard succeeded in promoting a productive dialogue situated at the crossroads of European, American, and Latin American theoretical perspectives. Without overlooking international debates, the *Revista*, whose final issue was published in December 2007, never strayed from its mission of highlighting the specificities of the Chilean transition and its multiple local problems. A group of intellectuals from various disciplinary fields contributed regularly to the *Revista*, hoping to generate a hybrid publication whose transdisciplinary nature not only reflected but debated the meanings and ramifications of the practice of "cultural critique."

In genealogical terms, Richard's cultural critique has its origins in an eclectic mix of European and Latin American intellectual currents. On one hand, one clearly observes in her writings the legacy of a brand of Continental European thought (psychoanalysis, the Frankfurt School, British cultural studies, French structuralism, poststructuralism, deconstruction) that emphasizes concepts such as "textuality," "the discursive nature of any realm (be it culture, society, politics, or, even, economics)," the "politics of the critical act," or the inscription of subjective desire in writing (Sarto, "Cultural Critique" 235). At the same time, her work evidences Latin American roots that likely date back to certain nineteenth- and twentieth-century essayists (Martí, Hostos, Mariátegui, Ortiz, Rama, and others) who convey a multidisciplinary approach to political and cultural phenomena and, even more important, are interested in both social marginality and the production of subjectivities and discourses that stand in a tense relationship to power.

Richard's work wishes to open a dialogue with both metropolitan and peripheral theoretico-cultural productions. In emphasizing the aesthetic materiality (that is, the linguistic configuration, lapses, slip-ups, and desires) of various discourses emanating from different points of origin, Richard succeeds in registering a "critique of criticism" that positions itself on an intellectual battlefield conceptualized as being both *of* and *from* the margin. Thus the apparent contradiction—one that some have imputed to Richard—of analyzing Latin America using metropolitan theoretical tools is nullified when one considers that Richard wants to resituate, threaten, and adapt these theories in the service of an eminently Latin American project. Finally, notwithstanding her eclectic theoretical lineage, it is important to recognize, too, that Richard's cultural critique assumes its initial form and affirms its basic ideological tenets in Pinochet's Chile of the 1980s because of a concrete, in situ debate with a very specific strain of the Chilean social sciences, led by the distinguished sociologist José Joaquín Brunner.

The cause of this debate between the Escena de Avanzada's aesthetic neo-avant-gardism, advocated by Richard, and the "renovated" sociology practiced in the Latin American School of Social Sciences (FLACSO) under Brunner has its roots in the supposed existence of an ideological common ground between the two groups during the dictatorship. Despite their differences, both the sociologists and the Escena de Avanzada sought to open spaces for reflection on the dictatorial catastrophe and possible routes toward democracy's restoration. In principle, the sociologists "à la Brunner," as representatives of the new (post-Marxist) Left, seemed to share the *post* perspective with those postmodern (neo-avant-garde) artists whose thought was characterized by a deep skepticism toward the traditional revolutionary Left's prevailing politico-utopian narratives. According to Richard, the presence of common ideological enemies—particularly on the political Right and on the traditional Left, like the Socialist and Communist Parties—along with a "shared framework" that bound the Escena de Avanzada to the renovated sociologists, "could have fed some type of complicit dialogue about a shared horizon of theoretical and cultural reconceptualization. This did not take place, however. Despite the fact that the theoretically renewed sector of the social sciences headed by José Joaquín Brunner demonstrated a greater perceptiveness and receptivity to the socio-aesthetic reformulations of the 'new scene,' a broader dialogue of productive communication . . . did not follow. Instead, mutual distrust and suspicion prevailed" (Richard, *Insubordination* 56).

The source of this "mutual distrust" had to do, on one hand, with a debate about which modes of expression would be most "appropriate" to think and speak about the dictatorial catastrophe and, on the other hand, with the radically differentiated speaking positions of the two groups. While Richard and the Escena de Avanzada, disconnected from academic institutions and state financial support, favored "the minimalism of syntactic breaks and fragments, opposing the epic of metasignification," the social scientists preferred "to *order categories* and to *categorize* disorder—to reframe the crisis of meaning in a secure language and a general framework that could in turn discipline the meaning of the crisis" (*Insubordination* 61, 58). This "postmodern" stance taken by the Escena de Avanzada, which mistrusted any utilitarian, functional, or instrumental rationalization, found itself in a strong ideological tension—in the end irresolvable—with the sociologists' zeal for reestablishing "consensuses" and subjecting political and social phenomena to *explanatory* criteria.

According to Richard, while it may be true that Brunner and the sociologists, especially in their later reflections, have dealt with topics and employed stylistic techniques that could be called "postmodern"—promoting, in turn, lively reflections on Latin American modernity and its "residual, decentered, anomalous, and so on" character—when the renovated sociologists "found themselves faced with the 'new scene's' *stylistic operations*, detached—critically and parodically—from the languages of modernity, these very same social sciences opted to protect themselves from such an adventure by taking shelter behind the screen—almost unchanged—of a 'quantitative methodology' tracing 'a statistical outline of the global development' of cultural transformation" (*Insubordination* 61). The desire to break free from the institutionalized and discursively normalized nature of the social sciences gave rise to cultural critique and served as its theoretical impetus.

In order to strengthen itself as a critical practice, Richardean cultural critique has subsequently tried to outline its differences and affinities with cultural studies. In what do these convergences and divergences consist?

First, it is evident that the two practices are related and that, additionally, cultural critique, in its most recent phase, has established some of its most productive debates with U.S. cultural studies. There is no doubt that the two practices share a desire to redraw the boundaries of academic knowledge and to reconfigure traditional forms of knowledge through a transversal and transdisciplinary lens (Richard, *Cultural Residues* 95–96). In turn, both cultural critique and cultural studies would like to dismantle hegemonic forms of power by engaging in a dialogical, resistant, and interrogatory rebellion (96).

Notwithstanding these points of contact, according to Ana del Sarto, while cultural studies "construes [its locus] from social materiality in order critically to produce social reality," cultural critique does it "from aesthetic materiality" ("Cultural Critique" 236). Consequently, a central disagreement that Richard has with certain currents in cultural studies concerns the ways in which it neglects aesthetic specificity and privileges the social excessively. Cultural critique, without becoming elitist, advocates against the relativization of aesthetics and in favor of literature and art, not as mere "textual" instances, but rather as unique discursive modes that speak in their own way and from their own place.

Other distinctive traits of Richardean cultural critique are:

1) *A focus on the extra-institutional and the marginal*: While Richard sees cultural studies as a practice limited to metropolitan university spaces, cultural critique, without completely turning its back on the university, wishes to call attention to the limits of the "system" and to speak from lateral, decentered positions (the feminine, sex- or gender-based heterologies, the subaltern).
2) *An anti- or transdisciplinary character*: From this perspective, cultural critique must not understand itself as a homogeneous or programmatic practice, but instead as a practice that questions procedures of constructing and disseminating academic knowledge. Cultural critique, in opposition to university-based philosophy, academic literary criticism, and the social sciences, dialogues with and takes (fragmentary) advantage of each one of these disciplines, while constantly interrogating both the content and the forms of transmission of institutionalized, professional knowledge (the paper, the academic citation, sanctioned editorial norms). According to John Beverley, "radical skepticism regarding the university's authority and academic knowledge" would be the main point of contact between Richardean cultural critique and subaltern studies (339). The two tendencies also share an "explicit, combative politics" that Beverley sees as healthy (338). Nevertheless, Beverley questions cultural critique for overprivileging the intellectual as a figure "necessary for revealing the complicities and complications of the coloniality of power" (339). Returning to Richard's vision, cultural

critique would create hybrid texts that aren't easily classifiable, blending the essay genre with deconstructive analyses and critical theory to "examine the crossroads between social discursiveness, cultural symbolizations, power formations, and constructions of subjectivity" (*Cultural Residues* 96). Instead of speaking *about* the Latin American crisis through the lens of "controlled knowledge" (*un saber controlado*), Richard argues in favor of speaking *from* the crisis and the destabilized spaces of "uncontrolled thinking" (*el descontrol del pensar*); she emphasizes the fragment, the margin, the fissure, and flight (in the Deleuzian sense) as central concepts of her critical practice (*Cultural Residues* 93). From the preceding observations, the affinity between Richard's own theoretical gaze and certain of the postmodern aesthetic practices that she analyzes becomes clear. Without establishing exact equivalencies, Richard's intellectual proximity to certain Chilean neo-avant-garde artists like, for example, the writer Diamela Eltit or the visual artist Carlos Leppe has been pointed out frequently by critics.

3) *A concern for the enunciative positionality of theoretical discourse*: Richard repeatedly underlines the importance of the local as a strategic site from which to think, theorize, and act. If cultural studies and "Latin Americanism" speak *about* Latin America, cultural critique tries to speak *from* Latin America, always conscious that "a Latin American theory that believes itself independent of the conceptual tapestry of metropolitan academic discourse is no longer possible" (Richard, "Intersectando" 1–2). Without discounting key concepts from cultural studies like alterity, marginality, and subalternity, Richard demands that debates like center/periphery, local/global, original/copy remain open in order to consider the tense relationship between "contextual placement and discursive position" ("Intersectando" 2).

4) *A nonessentialist identity politics*: In a context characterized by the crossbreeding and mutation of national, sexual, and ethnic identities, Richard warns against the essentialization of the Latin American subject. Cultural critique perceives the potential danger that concepts like "otherness" and "marginality" might be co-opted by metropolitan knowledge under the guise of democratic inclusion while, in practice, the "real other," embedded in specific, local contexts, is forgotten. Richard, additionally, expresses a fear that these concepts can be trivialized or emptied of meaning by their

excessive repetition in academic circles. As a consequence, a careful examination of Richard's critical lexicon reveals that words like "volume," "density," and "weight" are often linked to the idea of "experience" in order to remind readers that real experience, lived by subjects in crisis, should never be eclipsed or whitewashed by the powerful discourses of globalization and metropolitan theory.

Challenges and Discrepancies: Critiques and Self-Critiques of Richardean Thought

Since the publication of *Residuos y metáforas* (1998), Nelly Richard, without diverging from the central tenets of her thought, has begun to nuance some of her stances self-critically. These subtle self-critiques appear scattered across several articles written after Pinochet's arrest in 1998 in London ("Language"; "Reconfigurations"). Pinochet's capture—an unlikely and until then unanticipated event, given the amnesiac Chilean transition—caused Richard to reflect on the aptness of the margin as a site for rebellion and political transformation. If, in principle, rebellions from the margin seemed to be sufficient for producing the "lines of flight" (Deleuze) necessary for political and social change, Richard now indicates that Pinochet's arrest in London teaches that disruptions of power can originate, not only from lateral positions, but also from within the very epicenter of the political. In a Foucauldian gesture, Richard admits that the neoliberal machine is not impenetrable and that any "totalizing" system is not entirely so: "That there is no exteriority, that nothing is left outside, does not mean that the interiors of institutions do not present dislocations of frames and breakages of diagrams that stimulate and dynamize the game of forces between uniformity and deformity" ("Language" 260). At the same time, Richard recognizes that "lines of flight," in their Deleuzian sense, aren't always necessarily liberating (Nazism, for example, can be understood as a "line of flight" that distances the human being from logical behavior); neither must marginality necessarily be a liberating or politically effective subject position (Beasley-Murray 270).

In recent years, Richard has also questioned whether the fragment and the privileging of the catastrophe of meaning are, in fact, adequate strategies for combating amnesia and discursive normalization. If the imperative of postdictatorial societies is to carry out the work of mourning (Freud) and to avoid becoming trapped in unbearable loss and melancholy, then it is necessary to do something productive with the remnants of the catastrophe in order to transform the present critically.

One last self-critique includes the relationship between cultural critique and institutional power. According to Richard, every public intellectual runs the risk of being absorbed by the prevailing hegemonic system and, therefore, cultural critique wants to remain a practice that, in principle, distances itself from the academic institution and its normalizing impulses. Nevertheless, if the intellectual completely rejects power's normative apparatuses, she both risks losing an important route for political intervention and saps the university of its potential as a possible site of political commitment and resistance. In this sense, it is worth pointing out that Richard has recently assumed the post of vice-chancellor of Extension, Publications, and Research at the University of Arts and Social Sciences (ARCIS) in order to promote, from there, an informed and democratic dialogue between the university space and the "outside" (see http://vepi.universidadarcis.cl). It is also worth noting that Richard founded the Master in Cultural Studies program (formerly known as the Diploma in Cultural Critique) at ARCIS. This degree's name change, without sacrificing the spirit of its contents, seems to reinforce the kinship between cultural studies and cultural critique.

From other perspectives, perhaps the most intense criticism of Richard's thought has come from the traditional Marxist left, represented by the Chilean critic Hernán Vidal. Vidal points to an irresolvable contradiction between the political avant-garde (the militant Marxist left) and the artistic (neo-)avant-garde (the Escena de Avanzada, Richard, and the *Revista de Crítica Cultural*), while characterizing the *Revista* as a project that takes place "behind the back" of the Chilean left's institutionalized parties and abandons "the great narratives of human redemption" (291, 304). Vidal sees a certain value in what he calls the "testimonial function" of the postmodern left, precisely because the Escena de Avanzada "assum[es] consciously, in its theory and practice, the consequences of the political defeat of the Left starting in 1973" (302). Nevertheless, he sustains that the artists' micropolitical interventions and postmodern "theatricality" have not substantially changed Chile's political situation and that, strictly speaking, human rights organizations and not the artists were the ones who caused Pinochet's fall (304). Although Vidal's criticisms are valid, it is odd that he doesn't mention the work of the CADA group (Colectivo de Acciones de Arte) whose "art actions," realized in the urban space of Santiago in the 1980s, sought to explore possible connections between art and politics.

Without closing the debate, it seems that despite the possible differences between cultural studies and cultural critique, the key to Richard's project is found in its sense of alterity with respect to dominant discourses (Sarto, "Cultural Critique"). What Richard proposes, from the local, Chilean context, is a kind of call to arms and a warning that dissidence is something that may be disappearing in a Latin America characterized by phenomena as diverse as authoritarianism, neoliberalism, globalization, and the professionalization of academe. Conscious of its own conceptual limitations, Richard's cultural critique resists any compromise with power and strives unequivocally not to become yet another macronarrative.

Suggested Reading

Adorno, Theodor. "Cultural Criticism and Society." Translated by Samuel and Shierry Weber. In *The Adorno Reader*, edited by Brian O'Connor, 195–210. Oxford: Blackwell, 2000.

Beasley-Murray, Jon. "'El arte de la fuga': Cultural Critique, Metaphor and History." *Journal of Latin American Cultural Studies* 9, no. 3 (2000): 259–71.

Beverley, John. "La persistencia del subalterno." *Revista Iberoamericana* 69, no. 203 (2003): 335–42.

D'Allemand, Patricia. *Latin American Cultural Criticism: Re-Interpreting a Continent*. Lewiston, N.Y.: Edwin Mellon Press, 2000.

Richard, Nelly. *The Insubordination of Signs: Political Change, Cultural Transformation, and Poetics of the Crisis*. Translated by Alice A. Nelson and Silvia Tandeciarz. Durham, N.C.: Duke University Press, 2004.

———. "Intersectando Latinoamérica con el latinoamericanismo: Discurso académico y crítica cultural." In Castro Gómez and Mendieta, *Teorías sin disciplina*.

———. "The Language of Criticism: How to Speak Difference?" Translated by Alessandro Fornazzari. *Nepantla: Views from the South* 1, no. 1 (2000): 255–62.

———. "The Reconfiguration of Post-Dictatorship Critical Thought." Translated by John Kraniauskas. *Journal of Latin American Cultural Studies* 9, no. 3 (2000): 273–81.

———. "Reply to Vidal (from Chile)." In Beverley, Aronna, and Oviedo, *Postmodernism Debate*, 307–10.

Sarto, Ana del. "Cultural Critique in Latin America or Latin-American Cultural Studies?" *Journal of Latin American Cultural Studies* 9, no. 3 (2000): 235–47.

———. "La sociología y la crítica cultural en Santiago de Chile: Intermezzo dialógico: De límites e interinfluencias." In Mato, *Estudios y otras prácticas*, 99–110.

Vidal, Hernán. "Postmodernism, Postlefitism, and Neo-Avant-Gardism: The Case of Chile's *Revista de Crítica Cultural*." In Beverley, Aronna, and Oviedo, *Postmodernism Debate*, 282–306.

Yúdice, George. "Contrapunteo estadounidense/latinoamericano de los estudios culturales." In Mato, *Estudios y otras prácticas*, 339–52.

Cultural Field

GRACIELA MONTALDO (TRANSLATED BY EDUARDO RABASA)

The temporality that marked the study of culture of the 1950s and the 1960s in Latin America was linked to a political outlook articulated by Marxist thought and powered by the impulse of the anticolonial and radical revolutions of the period. That outlook was especially interested in the historicity of the processes that contributed to the definition of a given culture and to the relationships between cultures. The ideas of change, crisis, transformation, vanguard, and ruptures were thus linked to an accelerated temporality that used the concept of change both as an engine and as an instrument to think history and culture. The onset in Latin America, with the Cuban Revolution of 1959, of a revolutionary process that conceived the Americas as a place for its concretion and spread is a testimony to the expectations and faith in the power of history. "Latin America" is thought of as a whole, and as an alternative in a world dominated by polarities. Both the utopias and the revolutionary projects belong to the axis of temporalities and the homogenizing impulse of modernizing processes that conceived the future as the locus of all transformations.

However, far from becoming a unifying and universalist model, the critical thought of Latin America installed itself along the axis of temporality in order to reflect upon the complexity of the cultures. Endowed with a good Marxist library and supported by a literary phenomenon—the Boom of the Latin American novel, which gave it an unexpected visibility—literature became an especially malleable object to think about the cultural problems that fiction attempted, in a symbolic fashion, to resolve. Ángel Rama carried out a profound reflection on Latin American culture from the perspective of cultural heterogeneity. These projects were enunciated in terms of "multitemporality," of dense times, of synchronicity. The book that perhaps best exemplifies this conception of culture is *La literatura latinoamericana como proceso* (1985), edited by Ana Pizarro, in which Rama dialogues with key representatives of criticism of that epoch, such as Pizarro, Antônio Cândido, and José Luis Martínez. Its title summarizes the concerns of the times: literature is not only conceived as an autonomous and identity-giving practice, but its experience of temporality lies at the center of interpretation. Antonio Cornejo Polar stated in these same terms, in something of a critical testament, that in Latin American texts "various times are at work; or, to put it in another way, they are historically dense because they are bearers of social times and rhythms that sink vertically in their own constitution, resonating in and with voices that can be separated from each other by centuries of distance" (*Escribir* 18, translation ours). In *Transculturación narrativa en América Latina* (1982), Rama reorganized many of the ideas of the period regarding Latin American culture, focusing on literary practice in order to establish the model of coexistence of times and experiences: "the concept [of transculturation] is elaborated upon a double gesture: on the one hand, it registers the fact that the present day culture of the Latin American community (which is largely a transcultured product and is in permanent evolution) is made up of idiosyncratic values. . . . It is precisely that capacity to elaborate with originality, even under difficult historical circumstances, that shows that it belongs to a lively and creative society" (35, translation ours). He borrows the term "transculturation" from anthropologist Fernando Ortiz, and later borrows the term "alluvial" from historian José Luis Romero, in order to describe the same process of accumulation of cultural and social differences.

It is evident that the particular analysis categories of the different disciplines break apart and form a bigger entity: *culture*. The interdisciplinary attempts of the sixties resulted in the progressive disintegration or debilitation of disciplinary limits. The reading of Raymond Williams in the eighties conferred a critical statute on a critical practice that had already been taking place in Latin America, as he posited the idea of culture as a conglomerate of practices that regulate and rule the relationships of different social actors among each other and with institutions. Williams's work together with the reflections on the culture industry by Theodor Adorno and Walter Benjamin inspired critics of Latin American culture to search for new objects of study across disciplinary boundaries.

The idea of field was introduced in Latin American at the end of the seventies. Critics connected specific cultural phenomena with an ever widening outside; those connections ceased to be thematic, becoming functions linking the various cultural discourses with other, not necessarily similar practices. The idea of culture actually began to become plural, and the emergence of "mass culture" redefined the limits separating the practices of the elite from those of the rest of the social sectors; the categories of author, artist, intellectual, audience, and consumer likewise began to break away from the modern tradition and take on new meanings during a period of little political enthusiasm, military dictatorships, and lack of utopian or revolutionary political projects.

The categories of intellectual and artist came into crisis, and the idea of aesthetic value became more and more relative vis-à-vis the production of the mass media. With the advent of media culture, it was no longer possible to think in terms of pure autonomy, and it became necessary to acknowledge relationships and negotiations. At the same time, institutions of critical studies became stronger since they provided a framework to connect different cultural practices. The dissemination of the work of Michel Foucault and Raymond Williams at the end of the seventies played a central role in the deconstruction of the centrality of aesthetics and in the mounting of a critical discourse on cultural relationships. The idea of intellectual field, developed by Pierre Bourdieu, made it possible to draw a cartography of these relationships, and consequently to understand the dynamics in the movements and structural functions of the different cultural actors, a web of interactions ruled by power relationships.

The idea of field now allowed for the study of cultural dynamics as something more than the exclusive property of the elite, viewing them instead as the dynamics of the different cultures that compete for hegemony. Bourdieu began to define the idea of "field" in *Distinction* (1979), along with the related categories of "habitus" and "capital." A field is a system made of individual positions (characterized by the habitus of its members) that are defined by the structure and amount of capital owned. Capital may be economic (stocks, land, job, wealth), cultural (knowledge, grades, family education, schooling), social (friends, relationships, networks), symbolic (reputation, prestige, more or less ritualized acts of recognition). A field cannot be thought of outside structures of domination, since it is characterized by inequalities. Thus, a field is always a space where there is a struggle for domination that generates strategies of conservation, resistance, and subversion. Domination, in conjunction with habitus and capital, is not unidirectional, and actors may hold different positions depending on the structure that is analyzed. Moreover, there are fields and subfields with their own specific logics that simultaneously share common rules. Fields are defined on the basis of the capital at stake.

Bourdieu focused on the study of intellectuals and artists, and in Latin America the idea of field has generally been confined to the intellectual field. Intellectuals have been defined as the dominated segment of the ruling class; inasmuch as they possess class habitus and an elevated amount of symbolic capital, they are a dominant element of the cultural field, but since they are subdued or are required to negotiate with institutions and economic actors, they are dominated actors. From this ambivalent position Bourdieu derives the ambiguity of intellectuals and artists in modernity.

The field is a sphere of social life that has been authorized through history. The concept of institution is fundamental for the understanding of the dynamics of cultural fields. Institutions are the configuration of relationships between individual and collective actors. Bourdieu does not posit a univocal representation of social space but rather a multidimensional one, since social space is formed by a plurality of autonomous fields defined by certain modes of domination. Some forms of domination—for example, masculine domination—traverse different fields. Indeed, Bourdieu's theory makes an attempt to give new meaning to categories of classical Marxism (domination, capital, class) by opening their semantic reach into more complex societies, where social actors are valued differently in different situations. In the Marxist context of Latin American cultural criticism, Bourdieu's categories turned out to be very useful for studying cultural contexts in which social actors and institutions are characterized by the instability and the ambivalence of their roles.

Together with a rereading of Gramsci, Bourdieu's texts supplied tools to examine the function of the intellectual in Latin America. The works of Ángel Rama, Antonio Cornejo Polar, Néstor García Canclini, Jesús Martín Barbero, Beatriz Sarlo, Renato Ortiz, Nelly Richard, and Oscar Terán, among others, used Bourdieu's texts in a productive and critical way. Bourdieu's categories inspired studies that incorporated multiple outlooks and crossed disciplinary borders in order to better understand complex objects.

In Mexico, Néstor García Canclini used Bourdieu's categories most productively in foundational works of a culturalist perspective about the present. In such works as *Culturas híbridas* (1990), *Consumidores y ciudadanos* (1995), and *Latinoamericanos buscando lugar en este siglo* (2002), he set forth the idea of cultural field as a tool to interpret phenomena that cut across urban experience, culture producers, the cultural industry's relation to transnational capital, the relationship between high culture and the media, the organization of the past, multiculturality and multilinguism, the idea of nation, and the links between culture and popular art in state institutions. It is only through the idea of the field that he can explain the plurality of a country with many ethnic groups, languages, and traditions, with close and unequal connections to the United States, with an unbridled urban growth, and with a basically conflictive and ambiguous relationship with modernity, to name some of the many directions his work has taken. His studies always aim to put into play the plurality of experiences and discourses that make up cultures.

In Argentina, Beatriz Sarlo reinterpreted culture in light of Bourdieu's theories. Her books *El imperio de los sentimientos* (1985) and *Una modernidad periférica* (1988) gave impulse to a model of reading culture as a meeting point of tensions, and a battlefield. She dismantles the traditional distinctions between elite and popular or mass culture by showing, along the same lines as García Canclini in his analysis of the present, the ways in which interactions among diverse actors and practices presume intense negotiations and struggles for symbolic power.

Although we might make an outline of the archaeology of the idea of cultural field in European thought, it is worth remembering the way in which the majority of cultural analyses during the second half of the twentieth century in Latin America were handled with a wide cultural perspective that sought to understand the complexities of diverse phenomena. Tension between Eurocentric models and national or regional perspectives marked the majority of the critical studies on Latin America; the category of *culture* illuminated a good share of the foundational analyses. The works of David Viñas, Ángel Rama, Antonio Cornejo Polar, and Antônio Cândido are among them.

Suggested Reading

Altamirano, Carlos, and Beatriz Sarlo. *Literatura/Sociedad*. Buenos Aires: Hachette, 1983.

Bourdieu, Pierre. *Distinction: A Social Critique of the Judgement of Taste*. Translated by Richard Nice. Cambridge, Mass.: Harvard University Press, 1984.

———. *The Rules of Art: Genesis and Structure of the Literary Field*. Translated by Susan Emanuel. Stanford, Calif.: Stanford University Press, 1992.

Cornejo Polar, Antonio. *Escribir en el aire: Ensayo sobre la heterogeneidad socio-cultural en las literaturas andinas*. Lima: Horizonte, 1994.

Foucault, Michel. *The Order of Things: An Archaelogy of the Human Sciences*. New York: Pantheon, 1971.

Pizarro, Ana, ed. *La literatura latinoamericana como proceso*. Buenos Aires: Centro Editor de América Latina, 1985.

Rama, Ángel. *Transculturación narrativa en América Latina*. Mexico City: Siglo XXI, 1982.

Sarlo, Beatriz. *Una modernidad periférica: Buenos Aires 1920 y 1930*. Buenos Aires: Nueva Visión, 1988.

Williams, Raymond. *Keywords: A Vocabulary of Culture and Society*. Oxford: Oxford University Press, 1983.

Cultural Imperialism

HÉCTOR FERNÁNDEZ L'HOESTE

According to Armand Mattelart, cultural imperialism theory emerged in the 1960s from communications research focused on economic development and its corresponding policies and influenced various studies examining relations between countries. It was only in the 1980s, thanks to the increased popularity of a global lifestyle, that research on this theory began to grow in an accelerated fashion, motivated by the tangible presence of great media conglomerates. Within this context, communications nurtured the development of Latin American cultural studies.

Its theoretical evolution is marked strongly by events related to international politics and economics during the Cold War, and it focuses on the imbalances and inequalities in international flows of information. According to dependency theory, the failure of Latin American state economies results from the global economic system, which imposes continuous reliance on nonindustrialized nations. Following this argument, cultural imperialism proposes that the flow of information from rich to poor countries promotes a consumerist civilization, an accomplice to capitalism with little regard for national borders, benefiting the industries owning the mass communication media, mostly established in metropolitan enclaves.

In effect, as an interpretive theory, cultural imperialism was applied in various areas, including international relations, anthropology, education, the sciences, history, literature, and even sports. Reflections on "the order of the modern world" (capitalism), "society" (usually, in countries or communities with growing economies), "the dominant center of the system" (industrialized countries), and "values and structures" (cultures and organizations alien to growing countries), as well as "dependency" and "media imperialism" (which are sometimes synonymous), belong to its vocabulary.

Cultural imperialism is often criticized for its vague methodological framework, hard to measure and with little descriptive capability. Unfortunately, as initially proposed, in a linear and almost unilateral sense, cultural imperialism discards nearly all possibility of media production by peripheral nations. Part of this critical limitation lies in the hypothesizing of a single direction in the flow of information, an aspect that, even if it was once true, has changed greatly with the advent of new technologies. In addition, cultural imperialism does not contemplate the capacity of an audience to process information and interpret messages. Thus, the cultural dependency arguments sustained by this theory ignore research on reception and consumption by Latin American audiences. According to José Carlos Lozano, all influence favoring foreign ways imposed by communications media is evaluated without taking into account opposing local alternatives.

In the 1960s, cultural imperialism frameworks gained popularity in communications research in Latin America and gained many followers, including Venezuelan researcher Antonio Pasquali, author of the first comprehensive study of communications in Latin America in 1963; Bolivian scholar Luis Ramiro Beltrán, who contributed a Latin American definition for cultural imperialism in 1978; Mexican academic Javier Esteinou Madrid, a critic of Mexican communications; Chilean author Fernando Reyes Matta, an expert in international journalism; and Uruguayan intellectual Mario Kaplún, a proponent of educational communications. For Latin American pioneers like Beltrán, cultural imperialism is a verifiable process of social influence through which one nation imposes its sets of beliefs, values, knowledge, and behavioral norms, as well as its lifestyle, on other countries. In Latin America, the great milestone text is *Para leer al Pato Donald* by Ariel Dorfman and Mattelart, who, from Chile, challenged the imperialist nature of Disney's production; to a certain extent, this volume sets a precedent for Latin American cultural studies. Its proposal, it must be pointed out, emerges amid the desire to legitimate the Unidad Popular administration, wielding a consciousness of identity opposed to capitalist excess.

Given its proximity to the United States and its patent inequality in many aspects, Latin America was one of the first regions of the so-called Third World to develop an interest in communications policies and implement structural reforms of its media. In 1976, largely as a response to the claim for legitimacy of those who argued for cultural imperialism as a critical framework, representatives of twenty Latin American countries met, under the sponsorship of UNESCO, to study matters pertinent to communications policies. Some of those who contributed to this process of media regulation were Beltrán, Pascuali, and Paraguay's Juan Díaz Bordenave; their research identifies tensions between commercial growth and democratic development. Mattelart's work also provided a theoretical framework and evidence for media reform, strongly embracing viewpoints of economic dependence, class interests, and transnational domination. Proponents of reform championed a less unequal flow of media products and recommended increased democracy in access to media, favoring freedom of speech and more support to national development. Nevertheless, resistance to cultural imperialism was based largely on a defense of national communications policies, hoping to counter the dominance of U.S. culture; the feasibility of a rational proposal in the field of culture; and the possibly integrating impact of regional cultural production. Along the same lines, the MacBride Commission, a body of thinkers chaired by Irish Nobel laureate Seán MacBride, issued its guidelines in 1980, following years of research on the communications gap between the metropolis and the rest of the world. It sought to promote a more balanced communications order, New World Information and Communication Order (NWICO), less biased toward countries of the industrialized world. This approach would be criticized later—once its naiveté became evident—by a large number of Latin American scholars. From this point on, many things changed, starting with the demise of the Soviet Union, together with the end of the Cold War, and the extensive implementation of new mechanisms of hegemony—in particular, the propagation of neoliberalism—throughout the world.

In the 1980s, with the advent of democratic Latin American regimes, there emerged a new critical perspective interested in the analysis of reception processes and the consumption of cultural products. In locating communications in the context of the struggle for hegemony, its followers revitalized the issue, emphasizing processes of assimilation, rejection, and the repackaging of contents produced by subaltern sectors of society. There was a shift from semiotic or ideological models, according to which communication embodies an act of transmission, to a reassessment of the subject, in which the cultural studies approach was extended into the field of communications. The shift is evident even in the work of champions of cultural imperialism theory, such as Mattelart. Though cultural imperialism functioned early on as a motivation for the study of culture, the eagerness to give up its dogmatism soon led to the rise of Latin American cultural studies. As a matter of fact, there was a change from strictly media matters to a wider cultural scope, an expanded outline that made it possible to understand communications as a complementary cultural practice, and to value dynamics and articulations that, going beyond communication, support culture.

A very significant contribution to the consolidation of this new tendency was the work of Stuart Hall. One of his key achievements was a revised conception of audiences—previously viewed as passive, indistinguishable entities—reproduced and expanded in Latin America in the work of Chilean researcher Valerio Fuenzalida. To Fuenzalida, the collective influence of the family unit is particularly important, as is the sociocultural context of the communications media. Within this focus, through diverse methodological approaches, an active role was envisioned for the audience in Latin American cultural and communications research, establishing a greater capability for the rejection or negotiation of the media's hegemonic messages.

Unlike the critical approaches of the English-speaking world, supported by matters of class or gender, in Latin America the study of culture was redefined by a more ample problematization of its popular nature. For the most part, this strategy emerged from the updated meanings of theories like dependency or cultural imperialism within the context of globalization. For Tomlinson, for example, globalization suggests that "the interconnection and interdependence of all global zones happens in a less premeditated fashion than the intentional control attributed to imperialism" (175). In the early 1990s, as a result of the incontestable expansion of the market, there was a palpable need to rethink the role of the state. Responses fluctuated between support for continuous government intervention, with nationalist leanings, as in the case of Brazilian author José Marques de Melo, and more skeptical positions, such as those of Esteinou Madrid, who questioned the strength of government under the influence of free trade, or even Mattelart himself, who denounced an eventual lessening of difference as a result of accelerated world economic integration. On the other hand, Peruvian academic Rafael Roncagliolo questioned the rush to liberalize economic measures, insisting that "all Latin American countries are dependent, though some are more dependent than others" (338).

In this sense, there are multiple Latin American contributions. Jesús Martín Barbero highlighted the importance of the conditions of production and reproduction of meaning ignored by the conventional frameworks in the study of communications throughout the 1970s. The general framework of Martín Barbero's proposal is that there are points of access to the dominant culture and its structure of power from which it is possible to subvert and reorient its order. Martín Barbero suggests the idea of mediation to rethink the processes of symbolic production and points out that the rediscovery of the popular in communications has much to do with the validity of certain communications practices among the working classes. To him, mediations are "where the social materialization and the cultural expression [of media] are delimited and configurated" (*Communication* 215). As examples, Martín Barbero proposes three key locations: a family's daily routine, social temporality, and cultural competence. Altogether, what

Martín Barbero proposes is to rethink cultural identity starting with concepts like the city, nation, state, and mass and popular culture. In the same way, for Martín Barbero, new information technologies pose a formidable challenge to the reconfiguration of the Latin American imaginary, in which the media largely replace the state. Following this approach, it would be pointless to embrace globalization in a festive manner or to adopt a pessimist attitude.

Néstor García Canclini criticizes the omission of "the various ways in which different sectors appropriate messages" ("Ni folklórico" 8, translation ours). According to García Canclini, research shouldn't center only on electronic media, but also on popular cultures. Alluding to work by Pierre Bourdieu and Manuel Castells, García Canclini proposes the problematization of identity from the perspective of hybridity and consumerism. The hybrid sphere designates the new intercultural mixes, the product of various processes of reconfiguration of identity in which new actors come into play, like the de-collection of symbolic goods (the reorganization of cultural products according to personal preferences, paying little attention to the canon) and deterritorialization (the loss of relation between culture and a geographic or social space). García Canclini points out that the guiding principles of social relationships have changed, as well as the relations between national and popular character, and between identity and territory. Like Martín Barbero—though with a different focus—García Canclini concludes that, between decenterings and multi-determinations, what changes is the form of generating codes and thinking of culture. Popular and elite cultures persist, and they coexist with mass culture, promoting a more heterogeneous cultural reality, still far from being democratic or immune to hegemonic advances.

Facing a process of globalization that changes relations between economy and culture, cultural citizenship may offer alternatives to generalized market neoliberalism, states García Canclini. In a nutshell, his goal is not just to demonstrate that things have changed, but that sociocultural circuits are linked in multiple ways with the processes of transnationalization. Old categories like nation and ethnicity are still viable, but new identities rearticulate them in their own way, incorporating content from new systems of communication, rendering them less open to dependency or cultural imperialism. Echoing Roncagliolo, García Canclini advocates a new role for government as the arbiter or guarantor of informative balance, with a motivation beyond profit and a diminishing of the cultural inequity among Latin American countries.

There are other outstanding contributions, like those of Mexican scholars Jorge González Sánchez and Guillermo Orozco Gómez, who propose, respectively, cultural fronts and complex identities, and an integral focus on the audience as working concepts. González approaches the stratification and interactions of consumerism, insinuating a return to structuralism. From a pedagogical viewpoint, Orozco studies the individualized appropriation of cultural messages by way of multiple mediations.

Following these criticisms, the suppositions of cultural imperialism pertaining to dependency, based on the supremacy of foreign cultural production, are rejected along two main lines: the analysis of mediations that qualify reception and the studies that demonstrate the great variety of meanings of hegemonic cultural products, once subordinate sectors attach new traits to them. In this sense, limitations are obvious: an effective problematization of Latin American culture—and its consequent integration to media—is rendered impossible, as it takes place in the unequal context of globalization.

Suggested Reading

Beltrán, Luis Ramiro. "Communication and Cultural Domination: USA–Latin American Case." *Media Asia* 5 (1978): 183–92.

Dorfman, Ariel, and Armand Mattelart. *Para leer al Pato Donald.* Valparaíso, Chile: Ediciones Universitarias de Valparaíso, 1971.

García Canclini, Néstor. "Ni folklórico ni masivo: ¿Qué es lo popular?" *Dialogos de la comunicación*, no. 17 (June 1987): 6–11. www.infoamerica.org/documentos_pdf/garcia_canclini1.pdf.

Lozano, José Carlos. "Del imperialismo cultural a la audiencia activa: Aportes teóricos recientes." *Comunicación y sociedad*, nos. 10–11 (September–April 1991): 85–106. www.allbusiness.com/sector-61-educational-services/133876-1.html.

Mattelart, Armand. *Mapping World Communication: War, Progress, Culture.* Translated by Susan Emanuel and James A. Cohen. Minneapolis: University of Minnesota Press, 1994.

Mattelart, Armand, and Michèle Mattelart. "La recepción: El retorno al sujeto." *Diálogos de la comunicación*, no. 30 (1991): 10–17.

Roncagliolo, Rafael. "Trade Integration and Communication Networks in Latin America." *Canadian Journal of Communication* 20, no. 3 (1995). www.cjc-online.ca/viewarticle.php?id=305&layout=html.

Tomlinson, John. *Cultural Imperialism.* London: Pinter, 1991.

Cultural Industry

VICTORIA RUÉTALO

The concept of culture industry was coined in a 1944 essay by Frankfurt School critics Theodor W. Adorno and Max Horkheimer titled "The Culture Industry: Enlightenment as Mass Deception" describing how mass culture (in German fascism and in North American capitalism) produces desires, tastes, and attitudes, which reproduce its own all-encompassing system. The "culture industry" (Adorno and Horkheimer refer to *one* industry belonging to the system in general), whose main objective is to sell products through mass media, has a clearly ideological function: to induce the masses to buy into the system and assure their obedience to the interests of the market.

Their essay establishes three fundamental ideas, which would become points for debate throughout the global history of cultural studies. Firstly, it links culture directly to capitalism, seen as another product deriving from a hegemonic source, mainly the United States. Secondly, it expresses a stark pessimism as it rejects the utopian Marxist vision of the future proletariat revolution. Lastly, it implies that profit-based "art" for the masses lacks aesthetic value, lamenting the substitution of what Ángel Rama would refer to as a "lettered" art with a mass art.

Adorno and Horkheimer's theory is blind to possible acts of resistance within the system that they describe. What may at first explain this oversight is that, apart from radio and film, the other industries at the moment of the essay's conception were still in their infancy; furthermore, the youth market, which would emerge in the 1950s, creating a space for resistance against the status quo, had still not arrived. Nonetheless, the essay inaugurated a critique of the social and ideological role of the mass media that would become central to cultural studies. British cultural studies in its inception also recognized the possible threat of the cultural industry, as it produces a cultural standard that attracts the masses. However, contrary to the apocalyptic stance taken by Adorno and Horkheimer, British critics redeem national proletariat culture as a possible resistance to the hegemonic power of the foreign cultural industry. The Centre for Contemporary Cultural Studies (CCCS) at the University of Birmingham (founded 1963) shares with the Frankfurt School the notion that mass culture fulfills its role by integrating the working class into capitalist society. Conversely, the CCCS would find opportunities for other types of creativity and new ways of decoding culture at both individual and collective levels, despite its implicit organization of capital.

Cultural Industry in Latin America

From its inception Latin American critics saw the cultural industry as part of a foreign hegemony; however, from early on there were local attempts to offer an alternative. Local cultural industries and their critics can be divided into three historical periods. Firstly, there were aspirations to integrate modernity by producing local industries (film, press, radio, music) with national "brands." Secondly, the Cold War produced local left-leaning postures opposing the growing imperialism of the United States. The moment of globalization and its late capitalist phase provided new opportunities and spaces for resistance. Critically, in this third phase the concept of cultural industry was reevaluated, and the dichotomy between popular art and lettered art debated.

Although often thought of as foreign, there exist strong cultural industries in Latin America. Illustrating the development of local companies that dominate the cultural field in their respective countries, starting small and growing to offer an array of cultural products as technology improves, is the group O Globo in Brazil, with the newspaper *O Globo* (1925), Radio Globo (1945), TV Globo (1965), the satellite channel Globosat, the publisher Editora Globo, the phonographic company Som Livre (1969), and Globo Video (1981). However, despite TV Globo's current position as the largest network in Latin America and fourth in the world, there is a great gap between industries in the South and those in the North. According to a study carried out by UNESCO, Latin America and the Caribbean represented only 3 percent of the global market in cultural goods in 2002, while the United States, Britain, and China produced more than 40 percent of cultural goods the same year. Precisely for this reason, Latin American intellectuals continue to discuss the hegemonic and thus foreign role of the cultural industry with its implicit dominance of the English language.

Nationalization and Industrialization

When Adorno and Horkheimer developed their ideas in 1944, Hollywood dominated the nexus of production, distribution, and exhibition of film. In Latin America, Hollywood's authority made local production very difficult. However, the coming of sound in 1927 introduced the problem of language, and the popularity of the radio and its local stars provided a space for national and regional music and would help to convert the cinema into an important business in Brazil, Argentina, and Mexico. In the 1930s and 1940s an industrial model of film production began to dominate as companies took advantage of the popularity of radio stars (Libertad Lamarque, Niní Marshall, Jorge Negrete, Agustín Lara, Pedro Infante) and studios like those of Hollywood emerged, devising a formula to make money by offering local product with a strong national character.

Early critics dismissed this period as one of imitation and dissemination of foreign recipes from a local perspective. However, by the 1980s, Carlos Monsiváis was showing how mass culture came to grant an important value to popular expressions. Ana López argued that Golden Age cinema (1930s–1950s), for the first time ever, circulated Latin American images, histories, and themes, thereby challenging the omnipresence of Hollywood and maintaining regional interest.

The Struggle between Imperialism and Anti-Imperialism

In the 1950s, in the midst of the Cold War, the cultural milieu began to change. Film studios were declining, as is seen clearly in the failed attempt of Brazil's Vera Cruz (1949–54), a studio importing both technicians and equipment from abroad to produce an internationally viable, quality cinema, while television and music industries experienced major growth. The United States, wanting to maintain ideological solidarity throughout Latin America, pressured local industries and governments to promote an anticommunism that simultaneously admired a modern and North American way of life. This complicity between local governments, the United States, and the mass media is evident in the Mexican firm Televisa's support of the Mexican president Gustavo Díaz Ordaz during the student massacre in 1968 in Tlatlelolco.

Critical local responses vehemently challenged the growth of U.S. cultural imperialism. Chilean writer Ariel Dorfman and Belgian cultural critic Armand Mattelart published *Para leer al Pato Donald* (1971), an analysis of Disney comics. Inspired by a Frankfurt School reading, they criticized this mass literature's sustenance of ideological paradigms between the domineering First World and the dominated Third World. Meanwhile, a Latin American culture began to emerge with a new worldwide visibility. The literary Boom fostered the local publishing industry and produced new national literary talent and bourgeois cosmopolitan culture. Nonetheless, Boom writers such as Gabriel García Márquez, Julio Cortázar, and Carlos

Fuentes became popular as they criticized capitalist modernity and forecast its end. This effervescent era created many counter-hegemonic movements that sought to produce alternative methods to distribute their products. The *nueva canción* in Chile, protected and promoted by the leftist government of Salvador Allende, created Discoteca del Canción Popular for recording the movement's artists; in Argentina, *La hora de los hornos* (1968) would be shown clandestinely during military dictatorships. The movie, along with its accompanying manifesto, criticized the cultural monopoly of the First World as a form of neocolonialism. These three examples reproduce a similar rhetoric typical of the period in their rejection of foreign mass culture, even as they themselves were becoming products in the process.

Globalization: New Industries and Interpretations

The 1980s brought a change from politicized societies with centralized economies and a strong military state to representative democracies with neoliberal economies vying for a share in the global market. The simple configuration of imperialism versus nationalism disappeared and was replaced with an interconnected and interdependent system dominated by global postures of consumption and production. In this fervent time new industries developed (video games, the Internet), creating different spaces for the distribution of culture which would change old methods of accessibility and produce new ways of reading, listening to music, and viewing images.

Nonetheless, globalization has not diminished the power of cultural industries; indeed, it has helped them flourish: Venevisión, Televisa, and Rede Globo acquired a global, even more powerful role with the export of *telenovelas*. In part, the growing number of Hispanics in the United States has demanded the profusion of these media behemoths and the creation of others based in Miami (Univisión and Telemundo), which dominate the U.S. market with programming locally produced and imported from Latin America. The city of Miami, as administrative capital of the Spanish-language cultural industries of both North and South, has helped to diminish national and regional divisions to create a "Pan-Latin" identity (which includes Spanish and Brazilian) for the marketing of products. Taking advantage of the profit provided by the youth market, these industries promote movements ("rock en español," reggaetón), stars (Ricky Martin, Jennifer López, Shakira, Gael García Bernal), and spaces (Latin Grammys) that give a transnational façade to Latin American culture, not necessarily making them representative of a total homogenization as Adorno and Horkheimer argued, nor giving complete power to the local, but achieving a combination of the two (Yúdice).

Despite this global presence of the Latin, residues of a Frankfurt criticism with a more local and sophisticated voice still exist. Renato Ortiz finds in the globalization of popular culture the creation of an imaginary and a global mythology that, according to José Joaquín Brunner, has reached its limit in the creation of national and social inequalities. Meanwhile Beatriz Sarlo insists on a return to the state model of education and the reappropriation of the literary values of the 1960s to counteract the hegemony of the cultural industry. Nelly Richard also sees salvation through a vanguard art that provokes audiences to assume a more critical stance toward the mass media. From different perspectives these latter two critics propose a return to a lettered culture to escape the invasion of a foreign popular culture.

Other critics do not completely discard popular culture. Jesús Martín Barbero suggests that the medium is not the sole focus of the process of communication, but that the emphasis ought to be in the interdependence between different parts of its process: the transmitter, the message, the channel, and the receptor. For Martín Barbero this interdependence, what he calls mediations, is necessary in the act of reading the significance of popular culture, complicating the static model of 1944. On the other hand, Néstor García Canclini, William Rowe, and Vivian Schelling note how the modern and the traditional negotiate new cultural spaces, hybrid spaces, where it is no longer relevant to speak about the dichotomy between the industrial and the artisanal. Essentially, what they describe reaffirms local cultures, movements that have access to hegemonic media, which in some cases do not necessarily form part of the transnational circuit of products. In 1994 the Zapatistas launched a revolutionary challenge to globalization through the mass media, especially the Internet. Returning to one of the earliest and still most diffusive industries in Latin America, Gustavo Remedi examines community radio stations in Uruguay as a space of resistance that does not form part of the global circuit. Beyond creative consumption and active reception (Martín Barbero; García Canclini) one reaches a type of "imperfect" art, as Julio García Espinosa predicted earlier, an art that disappears into everything, eliminating the figure of the artist or the lettered intellectual. This reappropriation of the practice of citizenship finally acquires a public expression in an era where supposedly this space has disappeared as a result of neoliberal privatization. The pirate industries also challenge hegemonic cultural industries as they reproduce Latin American copies of foreign originals, creating an informal and new local business. More than producing local images (López), they threaten the center with what hurts most: cutting into the "bottom line."

Suggested Reading

Brunner, José Joaquín. *Globalización cultural y posmodernidad*. Santiago, Chile: Fondo de Cultura Económica, 1998.

García Canclini, Néstor. *Hybrid Cultures: Strategies for Entering and Leaving Modernity*. Translated by Christopher L. Chiappari and Silvia L. López. Minneapolis: University of Minnesota Press, 1989.

García Espinosa, Julio. "For an Imperfect Cinema." Translated by Julianne Burton. In *New Latin American Cinema*, edited by Michael T. Martin, 1: 71–82. Detroit: Wayne State University Press, 1997.

López, Ana M. "Tears and Desire: Women and Melodrama in the 'Old' Mexican Cinema." In *Mediating Two Worlds: Cinematic Encounters in the Americas*, edited by John King, Ana M. López, and Manuel Alvarado, 147–63. London: BFI, 1993.

Martín Barbero, Jesús. *Communication, Culture and Hegemony: From the Media to Mediations*. Translated by Elizabeth Fox and Robert A. White. London: Sage, 1993.

Monsiváis, Carlos. *Escenas de pudor y liviandad*. Mexico City: Grijalbo, 1988.

Monsiváis, Carlos, and Carlos Bonfil. *A través del espejo: El cine mexicano y su público*. Mexico City: El Milagro, 1994.

Ortiz, Renato. *Mundialización y cultura*. Translated by Elsa Noya. Buenos Aires: Alianza, 1997.

Remedi, Gustavo. "Production of Local Public Spheres: Community Radio Stations." In Sarto, Ríos, and Trigo, *Latin American Cultural Studies Reader*, 513–34.

Richard, Nelly. *Cultural Residues: Chile in Transition*. Translated by Alan West-Durán and Theodore Quester. Minneapolis: University of Minnesota Press, 2004.

Rowe, William, and Vivian Schelling. *Memory and Modernity: Popular Culture in Latin America*. London: Verso, 1991.

Sarlo, Beatriz. "Los estudios culturales y la crítica literaria en la encrucijada valorativa." *Revista de Crítica Cultural*, no. 15 (November 1997): 32–38.

Yúdice, George. *The Expediency of Culture: Uses of Culture in the Global Era*. Durham, N.C.: Duke University Press, 2003.

Cultural Participation

SILVIO WAISBORD

To paraphrase Raymond Williams's observation about culture, the concept of participation is one of the most difficult to define in the field of cultural studies. In political science the meaning of participation, a classic subject of analysis, has been extensively discussed. The concept of "cultural participation" is thus complex, as it refers to two ambiguous and contested notions.

Our goal is not to propose an ecumenical definition that settles existing debates, but to suggest that the idea of cultural participation is a point of entry to reflect upon central debates in cultural studies in Latin America. It is an idea that gives a sense of the richness of theoretical and disciplinary traditions as well as the kind of questions that have attracted interest from academics, activists, politicians, and intellectuals in the region.

The genealogy of the concept in Latin America can be interpreted as the progressive shift from consumerist to "productivist" positions, from structuralist to "agency" perspectives. Although this shift makes the analysis more complex, it runs the risk of ignoring the significance of inequalities in power, resources, and access that provide context to opportunities for cultural participation. If we remove the idea of participation from emancipatory ideals and define it as a chain of sense-making processes, the challenge is to assess its relationship to power.

Cultural Participation as the Consumption of Produced Goods

One position typically associated with the "sociology of mass media and culture" in either its "administrative" or "critical" versions focuses on participation as the consumption of cultural goods such as concerts, television shows, newspapers, and art exhibits. Participation is synonymous with ticket sales in "cultural" functions, the size of television audiences, attendance at movie theaters, and the like. Underlying this conception is a consumerist understanding of cultural participation as related to the supply and demand for "culture" as objects, media or activities. Audiences are basically conceived of as consumers, as opposed to culture producers. Culture is understood as a series of objects and institutions, and "participants" as spectators or audiences, regardless of the kind of relationship they have with products. This perspective is found in studies of media audiences and "arts" audiences that commonly aim to demonstrate preferences for specific products among audiences, to document consumption patterns, or persuade advertisers (as in the case of commercial media) or funding agencies or donors (for programs that are free or subsidized by wealthy patrons) about returns on their investments.

A variant of this position is the idea of cultural participation as "cultural work" as understood in the neo-Marxist definition given by Dallas Smythe. Without active participation of audiences, who watch television or listen to radio, cultural products lack market value because they are not transformed into commodities. In a market system, in which audience segments and packages are sold to those who finance cultural industries, the value of exchange of products is generated by audiences through their role as consumers. Here participation is not a democratizing process, but rather is fundamental for the functioning of an unequal, market-based system of cultural production.

Consumerist perspectives on cultural participation are also found in scholarly studies that analyze consumption habits in order to show the situation of cultural industries in a region, and audience preference for different types of content. Studies on preferences for domestic or international content (literature, television, movies) or entertainment or news (newspapers, television, radio) aim to produce a snapshot of practices of cultural consumption. Such studies are based on various theoretical approaches. From perspectives rooted in sociology of culture à la Bourdieu, some analyze the formation of cultural capital and forms of cultural distinction related to mechanisms of socioeconomic stratification. Thus, participation is seen as a way of establishing criteria for cultural classification according to the kind of cultural objects that are consumed.

Such perspectives on cultural consumption are also expressed in studies concerned with the situation of cultural industries. This line of research approaches participation as the consumption of available offerings made by cultural industries. Two conclusions are offered. First, there is very high foreign content in most countries in the region, particularly in film and music. Second, participation is focused on the consumption of foreign content as a consequence of market domination. Exceptions to this pattern are found in countries with more "developed" industries such as television and publishing and, to a lesser degree, film in Argentina, Brazil, Colombia, and Mexico, or industries such as radio where low production costs allow for the mass media presence of local content.

A similar perspective is found in official policies in support of "culture" and "the arts" at national, provincial, and municipal levels. Those policies typically promote the idea of cultural participation as a citizen's right that stimulates cultural democracy through the expansion of access to different cultural offerings, such as "the democratization of the arts" or support for cultural expressions that are ignored by the market. Also, they reaffirm cultural distinction within nation-states in a globalized world of increased cultural hegemony of products made in the global North. Those statements identify the need to stimulate the production and consumption of cultural goods to build and consolidate a national cultural space. Underlying this perspective is the premise of cultural autonomy as the guiding principle of national policies to expand and protect cultural production and history. Here participation is synonymous with cultural citizenship as membership within the nation defined as a cultural community. Such ideas also aim to achieve another objective: to promote democratization of access through increased participation in cultural spaces, traditionally reserved for the arts of "high culture" such as classical music and painting exhibits. Such a perspective aims to achieve cultural democracy as increased participation of a given country at both regional and global levels as a cultural producer, as well as public participation in the consumption of cultural goods typically accessed by elites or specific publics defined by socioeconomic status.

Cultural Participation as Sense-Making

"Consumerist" views of cultural participation are opposed to "productivist" views rooted in anthropological and constructivist positions that suggest that it is impossible to understand culture outsider the idea of participation. If culture is defined as "ways of life," a concept widely found in anthropological writings, the idea of "cultural participation" is tautological: there is no culture without participation. Everybody "participates" in culture whether through talking, practicing rituals, or choosing forms of dress and eating.

From this perspective, the analytical premise is that culture is related to sense-making networks that are activated by individuals and communities. Culture as habits, norms, and practices exists only as a participatory process. Obviously, there is "crystallized culture" in institutions or norms that exist beyond the processes through which they are experienced. The most extreme version of this position offers a processual conception of culture. That is, any cultural artifact (clothing, television show, book, symphony) has meaning only as it is experienced in active processes of participation. Those artifacts are references and resources within processes of cultural creation.

Studies on "active audiences" representing this concept of participation are influenced by diverse positions, from social constructivism to post-structuralism. While "participation as consumption" means a view of the audience as "listeners/receivers" (how many, when, how, who), the idea of "participation as production" considers the audience as taking part by giving meaning to cultural objects.

In Latin America, this position is identified with the work of Jesús Martín Barbero. In fact, not only does his classic book *De los medios a las mediaciones* figuratively suggest shifting from the study of communication to the study of culture, epistemologically it asserts that the task is to understand sense-making processes to understand the role of institutions (such as the media) and cultural products (such as *telenovelas*). Participation does not happen inside media and institutions; rather, cultural participation is linked to the use of resources and cultural capital.

It is also important to recognize the contribution of anthropological studies to the notion that the absence of "cultural participation" is impossible. Social life determines that human beings cannot refrain from participating culturally as they are immersed in sense-making networks. Cultural participation is unavoidable. This is a key difference compared to political participation which, according to recent sociological and political studies, is an option, as exemplified by citizens who decide not to vote or express their opinions publicly. Studies on the quality of public life in contemporary Latin American democracies have been concerned about the decrease in the quality and quantity of political participation as measured by various indicators (low voting rates, poor participation in political parties and civic organizations, lack of interest in politics). Regardless of whether such conclusions are correct in describing the present state of "political participation," it is important to indicate that, in contrast to politics, apathy and withdrawal are not possible options in "cultural participation" if we adopt a "productivist" perspective.

Participation and Cultural Citizenship

If our starting point is that "cultural participation" is unavoidable, how do we reconcile it with the persistent concerns about the state of participation in public life? How do we bring together the idea of cultural citizenship, either as democratic right or normative value, with the notion of cultural participation as sense-making action? If citizenship supposes participation as a member of certain political communities (the nation-state, multicultural states, and indigenous, religious, or ethnic communities), is it possible that there are no alternatives to being a cultural citizen/participant? Isn't cultural citizenship everyday participation through membership in various communities?

Understandings of "cultural participation" differ because cultural studies has debated different questions, and used different theoretical tools and examples to answer them. If we ask questions about how participation works in processes of identity construction and affirmation, participation is understood as sense-making production that uses and creates various resources to negotiate definitions. If the interest instead lies in the state of cultural production or the utilization of various institutions, participation is defined as a question of consumption.

Therefore, the pending questions are about what type of "cultural participation" exists, is desirable, and is linked to the situation of cultures, particularly regarding issues of inclusion and tolerance in contexts of migration and diversity. While "cultural citizenship" exists as long as individuals and groups actively participate in cultural life, the challenge is to identify what opportunities communities generate for sense-making. This is a question not only of individuals or groups as "active subjects" of sense-making practices, but also of the existence of resources to support diverse forms of cultural participation and minimize barriers to access the expression of cultural pluralism.

This implies deromanticizing the notion of cultural participation. Cultural participation, whether in youth or migrant "subcultures" or in the interaction and interpretation of products made by cultural industries, just to mention issues that have attracted attention from researchers in the region, doesn't imply democracy. Cultural participation must not be associated with an emancipatory vision, as culture "built from below" against power, but, above all, is a strategy of social belonging with diverse implications. There are forms of cultural citizenship that are not civic, but rather imply violence and oppression through mobilization of exclusivist and authoritarian sentiments. Cultural participation as a fact of social recognition and construction of communities and citizenship isn't necessarily democratic. Neither the notion of community nor the idea of citizenship implies democratic civility in the sense of the promotion of equal opportunities, tolerance of difference, and the inclusion of "Others."

Thus, it is necessary to interrogate the implications of cultural participation. The act of participation, being a citizen in cultural communities, cannot automatically be identified with democratic potential. The latter is about both production and consumption of cultural goods, public policies (the promotion of different artistic expressions), and the politicization of identities and interests. From the use of certain jargon to attendance at musical events, participation has unanticipated consequences. It can facilitate empowerment of socially excluded sectors or crystallize sentiments of hate and exclusion; it can demonstrate entertainment or the opposition to forms of domination.

If culture doesn't exist outside participation, the latter cannot be made synonymous with processes that push for recognition, autonomy, and expanding diversity. The implications of participation cannot be assumed; rather, this is precisely the question that needs to be answered.

Suggested Reading

Aguilar, Miguel Ángel, Adrián de Garay, and José Hernández Prado, eds. *Simpatía por el rock: Industria, cultura y sociedad.* Mexico City: Universidad Autónoma Metropolitana–Azcapotzalco, 1993.

García Canclini, Néstor, ed. *El consumo cultural en México.* Mexico City: Grijalbo/Consejo Nacional para la Cultura y las Artes, 1993.

Getino, Octavio. *Cine y televisión en América Latina: Producción y mercados.* Buenos Aires: CICCUS, 1998.

Maass, Margarita, and Jorge A. González. "Technology, Global Flows and Local Memories: Media Generations in 'Global' Mexico." *Global Media and Communication* 1, no. 2 (2005): 167–84.

Medina Carrasco, Gabriel, ed. *Aproximaciones a la diversidad juvenil.* Mexico City: Colegio de México, 2000.

Reguillo, Rossana. *Emergencia de culturas juveniles.* Buenos Aires: Norma, 2000.

Smythe, Dallas W. "On the Audience Commodity and Its Work." In Durham and Kellner, *Media and Cultural Studies,* 253–79.

Sunkel, Guillermo, ed. *El consumo cultural en América Latina.* 2nd ed. Bogotá: Andrés Bello, 2006.

Yúdice, George. *The Expediency of Culture: Uses of Culture in the Global Era.* Durham, N.C.: Duke University Press, 2003.

Cultural Policy

GEORGE YÚDICE (TRANSLATED BY NICHOLAS SANCHEZ)

Cultural policy is one of several forms of public policy, and as such it responds to government objectives (ensuring economic and social well-being, public health, public safety) by means of the design, planning, administration, and evaluation of relevant programs (such as public works—dams, freeways, bridges—that provide a foundation for economic growth and job creation). In general, a state institution implements cultural policy at a national, state, or local level, but in the last three decades the nonprofit sector (foundations and NGOs) has come to handle some of these functions with or without specific authorization from the state. The private sector also enters into the implementation of cultural policies by default (as when a transnational conglomerate like SONY, Time Warner, Bertelsmann, or Televisa distributes music, films, books, and television programming in a way that affects large public audiences and determines whether or not certain goods and services will survive in the market) or in agreement with the state (as when public-private foundations such as Mexico's National Foundation for Culture and the Arts are established, or when the private sector takes advantage of fiscal incentives via state legislation to function as a public subsidizer, as in the case of the Mecenazgo Rouanet Law or the Audiovisual Law in Brazil).

Compared to other types of public policy, cultural policy has historically received greater ideological intervention from governmental institutions: the formation of citizens through cultural-behavioral engineering in revolutionary France, Nazi racial and cultural hygiene, Soviet social realism, Mexican *indigenismo*. In the United States during the Cold War, the State Department waged a cultural war against communism, channeling funds to seduce the non-Stalinist left in roughly twenty countries, Mexico and other Latin American nations among them. Only beginning in the 1980s and 1990s were the projects of decentralization and democratization that had been outlined in the 1960s gradually put into practice. These projects imply a complete revision of the "ministry of culture" model adapted from those of Europe, particularly France.

Until very recently a ministry of culture's portfolio consisted of (1) high-cultural, Eurocentric arts that for the most part reproduced the values of elite minorities and (2) the folklore and popular arts that, together with (3) historic patrimony (colonial buildings and pre-Columbian remains), provided the particular identity of nations. Almost no ministry included the culture industries (radio, film, television) or telecommunications (which are increasingly integrated with television and the Internet in a distribution triad for the majority of culture that "is consumed" (Getino).

The suggestion that cultural diversity is an important asset not just in the democratization of nations and of culture in a global setting, and that culture as such is a factor in social and economic development, has transformed what is understood by the term, and increasingly ministries and nonprofit organizations, above all UNESCO and foundations like Ford and Rockefeller, and even the private sector promote an enormous expansion of what is included in this category. Today it has been proposed that the essence of culture is not the high-culture arts alone, but rather creativity as such, which can lie in any person or community. In fact, a new subsector has been created—the creative industries—that seeks to take advantage of this creativity to improve the economy, create employment, and produce a more cohesive society.

Increasingly, there is greater convergence among the arts, culture industries, entertainment industries, and embodied and performative practices. This increasing convergence obligates the researcher to employ a transdisciplinary methodology. And the economy figures here with greater importance because culture contributes between 5 percent and 9 percent of gross domestic product, in many cases surpassing all industries except tourism and biotechnology. In Mexico, industries based in intellectual property rights contribute 6 percent to the GDP (Piedras). And if one adds the piece of the tourism industry that corresponds to culture (museums, visits to indigenous cultures, purchase of handicrafts), the cultural sector occupies the first or second place within the economy.

We will come back to this new paradigm, but we must also elaborate on the preceding one, which refers to the consolidation of modern nations. Before this cultural consolidation, which for the most part took shape as a project in the 1920s, the countries of Latin America had already experienced the default cultural policies of their colonizers: imposition of the Spanish or Portuguese language, Christianization, and racial hierarchy. Even though the case of Mexico may not be not representative of other countries in the region, the notion of cultural policy can be effectively illustrated by the Mexican example because it was this country that contributed the most to the creation of a national identity by means of institutionalization and very high levels of public financing—a process that Octavio Paz once called the "philanthropic ogre."

The reconstruction of history was the principle vehicle used by Mexico to establish a new, more inclusive national identity when it broke with its nineteenth-century postcolonial legacy. The Mexican Constitution of 1917 announced a new national project of mass education with the aim of jump-starting the economy, incorporating the masses, and creating a sizable, educated, and nationalistic middle class capable of resisting the power of caudillos as well as national and foreign oligarchies. The cultural-educational projects included the artistic expression of the muralist movement sponsored by José Vasconcelos, who was appointed director of the University Department of Fine Arts by presidents Huerta and Obregón. This department included the Secretariat of Public Instruction and Fine Arts (later the Secretariat of Public Education). Cultural and educational policies were intensified and later institutionalized in the 1930s under the populist presidency of Lázaro Cárdenas, whose principal priorities were the incorporation of indigenous populations, the expansion of artistic education, the defense of the national patrimony, and the regulation of the film industry (Johnson 136). This project of national identity became stronger and stronger over time with the creation of the National Institute of Anthropology and History of Mexico (1939), the National Institute of Fine Arts (1946), and the National Museum of Anthropology (1964), which was the culmination of the process of national articulation, uniting the grandiose past with the modernity of the present. The results of this enormous labor advanced by the state are 6,000 libraries and 1,058 museums of anthropology, history, and art, in addition to the administration of a historic patrimony that consists of more than 200,000 archaeological sites and 80,000 historic and artistic monuments (Cervantes Barba).

This vast institutional structure underwent a number of transformations that give it a special character within the context of the Americas. The first is the questioning of traditional concepts and categories of cultural management—art, traditional culture (folklore, popular culture), and (tangible) patrimony—beginning with Mexican anthropology in the late 1970s and early 1980s. With the creation of the General Directorate of Popular Cultures (1978), the traditional was pluralized; with the creation of the National Museum of Popular Cultures (1982) and the first call for applications to the Program of Aid to Municipal and Community Cultures (1989), cultural management was confronted with institutionalized "cultural control"; and with the creation of the National Program for the Formation of Cultural Promoters (1984), the training of administrators was begun. Perhaps the theoretical reflection that best formulated the need to move beyond this restricted conceptual triad of culture is the book *Culturas híbridas* (1989) by Néstor García Canclini: we see in this book how popular cultures intermingle with high culture and the culture industries. But as we shall see, this conceptual opening remains distant from the current, larger expansion of what is understood as culture, which would not occur in Mexico and the rest of Latin America until the effects of the North American Free Trade Agreement (NAFTA) and globalization were felt. And this broader understanding has had important repercussions for the way in which development is conceived. As Cervantes Barba indicates, this cultural subsector, consolidated in the 1980s through efforts led by the Secretariat of Public Education, also received the modernizing and reformative imprint of the policies of development and decentralization of UNESCO. With the new government of Carlos Salinas de Gortari, the basis for entering

NAFTA was established, the context that would transform Mexico from an economy protected by the state to one of deregulation, privatization, an opening up to civil society and the free market, and other steps that harmonize with economic policies of the United States.

In the area of culture, the inauguration of the National Council for Culture and the Arts in 1988 as the coordinating organ of Mexico's vast institutional structure had the purpose, according to its president at the time, Rafael Tovar y de Teresa, of serving as a bridge between creators and society. And even as it did its utmost to aid in the decentralization of cultural institutions and to open itself up to private initiative through the creation of the National Foundation for Culture and the Arts, the principal agent of cultural management remained the state. The development of cultural management in the 1990s is staggering: "the national network of libraries; the network of institutionalized and community museums; programs to promote reading; a variety of activities in theaters, auditoriums, and plazas; workshops in cultural and community centers; innumerable contests, festivals, and programs of cultural invigoration, of promotion and diffusion of popular and indigenous culture; arts education; grants for study abroad; regional artistic circuits; new and better uses of mass media; stimuli for cinematic production and international cooperation" were all created (MacGregor).

It could be argued that the emphasis placed on the management and promotion of Mexican culture not only responded to the call for renewed interest by the community and civil society, but also had the purpose of mitigating fear in the face of the probable loss of sovereignty occasioned by NAFTA. In the words of Tovar y de Teresa, "the solidity of our culture constitutes the substratum of our identity . . . and the bulwark of our sovereignty" (17). In fact the mega-expositions promoted through the international cultural policy of the Salinas government used the bulwark of identity to garner success in a globalized world, as Tovar y de Teresa argues (19–20). According to him, a "return to cultural roots" was needed as a "unique and irreplaceable point of reference in order to assume changes [deregulation, political liberalization, and institutional decentralization] in a way that would not jeopardize our national identity" (12–13).

The protests against NAFTA and its international cultural policies—such as the mega-exposition "Mexico: The Splendors of Thirty Centuries" that, according to Paz ("Power" 19), conciliated the "otherness" of the Mexican past with the future of its modernity—and the irruption of the Zapatista Army of National Liberation that coincided with the implementation of

NAFTA, added to serious questionings on the part of anthropologists and others who proposed to introduce alternatives to the ideological use of cultural policy, among them Guillermo Bonfil Batalla, García Canclini, José Manuel Valenzuela Arce, and Carlos Monsiváis. In 1992 these critics published an analysis of the possible effects of free trade on education and culture. They questioned participation in a treaty whose only effect, at least on the cultural plane, consisted of the intensification of an ethos of consumerism in the minority that possessed sufficient means, and the exclusion of, out of 85 million Mexicans, the 17 million who lived below the official poverty line and 30 million others who lived at its doorstep (Monsiváis, "De la cultura" 194). They greeted the decentralization of Mexican culture with extreme caution, and furthermore called into question the neoliberal conditions under which private and transnational mass media were establishing the bases for a new cultural formation.

NAFTA is fundamental to understanding the enormous shifts in the concept of culture. It obliged the artists, researchers, and intellectuals interested in culture to recognize that the objective of development had a double or triple meaning—matrix of identity, agent of social cohesion, economic asset—in placing culture at its center, as UNESCO and even the World Bank recommended. James D. Wolfensohn, president of the World Bank, led the trend of multilateral development banks in including culture as a catalyst of human development. For Wolfensohn, a "holistic perspective of development" must promote the empowerment of the poor in such a way that they can count on the social and human resources that allow them to withstand "trauma and loss," to halt "social disconnection," "to maintain self-esteem," and at the same time to generate material resources. "Material culture and expressive culture are underappreciated resources in developing countries. But they can generate income through tourism, handicrafts, and other cultural activities" (World Bank 11). "Patrimony generates value. Part of our collective challenge is to analyze the local and national returns on investment that restore and derive value from cultural patrimony, be they buildings and monuments or living cultural expressions such as music, theatre, and indigenous handicrafts" (World Bank 13).

But instead of empowering cultural producers, NAFTA had disastrous effects. Eduardo Nivón Bolán observed three major general transformations, all of them negative: (1) the loss of industrial vigor; (2) a reorientation toward financial, commercial, and service-oriented activities; (3) the deepening of inequality because NAFTA did not generate equal benefits for all regions. Furthermore, he observed three specific effects in the area of culture: (1) the competition of private businesses with the state in the production of cultural goods and the concomitant predominance of privatized culture in homes; (2) the accelerated and less-regulated entrance of large global conglomerates and their cultural offerings within national territory; and (3) the reduction of the presence of the state in the "arrangement of norms, aid for infrastructure, and subsidies."

Today, cultural producers and managers, along with many intellectuals, are asking that certain aspects of NAFTA be renegotiated, above all those that make it difficult for the state to subsidize Mexican culture. A cultural exception that would exempt specifically *Mexican* culture from the laws of commerce is no longer the goal; rather, Mexico, like almost all of Latin America, has signed a Pact for Cultural Diversity that places cultures' access to internal and international spaces ahead of economic profit. What large conglomerates and the institutions that support their causes put in danger is diversity of expression. From this reality come the increasing attempts to strengthen diversity through support for small businesses that produce records or movies or books that the major production companies would not risk launching on the market. Cultural policy is no longer about only one national identity, but about national identities, which in turn are connected to the productive sector and legislation regarding goods and services on national and international scales.

Suggested Reading

Cervantes Barba, Cecilia. "Política cultural y ¿nuevos movimientos culturales en México?" Paper presented to the panel "Hegemonía cultural en América Latina," Latin American Studies Association conference, Las Vegas, October 8, 2004.

Getino, Octavio. "Aproximación a un estudio de las industrias culturales en el Mercosur (Incidencia económica, social y cultural para la integración regional)." Paper presented at the international seminar "Importancia y Proyección del Mercosur Cultural con miras a la Integración," Santiago, Chile, May 3–5, 2001. www.campus-oei.org/cultura/getino.htm.

Guevara Niebla, Gilberto and Néstor García Canclini, eds. *La educación y la cultura ante el Tratado de Libre Comercio*. Mexico City: Nueva Imagen, 1992.

Johnson, Randal. "Film Policy in Latin America." In *Film Policy: International, National, and Regional Perspectives*, edited by Albert Moran, 128–47. London: Routledge, 1996.

MacGregor, José Antonio. "El Promotor Cultural del Nuevo Siglo." *Sol de Aire* (Instituto Coahuilense de Cultura), no. 3 (2002).

Monsiváis, Carlos. "De la cultura mexicana en vísperas del Tratado de Libre Comercio." In Guevara Niebla and García Canclini, *La educación y la cultura ante el Tratado de Libre Comercio*, 190–209.

Nivón Bolán, Eduardo. "Cultura e integración económica: México a siete años del Tratado

de Libre Comercio." *Pensar Iberoamérica*, no. 2 (October 2002–January 2003). www.campus-oei.org/pensariberoamerica/ric02a02.htm.
Paz, Octavio. "The Power of Ancient Mexican Art." Translated by Anthony Stanton. *New York Review of Books*, December 6, 1990, p. 1821.
Piedras, Ernesto. *¿Cuánto vale la cultura? La contribución económica de las industrias protegidas por el derecho de autor en México.* Mexico City: Consejo Nacional para la Cultura y las Artes, 2004.
Saunders, Frances Stonor. *Cultural Cold War: The CIA and the World of Arts and Letters*, New York: New Press, 2000.
Tovar y de Teresa, Rafael. *Modernización y política cultural: Una visión de la modernización de México.* Mexico City: Fondo de Cultura Económica, 1994.
World Bank. *Culture Counts: Financing, Resources, and the Economics of Culture in Sustainable Development: Proceedings of the Conference.* Washington, D.C., 1999.

Cultural Production

ISABEL QUINTANA (TRANSLATED BY ERIK LARSON)

Beginning in the 1940s and 1950s, two theoretical movements appeared in Europe: the critical theory of the Frankfurt School, and cultural studies of the early Birmingham School. Both redefined the term "production" in relation to culture in the context of the burgeoning cultural industry. From this perspective, the traditional Marxist formulations that consider symbolic products (superstructure) to be mere reflections of economic production (infrastructure) were criticized. Both schools questioned the idealist conceptions of culture as a transcendent and abstract good and in doing so came to reformulate the differences between high and popular art to better account for the emergence of new social articulations. Critical theory, which originated in the context of Nazism and capitalist domination of economy, politics, and culture, would reflect on changes in high culture, as well as on the rise of the so-called culture of entertainment (film, music, radio). Theodor Adorno, founder of the Frankfurt School and its most salient representative—who with Max Horkheimer wrote *Dialectic of Enlightenment*, one of the pioneering books of cultural studies—and Walter Benjamin, who maintained a problematic relationship with the other members of the Frankfurt School due to his heterodox thought, developed two analytically distinct perspectives that have had a decisive influence on Latin American academic debates.

Adorno rejects mass culture and maintains art's privileged place: that of the critical conscience of society (negative dialectic). Benjamin, on the other hand, concentrates on art's possible use of technological innovation in order to transform both the auratic character of art and its own mechanisms of production and reception (*The Work of Art in the Age of Its Technical Mechanical Reproducibility*). The mass production of cultural artifacts makes possible a democratization in the use of productive forces as well as a substantial transformation in the experience of a public that, for the first time, gained access to mass culture and had to significantly organize their perceptions in relation to it. In "The Artist as Producer" (*Illuminations* 768–82) Benjamin posits that the artist, by utilizing the modes of production should, in the process, transform them; the example par excellence would be Brecht's montage technique within epic theater. The method of mechanical reproduction incorporated into bourgeois aesthetic forms provokes eclosion and critical distancing. For Adorno, such an experience is impossible. On the contrary, the Taylorist system of production applied to culture brings with it a process of reification, which leads to normalization, identification, and public fantasy. In addition, the work of art, by losing its use value to exchange value, can only be assessed in relation to market demand.

From a different perspective, English culturalists like E. P. Thompson and Raymond Williams became interested in the manner in which working-class and popular culture demonstrate resistance to the advancement of industrial power. In *Marxism and Literature*, Williams presents a theory of culture as a process of production (material and social) and of artistic practices as social uses of material means of production (language, writing technology, electronic and semantic systems of communication). He especially considers language and the processes of meaning to be the fundamental elements of society's material conformation. His theory implies a critique of the traditional notion of culture (as a privileged dominion, homogenous and consolidated) as well as a revision of Marxist formulations concerning the concept of production. He displaces the false dichotomy between a stable, objective, material world and the subjective dimension, which is rationally inapprehensible. In *Culture and Society* he questions the notion of a monolithic, compact, fixed economic base that would not permit human action because the symbolic products would only recreate that order. Following in Gramsci's footsteps, Williams posits that in the hegemonic practices through which the dominant class seeks to organize and control the people's experience lie residual and emergent elements. In this point he realizes a critique of the concept of ideology as a stable system of ideas that produces a false consciousness and a passive attitude in the masses. Thus he insists on analyzing that which escapes hegemonic dominion, which he terms "structure of feeling." Art and literature formalize these emergent structures, always diffuse yet signaling a certain intellectual current or a new historical period. The critic's job, or what he calls "the long revolution," consists, therefore, of dismantling the systems of meaning and values that capitalist society produces.

While these theories of cultural criticism were developed in England and Germany (and later on in the United States after the forced exodus of the members of the Frankfurt School), in the late sixties poststructuralism appeared in France as a product of a profound social and political crisis, marked by the optimism of the worker-student revolt in May of '68 and its subsequent failure. Beginning with a weakening of theoretical and ideological models conceived of as closed universes of meaning (including Marxism), and given the impossibility of a substantial transformation of society, writing became the final place of resistance. Among the numerous representatives of this current, two have more systematically developed a theory of literary production: Pierre Macherey and Julia Kristeva. In *A Theory of Literary Production*, Macherey considers critical work to be a form of production of meanings at the level of the superstructure. He also offers a critique of the monolithic concept of ideology by postulating, in accordance with Althusser, that what is of interest within a text is the moments in which ideology reveals its limits and secrets. These are the moments when ideology reveals itself as such and is, therefore, produced. The critic's job consists of giving an account of a web of meanings that is never conclusive. In this way, becoming familiar with a text is not revealing the supposedly hidden truth underlying it, but producing new knowledge concerning it. The goal is to discover the laws of its self-production as well as the conditions that make possible its autogeneration, a task that is realized through its relation to what is not present within the text. While Macherey recognizes that no text is absolutely independent, since it is inscribed within its social and linguistic framework, said relations do appear within, through their absence. It is precisely this lack that shapes it as an object. In this manner, as Eagleton suggests, Macherey (as well as Althusser) preserves the privileged status of art and theory by placing them in an avant-garde position from which ideological frameworks may be broken down.

In this sense, Kristeva's semiotic focus (*Sēmeiōtikē*) seeks to expose the articulations of theory; in other words, its own production, given that all theory is constructed and permeated by ideology. She proposes in her analysis to transform the terms she adopts. In this manner, the concept of production espoused by Marx does not interest her from the perspective of products but rather from their interiority. Assuming a hermeneutic and psychoanalytical perspective, Kristeva focuses her analysis on the instances prior to the formulation of meaning. These moments are what she terms the other scene where desires are formed before they become language, communication, or products. In this manner, language and the subject that produces it are considered in the processes of meaning (signifying practices). Art and literature also occupy a privileged space within this theory because, by their exposition of the heterogeneity of forces that invade and conform language, they make impossible any coagulation of determined meaning.

This textualist orientation, principally developed in France, went on to have effects in the larger field of cultural studies, both in Europe and in Latin America, with the translation of key works by Roland Barthes and later Michel Foucault. On one hand, Antonio Gramsci and Louis Althusser had an enormous influence regarding the concept of ideology. The essay *Producción literaria y producción social* by Noé Jitrik, in which the Argentinean analyzes the relationship between the modes of production of a given society and the modes of production of a text, is inscribed in this tradition. Jitrik posits that writing is developed according to techniques that are related to the general techniques of production. If the writing techniques are the product of the dominant class's development of productive forces, the writer may elect whether or not to change the sign (for example, the literary movement naturalism with respect to the positivist bourgeois ideology). Critical literature, by accentuating its distance from the ideology that accompanies the techniques of production, is able to separate itself from notions of consumption (59). In Jitrik's analysis, the idea of the sign implies a task of meaning production not contemplated in Saussure's linguistic theory (the signified reproduces, signification produces). At the same time, critical work produces new meaning (knowledge) in its reading and ultimately helps to transform the world.

Since the 1980s the development of sociological theories, also originating in France as in the case of Pierre Bourdieau and Michel de Certeau, have played a decisive role in the conceptualization of the cultural field as a tension between the expressions of high and low cultures. These theories assume a more decentered perspective vis-à-vis society, where those institutional formations that regulate individual behavior, if indeed they exist, possess their own symbolic patrimony. Also, communications theory (which began to rise to the fore in the seventies), upon observing a considerable growth in leisure time among spectators, would emphasize the role of the recipient as a producer of meaning, which implies a substantial change in the culture industries' administration, in which becoming familiar with the audiences' tastes and interests is fundamentally important.

These analytical models have had a substantial effect on Latin American thinkers regarding such concepts as production, circulation, and consumption, especially within popular culture. Néstor García Canclini postulates a materialist theory of cultural production, rejecting idealist notions of culture and cultural relativism, as well as the mechanistic approaches of Marxist theory. In *Las culturas populares en el capitalismo*, he presents the profound connection between cultural and socioeconomic processes. In this manner, one can principally observe the forms in which culture, in the era of capitalism, through distinct cultural apparatuses, the family, school, but also the media, prolong the hegemonic order through complex operations (administration, transmission and renovation) that create habits—the manner by which subjects internalize meaning structures according to their class position and social determination. According to García Canclini, the cultural apparatuses in which every class participates produce aesthetic habits that will lead some to high art and others to crafts (17).

In the field of communications, Jesús Martín Barbero has produced a substantial change in popular culture studies in Latin America. In *De los medios a las mediaciones* he signals how the Frankfurt School was the first to consider the processes of the masses as constituents of society's structural conflicts. At first, this idea had a profound impact on Latin American debates. Later on, however, the model was subject to numerous critiques, which made its limitations apparent. What prevailed in the end was the dissident Benjaminian line in which Martín Barbero positioned himself, which would also be a starting point for his own reflections (53).

Martín Barbero's methodological displacement in communications studies meant a switch from the study of media to that of mediations, in other words, concentrating his research on the reception, recognition, and appropriation on the part of the audience. To this end, his research is supported by Edgar Morin, who considers the culture industry to be an ensemble of mechanisms and operations through which creation becomes production. Martín Barbero proposed a concept of consumption that, neither reproductionist nor culturalist, coincided with the conjectures that García Canclini was developing at the same time in works such as *Desigualdad cultural y poder simbólico*, "Culture and Power: The State of Research," and later *Consumidores y ciudadanos*. For both thinkers, consumption must be considered as a social process of appropriation of products, and an ordering of meaning. Martín Barbero's proposal analyzes the logic of the productive system: the specific conditions of cultural production, their impact on the format of media genres (especially the soap opera), and the mode by which the productive system responds to and resignifies the public's demand.

The attempt to remove media studies from functionalist and reductionist analyses of culture in benefit of its recipients does not suppose, in this line of research, a naive view of consumption. In *Culturas híbridas* García Canclini signals the problems of segmentation, stratification, and spatialization of consumption, as well as the tension generated by the dissolution between high and mass culture in the presence of those who valiantly strive to defend symbolic capital. Along the same lines, Mexican researcher Rossana Reguillo has emphasized the difference in opportunities in generating symbolic configurations (especially of identities) between First and Third World countries by calling attention to production processes of visibility. For Reguillo, control of technology creates not only inequality but monopoly conditions within politics of representation, due to an ignorance of other communities; hence the necessity to implement more respectful and democratic politics.

In the last few decades, the process of globalization and the development of new technologies in the area of communications and services has led both to a permanent revision of the modes by which such phenomena affect cultural production, circulation, and consumption and to more in-depth studies of reception. In this sense Guillermo Orozco, who has focused on the areas of social communication and education, has posited that the audience's emancipation can be obtained only through a deeper knowledge of its role in the process. However, he also cites education as a decisive factor in that transformation ("La audiencia" 62). Concerning this last point, Beatriz Sarlo has indicated in *Escenas de la vida posmoderna* that the deterioration of the public school system, especially in Argentina, prevents an increasingly vast sector of society from gaining access to the manipulation of traditional symbolic goods and new technology. This inaccessibility is due not only to a lack of material resources but also to fundamental deficiencies in reading-writing abilities (this does not refer to oral communities, but rather to sectors that in times past could have had access to education). Thus the possibilities of appropriation and production of meaning for these popular sectors are quite restricted.

These reflections, wherein the political dimension of culture is underlined, make evident the need to recapture the public sphere—or to create one that is different—and to reformulate institutions involved in cultural processes in an era of the privatization of production by mostly transnational companies. Nevertheless, they also evoke a consideration of a new, broader concept of culture along the lines already drawn by Martín Barbero and García Canclini. For example, José Joaquín Brunner of Chile has proposed taking into account areas that have traditionally been excluded from the cultural sector and have fallen under the control of expert technocrats. George Yúdice, for his part, has argued in *The Expediency of Culture* that, in the era of globalization, a definite "instrumentalization of culture" has been produced that implies its use as a source of legitimacy in the most heterogeneous social sectors—urban development, economic growth, and even a space for resolving social conflicts (9–11). In this last vision, cultural production becomes a resource to which transnational companies as well as the groups opposed to the system appeal.

Suggested Reading

Bourdieu, Pierre, and Jean-Claude Passeron. *Reproduction in Education, Society, and Culture*. Translated by Richard Nice. London: Sage, 1977.

Brunner, José Joaquín. *Un espejo trizado: Ensayos sobre cultura y políticas culturales*. Santiago, Chile: FLACSO, 1988.

García Canclini, Néstor. *Las culturas populares en el capitalismo*. Mexico City: Nueva Imagen, 1982. Translated by Lidia Lozano as *Transforming Modernity: Popular Culture in Mexico* (Austin: University of Texas Press, 1993).

Horkheimer, Max, and Theodor W. Adorno. *Dialectic of Enlightenment*. Translated by John Cumming. New York: Herder and Herder, 1972.

Jitrik, Noé. *Producción literaria y producción social*. Buenos Aires: Sudamericana, 1975.

Kristeva, Julia. *Sēmeiōtikē: Recherches pour une sémanalyse*. Paris: Seuil, 1969. Translated by Thomas Gora, Alice Jardine, and Leon S. Roudiez as *Desire in Language: A Semiotic Approach to Literature and Art* (Oxford: Blackwell, 1980).

Reguillo, Rossana. "Pensar el mundo en y desde América Latina: Desafío intercultural y políticas de representación." *Diálogos de la Comunicación*, no. 65 (2002): 61–71.

Williams, Raymond. *Culture and Society: Coleridge to Orwell*. London: Hogarth Press, 1982.

———. *Marxism and Literature*. Oxford: Oxford University Press, 1977.

Culture

NARA ARAÚJO (TRANSLATED BY EDUARDO RABASA)

Derived from Latin, the word "culture" is associated with the action of cultivating or practicing—and with honoring as well; hence its fundamental meaning, related to "cult": both to a religious divinity and to the body or the spirit. According to the definitions in the dictionary of the Real Academia de la Lengua Española, *cultura* is the result or the effect of cultivating human knowledge, and also the set of ways of life and traditions of an epoch or social group.

Culture is defined by its humanness, as opposed to nature, forming one of the fundamental binary oppositions of Western metaphysical thought. From the perspective of structural anthropology (Levi-Strauss), the transition from nature to culture is associated with the incest prohibition and thus with blood relationships. Myth frequently treats such issues, as in the case of Oedipus and his mother Jocasta. What is converted into artistic material in Sophocles' tragedy *Oedipus Rex* has its origins in a mytheme in which the constant is the kinship structure. Cultural representation often draws from anthropological understandings of culture, and it can thus become a field for the elucidation of topics concerning culture in anthropological terms.

For semiotics, culture is a network of signs; it is a communicative action, an exchange that constantly assumes the presence of another, who serves as a necessary partner in the relationship between speaker and recipient. From the point of view of communications, one of the fundamental problems of culture is the naming and the drawing of frontiers of the subject of communication, as well as the process of construction of its counter-agent. Based upon this communicative value, it is possible to envision the idea of the value of culture as an informative mechanism, as well as the idea of culture as a self-organizing system that on a metastructural level describes itself through the action of critics and theoreticians, of "legislators of taste" whose descriptions tend to identify the "metadescription" with the actual fiber of culture as such (Lotman).

The term "culture" spans a wide range of uses. Culture, in the sense of cultural diversity, is the object of empirical knowledge; and culture, as cultural difference, is that which is conceivable and enables the construction of systems of cultural identification (Bhabha). Culture can be understood as a dimension and expression of human life, through symbols and tools; as the field of production, circulation, and consumption of signs; and as a praxis articulated within a theory. One can speak about urban culture, media culture, popular culture, mass culture, lettered or high culture. These last three categories have perhaps been among the most polemical, with both popular and mass culture being opposed to artistic and literary culture, and popular culture being more associated with grassroots traditions (culture "of the people"), usually seen in the context of Latin America as different from mass media culture (culture consumed by, but not produced by, the masses).

The twentieth century has given a great importance to popular and mass culture, considering both as fields of action and human transformation that affect the limits and the nature of artistic and literary culture, which are inseminated and transformed by them, while remaining fields of interest for their practical praxes and for research purposes as well. One of the sharpest critiques directed at mass culture, its standardization of stereotypes derived from the market and its relationship to capitalism, took place during the first half of the past century (Adorno).

In the case of lettered culture, the examples of the filmic melodrama as a semantic backbone to the plot of the novel *El beso de la mujer araña* (1976), by the Argentinean writer Manuel Puig, and of the popular dance called the guaracha in Puerto Rican writer's Luis Rafael Sánchez's *La guaracha del Macho Camacho* (1976), illustrate the interaction between different fields—lettered culture, popular culture, and mass culture—which take part in the formation of a new discursive entity that is created as a result of a celebrated fusion to produce a new semiotic reality. However, the Latin American context has witnessed the growth of a concern for the invasion of the mass media culture that is characteristic of the second (postmodern) half of the twentieth century, while at the same time there has been an attempt to recover the importance of aesthetic values, in recognition of the symbolic-political dimension of culture (Sarlo).

Thus, the set of beliefs and practices that constitute a given culture may be utilized as a technology of control, as a microphysics of power, as a set of limits within which social conduct must be contained, as a collection of models to which individuals are subjected. Culture is then a vehicle or a means by which relationships between groups are negotiated (Jameson), and a space in which conflict takes place and becomes a mechanism of power. Systems of domination find a vehicle in culture conceived in its widest meaning—fashion, sports, food, arts and literature—in taste (Bourdieu), or in a semiology of everyday life (Barthes).

Culture is the space of symbolic movements of groups that weave power relationships, with power understood not only in its vertical projection but also as a reticular or weblike design (Foucault), where every point in which power is exercised generates a focal point of resistance. Culture is associated with hegemonic discourses and, at the same time, with those that destabilize hegemony: culture as a space for intervention and agony, but also as a zone of resistance in postcolonial processes, that is, as a decolonizing force, even after the establishment of independent nation-states (Said). The position of the dominated culture and the role of the intellectual are expressed through the opposition that in the context of Latin American culture is identified with the couple Ariel-Calibán (Fernández Retamar).

Even though culture cannot be reduced to social processes, it is not distinct from them. Hence the utilization in cultural studies of terms like "identity," "representation," "ideology," and "hegemony," as well as the idea of the possibility of culture assuming a specific political function both in the construction of hegemonies and in their destabilization, and the criterion, originating in cultural materialism, that states that culture—its methods of production, its forms, its institutions, and its types of consumption—is vital to society since there is no such separation, as implied by the concepts of economic base and superstructure, between culture and social life as a whole (R. Williams).

In this way, material culture acts on spiritual culture. Gutenberg's printing press accelerated and democratized printing processes and hence those of reading as well; improvements in rotary mechanism made possible an increase in the number of newspaper pages and hence the publication of serialized novels, proving wrong the expectation that the printing press would be the end of lettered culture. The advent of the printing press, the reduced cost of paper, and the increase in the number of universities, as well as the development of engraving and stereotypy technologies, and the mass circulation of newspapers and illustrated magazines, all contributed to the increase in circulation of artistic and literary culture: from stone to papyrus, from quill to graphite, from typewriter ribbon to computer keyboard.

The imprint of material culture, seen in the material possibilities of its reproduction, led to the loss of the sense of a work of art's "aura," the distancing effect produced by belief in its authenticity, and thus art saw its ritual function transform into one of exposure (Benjamin). During the second half of the twentieth century, the distance between scientific and artistic-literary culture was shortened by the challenging of the limits between art and non-art, literary and nonliterary culture. It is a move from Arnold's concept of art, as a critique of life, to one of art as an extension of life (Sontag).

Within the projects of modernity, culture has been seen as a way to reach emancipation: to be educated is the only way to be free (Martí). Within the framework of the old desire that assigned a determining role to learning and to knowledge, culture was associated with erudition and freedom. The mistrust generated by the fact that culture does not guarantee the end of savagery, of violence (concentration camps, military dictatorships), is refuted by the links between knowledge and the creation of new forms of social conscience that are infused by newfound forms of a culture of life, represented by social movements such as the Mothers of Plaza de Mayo.

In the current and tense dialogue between local and global ("glocal"), between rural and urban, between oral and written, national and regional, as well as national and transnational, culture is expressed in every scenario of symbolic exchange: in the many forms of artistic and literary production, in religious practices, in the displacement of the margins toward the center, in the appearance of its new subjects (producers and consumers) in its expansion toward film and television (Monsiváis).

The important celebration of popular and mass culture advocated by the Birmingham School (R. Williams; Hall), and taken on by cultural studies in the United States, is a response to the crisis in those spaces, in the humanities and, more specifically, in literary studies that focus their attention on canonical works. Even if in the United States cultural studies brought about a democratization of knowledge, the field's increasing institutionalization and its sometimes superficial celebration of "pop" and mass culture have undermined the critical edge of its interventions in the academic and public arena (Hall; Jameson).

Latin American cultural studies took up a dialogue both with Anglophone sources of cultural studies and with the Frankfurt School, as well as with diverse currents of theoretical thought of the twentieth century. But its roots lay in the various preceding forms of cultural analysis within Latin Americanism, assuming its own profile due to its specific object of study, and a focus on culture/cultures as institutions and lifestyles, symbolic and concrete, overdetermined by history and geography and linked to concrete social formations that develop through specific modes of production, distribution, and consumption of goods and artifacts with symbolic value (Trigo). Along with radical positions "against literature" (Beverley) and critiques of mass culture (Sarlo), there have been warnings against an eventual relativism and fetishization of the fragment (Richard).

Various interrogations and early projects of cultural critique make up the body of work that forms important foundations of Latin American cultural studies. Both from anthropology (Ortiz) and from the very distinct field of literary criticism, linking political and aesthetic dimensions, there was articulated a theoretical model, heterogeneity, to explain the heteroclite universe of Latin American cultural discourses (Cornejo); also, by relying on interdisciplinarity—history, cultural anthropology, sociology, psychology, linguistics—to explore different expressive forms of regional subcultures, or the relationship between literary institutions and power, seeing culture as a battlefield (Rama).

There have been two poles in understanding the word "culture" as an object of study in the field of Latin American cultural studies: the anthropological, sociological, communicational (García Canclini, Brunner, Martín Barbero), and the artistic-literary (Beverley, Sarlo, Richard); these poles switch positions and their discourses overlap as they share the stage in the cyclical tension of cultural criticism. Also prominent in the agenda of Latin American cultural studies is the debate on the role of culture, seen in its broadest sense, as agent of transformation or resistance through its capacity for social action. Faced with the scenario of the (dis)(semi)nation, the deterritorialization and the consequent dislocation of symbolic products, of in-between places and interstices, it is impossible to speak of a homogeneous culture. And an effort should be made not to allow the word "culture" to turn into a facile guarantee of a synthesis (Rowe). As George Yúdice points out, in globalization, culture serves not only to consolidate identities and to control social access, but also as a fundamental resource for economic and social development.

In Latin American cultural studies, culture has been understood in the framework of its connections with the social sphere, in the transformations of popular culture and cultural industries, as an intersection of social discourses and symbolic processes, structures of power and constructions of subjectivity: gender, race, citizenship. Culture has been seen from protean perspectives that, from diverse places of enunciation and with crossed and opposing outlooks, aim to think about the place occupied by culture in the constitutive process of Latin America and Latin Americanism.

Suggested Reading

Bhabha, Homi K. *The Location of Culture*. London: Routledge, 1994.

García Canclini, Néstor. *Las culturas populares en el capitalismo*. Mexico City: Nueva Imagen, 1982.

Hall, Stuart. "Cultural Studies and its Theorethical Legacies." In *Cultural Studies*, edited by Lawrence Grossberg, Cary Nelson, and Paula A. Treichler, 277–85. New York: Routledge, 1992.

Jameson, Fredric. "Sobre los 'estudios culturales.'" In Jameson and Žižek, *Estudios culturales: Reflexiones sobre el multiculturalismo*, 69–136.

Lotman, Yuri. "Para la construcción de una teoría de la interacción de las culturas (el aspecto semiótico)." *Criterios* 32 (1994): 117–30.

Said, Edward W. *Culture and Imperialism*. New York: Knopf, 1993.

Williams, Raymond. *Marxism and Literature*. Oxford: Oxford University Press, 1977.

Yúdice, George. *The Expediency of Culture: Uses of Culture in the Global Era*. Durham, N.C.: Duke University Press, 2003.

Deconstruction

ROMÁN DE LA CAMPA

The textual revolution, often understood as the "linguistic turn," ultimately came to be known for its epistemological rather than its literary force, but its initial impulse owes much to a new era of literary analysis marked by deep breaks within the philological tradition and transcendental humanism. Perhaps this was foreseeable. Since romanticism, followed by various modernisms, one can trace changes in the way Western literature and its philosophical traditions were conceived. Even the idea of the soul found a different articulation from that point on, inasmuch as it became part of the inherent logic of textual production, a linguistic embodiment later brought to light in Latin American literature by writers such as Jorge Luis Borges, Octavio Paz, and Severo Sarduy. The notion of a hermeneutic center gave way to that of poetic, narrative, and mythological structures, eventually yielding to early modes of semiological analysis. This ongoing development, largely driven by the Sausurrean legacy throughout the twentieth century, reaches further articulation in what came to be known as deconstruction, a way of thinking the very act of writing that shifts our understanding of signification from themes and referents to a closer analysis of verbal constructs, always bound to excess, a new ground that also called for a more heretical and creative understanding of archives, histories, and canonical texts. Within literature, the object of study took on a new meaning as well. Tried and true approaches grounded in biography, authorial intention, and spatiotemporal context gave way to more immanent looks at creative work. It is safe to say that these were the first steps of the deconstructive impulse, in large part framed by Borges through that fascinating reader-writer called Pierre Menard.

The representational prism of humanism, its appreciation of art, beauty, harmony, and transcendental presence, undergoes a metamorphosis from this point on. Literature suddenly finds itself in a new economy of signification, no longer as plenitude or fullness but rather as what subverts ways of reading inspired in a logic of aporia governing the pursuit of knowledge, pleasure, and even ethics. Literature provided a special theater for this interplay between history, aesthetics, and epistemological indetermination. Texts afforded a dramatic unhinging of discursive order that had a direct application to literary history, or history proper. The lettered intellectual found his or her work caught in a more immanent trace of the complex relation between language and historical emplotments. At first this pursuit found a natural ground within the literary archive of postmodernity; later it moved toward more interdisciplinary contours of that epochal construct, ultimately yielding a broad array of new work in feminism, postcolonialism, and cultural studies. As this paradigm came into its own during the eighties, the inevitable mainstreaming of poststructural critique came into play, ultimately yielding to a type of academic marketing that led a figure like Derrida to decouple himself from any "posting," particularly the postmodern ("Marx and Sons"). Indeed, the force of that link is evident in Derrida's concern over the future of deconstruction in the age of marketing and globalization, a question that looms large over his *Specters of Marx*, arguably the most important book of his last period.

When it came to literary studies, some saw a substantial loss in new modes of knowledge production, others a transformative gain. The field no longer responded to well-established disciplinary methods but rather to the adventure of anti-teleological exploration, a new realm of conflictive interiority particularly inclined to questioning the claims of external causality. Indeterminacy thus found an inexhaustible terrain in the humanistic legacy, given the latter's breadth and weight. With it came a new anti-disciplinary force framed around the idea of deconstruction. Its modes of reading modeled a politics as well, but its stage was not that of social action or even commentary, but rather a closer look at language, a new vigilance toward its imbrications within epistemology and literature, as both disciplines framed a new praxis in search of the most constitutive subtleties of verbal constructs. In this new mapping of knowledge, deconstruction not only pronounced itself on the matter of literature but rather on all of writing, as Paul de Man reminded us, and most particularly on the modes of truth claimed by the social sciences. Needless to say, the latter questioned this challenge, as not all disciplines were ready or willing to alter the ways in which verbal constructs and cognitive power translate into knowledge production.

The story of Saussurean signification can't be easily left behind, even by those who recognize its capacity to turn into self-referential myth. The paths from formalism to structuralism to poststructuralist deconstruction resist cut-and-dried periodization, but they continue to imbue each other in unsuspected ways. One could place many important figures in this fluid chronology. Roland Barthes, Michel Foucault, and Louis Althusser provide extraordinary instances for this paradigm change in literature, history, and Marxism. All embody shifts between the initial semiological pursuits and subsequent notions of discourse. One could include here Edward Said's work, as well as Ángel Rama's (see de la Campa, "El desafío inesperado de *La ciudad letrada*"). Another example would be Gilles Deleuze's *The Logic of Sense*, which embodies an enticing slippage between the structural moment of its writing (1969) and the deconstructive moves it already suggests, as evidenced by its 1990 English translation from Columbia University Press and the critical acclaim it demands even today by theorists such as Badiou and Žižek. The primacy of the reader has extended to the twenty-first century, though along the way it may have replaced the literary domain with models of performance less driven by coherence, aesthetic willfulness, or expressive exuberance than by a more ambiguous approach to discursive materiality always already caught in internal slippages and aporetic moments.

The role of the 1960s can be misleading. The decade did not simply usher in the Latin American Boom or left-wing movements roughly associated with it, but rather the inauguration of a discursive terrain that entangles disciplines and art forms in all of the Americas, as well as Europe and other sites (see, for example, Glissant's articulation of Caribbean discourse). France is often seen as the source of it all, but this is a key moment caught in divergent approaches such as New Criticism in the United States, *explicación de texto* and stylistics in Spain and Latin America, semiotics in Italy and Russia, and Bakhtinian narratology, an array of work derived from a Saussurean legacy that had been gathering steam since Russian formalism. It is not difficult to see how the relation between Continental philosophy and literary studies grew closer. Unhinging the transcendental anchors of meaning, disassociating them from external factors, implied a greater proximity to the process of signification on the part of the reader, one that understood not only literature but reality as verbal construct. This was an extraordinary step. Its ramifications would become evident only much later.

Latin American literature and criticism provide an important chapter here. It is generally assumed that the Boom comes into being as the embodiment of literary and political experimentation of the 1960s, though one must also include the extraordinary role of that particular literary corpus in the United States, as well as the advent of semiological play throughout the Americas. In Latin America itself, always an aggregate of many different nations with their respective academic needs, one can also trace the critical avant-garde. Structuralist theory, inspired by the work of Wellek and Warren, for example, found fertile ground in Chilean, Argentine, and Mexican universities, while semiotics found its way in those as well as other Latin American nations. Of course, one could not fail to account for the novel ways of understanding literature invoked first by Borges and then by other writers such as José Lezama Lima and then Severo Sarduy during the 1970s. All of these could be seen as forms of critical and creative thought imbued by the Saussurean legacy. This engagement with new theoretical work in Latin America, it should be underlined, matched or surpassed the critical acumen of New Criticism and stylistics, which were more prevalent in the United States and Spain. The role of criticism in the sudden interest in Latin American literature during this period thus requires more attention. The Cold War and its funding for area studies created conditions for the Boom with the demand for scholars trained in Latin America who came armed with firsthand knowledge of a new theoretical capital and who later stayed, first as visiting professors and ultimately as immigrants who in time took up tenured appointments. Literary Latin Americanism owes considerably to this exceptionally hybrid moment of symbolic capital accumulation.

It is generally assumed that by the end of the 1970s, Latin American literary theory was overwhelmed by the editorial event known as the Boom and that its lettered sensibility had been subsumed by the commercialized poetics of exotic realisms. This notion often goes unexamined, thereby confirming a neat but unsuspected binary: first came the unconditional celebration of the Boom as a transcendental expression of Latin American ontology, then came its absolute disavowal as the deepest expression of error and self-deceit. The story could be retold as "The Route from Macondo to McOndo," the latter term coined by the Chilean writer Alberto Fuguet as title for an anthology of new Latin American literature. Told in the 1990s, it captures his struggle to establish himself as a Latin American writer unwilling to identify with a modality that seemed to have turned obligatory by the 1980s, particularly in the United States. The need to distance himself from Macondo, that quintessential town in *Cien años de soledad,* brought him closer to American fast food, but perhaps there was more to it. Within theory, much Latin American deconstructive work since the 1990s has looked upon the Boom as not just an imposed stereotype but also as a compensatory aesthetic for failed Latin American states. This deeper critique seeks to turn that literary event into an archive of misbegotten premises: a tightly held set of errors made up of criollo identity, lettered traditions, backward rural imaginaries, defunct modes of magical realism, dependency theory, misbegotten revolutionary triumphalism, and badly dissimulated modes of patriarchal impulses. In that setting, McDonald's came to represent freedom.

It is still a question whether a literary corpus can be held accountable for the political frustrations of an entire continent, or even more if deconstructive work can find itself unguardedly caught in a sociological approach to literature and development seemingly inimical to its modes of analysis. It is therefore important to take a closer look at Latin American work that paved the way for debates that continue to inform the field, which include names such as Ángel Rama, Josefina Ludmer, Silvia Molloy, Beatriz Sarlo, Silviano Santiago, Roberto Schwarz, and Irlemar Chiampi. Latin American literary studies evidence a growing transnational realm during this first wave of textuality, which corresponded not only to the Boom but also to the Cold War and more particularly to the creation of area studies in the United States. These structures, motivated by national defense, the nuclear threat, and competition with the Soviet Union, spearheaded by the launching of Sputnik (1957) and the consequent creation of the federal program known as the National Defense Education Act (1958), multiplied the number of programs dedicated to Latin American studies, thereby generating a demand for symbolic capital never seen before in the Americas. There is no doubt that "Latin Americanism," understood as an object of hemispheric study articulated both inside and out of Latin America, opened a new and different chapter at this moment. One could also postulate an earlier Latin Americanism in the historical and literary realm in the nineteenth century, a key to understanding Latin American letters that also remains quite fluid and often unread. Such would be the import of Julio Ramos's *Desencuentros de la modernidad,* though his reading of *modernismo* owes considerably to his novel reading of Ángel Rama and Foucault. Implicit in its fabric, therefore, is the radical break of Latin American criticism after the 1960s, which requires us to see Latin Americanism as a discursive community inscribed in a far-reaching order of critical, theoretical, and editorial strategies that transform the field in unsuspected ways (de la Campa, *Latin Americanism*).

The Cold War mode of knowledge production, fundamentally defined by new area studies, invites further examination: It opened a new market of texts and readers, as well as new forms of exile and diaspora, leading to a multitude of scholars, young and old, that now claim a new space in the role of Latin American and Latino constructs. This pertains not just to politics but also to the arts and media, in both the North and the South. It was also a time in which English came into its own as a main interface in the production of Latin Americanist discourse, as many Latin Americans began to make their presence felt in their own English-language manifestation of Latin American and even U.S. cultural matters. Translation acquired a new interhemispheric role as well as new theoretical attention regarding what it portends for the frontier of textuality. Viewed in this larger context, one must ask whether the Boom spoke to a broader American or inter-American aesthetic, and whether magical realism and McDonald's may be coterminous.

Comparative frameworks promise a more complex Latin American history both of literary criticism and of the hemispheric context in which it operates, the deep-seated academic threads that bind the Americas, not only in terms of languages and cultures but also of conceptual flows. This allows one to see that the so-called Latin American Boom, as well as the critical apparatus at the time, already corresponded to an intricately globalized domain, one that pertains not only to the political and cultural zeal inspired by the Cuban Revolution but also to Spanish and Catalan publishing efforts on the other side of the Atlantic, as well as to the complex academic market commanded by area studies from the sixties until the late eighties. This web of political, editorial, and academic flows was met by the early modes of immanent textual critique, which later found itself in modes of deconstruction.

A broadly conceived inter-American mapping suggests early deconstructive manifestations in Latin America from which one could trace crucial elements inherent to that history in later decades. An opening of the

Western canon from the Latin American margins of First World modernity takes place at this moment, a time in which the former begins to exercise, through this shifting Saussurean paradigm, a new and more critical exegesis of its own teleological history. That would be one of the main paradoxes inherent to deconstruction as a model of criticism. Its initial force crystallizes precisely at the moment in which Latin American literature is codified as the quintessence of postmodern literature (Zamora and Faris; de la Campa, "Magical Realism"). At this point, literature and theory imbue each other as never before, as Nietzsche, Borges, de Man, García Márquez, Foucault, Lispector, Irigaray, Kristeva, and Derrida, among others, spell a new and unexpected constellation of writers and theorists. By the end of the 1970s and early 1980s, however, we see in Latin America another unsuspected element, in this case political, that has left its indelible mark in debates over literary Latin Americanism ever since: Southern Cone dictatorships, subaltern indigenous struggles, and the waning of the revolutionist model in Central America's Sandinista movement.

How does one situate this history of political conflicts and failures within deconstructive critiques of Latin American models of development on one hand and the advent of a literary corpus that was welcome and praised throughout the world on the other? How does one approach this question while taking into consideration the transnational web of literary and editorial markets exposed earlier? There are, obviously, different ways to read such a complex web of texts and events. Deconstruction invites such entanglements; it sees itself as neither a literary pursuit nor just another philosophical mode but rather an epistemology that, as Paul de Man showed from the beginning, moves from literary to historical texts in order to arrive at the scene of writing. Once there, it reaches all modes of signification. The question therefore is not to take literature outside itself, nor to submit it to geopolitical calculations, but, on the contrary, to recognize the extraordinary textual ambition that ensues from it at this point, the attempt to unhinge the world through new modes of reading stemming from literary immanence, an impulse that may have begun in Latin America with the Boom but then began to see it as a corpus eminently worthy of deconstruction for what it meant, not just as literature but rather as a compensatory aesthetic pertaining to models of modern Latin American development.

Many specialists see this political injunction as a strictly Latin American phenomenon which has turned into a theoretical site for either mourning or celebration, or even an unusual combination of the two, as states must now turn to the market to find their bearings while liberal nationalism loses ground. My aim here is to examine this late deconstructive turn as well as its potential contradictions. One is led to ask if it is possible to decouple modern Latin American literature from the cultural utopia of its criollo, lettered upper classes, or if the latter is being conceived as an author whose intention exhausts the former by definition or necessity. A failed modernity sustained by a failed literary corpus might seem like another way of enclosing literature within historical destinies. Moreover, if one thinks of epistemic error, failure, or a perennial crisis of identity, it seems opportune to ask if this is not now the condition of globalization, rather than just what is found in the postcolonial Third World. Could the same critique of literature be applied to sites whose political state formation yielded greater levels of development, such as Europe or the United States? If we say yes, then all of modern literature fails, even when politics seems to have succeeded. If we say no, then literature fails only when politics fails, and we are once again, even in the age of deconstruction, equating literary failure to failures of modernization and development.

Menard, Bustrófedon, Melquíades, Auxilio, Socorro, these are not only literary figures of what was once seen as a Latin American textual revolution, they also stand for gestures that brought an uncertain modernity closer to the terrain of literary immanence, perhaps leading to a shift from universal humanism to postmodern cosmopolitanism. Needless to say, the nexus between negative dialectics and literary excess has no doubt tightened, just as that between metropolitan centers and their margins. Hybridity, heterogeneity, and otherness subsumed each other in the interplay of literary signification, a movement that ultimately found conflation in multiculturalism. One could therefore wonder if Latin American deconstruction was destined to be normalized by the academic power it acquired, thereby risking its destabilizing power, its newness as literary language.

The celebrated disciplinary fissures of the 1960s and 1970s may have foretold a capitulation that would become clearer in the 1980s and 1990s, to wit, a crack in the notion that an alternative path to modernization awaited Latin America on the other side of the Cold War. Current tensions between cultural studies and literature provide a telling window here, for techno-mediatic culture continually challenges how humanism responds to symbolic capital production. The early bet, initially articulated within literature (one thinks of Foucault's reference to Borges and his inchoate listings, for example), intuited the repercussions of what later came to be known as the "cultural logic of late capitalism." Before Jameson coined that term to describe postmodernism, one could already see its lineaments in his earlier work dedicated to literary theory (see *The Political Unconscious*). Two apparently opposite impulses were thus nearing each other: the usual concern of Marxist poetics for "ultimate instance"—a sense of totalization now claimed, ironically, by global capitalism itself—and a fusion of epistemology and literary studies that questioned Western humanism more deeply than ever before. Yet, as Jameson's turn from literature to culture intuited, the site of deconstruction for literary studies as a field of knowledge had grown more ambitious precisely as it was moving away from literature. It turned instead to a new scene of writing, or even history, unable to bank on an archive of reliable metanarratives.

The deepened link between literary criticism and epistemology found an even greater challenge as it focused on the discourses that narrated nations, particularly in areas such as Latin America, in which literature held a privileged plane of reference, as opposed to areas in which political texts had accrued greater value. A close reading of that fundamental structure meant looking for deep-seated contradictions. Latin American *testimonio*, for example, became a primary site of speculation. At first the genre invoked a rejection of the Boom that still spoke to the possibilities of national emancipation, later it became the site for a post-literary juncture that perhaps coincided with a post-national configuration. Similar tensions could be found in various postcolonial and subaltern critiques, notwithstanding the deep and perhaps diametrical theoretical differences between those who see deconstruction as a politics opening the way to new indigenous or alternative subjects and those who see it as opening to a notion of excess in which all subjectivities are suspect, including those defined as indigenous.

As one might suspect, Latin American "post-literary" mapping remains caught up in literature. Like the nation, literature relies on institutions that guarantee passage from one state or market to another, even if one no longer believes in them. In any event, it seems clear that the textual revolution led to forms of deconstruction that have gathered greater momentum since the eighties, particularly around the critique of the nation, the waning of revolutionary models based on state socialism in Latin America, and the increasing role of cultural studies, whose aim includes the study of the expanding role of techno-mediatic production under global capitalism, a difficult task that requires both description and analysis at once, given the constant flow of images that subjects now encounter in a range of important realms including performance and gender studies. One must therefore ask how this "cultural" turn fits in the literary-philosophical mapping discussed in this essay. Historically, Latin American cultural studies has been more inclined to social science methodology, but newer modalities within this field could be seen as a line of flight within humanistic epistemology that was initiated by literary studies, not only theoretically but also institutionally. It seems possible to trace the history of sliding signification between aesthetics and contemporary art forms leading to image production, a nexus that has deeply challenged the academic apparatus sponsored by the state. In time the role of lettered disciplines, which include some social sciences, found itself enveloped in the performative manifestation of audiovisual ontology prevalent in the life world of global capital.

If culture is understood as caught within the polysemy of performance, its study seems to call for a continuous engagement with the theoretical legacy inspired by literary texts, even if the latter are no longer protected by the national context that upheld the disciplinary status of literary criticism. The Latin American institutional apparatus resisted this turn, or may have seen it at first as an imposition coming from the North American academy. One should point out, however, that cultural studies had many sites of production in the twentieth century, including of course the Frankfurt and Birmingham Schools in Germany and England respectively, both of which left their mark in the Americas. All of these efforts found it necessary to look at culture through intradisciplinary prisms. All of them sought to engage the new production of symbolic capital and the waning of humanistic symbolic order. In that sense, the new cultural studies scene can be seen as intensification as well as a challenge, particularly if one thinks of how deconstruction has evolved through the textual revolution, Latin American literature, and the critique of national teleology. In that light, one is bound to recall the work of Nelly Richard, a prominent deconstructionist working in Latin America, who initially saw an opening in cultural studies that allowed deconstruction to gather a more incisive look at the "verbal scene" that included the arts, feminist work, and other important new approaches ("Signos culturales"). Later she began to doubt if the rigors inherent to deconstruction and its sophisticated work within language could be sustained by cultural studies.

By way of closing, I'd like to suggest that the topic of deconstruction and Latin America has turned literary and cultural studies into a particularly contentious academic endeavor. It is also a challenging one, though we don't really know if its reach is equal to its ambition. In that sense, I suspect it remains a tale to be told. We know that nationalism weighed heavily on the Latin American literary tradition and that politics overdetermined its academic culture. We also know that deconstruction attempts to divert both of these paths. I have argued, however, that it does not initiate this turn but rather intensifies it with a closer reading of the Latin American textual revolution that has been materializing, through literature, since *modernismo* at the end of the nineteenth century. Deconstruction promises that national hermeneutics, along with their extraordinary symbolic force, can't escape a new and profound sense of instability. Yet deconstruction and Latin America also remain caught in an uncertain embrace, given that modern literature continues to shadow an epistemology that would rather move past it or leave it behind as failed conceit. The history of this coupling is long, and it belies any attempt to relegate its rich past into mourning or to frame it in binaries such as native informants caught in the web of metropolitan imposition.

Suggested Reading

Barlow, Tani E. "Degree Zero of History." *Comparative Literature* 53, no. 4 (2001): 404–25.

De la Campa, Román. *Latin Americanism*. Minneapolis: University of Minnesota Press, 2000.

———. "Magical Realism: A Genre for the Times?" *Canadian Review of Hispanic Studies*, Summer 1999, 103–18.

Derrida, Jacques. "Marx and Sons." In *Ghostly Demarcations: A Symposium on Jacques Derrida's "Specters of Marx,"* edited by Michael Sprinker, 235–54. London: Verso, 1999.

Follari, Roberto. *Teorías débiles: Para una crítica de la deconstrucción y de los estudios culturales*. Rosario, Argentina: Homo Sapiens, 2003.

Glissant, Édouard. *Caribbean Discourse: Selected Essays*. Translated by J. Michael Dash. Charlottesville: University Press of Virginia, 1989.

Jameson, Fredric. *The Political Unconscious: Narrative as a Socially Symbolic Act*. Ithaca, N.Y.: Cornell University Press, 1981.

———. *Postmodernism, or, The Cultural Logic of Late Capitalism*. Durham, N.C.: Duke University Press, 1991.

Richard, Nelly. "Signos culturales y mediaciones académicas." In González Stephan, *Cultura y Tercer Mundo*, 82–97.

Wellek, René, and Austin Warren. *Theory of Literature*. New York: Harcourt Brace, 1949.

Zamora, Lois Parkinson, and Wendy B. Faris, eds. *Magical Realism: Theory, History, Community*. Durham, N.C.: Duke University Press, 1995.

Deterritorialization

NÚRIA VILANOVA

"Deterritorialization" has been used in the last few years both to refer to the relationship between subjects and physical territory at the moment of displacement and to reflect the idea of movement and change in relation to human beings as well as goods, symbols, and imaginaries. Although the fields of cultural studies, anthropology, and sociology have given this concept its widest dissemination, economists, political scientists, and a range of scholars have made use of the term to discuss ideas and phenomena related to migration and to the relationship between economy, society, and the state, as well as to talk about memory and anonymity in social dynamics unleashed by the process of displacement.

Originally the concept was used by the French philosophers Gilles Deleuze and Félix Guattari in the early 1970s to develop Marx's metaphor about capitalism as a voracious machine that would progressively absorb a diversity of "territories," such as agriculture, culture, education, and industry, to the point of "deterritorializing" them and leaving the proletariat (in the Marxist sense) without territory. According to Marx, at that point, when people are left without anything to lose, revolution would be possible. Deleuze and Guattari applied the idea of the unrestrained and voracious capitalist machine to the human psyche. They argued that human beings are always surrounded by diverse territorialities, some of which are imaginary, since territory is understood as subjectivizing and, thus, continuously exposed to being deterritorialized—that is, territory opens, escapes from itself, breaks down, or is destroyed. In a process of territorial restructuring, the human psyche is bound to be reterritorialized, which inevitably engenders recomposition and transformation. Capitalism is a system in a state of ongoing reterritorialization since it constantly attempts to take over—deterritorialize—multiple forms of interaction within a community, a group, or a family.

Deterritorialization has had a broader reach as it has become linked to other concepts. In Latin American cultural studies it has been used to study globalization, migration, fragmentation, and borders. It has also been used to evoke the very process undergone by academics and scholars displaced from their native Latin American countries to international universities, mainly in the United States, where they have established their careers. However, here the concept is restricted in use to the way it was understood by critics like Néstor García Canclini, Jesús Martín Barbero, Renato Ortiz, and Raúl Prada. They each developed ideas of deterritorialization that respond to the territorial-cultural realities that are the subject of their analysis.

In *Hybrid Cultures*, García Canclini formulates new parameters of analysis to deal with the complexity of the social and cultural dynamics of a continent that has been in profound transformation since the 1980s. He uses deterritorialization to develop his idea that millions of displaced Latin American migrants are entering and exiting modernity. This idea of entering and leaving modernity refers to two processes that develop in a joint fashion: the process of deterritorialization, which is to say the loss of what García Canclini calls the natural relationship—in the sense that it is predetermined and preestablished—between a culture and its geographic and social territory and, simultaneously, the process of reterritorialization, the territorial relocation of old and new symbolic productions (228–29). In order to understand these processes of deterritorializaton/reterritorialization, it is crucial to identify present-day dynamics that have thoroughly redefined the binary categories that had informed analytical approaches to Latin America through most of the twentieth century. Following García Canclini, the national is no longer recognized in opposition to the international; consequently, new concepts such as transnationality/transnationalization must be considered in reference to both migrant subjects and the market. García Canclini bases major components of his arguments on anthropologist Roger Rouse's research on the Mexican village of Aguililla (Michoacán). Aguililla is a small rural town whose inhabitants have literally lived in a transnational fashion since the 1940s when they started immigrating to Redwood City, California. The fact that a whole community settled together in the same destination (a common pattern for Mexican migration to the United States) transformed Aguililla's villagers into transnational subjects, in the sense that they lived between two populations. For many scholars working in the field of migration (James Clifford and Mike Davis among others), Aguililla became paradigmatic of the emerging social and cultural transformations brought about by migration: in this small Mexican town a transnational pattern was established, which included its inhabitants and its goods—both symbolic and tangible—already displaced and transformed through the process. Moreover, a process of transnationalization affected every single element, involving individuals as well as the whole community. Since the process of migration "uproots from their home territory" cultural and aesthetic practices, perceptions, and attitudes, which see themselves modified and reformulated when being inserted into another territory, Aguililla and its inhabitants exemplify the concepts of deterritorialization/reterritorialization through their very transnational pattern. In the same fashion, it is also true that those millions of migrants that both individually and collectively move from Latin America to the North constitute paradigmatic patterns of deterritorialization/reterritorialization. Because of this, García Canclini concludes that the most innovative analyses on deterritorialization are taking place in reference to the U.S.-Mexican border experience. The 2,000-mile strip of the U.S.-Mexican border sees the most migratory traffic of the Western Hemisphere—indeed, the U.S.-Mexican border is the busiest in the world.

In addition to individuals, symbolic and tangible goods, cultural practices, and imaginaries, we can also count cultures, perceptions, memories, and emotions among what is displaced by mass media and globalizing technology. Jesús Martín Barbero uses the concept of deterritorialization to elucidate the idea of a transformation that goes along with new cultural forms and modes of communication in a world in constant interaction. In his book *De los medios a las mediaciones,* Martín Barbero offers a new approach to mass communications and culture on the one hand and popular culture on the other, with interrelationships that establish themselves between these categories and hegemony/power. At almost the same time as García Canclini, Martín Barbero also breaks with binary categories of sociocultural analysis, which have been made obsolete by globalization and mass migration worldwide. In reference to the idea of cultural identity, Martín Barbero addresses what he defines as deterritorialized memories in order to describe the emergence and development of new cultures arising from transnational processes affecting markets as well as the media. Through these new cultures, cultural identities—particularly those linked to youth—are perceived in a more flexible and dynamic fashion, encouraging the permeability of different cultural forms stemming from diverse sources. A distinction is made between written culture, which is linked to language and therefore to territory, and visual and auditory cultures—music, image, TV, video, and we would add today the cybernetic industry—which are in constant displacement, inhabit no territory, and are therefore generators of the new cultural communities mentioned earlier.

Other groundbreaking work on the idea of deterritorialization has been done by Brazilian scholar Renato Ortiz. Ortiz's approach departs from the idea of nation and state in relation to globalization, and to what he calls the "mundialization" of culture. In his book *Mundialização e cultura*, Ortiz makes a clear distinction between globalization and mundialization. The notion of globalization is closely related to the economy and the market, and the determining impact of technology upon them. The idea of mundialization, in contrast, is linked to the displacement of cultures, more specifically cultures that are easily transportable through mass media and that break boundaries of national identity.

Essential to Ortiz's approach is a view of the role of the state not only in setting cultural policy and administering culture but also as an important "sphere of the production of meaning." Following this idea, one can argue that the nation, through its administrator the state, possesses the monopoly on the definition of meaning. Thus, since the impact of globalization breaks the specific meanings of national identities, the construct nation-state is reformulated by globalization.

Underlying the distinction between the globalization of the economy and the mundialization of culture that is so essential for Ortiz, we find a critique of postmodern criticism. From Ortiz's point of view, postmodernism celebrates difference without reflecting thoroughly on plurality or the asymmetrical relationships between identities. It is therefore crucial to distinguish between diversity and plurality. Following this argument, Ortiz sees deterritorialization as a movement of symbols and imaginaries shared by many identity communities through subjects who are spread out among diverse and distant locations throughout the world. Thus, having crossed national borders, humans have become world subjects who share fashion, TV programs, cinema, music, and a long list of items that no doubt includes the revolutionary cybernetic dimension of our lives at the very core of the "mundialization of culture."

From the specific perspectives of their distinct theoretical positions, García Canclini, Martín Barbero, and Ortiz develop the concept of deterritorialization through the dynamics of interrelationships between culture, subject, society, and state. In addition to these scholars, the Bolivian Raúl Prada proposes a new approach which is closely linked to the Andean world and the Bolivian context. Firmly adhering to Deleuze and Guattari's postulates, Prada in his book *Territorialidad* explores the notion of territoriality within ethnic groups native to Bolivia, in contrast to the Western concept permeated by capitalism. In that sense, territoriality is a collective and ecological space since it is ruled by communal experience (*ayllu*). Territoriality is, then, the social experience and the awareness of territory. It is not merely a geographic reference, but an essentially collective experience, internalized in the community conscience. Therefore, territoriality internalizes territory and makes territory symbolic. Following this argument, territoriality is a form and a hierarchy of power. No doubt this is a premodern perception of territoriality, since modernity is precisely what unleashes deterritorialization, which here means the loss of the territorial consciousness brought about by processes of modernization such as urbanization and commercialization. Nevertheless, deterritorialization is followed by reterritorialization, which results from resistance to the loss of territoriality—that is to say, to the loss of territorial consciousness. Thus the ideas of territoriality and deterritorialization are closely linked to memory, since Prada's notion of deterritorialization is, after all, the loss of territorial memory—in other words, of collective memory.

Prada's idea of deterritorialization as loss of territoriality–collective memory can be applied to the space of the northern Mexican border, the very region that generated García Canclini's first studies on the concept of deterritorialization in the Latin American context. One could argue that one of the outcomes of the border dynamics is that social memory, or the collective memory of a given place, is constantly reformulated in a process that erodes and rewrites the past, the present, and of course the future. Just as memory is determinant in the process of displacing the migrant subject's ethos and culture, so, since memory itself is also displaced, the social history of a territorialized memory—that memory which is located in the same physical, cultural, and symbolic space—is quintessential to shape what could be called a local tradition. In sum, territorialized memory is one that is shared by a collectivity.

In the process of displacement, migrants abandon their territorialized memory and insert themselves into a social anonymity. This is less dramatic for migrants who move in groups and settle down together, such as the Mexicans who have emigrated from places like Aguililla to Redwood City. For obvious economic reasons, this collective migration phenomenon has not been the case in the northern Mexican borderlands. In northern Mexican towns such as Ciudad Juárez, migration shapes a highly fragmented social space, where the absence of a shared memory and common traditions encourages a social dynamic dominated by anonymity and social dehierarchization. If, following Prada's arguments, we assume a notion of territoriality as a hierarchy of power, deterritorialization will also imply the loss of hierarchy.

On the Mexican-American border, social hierarchies can carry a very significant weight. This is especially true in urban areas that have traditionally been inhabited by the same families, with the same surnames, and where a collective memory is shared, such as the border towns of Matamoros, in Tamaulipas, and Monterrey, in Mexico's northern interior. But they now find themselves displaced by urban areas such as Ciudad Juárez or Tijuana where a very significant percentage of the population is always on the move and with them they displace their anonymity. New social hierarchies, with new parameters, emerge. Some of these hierarchies are related to transgression and violence, such as the powerful networks of organized crime, *polleros* and *coyotes* who smuggle undocumented migrants, drug traffickers, and hired killers into the United States. As a result, traditional identities and hierarchies linked to a fixed physical territory are disrupted by displacement. Such deterritorialization leads to new social, cultural and individual dynamics. Some of these are associated with violence and are linked to the most harmful face of uprooting, but others are generators of important, innovative artistic and cultural proposals. This has happened in the borderlands of northern Mexico over the last fifteen years, particularly in Tijuana.

Deterritorialization usually implies detachment and even uprooting. Moreover, it involves the reformulation and resignification of subjective specificities. Therefore, deterritorialization generates new dynamics of reterritorialization. Sometimes these are extremely dangerous and violently affect the most underprivileged. At the same time, in many respects deterritorialization/reterritorialization means innovation, progress, and the enrichment of a variety of social and individual aspects of life.

Suggested Reading

Clifford, James. *Routes: Travel and Translation in the Late Twentieth Century*. Cambridge, Mass.: Harvard University Press, 1997.

Deleuze, Gilles, and Félix Guattari. *Anti-Oedipus*. Vol. 1 of *Capitalism and Schizophrenia*. Translated by Robert Hurley, Mark Seem, and Helen R. Lane. New York: Viking, 1977.

———. *A Thousand Plateaus*. Vol. 2 of *Capitalism and Schizophrenia*. Translated by Brian Massumi. Minneapolis: University of Minnesota Press, 1987.

García Canclini, Néstor. *La globalización imaginada*. Buenos Aires: Paidós, 1999.

———. *Hybrid Cultures: Strategies for Entering and Leaving Modernity*. Translated by Christopher L. Chiappari and Silvia L. López. Minneapolis: University of Minnesota Press, 1995.

Ortiz, Renato. *Mundialização: Saberes e crenças*. São Paulo: Brasiliense, 2006.

Prada Alcoreza, Raúl. *Territorialidad*. La Paz: Punto Cero, 1996.

Diaspora

XIMENA BRICEÑO AND DEBRA A. CASTILLO

A Greek word that means dispersion, "diaspora" refers to any people or group forced to leave its homeland and to suffer dispersion in any part of the world. As an adjective, the term refers to the subsequent cultural development of these groups in the countries of arrival.

Because the diasporic process is always in dialectic relation to ideas of sovereignty, national identity, and nomadism, the classic model for the understanding of the phenomenon includes a recognizable ethnic group identity and an element of violent removal—most famously the African, Jewish, and Armenian diasporas. Applied also to institutions and disciplines, the concept of diaspora in the twentieth century acquires philosophical depth and creates explicitly diasporic forms of theory. Consequently, diaspora has gained specific kinds of institutional currency, in official units such as the Israeli Ministry of Diasporic Affairs, as well as in the consolidation of the academic field of diasporic studies and the founding of university programs in this field in many countries in both social sciences and the humanities. Moreover, in the most important sending countries like Mexico and Haiti, there are ministerial posts responsible for the affairs of their migratory populations.

Given this growing political attention, the academic interest in diasporic studies is not surprising. Comparative literature, anthropology, and history, as well as interdisciplinary and ethnic studies projects, give increasing importance to the study of diaspora through research units and formal courses of study in the field. While the social sciences focus on the dispersion of populations, with the psychological effects of rootlessness and disintegration, as much as on the reconstruction of the nation outside the national territory through cultural practices and political activities, the humanities concentrate on the analysis of diasporic cultural products and the role of memory and language in diasporic texts.

The field has established a productive intellectual dialogue with postcolonial studies, opening up new ways of thinking about nationalisms within the wider global context, and also with trauma studies, allowing for the exploration of the experience of displacement and relocation as fundamentally tied to concerns about trauma and affect. Hence diaspora shares prominence in recent critical discourse with concepts such as transculturation, hybridity, and frontier. Also, studies on the gendered aspect of diaspora show that a male, seminal nature underlies the term, as it implies a dispersion of seed, in contrast with the feminized culture—related to the ideas of cultivating, inhabiting, protecting—that remains at home.

In Latin America, while the phenomenon is a familiar one, the term is somewhat less current. Four major aspects of Latin American ethnic diaspora are:

1) Immigration to Latin America by specific ethnically identified groups. These prominently include African, East Asian, and Jewish populations.
2) Internal displacement of indigenous peoples as well as peasants from traditional lands, especially when accompanied by violence. Brazil's Movimento dos Trabalhadores Rurais Sem Terra, or Landless Workers Movement, with more than 1.5 members the largest social movement in Latin America, is a prime example.
3) Out-migration, whether within Latin America (Bolivians in Argentina), within individual nations from rural to urban areas (*cholos* in Lima), or from Latin American countries to foreign metropolises (especially the United States), comprising both the so-called brain drain and the emigration of undocumented workers. Special cases of such ethnically marked diasporas from Latin America to the United States include the cases of Cuba, where U.S. refugee policy has been extremely favorable, and Puerto Rico, which because of its colonial status confers U.S. citizenship by birth on its inhabitants. There are also significant ethnically marked diasporas of citizens from several Latin American countries to Europe, such as the exile of Southern Cone political activists during the authoritarian regimes of the 1970s–1980s, and the economic migration of Caribbean people to former colonial powers like Great Britain and Spain from the mid-twentieth century to the present.
4) The increasingly important transnational effect of cybernationalisms on national politics and culture in both sending and receiving cultures, ranging from the effect of cash remittances on local economies to the boom in global music.

Examples of academic discussion on Latin American diaspora may be found in several recent works (Duany; Durand and Massey; Trigo). Jorge Duany interprets the Puerto Rican case in terms of "divided nation" and "nation in movement," where the concept of nation is not linked to a geographical territory but to a translocal phenomenon. Conversely, with respect to the Mexican situation, Jorge Durand and Douglas Massey describe the crucial symbolic importance of crossing the border itself, something most undocumented Mexicans today experience as a traumatic event, even though the political boundary is arbitrarily imposed on a continuous landscape. Abril Trigo, in his analysis of the Uruguayan diaspora, emphasizes how, for the moving and multisituated elements of contemporary diaspora, the Internet has become an axis of recomposition of pseudo-communities, producers of culture, which Trigo calls "the cybernetic homeland."

Thus the two components of the traditional use of the term—place and ethnicity—are continually in a state of renegotiation and flux as determined by the myriad and multiple relationships of exclusion and exchange. *Place*, a common analytic device, grounds all discussion about diasporic identity as based on an originary homeland. In many studies this place of origin is evoked with nostalgia, and the people whose identity is tied to that space are essentialized and, not infrequently, fetishized. The loss of the homeland is read as a traumatic event, accompanied by violence; the evocation of the lost homeland from the space of diasporic arrival serves as one of the most important elements uniting the dispersed members of the population. In the classic diasporic model represented by the Jewish diaspora, the dispersed community maintains a fierce loyalty to the lost homeland and pledges a primary goal of regaining and returning to it.

Desire to recuperate the lost place of origin has historically fueled a troubled relationship with the receiving society. Displacement is an experience essential to the definition; the immigrant is never at home in the new country. Diasporic populations trouble and reshape the territories of arrival while (unlike the traditional image of the immigrant) remaining lightly committed. From the perspective of the receiving societies, diasporics are marked as irremediably foreign to the national project. To the diasporic qua diasporic, the new homeland is never the place of belonging, the foundation of cultural practices. Identity derives from a particular shared cultural memory; originary rootlessness is substituted by unquestionable quotidian practices, languages, and foods that are valued as constituent of powerful affective relations. This fundamental rootlessness represents a special mode of mourning, named "cultural mourning" by Ricardo Ainslie, which involves the working-through not only of relations with loved ones but also of cultural forms.

The second element is *ethnicity*, generally imagined in racialized and often stigmatized terms from the perspective of the dominant culture in the receiving society. Reluctance on the part of the host society often inhibits immigrants' efforts to penetrate in it, and overwhelms their aspirations to assimilate—ironically, the only solution to the situation of displacement and exile. Self-defense, protection, and survival organizations appear as a response to marginality and rejection, typically persisting into subsequent generations of descendents of diasporic peoples. Often, native populations interpret this as suspicious signs of foreignness, isolation, and unwillingness to fully take on a host-country identity. The rejected diasporics may then reconnect with their countries of origin in a significant and no less problematic way. As they engage in active political participation in the original homeland, questions of ethnicity open out from concerns about diasporic populations and presumably temporary residence in host countries, to issues involving rights of citizenship (or dual citizenship) and relation to one or more governments.

Complications immediately emerge. If diaspora is defined by a yearning to recuperate the lost homeland, its status is put to the question when, as with the Jewish situation, the founding of the state of Israel seems to bring this historical and cultural moment to a close. The challenge in this particular case involves an understanding of the diaspora beyond the point of its logical demise. Another complication concerns the African diaspora, originated in the forced removal of vast numbers of people from Africa and their dispersion over a period of centuries as slaves in the Americas. The descendents of these peoples continue to identify ethnically, and they have created multiple and dynamic cultural expressions throughout the diaspora. Yet, despite a generalized identification through African descent, no particularly strong back-to-Africa movement animates them. Instead, their major struggles involve civil rights work in post-emancipation New World states.

Partly through consideration of these issues, many scholars support an expanded and more flexible definition, although it dilutes the precision of the classic term. Simultaneously, this expanded definition allows room for the examination of postmodern itineraries of dispersion, what Appadurai calls "the new global ethnoscape." The new diasporas include victim, labor, trade, imperial, and cultural communities, as opposed to those of exiles, expatriates, refugees, and migrants. Likewise, many scholars make the case for a temporal, rather than exclusively spatial, understanding of diaspora; they focus less on dispersion and more on forms and temporalities of dwelling in displacement.

In fact, while the study of diaspora is inseparable from the study of postcolonialism and imperialism, it no longer represents what James Clifford calls "old localizing strategies," which assumed cultural and power determination in relation to binary structures such as center/peripheries or metropolises/colonies. Recent scholarship complicates these oppositions, discussing diaspora as a multiple, creolized, flexible, contingent, situational, adaptable, and malleable phenomenon. Recent thinkers also put pressure on key concepts like "home," "movement," "identity," and "return," understanding diaspora as a category of practice. Important theorists include those like Marc Augé—whose analysis of non-places of transition like the airport, train station, or bus terminal opens up new possibilities of theoretical intervention—as well as an international group of academics including Benedict Anderson, Arjun Appadurai, Avtar Brah, James Clifford, Aihwa Ong, and Ella Shohat. New studies of diaspora venture beyond territorialization and deterritorialization, familiar concepts from readings of Deleuze and Guattari, into transterritorialization.

Consequently, diasporic studies enters into dialogue with several crucial strands of contemporary critical discourse.

1) The focus on diaspora poses a challenge to Western narratives about modernity.
2) It means giving less importance to the state and, of necessity, more attention to different, translocal political strategies.
3) It underscores the limits of monological theorizing, the importance of dialogue, the interplay of narratives and counternarratives.
4) The more nuanced analysis in contemporary diaspora theory provides an important corrective to traditional diaspora studies, too often characterized by blindness to issues of gender and diverse sexuality.

How far to go with the opening out of discourse from the classic cases is currently a matter of heated debate. Nevertheless, the promise of interdisciplinary diaspora studies lies in its ability to disrupt narrow understandings of disciplinary verities and to reinvigorate area studies as a field.

Suggested Reading

Anderson, Benedict. *Imagined Communities: Reflections on the Origins and Spread of Nationalism*. London: Verso, 1993.

Appadurai, Arjun. "Sovereignty Without Territoriality: Notes for a Postnational Geography." *Public Culture* 8 (1996): 40–57.

Bhabha, Homi K. *The Location of Culture*. London: Routledge, 1994.
Brah, Avtar. *Cartographies of Diaspora: Contesting Identities*. New York: Routledge, 1996.
Clifford, James. *Routes: Travel and Translation in the Late Twentieth Century*. Cambridge, Mass.: Harvard University Press, 1997.
Duany, Jorge. *The Puerto Rican Nation on the Move: Identities on the Island and in the United States*. Chapel Hill: University of North Carolina Press, 2002.
Durand, Jorge, and Douglas S. Massey. *Clandestinos: Migración México–Estados Unidos en los albores del siglo XXI*. Mexico City: Miguel Ángel Porrúa, 2003.
Kaminsky, Amy K. *After Exile: Writing the Latin American Diaspora*. Minneapolis: University of Minnesota Press, 1999.
Kaplan, Caren. *Questions of Travel: Postmodern Discourses of Displacement*. Durham, N.C.: Duke University Press, 1996.
Mitchell, Timothy. *Questions of Modernity*. Minneapolis: University of Minneapolis Press, 2000.
Ong, Aihwa. *Flexible Citizenship: The Cultural Logics of Transnationality*. Durham, N.C.: Duke University Press, 1999.
Shohat, Ella. *Taboo Memories, Diasporic Voices*. Durham, N.C.: Duke University Press, 2006.
Trigo, Abril. *Memorias migrantes: Testimonios y ensayos sobre la diáspora uruguaya*. Rosario, Argentina: Beatriz Viterbo, 2003.

Digital Culture

ROSALÍA WINOCUR (TRANSLATED BY RUTH HALVEY)

The term "digital culture," which has been circulating in academic literature only for the past three decades, alludes to two main currents of thought in Anglophone and Latin American literature on the subject. The first conceives of digital culture in a strict sense, labeling it "cyberculture" in reference to a specific type of symbolic content that developed and grew from interactions on the Internet, a content that can be understood only on the basis of its virtual nature. The second current of thought, much broader, inscribes digital culture within the tradition of anthropological and cultural studies about media. Digital culture is considered from a framework that takes into account the new technological and symbolic foundation that Information and Communication Technologies (ICT) provide. Nevertheless, digital culture is not reified or isolated from other traditional and emerging cultural dynamics with which it is intertwined (Morley).

Among proponents of this first current of thought, we see that all are in agreement that cyberculture is a specific type of culture generated in cyberspace (a neologism invented by cyberpunk author William Gibson). However, the meaning of "cyberculture" is varied. The term can be used as a label for the subcultures of hackers, a Web-based literary genre, and the "cyberpunk" aesthetic. It can also be used as an expression that describes groups of online computer users, or as a metaphor to imagine societies of the future transformed by ICT.

During the 1980s, when the word "cyberculture" was first used, ICT functioned as a kind of futuristic myth that had the power to dramatically and fundamentally transform the world of humans, as well as human beings themselves (Macek). For some, ICT meant a new hope for a more democratized society, brought about by the free circulation of ideas and the formation of horizontal networks of knowledge and cooperation. For others, ICT meant a threat of control and subjugation of the human mind and all orders of life.

The definition of cyberculture has always been marked by the assumption that technology pervades every aspect of our existence. This view coincides with postmodern theories that propose ICT as extensions of the body, or virtual prostheses, which have the potential to modify essential aspects of our sociability and relationship to the body.

> If the Internet can be understood as the site of any culture at all, it is not, presumably, culture in the sense either of an elitist enclave or of a homogeneous social sphere. The culture that the net embodies, rather, is a product of the peculiar conditions of virtual acquaintance that prevail online, a collective adaptation to the high frequency of anonymous, experimental, and even fleeting encounters familiar to anyone who has ventured into a newsgroup debate. The majority of one's correspondents in cyberspace, after all, have no bodies, no faces, no histories beyond what they choose to reveal. There are no vocal inflections, no signatures, no gestures or embraces. There are words, but they often seem words stripped of context, words desperately burdened by the lack of the other familiar markers of identity in this strange, ethereal realm. (Porter 11)

Macek proposes a typology (see table) to describe the most common uses of the term "cyberculture," producing four concepts: *utopian*, *informational*, *anthropological*, and *epistemological.*

	Utopian concepts of cyberculture	Information concepts of cyberculture	Anthropological concepts of cyberculture	Epistemological concepts of cyberculture
Brief character of concept	• cyberculture as a form of utopian society changed through ICT • anticipating ("futurologism")	• cyberculture as cultural (symbolical) codes of the information society • analytical, partly anticipating	• cyberculture as cultural practices and lifestyles related to ICT • analytical, oriented to the present state and to history	• cyberculture as term for social and anthropological reflection of new media
Examples of authors and books	Andy Hawks, *Future Culture Manifesto* (1993); Pierre Lévy, *Cyberculture* (2001 [1997])	Margaret Morse, *Virtualities: Television, Media Art, and Cyberculture* (1998); Lev Manovich, *The Language of New Media* (2001)	Arturo Escobar, "Welcome to Cyberia: Notes on the Anthropology of Cyberculture" (1994); David Hakken, *Cyborgs@Cyberspace?* (1999)	Lev Manovich, "New Media from Borges to HTML" (2003); Martin Lister et al., *New Media: A Critical Introduction* (2003)

Pierre Lévy, another key author for understanding the nature of connections on the Internet, uses the term "cyberculture" to refer to the collection of cultural systems that arose in conjunction with digital technologies. In this vein, the term "digital culture" or "the culture of digital society" can be used to name the culture of societies in which digital technologies configure the dominant forms both of communication and of knowledge information, as well as research, production, organization, and administration.

The transformation that time and space undergo on the Internet has shaped the symbolic foundations of cyberculture by profoundly altering the usual coordinates of face-to-face relations. When entities, whether "a person, community, act, or piece of information[,] are virtualized, they are 'not-there,' they deterritorialize themselves. A kind of clutch mechanism detaches them from conventional physical or geographical space and the temporality of the clock or calendar. . . . The contemporary multiplication of spaces has made us nomads once again. But rather than following tracks and migrations within a fixed domain, we leap from network to network, from one system of proximity to the next. Spaces metamorphose and bifurcate beneath our feet, forcing us to undergo a process of heterogenesis" (Lévy 29, 31).

Within this more restrained conception of digital cultural, Manuel Castells, one of the key theorists of the information and knowledge society, emphasizes the fleeting and volatile character of interactions on the Internet: "It is a culture, indeed, but a culture of the ephemeral, a culture of each strategic decision, a patchwork of experiences and interests, rather than a charter of rights and obligations. It is a *multi-faceted, virtual culture*, as in the visual experiences created by computers in cyberspace by rearranging reality" (*Rise of the Network Society* 214).

The other, broader perspective prefers to bypass the prefix "cyber-" and study the phenomenon of digital culture from a socio-anthropological viewpoint. When light is shed on the material and symbolic conditions that make this interdependency possible, interdependency itself is no longer seen as the unequivocal result of technology: "From a cultural studies perspective, we can investigate the way technology transforms social relationships and personal and communal experiences, and the way technology relates both to the processes of globalization and the construction of our identity through local daily practices" (Mackay 46).

In the theoretical, methodological approach assumed in research of this nature, the computer, Internet, and cellular phone are conceptualized as *cultural artifacts* (Hine 43). This implies reconstructing the meaning that these technologies have for users, privileging the study of the type of practical and symbolic appropriation that is achieved in diverse sociocultural contexts and realities. Discourses, narratives, representations, and social imaginaries about ICT are all objects of study, with an eye to how everyday practices in certain material and symbolic spaces shape them, and how these practices make the social, cultural, and political interactions within and outside the Internet possible.

In Latin America, the dominant themes of the theoretical and methodological discussion on digital culture share the same Anglophone model. However, the enormous digital breach and the dissimilar experiences of appropriation of the Internet by diverse groups have raised questions such as: Do only those who have access to the Internet participate in these new cultural imaginaries? Is merely having access to the Internet enough to affirm a new type of culture isolated from the real sociocultural environments of the users? How do ICTs resignify the various symbolic universes and cultural forms of belonging, and how do these forms of belonging resignify ICT? And also, as José Joaquín Brunner pointedly asks, "In and of themselves, do ICT effectively open new avenues of development? Does virtual space narrow or widen the breach of knowledge between countries? And does cyberculture give way to new forms of global integration and to the more symmetrical use of available information at a worldwide level? In short, can we share the almost biblical hope of Nicholas Negroponte that 'the third shall be first' and, consequently, that the South will leave underdevelopment, poverty, and dependency behind by means of bits and network connections?" (translation ours). These questions contain a profound critique of the technological determinism implicit in the belief in an ad hoc culture of interactions on the Internet that can be understood only from within that culture. Roger Silverstone articulates the limitations of this approach: "Infinite storage. Infinite accessibility. Smart cards and retinal implants. Users are transformed by their use. And what it is to be human is just as surely transformed as a result. Click. . . . But it misses the nuances of agency and meaning, of the human exercise of power and of our resistance. It misses, too, other sources of change: factors that affect the creation of technologies themselves and factors that mediate our responses to them" (21).

From this perspective, "real" and "virtual" experiences of informal communications highlight the difficulty of analyzing the "real" and the "virtual" as parallel worlds whose existence is determined by the technology of connecting and disconnecting: "It is not fair to say therefore either that the Internet maps straightforwardly onto the space of flows, or that an emphasis on connection automatically transcends concerns about location. . . . multiple spatialities exist but remain meaningful to culturally competent users" (Hine 114). The multiplicity of material and symbolic references in daily life and in the media involve users in both worlds, regardless of whether the computer is on or off.

However, Arturo Escobar is correct in noting that the virtual nature of interactions on the Internet presents unprecedented challenges to anthropology, introducing new forms of alterity and ways of practicing power and diversity. These forms cannot be understood from the perspective of traditional anthropological questions about the self and others. Likewise, as García Canclini points out, virtual interactions also oblige us to ask other questions about the new conditions in which differences, inequalities, inclusion-exclusion, and the mechanisms of exploitation in intercultural processes are negotiated (43).

Suggested Reading

Bell, David, Brian D. Loader, Nicholas Pleace, and Douglas Schuler. *Cybercultures: The Key Concepts*. London: Routledge, 2004.

Brunner, José Joaquín. *Cibercultura: La aldea global dividida*. Remarks for round table on Cyberculture, "Hannover 2000," October 1999. http://archivos.brunner.cl/jjbrunner/archives/CIBERCULTURA O UNA ALDEA GLOBAL DIVIDIDA.pdf.

Castells, Manuel. *End of Millennium*. Vol. 3 of *The Information Age: Economy, Society, and Culture*. 2nd ed. Oxford: Blackwell, 2010.

———. *The Rise of the Network Society*. Vol. 1 of *The Information Age: Economy, Society, and Culture*. 2nd ed. Oxford: Blackwell, 2010.

De Kerckhove, Derrick. *The Skin of Culture*. Toronto: Somerville House, 1995.

Escobar, Arturo. "Welcome to Cyberia: Notes on the Anthropology of Cyberculture." *Current Anthropology* 35, no. 3 (June 1994): 211–31.

García Canclini, Néstor. *Diferentes, desiguales y desconectados*. Barcelona: Gedisa, 2004.

Gibson, William. *Neuromancer*. New York: Ace, 1984.

Hine, Christine. *Virtual Ethnography*. London: Sage, 2000.

Lévy, Pierre. *Becoming Virtual: Reality in the Digital Age*. Translated by Robert Bononno. New York: Plenum, 1998.

Macek, Jakub. "Defining Cyberculture (v. 2)." Translated by Monika Metyková and Jakub Macek. 2005. macek.czechian.net/defining_cyberculture.htm.

Mackay, Hugh. "Symbolism and Consumption: Understanding Technology as Culture." Paper presented at Coloquio Tecnología y Procesos Culturales, UNAM, Mexico City, February 1997.

Morley, David. *Media, Modernity, and Technology: The Geography of the New*. New York: Routledge, 2007.

Negroponte, Nicholas. *Being Digital*. New York: Knopf, 1995.

Porter, David, ed. *Internet Culture*. New York: Routledge, 1996.

Rheingold, Howard. *The Virtual Community: Homesteading on the Electronic Frontier*. Reading, Mass.: Addison-Wesley, 1993.

Silverstone, Roger. *Why Study the Media?* London: Sage, 1999.

Winocur, Rosalía. *Robinson Crusoe ya tiene celular: La conexión como espacio de control de la incertidumbre*. Mexico City: Siglo XXI, 2009.

Discourse

GUADALUPE LÓPEZ BONILLA AND CARMEN PÉREZ FRAGOSO

During the first half of the twentieth century, the theories proposed by Ferdinand de Saussure in Europe and Charles Peirce in the United States laid the foundation for the emergence of new ways of thinking that called into question the seemingly transparent relationship between signs and their referents. Two major contributions for the study of the mediating function of language in the representation of reality were Saussure's separation of the linguistic sign into the signifier and the signified, and Peirce's three-part relation among the sign, the object, and the interpretant. These contributions opened the way for new theoretical proposals that problematized the transparency of language and the relation between the signifier and the signified. The works of Vološinov and Bakhtin, for their part, laid the foundation for recognizing the social nature of language. Vološinov emphasized the determining role that social relations play in the production of linguistic signs, whereas Bakhtin outlined the discursive network that frames every utterance. Discussions on the conditions that allow the construction of meaning, on the one hand, and the preponderant role that the studies of the linguistic turn lent to language as a structuring agent in the construction of reality, on the other, took the discussion of language to the arena of discourse and discursive practices—that is, to the social terrain. As a manifestation of this epistemological transformation, the notion of discourse acquired new weight and opened the way for examining the historical nature of language and the ideological load of the linguistic sign.

As an analytical tool, the term "discourse" is located at the intersection of several disciplines, which captures its polysemy: it may equally refer to a linguistic event, a social practice, a system of representation, or a means of constructing knowledge, among others. From a linguistic point of view, discourse refers to that which is done with language, manifested in interconnected clauses. Some authors identify this use of the term by writing it with a lowercase *d*, thereby circumscribing "discourse" to a linguistic event. "Discourse" with a capital *D*, on the other hand, implies a social practice that goes beyond linguistic expression and includes systems of belief and ways of thinking, acting, and interacting (Gee). In this wider sense, "Discourse" or "Discourses" refers to systems of representation that regulate what can be done with language in a specific situation or context. The work of Michel Foucault is the most representative of this latter way of conceiving the term. For Foucault, discourse constitutes much more than the linguistic manifestation of verbal utterances, since it sets the limits of linguistic conduct according to the historical moment in which it is situated; that is to say, this notion of discourse refers to what can or cannot be said in a specific "discursive formation." A discursive formation is the set of rules that in a particular moment in history regulates and determines the formation of enunciative modalities, concepts, strategies, and objects.

A particular set of statements in which these regularities are recognized constitutes a specific discursive formation. In this sense, discourse creates a place for the subject and determines the possibilities for constructing knowledge.

Because knowledge is constructed through it, discourse has a mediating role, according to Foucault, who was thus able to relativize the notion of truth and grant it its historical dimension. Social forces are what establish a "regime of truth," and with it the types of discourse that are acceptable in a specific context. This does not imply that things do not exist outside discourse, but it is precisely through discourse that they are intelligible. In other words, the "extradiscursive reality" is mediated by the representation activity of the discourse by which it is, in part, constituted. In this way, discourse creates objects of knowledge and, while regulating the possible ways of speaking about those objects, it becomes an authority waving the banner of "truth" over them.

This last aspect is important in Foucault's theory of representation since it reveals the power that discourse has over social practices. It is through knowledge—always discursive—that the guidelines of valid conduct in specific moments and contexts are fixed. *Power*, *subject*, and *identity* are thus concepts that are intimately associated with the concept of discourse.

As heir to the discourse analytical frame of Bakhtin and Barthes and, mostly, Foucault, cultural studies appropriated and problematized the relation between text and context, between discursive intertextuality and institutions, and between representation and formation of identities. Thus, from the perspective of cultural studies, discourse and the production of meaning always imply permanent displacement and struggle.

In British cultural studies, Stuart Hall points out that the field itself constitutes a particular discursive formation, one that has no clear limits. Hall's work was groundbreaking in its questioning of the traditional model of communication and in establishing four moments that articulate the communicative process: production, circulation, consumption, and reproduction. Hall stresses the relative autonomy of each of these moments within the circumstances in which they operate, paving the way for the analysis of the deterministic and conflictive relation between the moments of encoding and decoding the message. Analytically, this approach allows one to track the imprints that institutional structures impress upon discourses in the moment of encodification. It also permits the exploration of forms of resistance to the dominant readings inscribed to these discourses; however, such alternative readings, which are a product of the circumstances of decodification and the position of the subjects, are still constrained by encoding and therefore prohibit infinite interpretations.

For cultural studies, the turning point created by the linguistic turn as well as the semiotic paradigm gave great weight to discourse and its textual medium. Hall himself emphasizes that language and discourse are metaphors in the analysis of culture, and highlights the relation between the symbolic and the identities of subjects.

In the context of Latin American cultural studies, the term "discourse" has been used in a looser sense to refer to the linguistic expressions of cultural manifestations (discourses on national identity, for example) as well as to the systems of representation that convey them. Behind many of these conceptual frameworks there is, undoubtedly, a clear Foucauldian influence, and they would appear to be more a legacy of the British tradition than of other schools of cultural studies. According to the Mexican sociologist José Manuel Valenzuela, a common element of the different approaches to studying culture seems to be a questioning of the dominant discourses. Valenzuela points out that by questioning dominant discourses, cultural studies reformulated the interpretations of sociopolitical processes. García Canclini, for his part, states that it is impossible to speak of cultural manifestations without taking into account the new conditions of symbolic production and circulation, conditions that necessarily affect the "discursive meaning" that society grants to these manifestations. Both of these authors emphasize the need in Latin America to recognize the critical trajectories developed within the Latin American context in order to broach the manifestations of our culture, so that, from that perspective, we can initiate a dialogue with outsiders' representations of our reality. The assertions of Mabel Moraña follow in this same vein, stressing that cultural studies in Latin America are situated in an enunciative position from and to the Latin American reality.

The discussion about the place of the subject and the mediation of codes in the context of studies about culture in Latin America necessarily must include a reflection on discourse, understood as the possibility for construction of knowledge in its clearest Foucauldian expression. By centering the analysis of culture on social processes which allow the flow of significations, the term "discourse" is also utilized tangentially to describe practices, representations, imaginaries as well as their symbolic materiality. Renato Ortiz speaks of the discourse of modernity, which is understood as a particular discursive formation, as an obligatory referent through which Latin Americans become aware of the changes taking place. He considers modernity precisely as a narrative that configures and reconfigures itself according to the history of the people.

Jesús Martín Barbero, for his part, considers that current cultural practices can be explained only by taking into account their relation to new technological media. For him, discourse as a social practice cannot be dissociated from the formats and media that convey it. Accordingly, he analyzes the emergence of new discursive formations and new discourses that arise as categories of perception of space and time that are transformed with the use of information and communication technologies in Latin American daily life. These discourses are expressed through very diverse media: not only from oral to written, but also including audiovisual and telematic media in their ever more numerous combinations. Traditional institutions like family and school have been affected, the latter by the transformation of the means of circulation and production of knowledge, that is, by discourse. The current array of technologies and the use of information and communication tools outside school evidence a transformation or, more precisely, an alternative to the modes of traditional circulation of knowledge. Martín Barbero calls this phenomenon "the decentering of knowledge" on its two axes: time and space. Thus school, as a territorial center delimited by physical space and associated with specific social actors at predetermined times, loses its force, especially among certain groups of young people whose media experiences are more relevant for them as a means of relating to learning. Martín Barbero posits that we have before us a new student, qualitatively different from that in previous times. The individual and the collective now need to narrate their own history through a polyphonic discourse that is intersected by the discourses of the new technology. The current multicultural life of Latin American societies demands that these narratives be expressed in accordance with the various literacies—oral, textual, audiovisual—because it is through the crossbreeding of these means of expression that new discourses take form.

From the stance of studies on culture and power, Nelly Richard analyzes the discourses of cultural studies about Latin America in terms of the asymmetry implied by the locus of enunciation (the metropolis) and the referents named by that discourse (local territories, or what she calls *territoriedades prácticas*). For Richard, discourse as an analytical category refers to the place of the subject and access to power/knowledge. Richard also analyzes the discourses of Latin American academics and the spaces of resistance where some of their critical discourses are situated. These discourses with their varying nuances are inserted into the public space of some countries, particularly those in the southern part of South America, where they participate in the public political debate and contest the neoliberal measures of governments. According to Richard, the relation between the fields of knowledge and the fields of action of these actors is dynamic and on occasion allows them to move from academic discourse to political action.

Beatriz Sarlo, for her part, underlines the role played by early-twentieth-century literary discourses and literary criticism, whose social function contributed to the shaping of national identity in Latin American countries. Some decades later, Sarlo points out, these discourses fulfilled a different but equally relevant function in regard to the social and political movements that marked the 1960s, for example, covering the debate between ideologies. This social function of the specialized discourse of literary criticism apparently was diluted in the "processes of technification" which, according to Sarlo, rendered it hermetical and exclusive. For Sarlo, it is thanks to cultural studies that this discourse is able to insert itself again in the public sphere. In the current environment, where electronic discourses are showing up in all fields of knowledge, Sarlo suggests focusing our attention on that which makes literary discourse lasting.

The richness and diversity of current discourses—electronic, print, audiovisual—demand new ways of accessing and interacting with them. The notion of discourse contributes conceptual elements that allow for questioning the dominant ways of reading reality and simultaneously constructing alternative social readings and practices.

Suggested Reading

Bakhtin, Mikhail. *The Dialogic Imagination: Four Essays*. Translated by Caryl Emerson and Michael Holquist. Austin: University of Texas Press, 1981.

Foucault, Michel. *The Archaeology of Knowledge*. Translated by A. M. Sheridan Smith. New York: Pantheon, 1972.

García Canclini, Néstor. *Diferentes, desiguales y desconectados: Mapas de la interculturalidad*. Barcelona: Gedisa, 2004.

Gee, James Paul. *An Introduction to Discourse Analysis: Theory and Method*. London: Routledge, 1999.

Hall, Stuart. "Cultural Studies and Its Theoretical Legacies." In Morley and Chen, *Stuart Hall*, 262–76.

———. "Encoding/ Decoding." In *Culture, Media, Language: Working Papers in Cultural Studies, 1972–79*, edited by Stuart Hall, Dorothy Hobson, and Andrew Lowe, 128–38. London: Hutchinson; Birmingham: Centre for Contemporary Cultural Studies, 1980.

Houser, Nathan, and Christian Kloesel, eds. *The Essential Peirce*. 2 vols. Bloomington: Indiana University Press, 1992–98.
Martín Barbero, Jesús. "Saberes hoy: Diseminaciones, competencias y transversalidades." *Revista Iberoamericana de Educación*, no. 32 (2003): 17–34.
Moraña, Mabel. Introduction to *Nuevas perspectivas desde/sobre América Latina*. Santiago, Chile: Cuarto Propio, 2000.
Ortiz, Renato. "América Latina: De la modernidad incompleta a la modernidad-mundo." *Nueva Sociedad*, no. 166 (2000): 44–61.
Richard, Nelly. "Intersectando Latinoamérica con el latinoamericanismo: discurso académico y crítica cultural." In Castro Gómez and Mendieta, *Teorías sin disciplina*.
Sarlo, Beatriz. "Los estudios culturales y la crítica literaria en la encrucijada valorativa." *Revista de Crítica Cultural*, no. 15 (1997): 32–38.
Saussure, Ferdinand de. *Course in General Linguistics*. Translated by Roy Harris. La Salle, Ill.: Open Court, 1987.
Valenzuela Arce, José Manuel, ed. *Los estudios culturales en México*. Mexico City: Fondo de Cultura Económica, 2003.
Vološinov, V. N. *Marxism and the Philosophy of Language*. Translated by Ladislav Matejka and I. R. Titunik. Cambridge, Mass.: Harvard University Press, 1986.

Diversity

HORTENSIA MORENO (TRANSLATED BY EDUARDO RABASA)

The inclusion of sexual diversity as a crucial concept of cultural studies presumes the existence of a perspective that questions any attempt to naturalize sexuality, to hide its institutional quality and to transform it into an anthropological universal (Vázquez and Moreno 23). In contrast with the dominant view during modernity—which aimed to explain all human phenomena in terms of identifiable biological forces—the notion of sexuality implied by the term "diversity" is based on evidence demonstrating that sexuality is a social construction, a historical invention based on the possibilities of the body, but whose meanings are created in social circumstances.

Foucault and Weeks are among the main authors who have developed this perspective. In Latin America, the study of diversity has found its impulse in research on homosexualities (Mogrovejo). This line of inquiry, however, goes beyond the horizon of specific manifestations of sexuality as part of a pursuit exploring the enormous plasticity of human behavior and its cultural expressions.

Foucault's works apply a historical approach to the study of sexuality, as opposed to an essentialist outlook, which would consider sex as a natural force, asocial, eternal and immutable, preexistent to all social life. According to Foucault, it is impossible to understand the body without the mediations of culture. Sexuality implies a historical constitution uniting a multiplicity of biological and mental possibilities that are not linked in a natural form, and the capacities of mind and body become meaningful only when inscribed in social relationships (Weeks 20).

Foucault investigates how power affects individual behavior, how it infiltrates and controls everyday pleasure. He traces how discourses regulate sex and how, from the eighteenth century on, childhood and teenage sexuality became important targets around which "institutional devices and discursive strategies" were constructed (*History* 1: 30). At that moment, medicine and psychiatry appropriated perversions as part of their own domain, and sexual variations began to be identified with mental illness, replacing a previous interpretation that drew the dividing line between the licit and the illicit within the confines of sin.

Since the nineteenth century, sexual heterogeneities have been understood as being "against nature," with the introduction of the perverse as the subject that exhibits peripheral sexualities (nonconjugal, nonheterosexual, nonmonogamous). Its appearance "entailed an *incorporation of perversions* and a new *specification of individuals*" subject to the controls exerted by family, medicine, psychiatry, and pedagogy (Foucault, *History* 1: 42).

When Freud published *Three Essays on the Theory of Sexuality* in 1905, a sexological knowledge had been accumulated, guided between the eighteenth and nineteenth centuries by disciplinarian and regulatory mechanisms that transformed the body into a field of action in which sexuality was the bridge linking the individual with the collective (Vázquez and Moreno 126):

> By the end of the nineteenth century . . . *any* deviation . . . from *any* biological norm was pathological in the broad sense . . . ; medical sexologists continued to conceptualize sexuality with reference to a fixed, virtually uncontested norm—the mutual attraction of man and woman culminating in vaginal intercourse. With reference to this norm, *any* other form of sexual behavior—even between men and women—was pathological, though pathological did not necessarily mean diseased. (Sengoopta 96–97)

What Freud elaborated in *Three Essays* is a conceptual description of perversions based on the paradigm of "normal" (procreative) sexuality, a model that predominated during the twentieth century. The Freudian contribution to the knowledge of sexuality allows the untying of sexual impulse from a normal "end" or a normal or natural "object." The meanings we confer on the male and female organs, according to Freud, are demanded by culture and do not emanate directly from biology. What we describe as "sexual" is constructed by social relationships, each of which holds a different conception of what constitutes appropriate sexual behavior (Weeks 55, 60).

Sexuality is a multidimensional fact, which does not depend exclusively on biology, but imbricates historical, cultural, social, symbolic, and imaginary determinants. Physiology and morphology of the body provide the preconditions for human sexuality, and both represent potentialities that are transformed and acquire meaning in social relationships. From there, every culture classifies different practices as either appropriate or inappropriate, moral or immoral, healthy or perverted (Weeks 29–30).

The main challenge to the essentialist vision of sexuality is related to the conceptualization of sexual difference not as a simple and univocal indicator, but rather as a complex set of elements that settle in the body, yet do not exhaust themselves in anatomy: there is not a direct relationship between a biological, anatomical, or physiological sexuality and its psychosocial, symbolic, and cultural manifestations. Clinical investigation had made it possible to appreciate a dissociation between the physical aspect of sexuality and its cultural manifestations in society. Our identities as men and women, heterosexual and homosexual, are a product of complex processes of definition and self-definition. Masculine and feminine identities, far from being fixed for all of eternity by natural qualities, are fragile, hazardous, and contradictory (Weeks 53–54).

Anatomy itself is a problematic field. The elements that constitute the genetic and cellular level, the hormonal level, and the anatomical level are not combined in fixed and unalterable relationships, but can rather be the cause of results that do not correspond to our Platonic idea of a perfectly dimorphic sexuality. Biologically speaking, there are many gradations running from female to male, and depending on where the demarcation lines are positioned, one can argue that along that spectrum lie at least five sexes, perhaps even more (Fausto-Sterling 21).

Levels of masculinity and femininity—defined from a biological point of view—can be found to form almost every possible combination. The intersexual body redefines sexual difference not as a precise cut, but rather as a convention derived from recognizable phenomena that can be interpreted by those who have a necessity of subjecting them to a binary code.

Katchadourian lays out a series of biological, psychological, symbolic, cultural, and social variables whose combinations can be considered in determining a specific position in the sex/gender system: (1) genetic sex, (2) hormonal sex, (3) gonadal sex, (4) morphology of internal reproductive organs, (5) morphology of external genitals, (6) secondary sexual characteristics, (7) erotic conduct, (8) sexual experience, (9) private thoughts, (10) cataloguing and self-cataloguing, (11) polarization or orientation, (12) sexual preference, (13) sexual role, (14) core gender identity, (15) typology, (16) gender role, (17) gender identity, (18) behavior. There is no compendium of possible combinations, but this approach permits us to imagine a wide range of sexualities where the norm is variety and not uniformity.

One of the predominating trends of Western society during modernity has been to restrict the spectrum of "licit" erotic practices and identities to a simple "normal sexuality," which, on the one hand, has produced a set of disciplinary measures to "redirect" and "cure" any "deviations" but, on the other hand, has generated cultures of resistance to moral codes (Weeks 35).

Such resistance seeks the abolishment of the penalization of peripheral sexual practices. The most visible group in this pursuit are homosexuals, who from the beginning of the twentieth century have been organizing in order to obtain the benefits of full citizenship. Even if sex is still an oppression vector and the insertion in social life of those with peripheral sexualities is not yet equitable, the gay community has nonetheless managed to substantially modify the world's sexual culture. In modern Western industrial societies, homosexuality has acquired much of the institutional structure of an ethnic group—an elaborate experience that includes a self-conscious identity, group solidarity, a literature, a press, and a high level of political activity (Rubin 17).

Even if homosexual acts exist in every culture, and if in Western culture there is an uninterrupted history of homosexuality, the idea of the existence of something that can be called *the* homosexual person is relatively new. The search for valid sexual identities has been a constant of male and female homosexuality during the twentieth century. The emergence of the gay community has led to the development and recognition of a new identity. Furthermore, the expansion of the homosexual category has allowed the proliferation of new types of sexual identities: the transvestite, the transsexual, the bisexual, the pedophile, the sadomasochist (Weeks 38–40).

The evident existence of a great variety of sexual manifestations has generated new perspectives that make it possible to transcend the given categories and think of these categories as complex and not necessarily adjustable to the binary pairs feminine/masculine, normal/abnormal, heterosexual/homosexual, sick/healthy.

The claims of the gay community have extended to a much wider and more comprehensive movement, called by certain media "queer nation," embodying among others the "trans" phenomenon, which includes transsexuals, or people who show what Money and Stoller call a "gender dysphoria": the internal belief in a mismatch between the body and the sense of identity (they state that they "are" either a man trapped in a woman's body or a woman trapped in a man's body). It also encompasses transvestites (people who wear, to erotic purpose, garb that corresponds to the "other sex") and transgendered people (those who assume the sexual and identity role of the "opposite sex").

The so-called queer nation includes among its ranks sadomasochists, for whom sexual pleasure is associated with receiving and inflicting physical pain. Sadomasochism is not listed automatically anymore among homosexualities. The notion of the "queer" also generates discussion on such sexual expressions as commercial sex, intergenerational sex (pedophilia), exhibitionism, and voyeurism.

This diversity evokes a questioning of modern sexual ethics. Though it may be true that the spectrum of licit sexual practices should be widened, an unlimited field of action cannot be postulated. The limits would entail that, instead of expressing a judgment on the nature of the act, we consider the context and the meaning of the act for those involved in it. Sex in itself is neither good nor bad, but is rather a field of possibilities and potentialities, all of which must be judged by the context in which they occur. Moral pluralism opens the way to acceptance of diversity as the norm of our culture and the appropriate means of thinking about sexuality (Weeks 115).

A modern sexual ethics questions the idea that there is an optimal way of experiencing sexuality and that everybody should experience it the same way (Rubin 15). The search for a unique truth regarding sexuality and the body has led, for a very long time, to a denial of human diversity and its options, limiting individual autonomy and converting the pleasures of the body into an indecent secret (Weeks 12). A democratic morality should judge sexual acts by the way partners treat one another, the level of mutual consideration, the presence or absence of coercion, and the quantity and quality of the pleasures they provide (Rubin 15).

Suggested Reading

Fausto-Sterling, Anne. "The Five Sexes: Why Male and Female Are Not Enough." *The Sciences*, March–April 1993, 20–24.

Foucault, Michel. *The History of Sexuality*. Translated by Robert Hurley. 3 vols. New York: Vintage, 1988–90.

Freud, Sigmund. *Three Essays on the Theory of Sexuality*. Translated by James Strachey. London: Hogarth Press, 1962.

Katchadourian, Herant A. *Human Sexuality: Sense and Nonsense*. New York: W. H. Freeman, 1974.

Mogrovejo, Norma. *Un amor que se atrevió a decir su nombre*. Mexico City: CDAHL/Plaza y Valdés, 2000.

Rubin, Gayle S. "Thinking Sex: Notes on a Radical Theory of the Politics of Sexuality." In *The Lesbian and Gay Studies Reader*, edited by Henry Abelove, Michèle Aina Barale, and David Halperin, 3–44. NewYork: Routledge, 1993.

Sengoopta, Chandak. *Otto Weininger: Sex, Science, and Self in Imperial Vienna*. Chicago: University of Chicago Press, 2000.

Vázquez García, Francisco, and Andrés Moreno Mengíbar. *Sexo y razón: Una genealogía de la moral sexual en España (siglos XVI–xx)*. Madrid: Akal Universitaria, 1997.

Weeks, Jeffrey. *Sexuality*. 2nd ed. New York: Routledge, 2003.

Ethics

ERIN GRAFF ZIVIN

The contemporary resurgence of ethical theory on both sides of the Atlantic forms part of a long tradition of moral philosophy, which can be traced to the work of Socrates, Plato (*The Republic*), and Aristotle (*Nicomachean Ethics*), each of whom debated the question of how one should live, or the pursuit of the "good." Theories of the ethical have focused on notions of virtue, happiness, justice, value, duty, friendship, and responsibility, oscillating between descriptive and prescriptive, objective and relative, ideal and practical, universal and particular. Moral philosophy has alternately dwelled upon socially sanctioned norms and individual experience: while the Latin root *mor-* emphasizes customs or social expectation, the Greek term *ethos* privileges individual character. From the inception of ethical thought, then, there has been a lack of consensus on the definition of the ethical, as well as how it is to be practiced. Current discussions of ethics in the fields of philosophy and critical theory are equally varied, ranging from theories of the *formal structure* of ethical experience to the *content* of ethical practice.

The moral philosophy of Immanuel Kant introduces the concept of the "categorical imperative" as that which commands (imperative) and that which is unconditional (categorical). Kant's vision of the moral, grounded in the idea of the sovereignty of reason, stresses rationality and autonomy as central to the definition of the moral subject, who acts through his own free will. Immorality, being a rejection of the categorical imperative, is therefore irrational. Although Kant continues the tradition of linking ethics to an autonomous subject, Alenka Zupančič in *Ethics of the Real* and Gabriela Basterra in *Seductions of Fate* argue that Kant's philosophy anticipates an ethics of heteronomy in such twentieth-century thinkers as Emmanuel Levinas, Jacques Lacan, and Alain Badiou.

Friedrich Nietzsche also understands the autonomous subject as the epicenter of the moral, connecting the idea of "values" to what he terms the "will to power." Nietzsche reflects critically upon the history of ethical thought by arguing that the idea of the "good" is intrinsically linked to the aristocratic class, which he calls "master morality." "Slave morality," in contrast, favors characteristics that contradict the hegemonic values of the ruling class. Nietzsche's tragic hero Zarathustra moves "beyond good and evil" by transcending the good/evil divide present in slave morality, thus embodying a revalued ethics.

In the second half of the twentieth century, a simultaneous turn *away from* and turn *to* ethics can be distinguished, a phenomenon some have attributed to the genocidal violence of the Holocaust. Many critics have identified the work of Emmanuel Levinas as a turning point in Western philosophy. Levinas's primary contribution to philosophy lies in his recentering the idea of the subject around the other: rather than privileging an autonomous self whose engagement with the other is secondary to being, Levinas underscores the response to the other's demand as that which makes subjectivity possible. While his earlier work *Totality and Infinity* characterizes the ethical relationship between the same and the other in more anthropomorphic terms (the "face" of the other commands the subject), later in *Otherwise than Being* he describes the encounter with the other as an interruption of the self from within, or by the other within the same.

In his *Liberación latinoamericana y Emmanuel Levinas*, Enrique Dussel turns to the work of Levinas in order to articulate a theory of liberation that would take into account the notion of the ethical, grounding it in the broader geopolitical context of postcolonialism and inequality. Levinas offers Dussel a way out of what he perceives, in Kantian philosophers such as Jürgen Habermas or Karl-Otto Apel, as a limited view of subjectivity that does not take into account the body or sentience. Dussel is interested in articulating a theory of ethical subjectivity that would be responsive to the tangible suffering of the other, ultimately leading to the political liberation of this other. For Dussel, then, the relationship between the same and the other moves beyond the intersubjective relationship detailed in Levinas's *Totality and Infinity* to take on broader ethno-political significance in a specifically Latin American framework. His work brings together the Levinasian relationship between the same and the other with the center-periphery of Immanuel Wallerstein's "world-system" theory in order to create a geopolitical ethics.

Dussel's emphasis in his ethics of liberation on the other as subaltern or victim anticipates the cult of the other that dominates U.S. literary and cultural studies during the 1980s, culminating in the multiculturalist and identity politics of the 1990s. Here, too, we find a preoccupation with the historically situated and ethnically, economically, or sexually specific other that has been systematically excluded, not only from history but, more specifically, from the writing of history, literature, and culture. This trend marks, at least in theory, a shift within the fields of both the political and the academic, and seeks to establish or expose the relationship between these spheres. In both of these examples, Levinas is taken at face value; the other is a literal figure, identifiable by the intellectual: the "African American other," the "indigenous other," and so forth.

The 1990s surge in intellectual production on ethics which has commonly been referred to as the "ethical turn," perhaps not surprisingly, coincides with this increased attention to the other. But if Dussel's work emerges as political repression is taking over the continent, the turn to ethics in U.S. academic circles seems to respond to a crisis of the political following the decline of the political activism of the 1960s and 1970s. This is perhaps what has led thinkers such as Judith Butler, John Guillory, and Chantal Mouffe to raise concerns that the so-called turn to ethics signifies a turn away from politics, that the ethical comes to serve as a substitute for the political.

The emergence of deconstruction as a dominant mode of criticism in the 1980s adds a new, discursive aspect to debates on ethics. Grounded largely in the work of Jacques Derrida and Paul de Man, deconstruction elicits two ostensibly contradictory responses that can be understood as representative of broader tendencies in ethical theory. In the first, deconstruction is viewed as an amoral or antimoral practice for its nihilism and its privileging of the text above all else; contemporary literary studies in general, especially when it is punctuated by an interest in theory, is seen as anti-ethical, and deconstruction is primarily to blame. The second "camp," by contrast, aims to highlight a certain ethicity of deconstruction, an argument that can be seen in Simon Critchley's *The Ethics of Deconstruction*. Derrida himself shies away from both positions, which he views as equally moralizing. Rather than defending deconstruction as inherently ethical, however, Critchley instead attempts to underscore the strong, one might say haunting, influence of Levinas's ethical philosophy upon Derrida's thought, reading deconstruction as an ethical demand. Regardless of one's position, a crucial distinction is made here between the idea of ethical content (morality, whether universal or particular) and the notion of ethical experience (in Levinas's terms, the interruption of the same by the radical exteriority of the other).

Without overlooking radical differences between them, several theories of the ethical within recent Continental philosophy and psychoanalytic theory seem to coincide, at least on a structural level, with the idea of ethical responsibility in the interrupted subject described by Levinas. Derrida, as Critchley has argued, structures his philosophy of deconstruction around the idea of the gift and the unconditional. Jacques Lacan's dictum to not give way on one's desire and Alain Badiou's idea of ethics as fidelity to an event both describe an experience of ethical subjectivity in which a radically exterior force disrupts and, in doing so, constitutes the subject.

Two broad tendencies emerge from these debates. In the first, a liberal-humanist emphasis on ethical content, whether universal or pluralistic, can be found not only in literary circles but also in philosophers such as Martha Nussbaum and Wayne Booth, who mine literature for instances of the ethical. In the second, we see a more radical or deconstructive strain that hesitates to imbue the ethical with content, emphasizing instead the formal structure of ethical experience through the ideas of undecidability or unreadability.

Within recent Latin American literary and cultural criticism, both currents can be detected, but within a highly politicized context. Both emerge from a strong leftist tradition, so that differences between them cannot be properly characterized by adjectives such as conservative, liberal-humanist, or radical. Rather, their differences lie in their unique approaches to *difference* itself. A preoccupation with the ethical in thinkers like Dussel or

Walter Mignolo is motivated first and foremost by a concern with the historically specific other. The violated other of history—the indigenous, the subaltern, the woman—contrasts with an elusive or unreadable other. This tension between ontology and heteronomy to a certain degree mirrors the debates of the Latin American Subaltern Studies Group, the participants of which struggled to agree upon the definition of the subaltern as a political subject or as an empty, impossible category, leading ultimately to the group's dissolution.

Over the last decade or so, a current of Latin Americanist critical thought has engaged the latter tendency, while underscoring what has been perceived as a lack of political content in European and North American theories of the ethical. These thinkers emphasize the idea of undecidability, the secret, the unsayable, as that element of radical exteriority in the literary text that perturbs the reader, and serves as the impossible condition of possibility of interpretation.

Evaluating the limits of ethical theory in the Anglo-American tradition, Idelber Avelar argues that philosophers such as Nussbaum and Booth emphasize a liberal, cosmopolitan ethics that, while ostensibly favoring cultural pluralism, remains structured around an ethnocentric worldview that completely eclipses the other it purports to celebrate. Turning away from an ethics of empathy or friendship, Avelar proposes a way of conceiving the ethical that emphasizes an undecidable relation to the other. Through a close reading of Jorge Luis Borges's short story "The Ethnographer," he exposes the limits of well-meaning First World sympathy while signaling a Latin American tradition of theorizing the ethical from the space of the literary.

The question of the political remains central to theories of the ethical within Latin American critical thought, even when the content of the political or the ethical is indeterminate. Like Avelar, Alberto Moreiras turns to the realm of the literary in order to rethink the ethical as inseparable from the political. In his discussion of the genre of the Mexican thriller, in which the "secret" of murder is investigated, the thriller aesthetically codifies the ethical breach, thus dwelling within the space of ethics, albeit negatively. By investigating the scene of the crime, the thriller becomes, in addition to ethical, a political act that Moreiras calls infrapolitical. Infrapolitics, which involves the simultaneous deconstruction of the political by the ethical and the ethical by the political, is radically opposed to moralism, which aims to protect autonomy rather than privileging heteronomy—a distinction that

Moreiras deems central to any discussion of the relationship between ethics and politics. This most recent trend in Latin Americanist ethical thought brings together the literary, the political, and the ethical in a complicated triad that eschews the normative in favor of an empty but potentially liberating possibility of difference as radical interruption.

Suggested Reading

Avelar, Idelber. *The Letter of Violence: Essays on Narrative, Ethics, and Politics.* New York: Palgrave Macmillan, 2004.

Badiou, Alain. *Ethics: An Essay on the Understanding of Evil.* Translated by Peter Hallward. London: Verso, 2001.

Basterra, Gabriela. *Seductions of Fate: Tragic Subjectivity, Ethics, Politics.* London: Palgrave Macmillan, 2004.

Critchley, Simon. *The Ethics of Deconstruction: Derrida and Levinas.* West Lafayette, Ind.: Purdue University Press, 1992.

Davis, Todd F., and Kenneth Womack, eds. *Mapping the Ethical Turn: A Reader in Ethics, Culture, and Literary Theory.* Charlottesville: University Press of Virginia, 2001.

Deigh, John. "Ethics." In *The Cambridge Dictionary of Philosophy*, edited by Robert Audi, 2nd ed. Cambridge: Cambridge University Press, 1999.

Derrida, Jacques. "Passions: 'An Oblique Offering.'" In *On the Name*, translated by David Wood, John P. Leavey Jr., and Ian McLeod, 3–31. Stanford, Calif.: Stanford University Press, 1995.

Dussel, Enrique, and Daniel E. Guillot. *Liberación latinoamericana y Emmanuel Levinas.* Buenos Aires: Bonum, 1975.

Garber, Marjorie, Beatrice Hanssen, Rebecca L. Walkowitz, eds. *The Turn to Ethics.* New York: Routledge, 2000.

Lacan, Jacques. *The Seminar of Jacques Lacan.* Book 7, *The Ethics of Psychoanalysis, 1959–1960.* Translated by Denis Porter. New York: Norton, 1992.

Levinas, Emmanuel. *Otherwise than Being, or, Beyond Essence.* Translated by Alphonso Lingis. Pittsburgh, Pa.: Duquesne University Press, 1998.

———. *Totality and Infinity: An Essay on Exteriority.* Translated by Alphonso Lingis. Pittsburgh, Pa.: Duquesne University Press, 1969.

Moreiras, Alberto. "Infrapolitics and the Thriller: A Prolegomenon to Every Possible Form of Antimoralist Literary Criticism: On Héctor Aguilar Camín's *La guerra de Galio* and *Morir en el golfo*." In *The Ethics of Latin American Literary Criticism: Reading Otherwise*, edited by Erin Graff Zivin, 147–79. New York, Palgrave Macmillan, 2007.

Zupančič, Alenka. *Ethics of the Real: Kant, Lacan.* London: Verso, 2000.

Gender

MARICRUZ CASTRO RICALDE (TRANSLATED BY EDUARDO RABASA)

Gender is one of the main categories of analysis for feminism and women's studies because of its clarity in showing how society is organized into binary and oppositional schemes. A perspective of gender reveals how specific traits attributed to masculinity and femininity are constructed culturally by virtue of a presumed correspondence with biological features. The term "gender" tends to be presented as the complementary pairing of "sex," which is linked to the biological differences that distinguish men from women, whereas gender refers to the sphere of culture, since it makes reference to socially constructed features.

Through the category of gender it was possible to reflect on how inequality between men and women had been normalized throughout history, and how the adscription to one sex or the other determined the roles that the subject had to perform. It was an answer to essentialist theories that insisted upon irreconcilable, non-interchangeable, and intrinsic differences between men and women. It also permitted the analysis of how organizations and practices institutionalize sexual difference within societies. However, during the last fifteen years a discussion has ensued on whether these assumptions were not oversimplifying the problematic around identity by reproducing a scheme of differentiated pairings: nature/culture, body/meaning, given/acquired, woman/man, feminine/masculine.

The complexity became manifest during the debate around the precise moment in which the individual is gendered, in contrast to sexuation, which is established at the moment of birth. Sexual practice (age ranges of initial sexual activity, preferences toward a partner of a given sex, frequency of sexual activity, existence or absence of pleasure-producing devices, procreation as the ultimate goal, acceptance or rejection of new reproductive technologies) illustrates how certain structural dispositions bring about—or not—the exercise of sexual practices, just as one might imagine would occur through the association with a biological process, an imperative of the subject, determined by the fact of possessing a genital apparatus. The reflection on the fact that sex is not "given" nor gender "reached" put into question the social interaction and institutions as the determining variables for the generic constitution of the subject, as well as its distance from the process of sexuation. Hermaphroditism, the indetermination and the sexual ambiguity of the newborn, as well as the ever more frequent mutations from one sex to the other, debunked the idea that we are "born" sexuated or that sex is a biological given. Transsexuality produced a new understanding of sex, since it put to rest once and for all the nineteenth-century idea of a corresponding specific gender, unchangeable and opposed completely to the other gender for each sexuated body.

Anthropological research has shown that the set of meanings that points toward one or another gender operates differently in different societies, and even within communities and subsets of the same social group. These sets of meanings are not a handful of permanent features, nor can they be associated inextricably with the representation of a given role. Gender is rather constructed in a sustained way, is demonstrated in our choices, and can confirm or not (at least provisionally, given the temporal space and situation) the identifications associated with its normativeness.

Marks of gender are thus present at every moment of the human being's existence, immersed in a wide range of social practices and influenced by the historical moment and spatial context. Hence the interest in studying the multiple intersections of gender with other variables such as race, social class, and age.

Theories of gender assign crucial value to the social aspects of gender formation. The individual's learning process in his/her process of socialization, the acceptance of the rules that assign specific meanings to the feminine and masculine genders, and the legitimization that is obtained by respecting these rules underscore the preexistence of a set of meanings that the subject acquires gradually through a system of reward and punishment. This carries diverse implications: the individual is inserted in a structured and structuring social environment that transforms human beings simultaneously into oppressor and oppressed, victim and victimizer, and in which they reproduce the conditions that materially and symbolically tie them to that system.

Along this line of thinking, the mobilizing power of the "gender" category is cast aside, as it would only configure subjects without voice or agency, simple producers of a preexisting cultural script. If, however, this outlook not only would consider the implications of being and acting as collective subjects but also would involve the implicit power of their singularity, then it would be possible to undermine the hegemonic elements that contribute to the construction of similar identities. But at the same time, a view of gender as defined only by individual decisions would lose sight of its political side and of its high impact within social relationships. Gender's close link to cultural practices makes it a sort of representation and order of discourse susceptible to being read and interpreted by the subjects themselves as well as by the rest of the members of their environment. In itself, it accommodates agreements, differences, negotiations, and all kinds of interactions in the symbolic sphere, which are influenced by identity politics in the same way that they are influenced by gender configurations.

In her influential *Gender Trouble* (1990), Judith Butler proposes a way out of this apparent disjuncture between individual and collective, between subjectivity and the social. By coining the concept "gender performance," through which she recognizes subjects' capacity to intervene in the structuring of their subjectivity, she gave a new meaning to the regulatory practices that operate on the construction of identity. Because of the varied and repeated ways in which gender mandates are interpreted, gender is no longer something "given" or "reached" but a flexible category that includes a space for contradictions, affirmations, novelties, rejections, and changes both in subjectivity and in practices, gestures, and behaviors.

In *Bodies That Matter* (1993), Butler asks whether the body is, like gender, an effect of discourse built upon the basis of the exclusion of others. Her answer is affirmative and is centered on the analysis of the body as a material reality, shaped by gender and filtered through discourse. Bodily shape and corporal appearance are modeled upon socially constructed discourses, in relation to sex, sexuality, and race. This escapes suggestions of determinism, as gender is not imposed on the body, nor is the subject limited to accepting or rejecting what s/he is, according to his/her sex (male or female). Rather, the subject appropriates a bodily norm that regulates both matter and its meanings, based upon a heterosexual imperative that promotes certain identifications and repudiates others (*Bodies* 3).

Polysemy and Conceptual Diversity in Latin America

In Spanish, *género* means both "gender" and "genre," and furthermore is used generically to refer to cloth. The Latin American academy has also been witness to a debate on its necessity and its dispensability. For example, the perspective of many European theoretical thinkers, like Rosi Braidotti, has been that this discussion is unnecessary, as the model for the war of the sexes was imported from the United States, and the Mediterranean pattern of machismo presents a different type of problematic. According to Braidotti, emphasis should be placed on sexual difference as it demonstrates, within the same system, the asymmetric position between the feminine and the masculine with more clarity. A parallel stance criticized the universalization of that social asymmetry, the tendency to see it as an inevitable condition and to locate its subsequent reification outside sociohistorical practice. This type of debate reveals not only a distinct way of understanding these notions—and thus the world—but also the existence of different political agendas.

Jean Franco recalls a debate initiated by the Catholic Church, which rejected the use of the word "gender" as it "sought to provoke an ideological transformation and generate a new conception of the human being, subjectivity, marriage, family and society. In sum, it stands for a cultural revolution" ("The Gender Wars" 123). Franco claims that accepting that the differences between men and women are a social construction and are not exclusively due to biological aspects would open the door to a range of substantial changes with regard to legalized abortion, the acceptance of homosexuality, and the collapse of traditional family values. Not only has the Church repudiated the term, but the Catholic hierarchy came to use the terms "gender" and "feminism" indiscriminately during the nineties, after a long effort to associate this movement with communism during the sixties. The term thus acquired a polysemic trait that contributed to the understanding and reception of "gender" in diverse ways, varying by discipline, institution, and region. For example, without clarifying in what sense the term "gender" is utilized, governments started up programs, administrative units, and research centers, in which the intention of supporting a "perspective" of gender is usually emphasized.

Thus, if "gender" usually refers to women, "gender studies" is generally understood as research related to women. A derivation of this usage was its substitution for "feminism." The reductionist feature of both usages has had heavy implications, as it stripped the term of the agency associated with both concepts and made it an object of suspicion and mistrust. In Mexico, for example, dual streams seem to coexist. In a pioneering way, in 1983 the Colegio de México created the Interdisciplinary Program for Women's Studies; a decade later the University Program of Gender Studies appeared at the Universidad Nacional Autónoma de México. But it could be argued that the word "gender," by widening the field (and, in social perception, not referring only to women), points toward the debunking of essentialisms that allocate to each sex a script of cultural patterns and, furthermore, outlines the inclusion of alternative modes of subjectivity.

The use of this category has been largely fruitful for the construction of alternative canons, especially in the social and humanistic sciences. The recovery of the roles that women have played throughout time, in the most diverse disciplines and in a plurality of fields, has been one of the most exploited areas of research in gender studies in Latin America. Researchers have worked on recovering women left out of history, and also on elucidating the reasons for the exclusion of women. These types of studies have undermined such stereotypes as "compulsive heterosexuality" and "domesticity" and addressed the lack of complexity in cultural products that these stereotypes have generated along with their tendency to relegate women to those spaces traditionally considered feminine—the family, the heterosexual couple, motherhood—in their representations. Gender as a category has also played a decisive role in the analysis of social representations. Investigations carried on from this angle, especially those that evaluate media products, demonstrate the reiteration of gendered roles and environments, as well as their most visible consequences: gender's naturalization, its propagandistic function, and the divulgation of a negative fate for those who symbolically break with the order of their communities. Following from this vein of research, studies have centered on the fetishization of the feminine body, its objectlike character, as well as the demonstration of how gendered cultural repertoires have had direct implications on the reproduction of inequality in means of production, the generation of knowledge, spheres of public power, and even decision-making in relation to individual destinies.

Gender studies have also engendered a discussion on the construction of masculinities. The association of the patriarchal order with the masculine universe may be one of the reasons why studies of masculinity came later and are still at a very incipient stage in Latin America, and why they still do not generate the same enthusiasm as studies on the feminine. Contemporary studies on masculinities have centered upon questioning the ways in which male subjectivities are constructed, the relationships between male subjectivities and socialization processes, the implications of the denaturalization of theory and praxis on individual men, the diverse and plural character of male identities, and the ways in which gender dynamics are present in questions and research methodologies on these subjects, just to mention a few topics.

Cultural Studies in Latin America and Gender

In Latin American cultural studies, gender has barely begun to appear as a category of analysis. There has been a greater insistence on redefining culture in the context of the popular, of interethnic relationships, of the emergence of collective actors traditionally relegated to the periphery. Attention has also been paid to hybridizations and new identity configurations or the increasingly complex character of notions like nation, citizenship, and the impact of globalization. And even though gender traverses all these fields, its implications are just beginning to be grasped. It would seem as if the close association of the term with the feminist movement has brought about its cloistering within a restricted epistemological space belonging to a dated body of knowledge.

A quick glance at publications of the last few years dedicated to cultural studies (Hart and Young; Ríos et al.; Sarto et al.; Salas Astrain) shows a significant silence around gender. While it is true that it is present as a term, it is included as a given and it projects the appearance of an already concluded discussion. According to Sylvia Molloy, "Traditionally, gender as a category of analysis has not received the attention or the respect of Latin American criticism . . . and is still seen as a critical category that is not entirely legitimate, even abject, often cast aside when not subordinated to categories that are considered to be more urgent." These positions disarm "the intervening capacity of gender" and place it in the "outermost peripheries of national cultural projects" (translation ours). One of her main concerns lies in the fact that a biased reading of a cultural text systematically pushes aside every possibility of a change in established discourses. Following Nelly Richard, she proposes new inflections (*nuevas re-flexiones*) on the Latin American cultural text and the need to fracture established discourses.

On another note, Richard wonders whether there should not be fissures in the label of "Latin American cultural studies" as a possible power block, since its adoption and subsequent institutionalization was due to the influence of U.S. scholarship and not to Latin America's own projects of disciplinary criticism. In this sense, it could be more transgressive and political to talk about "gender studies" or "feminist criticism" by virtue of the sense given them within local traditions and the appropriation of these labels over that of "Latin American cultural studies" ("El conflicto" 444).

By stressing that in Mexico "in neither the intellectual nor academic fields" has there been an interest in taking up a rigorous theoretical discussion on the subject, which translates into a lack of essays and published reflections, Marta Lamas agrees with Braidotti about the lack of concern evinced by male critics in tackling the subject. This results in the creation of ghettos that "cater to a basically female clientele and also function as spaces for shaping units for political activity" ("Cultura, género" 340–43, translation ours). Lamas's despair about the lack of a properly Latin American theory and the dependence on literature emanating from the Anglo-Saxon world could be seen as the counterpart to Richard's position on the existence of operative detail and materiality, of a "critic *in action and in situation*, which is to say, necessarily imbricated within the practical functioning of a local structure" ("El conflicto" 444, translation ours). Both positions allow us to appreciate the breadth of the range in which gender moves: from the urgency to develop its own concepts or to construct them through the criticism of those already in circulation, to inquiry on how it works under specific sociohistorical conditions. The convergence of views on its possibilities as a category of analysis makes it necessary to define, interrogate, and reconceptualize all those notions that sustain and enrich it—sex, sexuality, sexual difference, identity, femininity, masculinity—instead of collapsing them into a unique term: "gender" (Hawkesworth 175).

Suggested Reading

Braidotti, Rosi. *Nomadic Subjects: Embodiment and Sexual Difference in Contemporary Feminist Theory*. New York: Columbia University Press, 1994.

Butler, Judith. *Bodies That Matter: On the Discursive Limits of Sex*. New York: Routledge, 1993.

———. *Gender Trouble: Feminism and the Subversion of Identity*. New York: Routledge, 1990.

Cranny-Francis, Anne, et al. *Gender Studies: Terms and Debates*. New York: Palgrave Macmillan, 2003.

Franco, Jean. "The Gender Wars." In *Critical Passions*, 123–30.

Fougeyrollas-Schwebel, Dominique, et al., eds. *Le genre comme catégorie d'analyse: Sociologie, histoire, littérature*. Paris: L'Harmattan, 2003.

Hawkesworth, Mary. "Confundir el género." *Debate Feminista* 10, no. 20 (October 1999): 3–48.

———. "Gender as Analytic Category." In *Feminist Inquiry: From Political Conviction to Methodological Innovation*, 145–76. New Brunswick, N.J.: Rutgers University Press, 2006.

Kaminsky, Amy K. *Reading the Body Politic: Feminist Criticism and Latin American Women Writers*. Minneapolis: University of Minnesota Press, 1993.

Lamas, Marta. *Cuerpo: Diferencia sexual y género*. Mexico City: Taurus, 2002.

———. "Cultura, género y epistemología." In Valenzuela Arce, *Los estudios culturales en México*, 328–53.

———. *Feminismo: Transmisiones y retransmisiones*. Mexico City: Taurus, 2006.

Ludmer, Josefina. "Las tretas del débil." In González and Ortega, *La sartén por el mango*, 47–54. www.isabelmonzon.com.ar/ludmer.htm.

Molloy, Sylvia. "La flexión del género en el texto cultural latinoamericano." *Revista de Crítica Cultural*, no. 21 (November 2000): 49–59.

Monsiváis, Carlos. "Crónica de aspectos, aspersiones, cambios, arquetipos y estereotipos de la masculinidad." *Desacatos: Revista de Antropología Social*, no. 16 (2004): 90–108.

Portugal, Ana María. "Feminismo." In Salas Astrain, *Pensamiento crítico latinoamericano*, 1: 355–60.
Richard, Nelly. "El conflicto entre las disciplinas." *Revista Iberoamericana* 69, no. 203 (2003): 441–48.
Scott, Joan. "Gender: A Useful Category of Historical Analysis." *American Historical Review* 91, no. 5 (1986): 1053–75.
Vargas, Virginia. "Declaración de América y el Caribe." *Debate Feminista* 6, no. 12 (October 1995): 75–83.
West, Candace, and Don H. Zimmerman. "Doing Gender." *Gender and Society* 1, no. 2 (1987): 125–51.

Globalization

REBECCA E. BIRON

The word "globalization" generally refers to the process by which economies and cultures around the planet become increasingly interdependent. The fifteenth century marked the historical beginning of globalization as a practice by permitting the types of navigation and commerce that linked human communities in spite of vast geographic distances and cultural differences. The European "discovery" of Amerindia in 1492 made the web of connections among all of the world's continents that we see today possible. Understood in this way, globalization is nothing new. However, the ubiquity of the term in political, economic, cultural, and academic discourse at the beginning of the twenty-first century indicates that it has taken on a quite specific meaning for more recent developments in geopolitics.

There are a number of ways to periodize and classify the expansion of capitalist relationships since 1492. Immanuel Wallerstein's "world system" locates that moment as the break from a previous, interregional system toward a properly global form of economic organization, with Europe in the center as the source of the "discoveries" and of capitalism itself. Much has been written about globalization as the culminating stage of a kind of Eurocentrism that aims to modernize the world according to a totalizing model of "civilization." Seen this way, both the positive and negative effects of globalization can be attributed to the Eurocentric system's arrival at its end point, or to the end of modernity per se. This end point is imagined as the moment in which natural resources are depleted, there are no new populations to exploit for ever cheaper labor, and it is no longer possible to control the proliferation of social differences or the forms of economic, political, and cultural resistance that those differences generate. Another way to situate globalization, however, restricts it much more in temporal and in philosophical terms, defining it as the postmodern structure of economics and culture. From this point of view, globalization refers to the Americanization of world economies and cultures after 1945 when the United States developed industries and capital flows that surpassed those of Europe.

Currently, the term "globalization" describes the vertiginous increase in inter- and transnational trade that, combined with a widespread privileging of free market forces over local and national protectionism, seeks the expansion of a unified capitalist economy with planetary reach. This process both depends on and produces rapid advances in communications technology that facilitate the almost instantaneous electronic transfer of capital as well as information. In parallel fashion, we see improved efficiency in the movement of goods and people around the world. This is how globalization condenses time and space, making the world smaller by reducing the time needed for people to reach one another regardless of their geographic location. Thus, since the 1980s, globalization has been used to describe the increased velocity with which experience of the local changes.

Economic globalization comprises transnational and supranational cooperation in the production, distribution, and consumption of goods and services, including financial services such as the International Monetary Fund or the World Bank. *Political globalization* concentrates administrative powers over public and economic policy through a wide variety of treaties and multinational alliances including the World Trade Organization, the North American Free Trade Agreement, Mercosur, and the European Union. It approaches local and regional policy issues from the perspective of the global context. Finally, *cultural globalization* refers to the worldwide dissemination of information, images, values, and tastes, along with the growing cosmopolitanism of urban life. Obviously, these three fields are interlinked.

For example, transnational economic ties often weaken the role of nation-states in the management of economic activity and the preservation of cultural heritage. Some theorists argue that globalization as the dominant economic force will destroy the modern nation-state by channeling power through extra-national organizations. Others, however, hold that globalization ironically strengthens national stability by promoting ever more efficient and productive international connections. In both views, the cultural and political conflict between homogenization on the one hand and autonomy on the other is the central question. Nevertheless, this question is no longer limited by geography. That shift opens up new possibilities for imagining groups and social movements, given that they increasingly find ways to form themselves anywhere on the planet without the traditional regard for national or regional boundaries.

With current globalization processes, the dichotomies that dominated geopolitical debates of the twentieth century, such as center/periphery, First World/Second (or Third) World, development/underdevelopment, seem more and more anachronistic. They refer to geographic zones and fixed concepts of cultural identity, whereas the new linkages and alliances that are appearing on a worldwide scale base themselves on a fluid sense of social relations. Super-rich capitalists from all over the world, for example, easily have more in common with each other than with their working-class compatriots. Groups—youth, the educated middle class, ethnic groups—identify themselves through their consumption patterns or through extra-national political activism. Even antiglobalization activists organize globally.

Some believe that globalization represents a profound threat to the kinds of local identities and customs that only nation-states can protect and nurture. Others see the decline of the nation-state as a form of liberation from modern and totalizing hegemonies. They hope that weakened national governments might cede their power to more democratic new types of social organization that are less limited by geography or rigid political systems. This last position underscores globalization's potential as a socially progressive force, while the first position stresses its potential as an engine of unregulated hyper-capitalism that will subjugate active citizenship under the anonymous control of the free market.

Individuals typically adopt one of these positions depending on the relative emphasis they assign to the three categories mentioned above (economics, politics, culture), as well as their ideological stance regarding capital, consumption, and labor conditions. For instance, those who emphasize the improved access that globalization provides to communication and consumption, whether material or cultural, see it as a source of more democratized and popular political power. But for those who attend more to the exploitation of workers in industries lacking adequate governmental regulation, globalization looks much more like a system that deepens socioeconomic inequalities and politically weakens the global working class.

Cultural studies began to figure centrally in academic discourse during this new accelerated phase of globalization. Globalization, understood as a vast network of inter- and transnational linkages of all types, poses a significant challenge to academia's disciplinary organization. With its inter- and transdisciplinary approach to the analysis of emerging forms of social organization and expression, cultural studies accepts that challenge. If modern literary criticism tended to affirm the link between literary production and the creation of modern nation-states, cultural studies analyzes how transnational processes in economics, politics, and communications generate new social alliances and forms of cultural expression. Moreover, it analyzes the ways in which these forms produce, in turn, new political and economic relationships. This focus allows us to see the flow of people, goods, and signs as a situation in which economics and politics become culture while at the same time culture becomes economics and politics.

Cultural studies recognizes that globalizing processes still occur in complex relation to the national, but it no longer privileges national borders as the primary determining factor in the establishment, structure, or extension of alliances among communities. Insofar as it emphasizes globalization as the dominant force in emerging forms of social organization and expression, cultural studies focuses on movement of all types. While electronic media continually accelerates communication, messages and images reach an exponentially expanding public. In addition, while capital travels with greater ease throughout the world in search of cheap labor and production costs, people also migrate more in search of work and socioeconomic stability. Therefore, along with communications and consumption, some of the main concerns of cultural studies in relation to globalization involve human migrations, the deterritorialization and reterritorialization of ideas, identities, and economic resources.

Latin American debates about globalization are heavily weighted with regional history. Given that the Conquest marks the beginning of the "500 year system" (Chomsky), the region's violent and abrupt entry into the "world system" paradoxically makes modernity possible even as it installs a structurally subordinate relationship, first with Europe, and then with the United States. Globalization's effects in Latin America are necessarily defined by five hundred years of exploitation, dependence, and inequality. All of these conditions pertain both internally to the region and in relation to the so-called center to which Latin America is positioned as periphery. Any progressive potential evidenced by globalization tends to be eclipsed by its intensification of regional vulnerabilities to capitalism's centers of power.

Neoliberalism dominated the policies of most Latin American governments in the last decades of the twentieth century. It advanced globalization insofar as it insisted on the power of a global open market, along with privatization and foreign investment, to solve local social and economic problems. As of 1990, most of those governments tried to follow the neoliberal recommendations of the Washington Consensus. However, in negative reaction to the effects of neoliberalism, different types of governments came to power at the turn of the century: Hugo Chávez in Venezuela (1998), Luiz Inácio Lula da Silva in Brazil (2002), Néstor Kirchner in Argentina (2003), Tabaré Vázquez in Uruguay (2004), Evo Morales in Bolivia (2005), and Michelle Bachelet in Chile (2006).

Although recent political events in Latin America indicate a popular resistance to unfettered globalization, a number of key questions remain unresolved. First, what does the phenomenon of deterritorialization really mean, given that intercontinental linkages structure the long history of world trade, and that Latin America occupies an originary geographic position in that history? What happens to our concept of place when we imagine a truly globalized society? Massive migrations toward urban centers on the one hand, and between countries on the other hand, lead to the development of multicultural identities and practices, as well as multiple citizenships. Carlos Monsiváis has described this situation as the emergence of a new "portable border." If new globalizing processes imply overcoming old spatial and temporal limits, where is the space for the defense of civil and workers' rights, governmental representation, or cultural creativity?

The Zapatista movement in Mexico, which first garnered broad public attention in 1994, the same year that NAFTA was implemented, provides a strong example of the intersection of the globalized economy, tensions within the modern nation-state, and a global web of extra-governmental connections. It was founded in order to defend economic, cultural, and human rights in agrarian and indigenous zones of southern Mexico and it challenged the legitimacy of national neoliberal policies from a specific site within the nation, but also by mobilizing a network of supra-national ethnic and ideological alliances. By the year 2006, the Zapatistas had achieved worldwide reach, linking with and supporting a wide variety of social movements with common conceptual frameworks and moral positions. The neo-Zapatista movement is no longer just an indigenous affair, or Chiapanecan or Mexican, but rather a global one.

In another example that reveals the complexity and urgency of such intersections, Mexicans living in the United States staged mass protests in

2006. They demanded public recognition of their presence and productivity in the United States. They also sought the implementation of new policies that would respect immigrants' economic and cultural contributions to the country. It quickly became clear, however, that no matter how visible and forceful the protests might have been, there were simply no transnational political structures in place that could respond to their demands.

An often-addressed issue in relation to cultural globalization is the degree to which the new stage in globalized capitalism reduces cultural identity and expression to mere consumerism, practices that are depoliticized and disconnected from their local contexts: "I buy, therefore I am." The association of extreme consumerism with cultural Americanization leads to critiques of globalization as an instrument of social control that disempowers people politically, denationalizes economies, and convinces the lower classes that they can (or should) think of themselves primarily as enthusiastic consumers.

One of the central figures in Latin American debates over the relationship between consumption and culture is Néstor García Canclini. He focuses upon the multiple mediations that allow globalization to be defined as "a complex of homogenizing processes and, simultaneously, of articulated fragmentation of the world, which reorganizes differences and inequalities without resolving them" (*La globalización imaginada* 49, translation ours). This definition underscores the indeterminate nature of the current hypercapitalist moment. That is, just as with the neo-Zapatista movement, the struggle over the rights of transnational workers, or the election of antineoliberal governments, globalization can produce new types of personal and economic agency at the same time that it can generate new forms of exploitation or impoverished cultural homogeneity.

Suggested Reading

Colclough, Christopher, and James Manor, eds. *States or Markets? Neo-liberalism and the Development Policy Debate*. New York: Oxford University Press, 1991.

Dussel, Enrique. *Ethics and the Theology of Liberation*. Translated by Bernard F. McWilliams. New York: Orbis, 1978.

García Canclini, Néstor. *Consumers and Citizens: Globalization and Multicultural Conflicts*. Translated by George Yúdice. Minneapolis: University of Minnesota Press, 2001.

———. *La globalización imaginada*. Mexico City: Paidós, 1999.

———. *Hybrid Cultures: Strategies for Entering and Leaving Modernity*. Translated by Christopher Chiappari and Silvia López. Minneapolis: University of Minnesota Press, 1995.

Mato, Daniel, ed. *Estudios latinoamericanos sobre cultura y transformaciones sociales en tiempos de globalización*. Buenos Aires: CLACSO/ASDI, 2001.
Monsiváis, Carlos. *Los rituales del caos*. 2nd ed. Mexico: Era, 2001.
———. "¿Tantos millones de hombres no hablaremos ingles? (La cultura norteamericana y México)." In *Simbiosis de culturas: Los inmigrantes y su cultura en México*, edited by Guillermo Bonfil Batalla, 500–513. Mexico: Consejo Nacional para la Cultura y las Artes/Fondo de Cultura Económica, 1993. Translated by Christopher Dennis as "Would So Many Millions of People Not End Up Speaking English? The North American Culture and Mexico" in Sarto, Ríos, and Trigo, *Latin American Cultural Studies Reader*, 203–32.
Ribeiro, Darcy. *Las Américas y la civilización: Proceso de formación y causas del desarrollo desigual de los pueblos americanos*. Caracas: Biblioteca Ayacucho, 1992. Translated by Linton Lomas Barrett and Maria McDavid Barrett as *The Americas and Civilization* (New York: Dutton, 1971).
Robertson, Roland. *Globalization: Social Theory and Global Culture*. London: Sage, 1992.
Wallerstein, Immanuel. *The Modern World-System*. 3 vols. New York: Academic Press, 1974.

Hegemony

CARLOS AGUIRRE (TRANSLATED BY EDUARDO RABASA)

The concept of hegemony holds a prominent place in contemporary theoretical and political debates and has exerted a great influence on the development of cultural studies in many places throughout the world. The starting point of the discussions on hegemony is usually the work of the Italian Marxist thinker Antonio Gramsci (1891–1937). In his *Prison Notebooks* and other works, Gramsci proposed a series of conceptual tools in order to understand the concrete historical forms through which certain groups or classes exert domination over others, as well as the political and cultural mechanisms that sustain these forms. Gramsci sought to analyze the dialectic between coercion and consensus within this process and, at the same time, to move beyond economicist interpretations of history and politics by giving central attention to the role of culture in the analysis of domination.

Gramsci came to an understanding of hegemony as a form of domination in which coercion and violence do not disappear, but coexist with ways of accepting power and domination that are more or less voluntary or consensual on the part of subaltern subjects. "In order to exert political leadership or hegemony," wrote Gramsci, "one must not count solely on the power and material force that is given by government" (quoted in Ruccio 3), but also on the seemingly voluntary acceptance by subaltern subjects, which is mediated in a crucial way by cultural forms of interaction between dominated and dominator. According to British literary critic Raymond Williams, the concept of hegemony not only refers to "matters of direct political control" but also "includes, as one of its key features, a particular way of seeing the world and human nature and relationships" (*Keywords* 118). According to Gramsci, hegemony implies that the values and world-view of the dominant classes turn into a sort of "common sense" shared by dominated groups by virtue of which they end up accepting—though not necessarily justifying—the exercise of power by the dominant groups. This common sense is disseminated and acquired through a complex process in which education, religion, and culture play a crucial role.

There are three elements to be highlighted in the Gramscian formulation of the concept of hegemony. One, the dynamic nature of the *process* that leads to hegemony; in other words, hegemony is not a static "moment" in a historical process but the result of a continuous interplay of complex and interrelated forms of domination and resistance. Two, the active role of subaltern groups within historical processes. Three, the articulation between economic, legal, and political forms of power, on the one hand, and the dynamics of exchange and cultural and ideological conflict, on the other.

Gramsci's main interest, however, lay in the possibility of building an alternative hegemonic project: one that, in his vision, would bring subaltern groups—a term he also coined, as a substitute for "working class"—into power. His formulation of hegemony as a process that included culture as a crucial element implied that he saw in this cultural dimension a crucial axis for the construction of a revolutionary project. Thus Gramsci's proposal contributed to overcoming the dominant economicist approach both in historical and political analyses and in proposals for the political mobilization of subaltern groups. In both senses, Gramsci would become a fundamental reference for the development of less rigid and dogmatic forms of approaching social theory and political practice.

In the 1970s a group of Marxist historians interested in overcoming the economicist and reductionist versions of Marxism rediscovered Gramsci and used the concept of hegemony in a creative fashion. Authors such as Eugene Genovese and Edward P. Thompson, for example, utilized the Gramscian concept of hegemony in order to emphasize the role of the legal system in the construction of a system of class domination that, at least partially, counted upon the acquiescence of subaltern groups—the slaves of the South of the United States, in the case of Geneovese, and the plebeian groups in eighteenth-century England, for Thompson. But it is important to stress that for these historians hegemony did not imply, as some authors had suggested, the absence of conflict, but rather the existence of a set of social parameters that allowed the conflict to be processed in ways that did not put at risk the continuity of the status quo.

Gramsci's concepts were thus particularly useful in this double task in which Marxist historians were immersed: on the one hand, they sought to rethink the most orthodox Marxism, which saw in domination merely a top-down exercise of power; on the other, they aimed at overcoming the reductionist schemes of "base" and "superstructure" according to which culture was a mere reflection of political and productive structures. The work of Raymond Williams, from the perspective of literary and cultural studies, was very close to these efforts.

A similar objective, that of illuminating the historical experience of oppressed classes, can be found in the collective work of the Indian group known as Subaltern Studies and, especially, of its main mentor, the historian Ranajit Guha. The group took its inspiration from the notion of subaltern "classes" or "groups" developed precisely by Gramsci. Though they were closely related to the so-called "history from below," the members of the group took on a much more radical political and epistemological stance. They directly criticized "elitist" versions of history—in both its colonial and Marxist manifestations—that had rendered the subaltern invisible. Influenced also by poststructuralist streams of thought, Guha and his followers paid special attention to cultural and discursive analysis. Finally, they put into question the nation-state as the privileged analytical unit, and at the same time placed the colonial question at the center of their concerns.

In various essays, some of them collected in the volume *Dominance Without Hegemony*, Guha proposed a way to understand hegemony as a "a condition of dominance in which the moment of persuasion outweighs that of coercion" (103), but his analysis led him to conclude that colonial domination in India constituted a case of "domination without hegemony," and he accused both colonial and nationalist historiography of inventing what he called a "spurious hegemony," which suggests the voluntary cooperation of the Indian population with the colonial project and the virtual absence of resistance (72). In the following years, Subaltern Studies would exert an enormous influence in other scholarly areas, including Latin American studies. Its innovative methodological proposals came along with a rather explicit political stance, albeit a very polemic one. The point was to adopt the subaltern not only as an object of analysis but also as the subject of theoretical and political reflection (Chaturvedi).

Two Latin Americanist scholars, anthropologist William Roseberry and historian Florencia Mallon, produced works that offered important contributions on the notion of hegemony as a tool in the historical analysis of domination. Roseberry warned that the concept of hegemony must be seen less as a tool to understand consensus than as an analytical instrument to understand the conflicts and struggles for power, insisting that hegemony is not "a finished and monolithic ideological formation but . . . a problematic, contested, political process of domination and struggle" (358). According to Roseberry, this way of understanding hegemony leads us to attempt to decipher "the ways in which the words, images, symbols, forms, organizations, institutions, and movements used by subordinated populations to talk about, understand, confront, accommodate themselves to, or resist their domination are shaped by the process of domination itself" (361). Thus the process of hegemony does not end in a situation of complete acceptance by the subalterns of the dominant ideology or its conditions, but rather in the construction of certain shared parameters under which domination acquires sense and they act against it.

From the perspective of history, Florencia Mallon proposed to understand the notion of hegemony in its double condition of *process* and *end point*. In other words, she posited the conceptualization of hegemony as a "hegemonic process" through which power and meaning are challenged, legitimized, and redefined, but also as the culmination (always provisional and contentious) of such a process, which results in the formation of a new hegemonic balance that gives birth to a new "common social and moral project that includes popular as well as elite notions of political culture" (6). On the other hand, Mallon also utilizes the concept of hegemony to analyze the contentious processes of power struggles, not only at the level of the nation-state, but also within indigenous or peasant communities. Her book *Peasant and Nation* represents precisely an effort to connect these processes of what she has called "communal hegemony" with the hegemonic processes that take place at the level of the nation-state in Peru and in Mexico.

But the Gramscian notion of hegemony, as we have already stated, not only has been employed in the historical analysis of domination but also constitutes a very important conceptual tool in debates about the diverse political projects that aspire to shape a new "hegemony" that is revolutionary in nature or that promotes radical social change. Within this effort,

Ernesto Laclau and Chantal Mouffe's book *Hegemony and Socialist Strategy: Towards a Radical Democratic Politics* represented a very important landmark. In this brief and dense book the authors began to rethink the question of political practice with the aim of giving shape to an alternative, radical, and socialist hegemonic project that was also democratic and popular. They put into question both the teleologism and the economicism of orthodox Marxism, as well as the emphasis on spontaneous action by certain romantic streams of the left. They proposed as an alternative a form of "radical democracy" as a new hegemonic project. Admitting that "every hegemonic position is based on an unstable equilibrium," they called for a rejection of "essentialisms" and saw the coming of a process of political struggles in the contemporary world that produces "the de-centering and autonomy of the different discourses and struggles, the multiplication of antagonisms and the construction of a plurality of spaces in which these can affirm themselves and develop" (192). Hegemony, Laclau and Mouffe conclude, is the name we give to a "game" that takes place in the field of politics and whose rules and actors are never predetermined. The conclusion is that it is an open process in which the forces of change must make an effort to construct—and control—the dynamics of such a game.

A central element of all these appropriations and uses of the concept of hegemony is the attention given to the cultural processes that go with or sustain the exercise of domination and resistance. The Gramscian notion of hegemony understands culture as a space of intervention and conflict that is crucial for the ways in which power is exercised and disputed. It also implies a form of analyzing the social as a whole in which the processes of constitution of the state, social classes, and popular cultures and the construction of hegemony are simultaneous, confluent, and mutually contentious, subjected to multiple tensions, in which strictly "cultural" dimensions cannot be dissociated from the political and power structures that contain them. Therefore, it is not surprising that in the development of cultural studies in Latin America, the concept of hegemony has played a central role in scholars' theoretical reflections. To a certain extent, the field of cultural studies has defined itself in relation to the need for articulating both theoretically and politically the notions (both coming from a Gramscian matrix) of hegemony and subalternity.

One of the seminal texts of Latin American cultural studies is Néstor García Canclini's *Culturas híbridas*. Among other things, this book is, as Renato Rosaldo writes in a foreword, an attempt to "bring Gramsci center stage in the study of Latin American social formations" (*Hybrid Cultures* xiii). It should be mentioned that Gramsci's influence in Latin American social sciences goes back a few years and can be traced to the work of the so-called Argentinean Gramscians—Héctor Pablo Agosti, José Aricó, Juan Carlos Portantiero, and others (Burgos). García Canclini's project was to analyze the ways in which dominant culture (identified by him with practices considered "high" and "modern") and popular culture (generally identified with the "traditional") intersect, and the extent to which both repression and appropriation of the latter by the former become central elements in the process of hegemonic domination. In this way, a main concern of his work is to understand "of what use culture is to hegemony" (*Hybrid Cultures* 93), which is to say, how can we really know whether or not culture plays a crucial role in the exercise of domination. We are acquainted, he says, with the "intentions" of modernizing politics, but not so much with their "reception," which leads to placing the analysis of popular consumption of cultural goods at the center of his attention. García Canclini suggests that neither the "reproductivist" perspectives, which see popular culture as an "echo" of dominant culture, nor the "idealistic" ones, which see popular culture as a manifestation of the autonomous creative capacity of subaltern groups, manage to capture the complexity of these processes. A correct appropriation of Gramsci, suggests García Canclini, should advocate for a "relativization" of the process, by granting the popular classes "a certain initiative and power of resistance, but always within the contradictory interaction with hegemonic groups" (181).

The work of García Canclini proposes an "oblique" look at the problem of the relationship between culture and domination: "The crossings between the cultured and the popular render obsolete the polar representation between both modalities of symbolic development, and therefore revitalize the political opposition between hegemonics and subalterns, conceived as if it were a question of totally distinct and always opposed groups" (259). In order to grasp this process in all its complexity, we should pay attention to "the dissemination of the centers, the multipolarity of social initiatives, the plurality of references—taken from diverse territories—with which artists, artisans, and the mass media assemble their works" (259). To answer this challenge, García Canclini proposes the notion of "hybrid cultures," a concept that would allow us to overcome the sterile dichotomies of "hegemonic" and "subaltern." The point is to analyze the "solidary or complicit activities" between the two groups, thus revealing the extent to which "hegemonic and subaltern groups are needed" (259). The concept of *hybridization* becomes García Canclini's theoretical proposition in order to understand the complex relationships between hegemony and resistance, a proposal that had a notable influence in the development of Latin American cultural studies in the nineties (Sarto, "The 1980s" 181).

The foundation of the Latin American Subaltern Studies Group in 1992 and, more generally, the influence of the Indian Subaltern Studies on Latin American cultural studies opened new perspectives in the reflection around the notions of hegemony and subalternity. Although it is not possible to find a homogeneous position among the members of this group (dissolved in 2000) or among those who have felt close to the work of Guha and his collaborators, we can outline as a common element the effort to rethink and dismantle the cultural logics that accompany and sustain the diverse forms of hegemonic domination, as well as the interest in contributing to the formation of counterhegemonic projects for social change. Regarding the former, as Ileana Rodríguez has said, subaltern studies emphasized the "impossibility" of separating the political and the cultural ("Reading" 6). Regarding the latter, "subaltern studies" in Latin America represented an effort to make a contribution to the construction, both theoretical and political, of a new hegemonic project sustained by a revalorization of the subaltern subject. The emergence of subaltern studies in the Latin Americanist scenario represented an infusion of theoretical and political energy, but it also prompted challenges and disagreements. On the one hand, it offered a possible solution to the impasse produced by the crisis of the Marxist and socialist left, although it quickly revealed the complexities and paradoxes of the attempt to construct an alternative project that connected subalternist scholars in the United States with Latin American subaltern subjects. On the other hand, it took on a theoretical perspective that some—among them García Canclini himself—would see as dichotomic and reductionist.

John Beverley has suggested that cultural studies would make it possible precisely to overcome the presumed rigid bipolarity between hegemony and subalternity by way of a greater attention to the complex cultural dynamics of civil society ("Im/Possibility" 53). At the same time, other scholars such as Hernán Vidal have questioned the insufficient political interest of many of those engaged in cultural studies ("Restaurar lo político"). This combination of a greater attention paid to culture and a certain disinterest in the political dimensions leaves us with a challenge: how to connect the scholarly practices of cultural studies with the debates around the set of new projects for social change for Latin American societies. John Beverley is optimistic: "cultural studies prepare/anticipate/legitimize the need/possibility of a cultural revolution" ("Postscriptum" 588). We believe there are reasons to cautiously share this optimism. Besides well-established concerns on issues such as human rights, collective memories, identity politics, and the relationships between culture and social change, there has recently been a notable interest in the study of "new knowledges" and "new epistemologies" (Mato, *Estudios y otras prácticas*). The Latin American Studies Association (LASA) has recently launched an ambitious transnational project on this subject, which has opened a huge set of possibilities to rethink politics and culture. On the other hand, the valuable collective work coordinated by Doris Sommer on "cultural agents" also reflects the concerns about how to connect new forms of cultural production with projects of transformation that are not necessarily "revolutionary" in the classical sense of the term, but that are engaged with efforts toward the democratization of Latin American societies (*Cultural Agency*). The confluence of the political and cultural that can be seen in these and other efforts is, perhaps, the main contribution of cultural studies to the challenge of building a new (hegemonic) project that is democratic, plural, and inclusive.

Suggested Reading

Beverley, John. "The Im/Possibility of Politics: Subalternity, Modernity, Hegemony." In Rodríguez, *Latin American Subaltern Studies Reader*, 47–63.

Burgos, Raúl. *Los gramscianos argentinos: Cultura y política en la experiencia de* Pasado y Presente. Buenos Aires: Siglo XXI, 2004.

Genovese, Eugene D. *Roll, Jordan, Roll: The World the Slaves Made*. New York: Pantheon, 1974.

Guha, Ranajit. *Dominance Without Hegemony: History and Power in Colonial India*. Cambridge, Mass.: Harvard University Press, 1997.

Laclau, Ernesto, and Chantal Mouffe. *Hegemony and Socialist Strategy: Towards a Radical Democratic Politics*. London: Verso, 1984.

Latin American Subaltern Studies Group. "Founding Statement." In Beverley, Aronna, and Oviedo, *Postmodernism Debate*, 135–46.

Mallon, Florencia E. *Peasant and Nation: The Making of Postcolonial Mexico and Peru*. Berkeley: University of California Press, 1995.

Rodríguez, Ileana. "Reading Subalterns Across Texts, Disciplines, and Theories: From Representation to Recognition." In *Latin American Subaltern Studies Reader*, 1–32.

Roseberry, William. "Hegemony and the Language of Contention." In *Everyday Forms of State Formation: Revolution and the Negotiation of Rule in Modern Mexico*, edited by Gilbert M. Joseph and Daniel Nugent, 355–66. Durham, N.C.: Duke University Press, 1994.

Ruccio, David F. "Unfinished Business: Gramsci's Prison Notebooks." *Rethinking Marxism* 18, no. 1 (January 2006), 1–7.

Williams, Raymond. "Base and Superstructure in Marxist Cultural Theory." *New Left Review* 1, no. 82 (November–December 1973), 3–16.

Heterogeneity

ESTELLE TARICA

The term "heterogeneity" as used in Latin American cultural criticism derives primarily from the work of Peruvian critic Antonio Cornejo Polar (1936–1997). However, as will be seen, there are other important uses of the term, especially in the work of anthropologist Néstor García Canclini. Cornejo defines "heterogeneous discourse" as a discourse marked by the cultural difference between the producer of the discourse and its referent. According to Cornejo, examples of this phenomenon include the chronicles of the Conquest, *indigenista* literature, *gauchesca* literature, and *negrista* literature. In each of these cases, the discourse distorts its referent—for example, the indigenous world—because it is produced by a world that is alien to the world it describes. Cornejo states that such discourses should not be dismissed because of their lack of verisimilitude; rather, their most profound truth resides in this very lack. Cornejo thus rejects referentiality as the basis for interpreting such texts. He argues that it is useless to expect that *indigenista* literature represent the indigenous world faithfully, because it is written from a perspective that is both alien and antagonistic to that world and occupies a hierarchically dominant position with respect to it. Speaking of those who, like Mario Vargas Llosa, criticize *indigenista* literature for its distorted vision of the indigenous world, Cornejo writes: "they consider what is the most profound identity of the movement as a defect and in the long run they demand that it stops being what it is—*indigenismo*—in order to become what it cannot be: indigenous literature" ("*Indigenismo*" 111). Cornejo argues that these heterogeneous texts reveal the fragmented and fractured condition of Latin American nations, a condition that literature reproduces but cannot resolve.

The concept of heterogeneity emerged in the 1970s as a response to two distinct situations. One, the political moment in Peru, especially the ideological bankruptcy of the term *mestizaje*, under whose rubric the Velasco military regime claimed to have achieved Peru's long-sought national unity. Cornejo insisted that this national unity was merely an illusion fostered by state propaganda and that the colonial legacy of the nation had yet to be overcome. Two, debates about Latin American literature taking place against the backdrop of the Cold War and amid the enormous changes in the literary landscape brought about by the so-called Boom of the novel in the 1960s. What kind of literature and criticism should be considered representative of Latin America? Some Boom novelists, spurred by their international success, begin to speak of the "universalization" of Latin American literature. This generated a counter-discourse launched by literary critics, materialist if not Marxist, who argued for a greater awareness of the cultural and historical specificity of the region and its manifestation in literature. A series of literary concepts emerged to name and explain this particularity, among them "literary heterogeneity."

Using the vocabulary of Peruvian thinker José Carlos Mariátegui, an enormously influential avant-garde socialist intellectual, Cornejo argued that the narratives that best represent Latin America are those that reflect the reality of its "non-organically national" societies. The phrase "non-organically national" refers to the cultural fragmentation of the nation into opposing, antagonistic worlds, its hierarchical division into a "lettered" world and an oral world, urban and rural, Western and indigenous. "Heterogeneous literatures" reflect this disintegrated national reality; they are "literatures that are situated in a conflictive crossing between two societies and two cultures" ("*Indigenismo*" 101). The conflict is reflected not at the level of content but at the level of literature's "mode of textual production"—that is, at the level of the literary system itself and its functioning within the nonorganic nation. Cornejo argued that the literary system participates in reproducing the national fracture because the raw material of national literature is writing, which means that literature is produced and circulated only within the culturally Western or occidental side of the nation, without crossing over to the indigenous side. In Cornejo's view, literature is a closed, exclusive system. It fails in its attempts to be inclusive because it cannot escape its written nature, and thus its alien condition vis-à-vis indigenous modes of expression, which are of an oral nature.

Cornejo further argued that such a literary system functions as a key part of the ideology that justifies the imposition of the West over the indigenous world. In emphasizing the technology of alphabetic writing, Cornejo insists that literary production is a social act or event for which criticism must account. And *written* literary production, says Cornejo, whether it be the sixteenth-century chronicles of Conquest or twentieth-century *indigenista* literature, has a particular historical significance: the letter is the sign of the difference between colonizers and colonized. Thus the growing symbolic importance that Cornejo attributes to the primal scene at Cajamarca in 1532 between the priest Valverde and the Inca Atahuallpa, when the Inca, after reportedly holding the Bible to his ear in a vain attempt to "listen" to its word, throws it to the ground and unleashes the Spaniards' violence (*Escribir* 20–43). Cornejo claims that each written Andean text forcibly reproduces this first encounter precisely because it is a written rather than an oral text. Such a text cannot but affirm the difference between colonizer and colonized, however much it seeks to denounce or eliminate that difference.

From the perspective of this concept of the literary, literature cannot resolve an antagonism of which it itself forms a part. The concept of heterogeneity offers a vision of literature as politically weak yet still carrying an enormous cultural and historical burden, a burden that is so heavy that it, rather than the intentionality of the author, determines the meaning of literature. Seen in this light, the power of literature to be a social witness resides in the text's unconscious, in what it communicates without meaning to—that is, in the reproduction of social conflicts at the national level that have yet to be resolved. We might say that the concept of "heterogeneity" presupposes the "death of the author" (Barthes, "Death").

In his last book, *Escribir en el aire* (1994), Cornejo concedes that the attempt to find a Latin American literary theory has failed, but he does not abandon his attempt to understand and explain those literatures "that function at the edges of dissonant and at-times mutually incompatible cultural systems" (11). He nuances the concept of literary heterogeneity in light of poststructuralist theories of subjectivity, eventually arguing that heterogeneity exists not only in the relation between two cultural worlds but also within each of those worlds and within those subjects who seek to transmit them. Although the concept started out as an attempt to understand the role of literature in the functioning of systems of social differentiation rooted in colonial structures, it ends up looking more like a simple appreciation and awareness of the difference, plurality, contradiction, and instability that mark all identities, individual and collective.

The concept of heterogeneity has proliferated beyond the Andes and in the years since Cornejo's death. The concept resonates with some of the arguments advanced by Latin American subaltern studies (see Beverley, "Siete aproximaciones"; Moreiras, *Exhaustion*), which turn to heterogeneity in order to critique another concept that had also emerged in the 1970s, namely, Uruguayan critic Ángel Rama's "narrative transculturation." Although Rama and Cornejo held many ideas in common, the two critics diverged in their views of Latin American national culture: Rama advocated for cultural unification within the nation, while Cornejo insisted on the deep fractures that national culture should not and cannot heal.

Another thinker whose work makes important references to heterogeneity is Néstor García Canclini, in his fundamental book *Culturas híbridas: Estrategias para entrar y salir de la modernidad* (1990; published in English in 1995). His concept of "multitemporal heterogeneity"—that is, "temporal heterogeneity" or "multitemporality"—refers to the presence of multiple historical temporalities, each characterized by specific socioeconomic conditions that coexist in Latin American nations. A temporality is not only a time period; it refers to a particular way of conceiving of time and of living in time. For example, a modern temporality is different from a postmodern temporality, and an artisan temporality is different from an industrial temporality. The concept appears to have been adopted from Marxist critic Perry Anderson, although in García Canclini's usage the term "multitemporal heterogeneity" goes beyond Marxism (*Hybrid Cultures* 45). Anthropological and sociological, it seeks to understand cultural and geographic diversity (ethnic and local identities) as well as the inequality created by the transnational political-economic system (subordinate participation in global capitalism) (182).

According to García Canclini, multitemporality creates Latin American modernism, rather than being an obstacle to it; multitemporality makes possible and gives shape to modernity's ideological and aesthetic expression. He writes that "modernism is not the expression of socioeconomic modernization but *the means by which the elites take charge of the intersection of different historical temporalities and try to elaborate a global project with them*" (46). García Canclini's goal is "to generate another way of conceiving of Latin American modernization" (2). Rather than seeing modernization as the implantation of an external force that destroys native or local traditions, García Canclini sees modernization as a process composed of diverse attempts to "take charge" of multitemporal heterogeneity: modernization as a process through which Latin Americans participate in the construction of their world.

As with Cornejo Polar, García Canclini starts from the necessity of recognizing the coexistence of diverse temporalities within each nation. He seeks to understand how this reality has created Latin America's modernity and to identify the political challenges to which this diversity gives rise. He criticizes all attempts to cover over these differences and inquires into the best way to respond to social inequality. But in contrast to the Peruvian critic, García Canclini sustains that this heterogeneity produces a fundamental "hybridization" of society, one in which a clear division between the traditional and the modern, or between high culture, popular culture, and mass culture, has disappeared. The multiple temporalities that exist within each nation end up creating a "hybrid" modernity.

The term "heterogeneity" has yet another genealogy, one that converges with Latin American cultural criticism in the work of Ernesto Laclau. In his book *On Populist Reason* (2005), Laclau uses the concept of "social heterogeneity" to describe a political situation in which subjects who are "exterior" to the common discursive space also participate politically (140). This use of the concept of "heterogeneity" emerges from the process undertaken in the 1980s of reexamining the Marxist concept of "lumpen proletariat," so as to offer a better account of the political practices of social subjects whom orthodox Marxist thinking has tended to marginalize and discredit (see Stallybrass). Although there does not seem to be a direct filiation between this use of "heterogeneity" and Cornejo's, the two share some important features. Both refer to a political situation marked by the lack of a discursive space common to diverse social actors and by the incommensurability that exists between such social groups, as for example the incommensurability between the ideological horizons that shape the demands of indigenous groups and those that shape the demands of the working class. The case of García Canclini is different, because his concept of heterogeneity ultimately boils down to a concept of hybridity—that is, García Canclini postulates the existence of some common discursive spaces created by the institutions of the nation-state, however imperfect or limited these spaces might be.

Regardless of their differences, each one of these concepts of "heterogeneity" emerges out of Latin America's heterodox Marxist tradition as it confronts new and evolving social movements. Still committed to the goal of social justice, these thinkers have sought to understand societies marked by the existence of subjects whose political consciousness and collective identities have not been created by the logic of social class, societies whose development has not occurred along the lines dictated by conventional models of modern progress.

Suggested Reading

Beverley, John. "Siete aproximaciones al 'problema indígena.'" In Moraña, *Indigenismo hacia el fin del milenio*, 243–83.

Bueno Chávez, Raúl, and Nelson Osorio Tejeda, eds. "La trayectoria intelectual de Antonio Cornejo Polar." Special issue, *Revista de Crítica Literaria Latinoamericana* 25, no. 50 (1999).

Cornejo Polar, Antonio. "El indigenismo y las literaturas heterogéneas: Su doble estatuto socio-cultural." *Revista de Crítica Literaria Latinoamericana* 4, nos. 7–8 (1978): 7–21.

Translated by Christopher Dennis as "*Indigenismo* and Heterogeneous Literatures: Their Double Sociocultural Statute," in Sarto, Ríos, and Trigo, *Latin American Cultural Studies Reader*, 100–115.

———. "Mestizaje, transculturación, heterogeneidad." In Mazzotti and Zevallos, *Asedios a la heterogeneidad cultural*, 54–56. Translated by Christopher Dennis as "*Mestizaje*, Transculturation, Heterogeneity," in Sarto, Ríos, and Trigo, *Latin American Cultural Studies Reader*, 116–19.

Higgins, James, ed. *Heterogeneidad y literatura en el Perú*. Lima: Centro de Estudios Literarios Antonio Cornejo Polar, 2003.

Laclau, Ernesto. *On Populist Reason*. London: Verso, 2005.

Mariátegui, José Carlos. *Siete ensayos de interpretación de la realidad peruana*. Lima: Amauta, 1928.

Mazzotti, José Antonio, and U. Juan Zevallos Aguilar, eds. *Asedios a la heterogeneidad cultural: Libro de homenaje a Antonio Cornejo Polar*. Philadelphia: Asociación Internacional de Peruanistas, 1996.

Moraña, Mabel, ed. *Indigenismo hacia el fin del milenio: Homenaje a Antonio Cornejo-Polar*. Pittsburgh, Pa.: Instituto Internacional de Literatura Iberoamericana, 1998.

Rowe, William. "Sobre la heterogeneidad de la letra en *Los ríos profundos*: Una crítica a la oposición polar escritura/oralidad." In Higgins, *Heterogeneidad y literatura en el Perú*, 223–51.

Stallybrass, Peter. "Marx and Heterogeneity: Thinking the Lumpenproletariat." In "The Margins of Identity in Nineteenth-Century England," special issue of *Representations*, no. 31 (1990): 69–95.

Hybridity

LEILA GÓMEZ (TRANSLATED BY EDUARDO RABASA)

Generally speaking, the term "hybridity" or "hybridization" speaks to the processes and results of the mixing of different cultures in Latin America. The term holds a prominent place in critical thought on Latin America, together with other terms that along the same lines have tried to explain the diversity of Latin American reality and its struggles between conciliation and conflict. Among the studies that have most vigorously shaped the vocabulary and the critical conceptualizations of literary and cultural studies are those on *mestizaje* (Vasconcelos; Rojas), transculturation (R. Ortiz; Rama), heterogeneity (Cornejo Polar), alternative literatures (Lienhard), and more recently contact zones (Pratt). Starting with Néstor García Canclini's book *Culturas híbridas: Estrategias para entrar y salir de la modernidad* (1990), the term "hybridization" attained a great conceptual precision in Latin American cultural studies, as well as a larger diffusion, acceptance, and controversy within intellectual debate. In *Culturas híbridas*, hybridization is thought of as a phenomenon fundamentally linked to modernity, in the way that it is configured within the logic of the market that produces consumers and rearticulates identities of citizenship in globalization. Hybridization can be observed in the intersections between elite culture, culture industries, and popular culture, as well as in the role played by the state and private organisms in the symbolic production of cultural goods.

In the discourse of conquest and colonization—full of Greco-Latin references—the forms that were produced by racial and cultural mixture were seen in a pejorative light. In Mexico, the Franciscan priest Gerónimo de Mendieta called the result of the mixture a "chimera," a "monster that spits fire from its mouth and that has a lion's head and neck, a goat's stomach, and a dragon's tail" (quoted in Lienhard 134, translation ours). In Latin America, the term "chimera" introduces and institutes the image of monstrosity associated with the exchange between the colonizer and the colonized, and therefore seeks to capture its highly conflictive character (Lienhard 133). In a similar way, the term "hybridity" carries pejorative connotations due to the burden of the influence of nineteenth-century thought, when it was also believed that hybridization was detrimental to racial and/or social development. The Peruvian critic Cornejo Polar warned of the risks of transferring biological terms and concepts into the social sciences and utilizing them as explanatory metaphors ("Mestizaje e hibridez"). Hybrids such as mules, admonishes Cornejo Polar, are sterile. However, García Canclini replied that in 1870 Mendel demonstrated that genetic hybridizations increased the quality and the performance of food and its derivates, as in the case of cereals, flowers, and coffee, as it improves their capacity for survival and their adaptation to their habitat ("Noticias recientes"). This importing of the concept of hybridization from biology into the social sciences would become useful by virtue of its explanatory power and its theoretical consistency. Also, Jean Franco has stated that the term "hybridity" has postulated a new semantic twist by transferring the explanations for *mestizaje* (miscegenation and social interaction) from the field of zoology (and the racist theories of positivism), where the concept of *mestizaje* was confined, to botany, opening the field to new possibilities and realizations of the concept. Acknowledging that both *mestizaje* and hybridity present theoretical problems in their translation from their original disciplines to the field of culture, Franco states that as opposed to the notion of *mestizaje*, "which suggests that culture sprang naturally from a copulation," hybridization is a botanical metaphor, "tightly related to the notion of culture as cultivation" (59, translation ours). For Canclini, the concept of hybridity contributes to identifying and explaining "multiple fruitful alliances" and to deviating from biologically oriented discourses on race. García Canclini clearly distances the concept of hybridity not only from racial mixtures "to which *mestizaje* tends to be limited" (*Hybrid Cultures* 11) but also from syncretism, a term normally used to designate religious fusions. Beyond the advantages or disadvantages of the transdisciplinary metaphor utilized by García Canclini, Cornejo Polar's criticism of the concept of hybridity points out that any celebratory vision of the fertile alliances of hybridization may obscure the real power asymmetries in Latin American worlds, which are "torn and belligerent" ("Mestizaje e hibridez" 8, translation ours).

The concept of hybridity is thus located within a tradition of Latin American theoretical propositions that seek to explain cultural mixing and interaction. This tradition was inaugurated in the twentieth century by such thinkers as José Vasconcelos, Ricardo Rojas, and Pedro Henríquez Ureña, with their dismantling of old and essentialist racial theories. A few decades later, in 1940, the concept of transculturation proposed by Cuban anthropologist Fernando Ortiz was articulated along these same lines. The concept of transculturation aimed to reformulate the passive role with which traditional anthropology thought about colonized cultures through the concept of acculturation. The concept of transculturation applies to the contact between African, native American, and European cultures in the new world, and underlines the originality and creativity of popular cultures, insisting on their active role of exchange with the culture of the colonizer (Lienhard 134). Ángel Rama, with his proposal of a transcultural narrative, extended Ortiz's anthropological concept to the study of the literary narrative of such authors as José María Arguedas, Gabriel García Márquez, and Augusto Roa Bastos. According to Rama, these authors assume a creative role in their appropriation of metropolitan models and their ways of rereading their own and other cultures in the processes of literary creation.

Antonio Cornejo Polar proposed the concept of heterogeneity or heterogeneous literatures to identify those literatures whose main elements do not belong to the same cultural universe. In heterogeneous literatures, at least one of the stages that Cornejo Polar visualizes in the literary processes—whether it is production, the referent, circulation or reception—does not correspond to the sociocultural universe of the others. Thus, indigenist literatures of lettered or erudite authors and readers and referents from the indigenous universe would be the clearest examples of a heterogeneous literature. It is in this same sense that Martin Lienhard proposes the concept of alternative literatures to describe those productions that circulate on the margins of hegemonic circuits and oral-popular subsocieties as well, precisely because they are directed toward a reader that is equally "alternative." In the case of Andean societies, that "alternative reader" would be a bilingual reader, capable of communicating both in Spanish and in Quechua (or Aymara) and capable of moving efficiently within both circuits. Arguedas, by integrating colloquial Quechua into his Spanish-language narrative, transgresses the canons of highbrow literature written in Castilian, as well as the traditional norms of ancient Quechua poetry. Thus, for Lienhard, Arguedas's narrative is representative of the corpus of alternative literatures.

In her 1992 book *Imperial Eyes*, Mary Louise Pratt gives the name "contact zone" to the temporal and spatial copresence of individuals belonging to cultures historically and geographically separated. Pratt utilizes the term especially to show the interaction and the formation of subjectivities in the cultural intersection of colonial encounters, in which copresence often means the existence of radically asymmetric power relations (7). The idea of the contact zone underlines the role of subjectivities within a sociopolitical, economic, and cultural system or framework, which is to say that it incorporates the multiple variables that condition and explain contact and its relational asymmetries. With this concept, Pratt links studies of imperial travel to analyses of colonial discourse and transcultural narrative.

The main contribution of *Culturas híbridas* to this stream of critical thought is the highlighting of the concept of hybridity within the context of modernity, specifically referring to transformations and negotiations of local cultures, whether popular or elite, in contact with culture industry technologies in a global market. Thus, hybridization is generally associated, according to García Canclini's study, with market logic, with technologies of mass diffusion and consumption, with the globalization of culture, with the decentering of homogenizing practices and ideologies of national states. While it is true that these considerations were implicitly contained in concepts such as transculturation and heterogeneity, García Canclini places an emphasis on the analysis of cases that cast some light on the relationships between the local and the global within modernizing processes. Therefore, hybridity cannot be understood as a conceptual proposal without taking into account the problems of modernity in Latin America. The concept of hybridity seeks to examine the way in which highbrow avant-garde art and popular culture are related to the symbolic and economic market, to technological advances, and to the traditional matrixes of deep cultural roots. García Canclini wonders: "What are painters looking for when, in the same painting, they cite pre-Columbian and colonial images along with those of the culture industry, and then reelaborate them using computers and lasers?" (*Hybrid Cultures* 2). García Canclini investigates the ways in which electronic media massively disseminate highbrow art and folklore and the ways in which music "renews itself" by incorporating popular Asian and African rhythms (14). In order to explain these processes or strategies of hybridization, García Canclini borrows a term from economics: "reconversion." Economic and symbolic types of reconversion are not utilized exclusively as strategies of hegemonic sectors or culture industries, but rather are also renewed in the everyday practices of popular sectors, such as when immigrant peasants adapt their knowledge for city life and their handicrafts and products for urban consumption. García Canclini sees in this "reconversion" strategies of hybridity to enter and exit modernity.

Culturas híbridas and the concept of hybridization brought into debate three main points. The first was the consolidation/dismantling of binarisms or absolute oppositions such as traditional versus modern, lettered versus popular, or highbrow versus mass culture. García Canclini emphasizes the impurity on which genres and cultural hierarchies are built. The second point that *Culturas híbridas* raises for debate is the role of the disciplines charged with the study of hybridization, and the traditional academic separations according to which art history and literature study erudite art, anthropology limits its investigations to the popular, and communications examines the mass production and consumption associated with culture industries. García Canclini proposes that hybridization must occur within disciplines so they may provide researchers with tools that enable them to navigate the different levels of cultural production. Communication among disciplines becomes important in explaining and defining ever more complex objects of study. This collaborative work across disciplines would allow for a greater understanding of the third matter debated in *Culturas híbridas*: the contradictory and complex processes of modernity in Latin America, their unevennesses and inequalities, their "truncated innovations," their "multitemporal heterogeneity," and the ways in which diverse national sectors are responsible for them. In order to speak about the coexistence of multiple temporalities in Latin America, García Canclini turns to Perry Anderson's study on the early-twentieth-century emergence of European modernisms. For Anderson, these avant-garde movements flourished and developed in contexts in which the political and economic modernizations were not structural or even, such as Parisian cubism or Italian futurism. These cultural modernisms arose within a continental Europe that was undergoing a complex structural modernization that combined forms of a classic or retrogressive past, semiaristocratic in nature, with technical advances that were abruptly changing the social relationships of production, and with insurgent political movements that created a vision of unforeseen political futures. In a similar way, in Latin America, cultural modernisms are not the expression of even socioeconomic modernities but rather the way in which "elites take charge of the intersection of different historical temporalities and try to elaborate a global project with them" (*Hybrid Cultures* 46). For García Canclini, the study of modernity in Latin America means examining the complexity of its contradictions, the coexistence of diverse temporal levels, and its "truncated innovations."

The concept of hybridization becomes especially useful for the examination of a "fluidly interconnected world" ("Noticias recientes"). García Canclini considers the study of hybridization to imply going beyond the analysis of identities that are "self-contained" within communities that imagine tales of their own origin and development in a closed way. For García Canclini, hybridity allows for the study of societies whose identity breaches ethnic, class, and national essentialisms, generating a complex repertory of heterogeneous messages and symbolic goods in social contexts of uneven modernization. In this way the concept of hybridity stems from an awareness of the staging of art and culture as it occurs in the intersection of the multidirectional flows, and of the porosity of frontiers in global processes. For García Canclini, the practice of Mexican vendors that used to sell Aztec calendars or Mexican handicrafts and now also offer Disney toys and Spiderman represents "the alteration of the common place of historical iconography and indicates the multidirectionality of the messages and the ambiguities produced by their media use" ("La épica" 36, translation ours).

From a different academic tradition, mainly British, postcolonial criticism has again taken up the concept of hybridity, with certain intersections and differences with Latin American critics. Hybridity has proven to be a useful concept to characterize colonial discourse—that is, the symbolic forms created by colonialism and imperialism in order to name, control, and govern their others. Drawing from a combination of Foucault's notion of discourse and psychoanalysis's concept of ambivalence, Homi Bhabha refers to colonial discourse as hybrid, or ambivalent. The ambivalence in the enunciation of colonial discourse is manifested in the interaction or inseparable fusion of its two levels: on the one hand, the level of a conscious and disciplined discourse about otherness, and on the other hand, an unconscious and phantasmagoric desire for the other. In order to explain this ambivalence in colonial discourse, Bhabha uses the discovery of the book by colonized cultures in India, Africa, and the Caribbean, a displacement that paradoxically renders prodigious the presence of the book as it is repeated, translated, misunderstood, displaced (*Location* 132). When native Indians receive the translation of the British Bible, they ask the missionary, questioning the "cannibalistic" rites of the Eucharist: "How can the word of God come from the flesh-eating mouths of the English? . . . How can it be the European Book, when we believe that is God's gift to us? He sent it to us at Hurdwar" (116). Thus the presence of the British book, colonial law, or English identity cannot be represented in its entirety; its signification is displaced when it is reproduced in the colonies. The colonial presence is divided between its appearance as something original and authoritative and its articulation as repetition and difference. Its reproduction in the colonial context, "its duplication" in a syntagma of differential knowledges, alienates the identity of English being, and produces new ways of knowing, as well as new places from which power may emanate. Other "denied" knowledges thus enter the dominant discourse, destabilizing its authority base and questioning its rules of recognition (113).

For Bhabha, hybridity, in the same way as for García Canclini, is not a third term that resolves the tension between two cultures. For Bhabha, hybridity is a problematic internal to colonial discourse. The questions of the native Indians regarding the British Bible, the use they make of the English book, generate uncertainty and a lack of firmness that afflicts the discourse of power. This uncertainty displaces the confidence in what it means to be an Englishman in the colonialized world. Thus the colonized subject becomes a terrifying, perturbing subject, of paranoid classification, a constant source of questioning of the images and presences of authority.

Following Bhabha, Robert Young postulates that in colonial discourse, all instrumental knowledge on otherness is founded on the protocols of desire and fantasy, in a constant fluctuation between what is desired and repudiated (161). In this way the marginal, what lies unclassified in the periphery, is manifested in the center of colonial discourse, making ambivalence its constitutive condition. Within postcolonial criticism, Young reconnects race and gender studies to the concept of hybridity, insisting upon the fact that social and pseudoscientific constructions of race (and of racial difference) have always been propelled by the corrupt conjunction of hybrid sexual and economic discourses within the discourse of colonial power. By rearticulating the debates on race and gender with the hybridity of colonial discourse, Young highlights the ambivalence between the desire of the white colonizer toward the male/female colonized natives and the horror caused by hybridization or racial mixture. Recently, Joshua Lund has proposed the need to rearticulate the concept of race vis-à-vis the theorizations on hybridity in Latin American cultural studies in fruitful dialogue with postcolonial studies.

The concept of hybridity has proved to hold a great theoretical productivity, stimulating critical debate in Latin American linguistic, anthropological, artistic, and cultural studies, in the works of John Beverley, Roberto Schwarz, George Yúdice, Jesús Martín Barbero, Renato Ortiz, and others. As García Canclini himself points out, "studies on hybridization modified the way of speaking about identity, culture, difference, inequality, multiculturalism and about the paired terms that organize conflicts of the social sciences: tradition/modernity, north/south, local/global" ("Noticias recientes").

Suggested Reading

Beverley, John. *Subalternity and Representation: Arguments in Cultural Theory*. Durham, N.C.: Duke University Press, 1999.

Bhabha, Homi K. *The Location of Culture*. London: Routledge, 1994.

Cornejo Polar, Antonio. "Mestizaje e hibridez: Los riesgos de las metáforas." *Revista de Crítica Literaria Latinoamericana* 24, no. 47 (1998): 7–11.

Franco, Jean. "Policía de frontera." In *Mapas culturales para América Latina: Culturas híbridas, no simultaneidad, modernidad periférica*, edited by Sarah de Mojica, 55–60. Berlin: WVB, 2000.

García Canclini, Néstor. *Culturas híbridas: Estrategias para entrar y salir de la modernidad*. Mexico City: Grijalbo, 1990. Translated by Christopher L. Chiappari and Silvia L. López as *Hybrid Cultures: Strategies for Entering and Leaving Modernity* (Minneapolis: University of Minnesota Press, 1995).

———. "Noticias recientes sobre la hibridación." *Revista Transcultural de Música/Transcultural Music Review* 7 (December 2003). www.sibetrans.com/trans/trans7/canclini.htm.

Lienhard, Martin. *La voz y su huella*. Havana: Casa de las Américas, 1990.

Lund, Joshua. *The Impure Imagination: Toward a Critical Hybridity in Latin American Writing*. Minneapolis: University of Minnesota Press, 2006.

Martín Barbero, Jesús. *Communication, Culture, and Hegemony: From the Media to Mediations*. Translated by Elizabeth Fox and Robert A. White. London: Sage, 1993.

Ortiz, Fernando. *Cuban Counterpoint: Tobacco and Sugar*. Translated by Harriet de Onís. Durham, N.C.: Duke University Press, 1995.

Ortiz, Renato. "Diversidad cultural y cosmopolitismo." In Moraña, *Nuevas perspectivas desde/sobre América Latina*, 43–53.

Pratt, Mary Louise. *Imperial Eyes: Travel Writing and Transculturation*. London: Routledge, 1992.

Schwarz, Roberto. *Misplaced Ideas: Essays on Brazilian Culture*. London: Verso, 1992.

Young, Robert J. C. *Colonial Desire: Hybridity in Theory, Culture and Race*. London: Routledge, 1995.

Yúdice, George. "From Hybridity to Policy: For a Purposeful Cultural Studies." Translator's introduction to García Canclini, *Consumers and Citizens*, ix–xxxviii.

Identity

NOHEMY SOLÓRZANO-THOMPSON AND CRISTINA RIVERA GARZA
(TRANSLATED BY VALERIE HECHT)

The word "identity" is derived from the Latin *identitas*, whose root is *idem*, "itself." More a relational label than a given fact in and of itself, identity as a category invites an analysis of the production of subjectivities, collective as well as individual, that emerge, or can be perceived, in the realm of daily social practices and the physical experiences of the body.

In order to understand the beginnings of identity studies in Latin America proper, it is necessary to consider their roots in the nineteenth and in the first part of the twentieth century. During the wars of independence and the subsequent nationalist eras, the new Latin American governments and criollo intellectuals dedicated themselves to the work of forging new nations. The heterogeneity of the Latin American population, comprised principally of Europeans, criollos (those people born in America without being of indigenous origin), indigenous peoples, Africans, and various blends of these groups, made this work difficult, compared to the case of the "Old World," whose populations were understood to be uniform. The liberal consensus consisted of uniting the inhabitants symbolically under one sole identity—in countries like Mexico and Peru national unity involved the necessity of integrating the indigenous peoples and mestizos into the new nation, assimilating them into the criollo customs, which were considered civilized. In countries such as Argentina, the process was more one of exclusion, marginalization, or even genocide of minority groups of indigenous and African origin. So, then, explorations involving identity during the nineteenth century often investigate the different negotiations that were carried out among a small, white elite, which intended to Europeanize the New World at all costs, and the large and heterogeneous majorities that not only resisted the processes of incipient modernization of the epoch but also proposed historic alternatives based on their local cultures and daily practices.

The confrontation between processes of modernization and popular resistance acquired more prominence toward the end of the nineteenth century and engendered social mobilizations, among which the Mexican Revolution of 1910 turned out to be the most violent and massive. After a decade of internal struggles, a new Mexican constitution was promulgated in 1917, and on this basis, and in the context of a polarized society, important debates were carried out about the matter of national identity and its relationship to modernity. In postrevolutionary Mexico, the figure of José Vasconcelos (1882–1959) was relevant not only in his role as minister of public education, charged with supporting the painters of the Mexican School, which through its art produced in Mexico a truly mixed identity that was later disseminated throughout the world, but also as the philosopher who in the 1920s coined the neologism "cosmic race" to describe in a positive way the outcome of the mix of races that was the product of more than four hundred years of colonization. Vasconcelos's discourse eventually was deployed by the governing classes in Latin America in order to continue their domination of marginalized groups. In countries like Mexico, Guatemala, and Peru, the idealized figure of the mestizo was established by the governing classes as the representative of modern society and the only national beneficiary, and thus justified their lack of attention to the problems of the indigenous population and other ethnic minority groups. In these countries, programs were initiated to integrate these groups into mestizo society and thereby "improve" their cultural and economic situations. In a fundamental way, these programs thwarted the continuation of indigenous and minority traditions, promoted migration to the cities, and realized no significant impact on the economic situation of many of these groups from rural areas.

Vasconcelos was not unique in theorizing a possible "Latin American" identity: Simón Bolívar (1783–1830), José Martí (1853–1895), and José Enrique Rodó (1872–1917), among others, also reflected upon this possibility. These intellectuals were influenced by the ideas of scientific racialism of the nineteenth century, responding to it by attempting to combat European positivism with their writings on Latin America. The "Latin American" identity produced by these theorists aimed to contradict the pseudoscientific ideas about the possible "inferiority" of the peoples of Latin America and, by extension, its governments. This production also became an important rhetoric for combating the continuation of influence of the United States and Europe in Latin America during and after the wars of independence.

Peru's José Carlos Mariátegui (1894–1930) was influenced by Marxism in his description of the Peruvian condition of inequality, which he called "the Indian problem." Peruvian anthropologist José María Arguedas (1911–1969) concentrated mainly on the situation of the Quechua of the Andes, depicting them as victims of society and the Peruvian government. Arguedas is one of the founders of modern *indigenismo*, a branch of literature and social sciences that attempts to improve the situation for indigenous peoples. In his essays on literature and culture, critic Antonio Cornejo Polar (1936–1977) proposed that Andean reality must be read by way of its cultural heterogeneity, taking into account how this heterogeneity contributes to the formation of collective subjectivities unique to the Andes.

In Brazil, similar debates occurred about the place of the descendents of African slaves in the national imaginary. Anthropologist Gilberto Freyre (1900–1987) is one of the central figures of this debate. His text *Casa-grande & senzala* (1933) promotes the idea of racial democracy—in other words, the argument that in Brazil there is no racism, only class problems. This theory characterizes the hegemonic notions of Brazilian national identity during through much of the twentieth century.

In the Hispanic Caribbean, Cuba's Fernando Ortiz (1881–1969) in *Contrapunteo cubano del tabaco y el azúcar* (1947) proposed the notion of transculturation—that is, the creation of a new culture in an imperialist process that originates in the metropolis and that devalues the dominated culture by imposing imperialist culture without completely annihilating the native. Transculturalism has become an important concept in postcolonial identity studies.

Mexico's Octavio Paz (1914–1998) in *El laberinto de la soledad* (1950, revised and expanded in 1959) searches for the roots of national identity in Mexico's colonial history. In the text's most well-known and controversial section, Paz explains that the Mexican is the bastard child of La Malinche, indigenous translator, collaborator, and lover of Hernán Cortés during the conquest of Mexico. The children of La Malinche are marked by the violence of conquest and colonization, and have not been able to overcome the stigma of being the product of a symbolic and large-scale rape.

The contradictions inherent in referring to Latin American identity, its relationship to modernity, its construction of nationality and race, and the exclusion of certain groups in the writings of Latin American thinkers from the twentieth century led to the emergence, in the 1960s and 1970s, of the first social movements concerned with identity politics. In this era two fundamental branches of criticism rose to prominence: one focusing on the situation of women and the other on ethnic Latin American minorities. The debate around identity and multiple identities based on race, sex, and ethnicity emerged in the Latin American civil sphere as a response to hegemonic narratives of national identity.

The persistent subaltern situation of Latin American ethnic minorities—in particular Afro-Latin Americans and indigenous groups—and the absence of their voices in nationalist cultural production have provoked the development of militant movements in Latin America. It is important to note here that many of the leaders of the indigenous movements of the eighties were women who felt marginalized by Latin American feminism. One of the first leaders of those movements was Domitila Barrios de Chúngara, who interrupted the conference on women sponsored by the United Nations in Mexico in 1975 to call feminists to task for their exclusion of indigenous women. Theories on indigenous Latin American identity are characterized by their affirmation of autochthonous culture, the defense of traditions and language, and protest against the social and military attacks by Latin American institutions and government that wished to integrate these populations into the nation. The Afro-Latin American movements respond to a concern with the social condition of their members and the devaluation of their traditional culture. These movements are located principally in Brazil and the Caribbean. In Brazil, much cultural debate revolves around uncovering the injustices veiled by the national doctrine of racial "democracy." In Cuba, the Revolution's influence made possible an analysis of the racist roots underlying the social condition of people of Afro-Caribbean origin.

Identity studies in the 1990s focuses on the effects of the market in the formation of Latin American identity. George Yúdice, one of the important critics of this era, argues that economic and political changes have created a new private market where identity and culture are manufactured in negotiation with this market, and not directly with the institutions of the state. The study of the identity of Latin American immigrants and their descendents in the United States was also important in this period. Initially, in effect, as in the case of Rodolfo Acuña and his *Occupied America*, the vision that came to be favored was one that called attention to the existence of an internal colonialism, generator of a rigid economic and social hierarchy that, taking advantage of class and race differences, exploited the labor force of conquered peoples. References to lost identities and territories abound in Acuña's bibliography. The growing influence of social history soon invited a focus that turned toward phenomena that, although developed in contexts of inequality, implied strategies of negotiation and/or accommodation among different social groups. In this manner, critical attention was directed with more frequency toward everyday activities and interpretations that made clear the active participation, though limited, of the poor, women, and children. Socially, nevertheless, the debates surrounding multiculturalism and the official use of the term "Latino" and/or "Hispanic" to denominate a plethora of immigrants of Latin American origin in the United States propitiated the existence of studies that, displacing once again the category of class, privileged, often in a schematic way, national and ethnic origins in their analyses of so-called Latinness. Those categorized in these groups did not hesitate to respond: one of the most common complaints was directed toward the homogenizing character of a term that, in its efforts to encompass, ignored and then later disdained the cultural differences and the political implications of the vast diversity of experiences and struggles of immigrants in the United States. One of the first important explorations in this sense was *Borderlands = La Frontera: The New Mestiza*, by Gloria Anzaldúa, which introduced the concept of the "new mestiza" building on Vasconcelos's "cosmic race." Such emphasis on mixing, the hybrid, and the tense situations that this kind of interactions produces socially has been of interest to prominent Latina/o theorists like Juan Flores, Frances Aparicio, Ilan Stavans, and Gustavo Pérez Firmat.

This time period also sees the beginnings of the elaboration of Latin American sexuality studies. Influenced by the work of France's Michel Foucault and U.S. theorist Judith Butler, many studies about Latin American homosexuality emerged in the twenty-first century. Among them, the works of José Quiroga and José Esteban Muñoz stand out. In his book *Tropics of Desire: Interventions from Queer Latino America* (2000), Quiroga argues that Latin American gay men and lesbians historically have not identified themselves on the basis of their sexuality as in the United States—rather, they have followed a political and social strategy of invisibility in order to subsist in society in general. Through a reading of performance artists, José Esteban Muñoz in *Disidentifications: Queers of Color and the Performance of Politics* (1999) suggests that racial and sexual minorities in the United

States have developed a process of creating their identities that does not depend upon the mere appropriation of mainstream culture, nor upon the total negation of it. In contrast, these groups transform the dominant culture in order to self-create their own cultural identity. Muñoz calls this process "disidentification."

The work of Yúdice, Quiroga, and Muñoz proposes a new direction of identity studies: the understanding of Latin American identity through performativity. Taking as a point of departure the affirmation that sexuality and gender are social constructions that coincide with certain *performances*, codified by culture, contemporary critics postulate that Latin American identity in all of its manifestations—national, ethnic, racial, cultural, sexual—is constructed on the basis of the conscious and strategic performance of the individual.

Suggested Reading

Anzaldúa, Gloria. *Borderlands/La frontera: The New Mestiza*. San Francisco: Aunt Lute Books, 1987.

Beverley, John. *Subalternity and Representation: Arguments in Cultural Theory*. Durham, N.C.: Duke University Press, 1999.

Franco, Jean. *Plotting Women: Gender and Representation in Mexico*. London: Verso, 1989.

Freyre, Gilberto. *The Masters and the Slaves*. Translated by Samuel Putnam. New York: Knopf, 1956.

Muñoz, José Esteban. *Disidentifications: Queers of Color and the Performance of Politics*. Minneapolis: University of Minnesota Press, 1999.

Ortiz, Fernando. *Cuban Counterpoint: Tobacco and Sugar*. Translated by Harriet de Onís. New York: Knopf, 1947.

Paz, Octavio. *The Labyrinth of Solitude: Life and Thought in Mexico*. Translated by Lysander Kemp. New York: Grove Press, 1961.

Quiroga, José. *Tropics of Desire: Interventions from Queer Latino America*. New York: New York University Press, 2000.

Vasconcelos, José. *The Cosmic Race: A Bilingual Edition*. Translated by Didier T. Jaén. Baltimore: Johns Hopkins University Press, 1997.

Yúdice, George. *The Expediency of Culture: Uses of Culture in the Global Era*. Durham, N.C.: Duke University Press, 2003.

Zea, Leopoldo. *El problema de la identidad latinoamericana*. Mexico City: UNAM, 1985.

Ideology

SEBASTIAAN FABER

Born under the sign of inversion, the concept of ideology is infinitely ironic. In the most common sense of the term, ideology mistakes the ideal for the material, injustice for justice, and appearances for reality (Eagleton 51–61). In *The German Ideology* in 1845–47, Marx and Engels suggested that the idealist philosophers saw the world upside down (26). If ideology is a form of mystification, however, its critics necessarily make a claim to nonideological knowledge. This is why Marxist *Ideologiekritik*, which reveals others' false consciousness, is not unlike the denouement of a good comedy.

Indeed, the evolution of the concept is itself marked by a series of quasi-comic inversions. First conceived by the French as a "science of ideas" that would allow them to discover the workings of the human mind and thus help liberate it from (religious) mystification, the concept was quickly mobilized to delegitimize the practitioners of that very science. Emperor Napoleon I argued in 1812 that the "*idéologues*" were lost in the fog of metaphysics, ignoring "a knowledge of the human heart and of the lessons of history" (quoted in R. Williams, "Ideology" 154). Two centuries later, it is still easy to invert ideology's critical vector. As Slavoj Žižek writes, ideology "seems to pop up precisely when we attempt to avoid it, while it fails to appear where one would clearly expect it to dwell. When some procedure is denounced as 'ideological *par excellence*' one can be sure that its inversion is no less ideological" ("Introduction" 4). Ever since Napoleon's times the concept of ideology has served the Right as much as the Left to delegitimize adversaries by portraying them either as fools duped by appearances or as hypocrites bent on deceiving others for their own benefit. "[I]n popular argument," Williams writes, "ideology is still mainly used in the sense given by Napoleon. Sensible people rely on experience, or have a philosophy; silly people rely on ideology" (157).

Still, the prominence of the concept in the last two centuries is due less to its usefulness as a rhetorical weapon than to its explanatory power. The theory of ideology aims to elucidate some of the most challenging enigmas facing reformists and revolutionaries since the beginning of modernity. How is it possible for a social majority to collaborate in its own oppression? How can oppressors and oppressed persist in fundamentally mistaken notions about reality? Revealing the root causes of these phenomena, moreover, the theory of ideology points to ways of overcoming them, making possible the transformation of society.

As a notion fundamental to Marxism, the concept has been rejected by competing schools of thought. In the 1950s, social scientists in the West—Aron, Shils, Bell, and others—proclaimed the "end of ideology," expressing their faith in the superiority of the "objective" sciences practiced in Western democracies, as opposed to their "ideological" counterparts under totalitarianism. Later, ideology was dismissed by poststructuralists and postmodernists such as Foucault, Lyotard, Baudrillard, Deleuze, and Rorty, who balked at its debt to Enlightenment thought: the idea that some can claim access to the truth, denouncing the blindness of others. Critics such as Eagleton, Žižek, and Larraín, by contrast, have argued that the concept of ideology—albeit an updated version—remains an indispensable tool of cultural and political critique.

The theory of ideology is at bottom perspectivist. It assumes that the circumstances and interests of particular groups limit or distort the way they conceive of reality and their place in it. This perspectivist dimension—which sometimes tends toward determinism—is the concept's greatest strength, but also its greatest weakness: It facilitates *tu quoque* arguments and makes it practically impossible to immunize oneself against its critical force. Who can presume to transcend the limitations of their historical and social situation? As we will see, the most important differences among the various versions of the concept come down to two questions: first, how much they allow for the possibility of a perspective that sees the world "as it truly is," and second, to whom they grant such a perspective.

The widespread twentieth-century use of the concept in the social sciences and humanities is due primarily to its central place in the critical analysis of capitalism as formulated by Marx, Engels, and their followers: ideology blinded participants in the capitalist system to its injustice. Still, Marxists use several different concepts of ideology that are not always mutually compatible. The main differences can be illustrated through three questions: Does ideology denote a false view of the world (implying that there is a true one), or simply a *particular* worldview—that is, is it a critical or a neutral concept? Is ideology a primordially mental phenomenon, or rather a material one—that is, does ideology arise in the minds of subjects, or does it have a concrete existence in the social world? And can ideology be overcome? How these questions are answered determines the usefulness of the concept of ideology as a tool for critique—as well as identifying the possible agents of social change and the margin of change possible.

For Marx himself, ideology denoted a false view of the world that, as such, could be criticized and overcome, both through the scientific analysis of social reality and through revolutionary practice. Although in *The German Ideology* Marx and Engels appear to see ideology as a purely mental phenomenon—a "falsche Bewusstsein" or "false consciousness," in Engels's words—Larraín underscores that for Marx the inversions of ideology reflect and hide the inversions and contradictions of social reality as constituted in specific practices (55). Unlike Marx's, Lenin's concept of ideology is neutral: it is a coherent vision of society, shared by a class, a group, or a party, inspiring a particular course of action; and the goal is for the revolutionary ideology to defeat all others. Gramsci's concept of hegemony similarly tends toward neutrality and is less concerned with the truth of ideas than with their political efficacy.

The most coherent case for ideology as a *material* phenomenon is made by Althusser, for whom ideology constitutes subjects as such, through "ideological state apparatuses" like the educational system and religion. For Althusser—influenced by structuralism—ideology is an inexorable prison. Although he postulates the possibility of a "scientific" perspective, even this only provides a provisional escape. Together with Gramsci and Lacan, Althusser paves the way for the neutral, discursive concept of ideology theorized by Laclau, Mouffe, and other post-Marxists. Rejecting the notion that ideologies "belong" to particular social classes, Laclau's notion of hegemony is conceived as a discursive articulation of diverse ideological elements—a tentative structure sustained by a central "empty signifier"—which in turn allows for temporary sociopolitical coalitions.

The fate of the concept of ideology in the field of cultural studies is closely tied to the changing influence of different Marxist legacies. British cultural studies emerged in the 1950s in part out of discontent with Marxist cultural criticism, particularly its materialist determinism (culture as a "superstructural" reflection of the economic "base") and its traditional privileging of high culture over popular or mass culture.

Early cultural-studies critics like Williams and Thompson recognized popular culture—conceived as a whole way of life—as an object worthy of study but also as a space that could harbor a certain level of autonomy and political agency. With Hall's arrival at Birmingham, this "humanist" paradigm was displaced by an Althusser-inspired structuralist one. (In 1983

Hall laid out his objections to the Marxist version of ideology: economic reductionism and the distinction between false and true consciousness. If ideology is indeed a distortion, he writes, one can wonder "why some people . . . cannot recognize that [their ideology] is distorted, while we, with our superior wisdom . . . can" (31).) Hall's neutral, Althusserian version became "the most important analytical category for cultural studies in the 1970s" (Castro Gómez, "Althusser" 740, translation ours). Larraín in turn rejected Hall's version, arguing for a critical notion of ideology as distortion. Larraín also questioned Hall's reading of Marx, who, Larrain argues, never suggested that intellectuals should "correct" mistaken views of the world. For Marx, ideology is rooted in social reality, and overcoming it implies the practical transformation of that reality (57).

In the 1980s and 1990s—with the rise of postmodern theory, the institutionalization of cultural studies in the British and U.S. academy, and the marginalization of the Marxist legacy—the concept of ideology lost prominence. Castro Gómez laments this development: "the abandonment of the category of ideology by some theorists of culture has contributed to weakening the critical and political potential that cultural studies used to have." For him, Althusser's legacy is most fitting to effectively formulate "a critique of the political economy of culture" (742, 738).

Within Latin Americanism, rigorous and original uses of the concept of ideology can be found in Marxist critics like Schwarz and Larsen, who are generally hostile to cultural studies. Schwarz, in *Misplaced Ideas*, theorizes ideology in the context of postcolonial Brazil, proposing the notion of "ideology to the second degree" to describe what happens when ideologies from the metropolis—such as liberalism in the case of nineteenth-century Brazil—are "imported" by the colony. If daily life in the metropolis *confirms* ideology—a "necessary illusion well grounded in appearances"—the incongruent appearances of Brazil *reveal* the imported ideologies in all their falsity. Because they are nevertheless adopted by the Europeanizing bourgeoisie, however, they become "ideologies to the second degree": illusions *not* grounded in appearances that nevertheless shape social practice (28). Žižek similarly argues that it is quite possible to be aware of the falsity of appearances and yet *act* as if one is not (*Sublime Object* 31).

The greatest challenge of the notion of ideology as distortion continues to be its implicit truth claim. How to perform a rigorous cultural critique without succumbing to epistemological arrogance? The critics that have weathered this challenge most skillfully are those who fully accept the irony inherent in the concept. "[A]lthough no clear line of demarcation separates ideology from reality," Žižek writes, "although ideology is at work in everything we experience as 'reality,' we must none the less maintain the tension that keeps the *critique* of ideology alive" ("Introduction" 17). In Latin America this position is most clearly embodied by Monsiváis, whose peculiar form of *Ideologiekritik* never ceases to insist on the creative and political potential of popular culture—which he analyzes, criticizes, and celebrates—and whose idiosyncratic combination of the lucid and the ludic goes a long way toward immunizing him against the temptations of elitism (Faber, "Estilo" 93–94, 101–2).

Suggested Reading

Althusser, Louis. *Lenin and Philosophy, and Other Essays.* Translated by Ben Brewster. London: New Left, 1971.

Castro Gómez, Santiago. "Althusser, los estudios culturales y el concepto de ideología." *Revista Iberoamericana* 64, no. 193 (2000): 737–51.

Eagleton, Terry. *Ideology: An Introduction.* London: Verso, 1991.

Faber, Sebastiaan. "El estilo como ideología: De la *Rebelión* de Ortega a los *Rituales* de Monsiváis." In *El arte de la ironía: Carlos Monsiváis ante la crítica,* edited by Mabel Moraña and Ignacio M. Sánchez Prado, 76–103. Mexico City: Era/UNAM, 2007.

Hall, Stuart. "The Problem of Ideology: Marxism Without Guarantees." In Morley and Chen, *Stuart Hall,* 25–46.

Marx, Karl, and Friedrich Engels. *Die deutsche Ideologie: Werke.* 3 vols. Berlin: Dietz, 1971. Translated by S. Ryazanskaya as *The German Ideology* (Moscow: Progress Publishers, 1964).

Schwarz, Roberto. *Ao vencedor as batatas: Forma literária e processo social nos inicios do romance brasileiro.* São Paolo: Duas Cidades, 1977.

———. *Misplaced Ideas: Essays on Brazilian Culture.* Edited by John Gledson. London: Verso, 1992.

Williams, Raymond. "Ideology." In *Keywords,* 153–57.

Žižek, Slavoj. "Introduction: The Spectre of Ideology." In *Mapping Ideology,* 1–33. London: Verso, 1994.

———. *The Sublime Object of Ideology.* London: Verso, 1989.

Latin/o Americanism/o

JUAN POBLETE

The term "Latin/o Americanism/o" as used in cultural studies originated in U.S.-based academic debates. However, it is not a foreign term for Latin

American intellectuals who, in a long nation-based continental tradition from José Martí to Hugo Chávez, have defined it precisely in a negative relation with the United States.

Latin/o Americanism/o (including Latin/o American cultures in Canada and the United States) is part of an effort within the North American academy to rethink the borders and the geopolitical and geocultural concepts defining Latin America, the objects, subjects, and processes thus involved, and the epistemic categories and methodological procedures used to study them. The context is what was first called the postmodernism debate in Latin America and is now conceptualized as the globalization of/in the Americas. The debate on postmodernity focused on the reexamination of the heuristic capacity of Western master narratives (progress, reason, progressive democratization, politics) and the disciplinary narratives of the social sciences and the humanities to give an account of the transformations of a world fast unraveling and seemingly incapable of finding a new shape as an intelligible totality. Along these lines the postmodern debate had a fundamentally temporal, vertical, and historical orientation centered on the notion of epochal change. The discussion on globalization, on the other hand, has focused on the supposed emergence of a homogeneous global culture, on the expansion of an experiential quasi-planetary horizon linked to the commodification of life, and on the emergence of the local as a layer different from the national, mediating the relations between the global and the national. In this regard, the terms "transnational," "postnational," and even "translocal" have been used to refer to the multiple flows of goods, capital, discourses, and populations through the world in general, and more specifically through the world region we call Latin America (Fox; Tomlinson). The discussion on globalization has brought to the debate the horizontal nature of spatial and geographic dimensions, and the concepts of flows and displacements. It shares with the postmodernity discussion a suspicion about the limits and consequences a state-centric perspective (liberal or socialist) has had, and continues to have, on our understanding of the actual heterogeneity of the social processes and phenomena it attempts to describe. In this way some of the issues any reconceptualization of Latin/o America in a global perspective must face are clearly highlighted. They include how—at a time of a reterritorialization of national life in the different Latin American countries and of their relations with Europe and the United States—to think the connections between, on the one hand, the colonial and postcolonial legacies at the intersection of the historical temporalities of multiple imperial projects and, on the other, the geocultural and geopolitical dimensions that have organized these projects into culturally homogenous and self-contained regions.

Latin/o Americanism/o in the Humanities

In a famous 1989 essay on *testimonio*, the U.S.-based critic John Beverley began by asking: "Do social struggles give rise to new forms of literature and culture, or is it more a question of the adequacy of their representation in existing forms?" (*Against* 69). Beverley posited that *testimonio*, associated for him with the Central American struggles of the 1970s and 1980s, was a new form of literary representation. In contrast to the novel, centered on its bourgeois presuppositions (the privileging of individual and nuclear family life, and of private and urban spaces), *testimonio* was the cultural form of a neopopular configuration manifesting itself in Central America. *Testimonio* as defined by Beverley is a literary form that narrates a real life in the words of its own protagonist or those of a witness, often an illiterate subject. As such, it requires the collaboration of an intellectual interlocutor. Later Beverley radicalized his hypothesis, proposing that insofar as it was a representation of subalternity, *testimonio* was a form of postliterature, or at least a sign of the end of the literary and of the traditional humanism on which it rested. As postliterary, *testimonio* was capable of doing away with the distinction between fictional and nonfictional issues characteristic of the aesthetic as a mode in order to embrace the struggles and voices of collective subjects long subjected to a history of subalternization, first by the Spanish colonial state and later by their postcolonial criollo inheritors. In this sense, the study of *testimonio* seemed to offer a radical alternative to contemporary U.S. efforts to develop a cultural studies agenda. In contrast to the latter—which Beverley saw as still situated within the cultural coordinates, now mass-mediated, of dominant capitalism—*testimonios* spoke of collective and emerging actors fighting on the ground with this capitalism and were the harbingers of the (re)emergence of a neopopular non- or at least anticapitalist culture. Thus, *testimonio* heralded a posthumanist and perhaps postliterary epoch, freed from the bourgeois subject and the cultural heritage of classical humanism (Beverley; Gugelberger).

Reacting too to the emergence of cultural studies that broadened the space of what was worth studying culturally under capitalism, Alberto Moreiras proposed his own version of subalternism. Inspired more by deconstruction than by Marxism, Moreiras saw *testimonio* as embodying less a positive proposal than a radical critique or pure negativity. Also building on the work of Indian subaltern scholars such as Gayatri Spivak and Ranajit

Guha, but above all on Derridean deconstruction, Moreiras believed *testimonio* revealed the aporias involved in the representation of subalternity under the epistemological apparatus of U.S.-based Latin Americanist critics. As a crisis of representation, *testimonio* was a symptom revealing the limits of any representation of Latin America within the American academy. In this sense, more than opposing it, *testimonio* shared with the best literature its capacity to explore the limits of the representable and to say in other words what can be said only indirectly (Moreiras, *Exhaustion*).

In this way, while Moreiras posited the unique capacity of literature to deconstruct representational apparatuses, Beverley declared the end of the literary and the beginning of a postliterary epoch. Moreiras found stronger representational powers in literature than in literary studies. Literature was here thought as the other side of critical thinking, which together with philosophy, seemed to be something quite different from the vested interests and the internal limitations of the social sciences "experts." In the traumatic context of Southern Cone postdictatorships and Central American violence, those powers were, for Moreiras, paradoxical insofar as they refer to literature's capacity to interrupt representation and question its status. Beverley, on the other hand, found the same capacity, but in *testimonio* much more than in literature. The two scholars shared, however, their suspicion toward what they called the populism of cultural studies and its alleged acritical inscription within advanced capitalism and its commodification of cultural differences.

Among other sources, the issue of the representational capabilities of dominant written discourses to account for Third World objects, processes, and subjects constituted by the same colonial and postcolonial state legacies underpinning those discourses, stemmed from the work of the Indian subalternists Ranajit Guha and Partha Chatterjee and from postcolonial critics including Homi Bhabha and Gayatri Spivak. From these sources, Latin/o Americanism/o inherited an emphasis on the categories of subalternity, colonial and postcolonial subjectivity, and ir/representability (Loomba). These new relational categories have the significant advantage of allowing the mapping of a series of questions that the Latin American tradition, with its strong sociological and state-centered orientation, had never explored adequately. The intersections of race, class, gender and ethnicity in the analysis, and of psychoanalysis, literary and cultural theory, feminism, and anthropology in the perspectives, allow a much clearer understanding of the true historical complexities of the processes of colonization/decolonization as they affected multiple and heterogeneously constituted social subjects—indigenous peoples, Afroamericans, sexual minorities, women, mestizos.

On the other hand, the Indian and Anglocentric origins of subaltern and postcolonial theory, and the empty relationality of many of their main categories, produced an interesting debate about their applicability in/to Latin America and their sometimes paradoxical metropolitan exportation toward the periphery as yet another form of intellectual neocolonialism and theoretical fashion (Thurner). Moreover, transformed in the English-speaking world in a convenient monolingual pedagogical practice that divides the world into a highly defined "us" and a strongly undifferentiated "them" capable of encompassing all Third World people, postcolonial theory has always been in need of its grounding in the specific historical, social, and cultural conditions of a concrete location (Loomba). Nevertheless, this specific knowledge produced in the United States by so-called area studies (African, Asian, and Latin American studies) was precisely—in its modernizing, and thus in its homogenizing state and Eurocentric orientation—one of the forms of knowledge that subaltern and postcolonial studies in their Latin Americanist versions had attempted to dismantle. A clear example of this program and critique can be found in the Latin American Subaltern Studies Group Manifesto. It highlights the need to distinguish among the state, the nation—which it sees in its historically dominant discursive shape as the almost exclusive result of the labor of the state and its institutions—and the people, which it defines as the ensemble of subaltern populations whose participation, and ways of cultural, social, and political organization, must be visibilized and deinvisibilized (Rodríguez, "Reading").

Latin/o Americanism/o in the Social Sciences

Another source of that critique of the traditional forms of studying things Latin American in the United States that Latin/o Americanism/o seeks to or can represent, is the globalization of Latin American populations and specifically its transformative impact on the national paradigms of ethnic assimilation in the United States.

Of all U.S. immigrants between 1992 and 2004, a third were of Mexican origin, and an additional quarter were from elsewhere in Latin America (Passel and Suro). In the last thirty years, the Latino population overall has gone from 14.6 million or 6.4 percent of the U.S. population (the equivalent of half the size of the African American population in the nation) in 1980 to becoming in 2003 the largest U.S. minority, and in 2010 comprising more than 50 million people, or 16.3 percent of the population. Between 1980 and 2000 the U.S. Latino population more than doubled, and it accounted in the same period for 40 percent of the total population growth.

This mass migration of Latinos in the last quarter of the twentieth century altered the social and political landscape of the United States and thus challenged previous U.S.- and Latin America–based ways of studying the national and international dimensions of Latin/o Americans. In the U.S. context, those forms of study were called ethnic studies and Latin American (area) studies. While the first dealt with populations recognized as "in the process of becoming" ethnic minorities in the nation, Latin American studies was focused on populations located in a different geocultural and geopolitical area, elsewhere. Central to the first paradigm was the notion of a dominant white majority and thus of ethnic minorities in the process of differential integration to that core. Crucial to the second paradigm was the bounded nature of the area and its internal coherence and logic. To put it briefly, these central tenets structuring U.S. ethnic studies and Latin American studies are now in need of serious reconsideration. Latino studies and Latin/o Americanism/o can be two of the spaces where that thinking takes place. In this way, Latin/o Americanism/o can now be conceived, at least in one of its possible and, for me, desirable forms, as the space for the conversation between the ethnic and area studies traditions and their counterparts in Latin America at an epochal moment of globalization of things Latin/o American.

The tasks of that Latin/o Americanism/o are many and have manifested themselves most convincingly within the social sciences or in empirically based cultural studies. They have to do, first, with the very large population displacements. What must be visibilized (because it was previously invisibilized) or reconceptualized (because so far it has been perceived from only one perspective) are the forms of belonging and affiliation of subjects engaged in their connections with the different levels of the communities within which they choose or are forced or invited to participate. The bibliography on citizenship—from its broadening to incorporate nontraditional forms such as cultural and social citizenship which go beyond formal political citizenship, to its multiplication into dual or multiple citizenships or its questioning in forms of differential inclusion/exclusion or even voided citizenships—is a good indicator of the set of problems opened up by such reconsiderations (Flores; Flores and Benmayor; Rotker; Shafir). This broadening in fact has been occurring in connection not only with

U.S.-based Latino populations but also in Latin America a propos internal and external migrations; the new geocultural and geopolitical maps; the racialization of labor forces at a continental level, including in countries that send migrants to others that are happy to exploit them under their highly flexible and productive form of indocumentation (Quijano; de Genova; Grimson); and, more generally, the challenges posed by the lack of fit between the cultural and social geographies of central and peripheral capitalisms (Quijano).

That lack of fit manifests itself in the life of those who "travel" every day without leaving their locations or are relegated to a form of marginalization that excludes them in a quasi-structural way. The topics of this new agenda include: the daily consumption of transnational products or of products heavily influenced by their formats, contents, and techniques (García Canclini, *Diferentes*; *Consumidores*); the emergence of a complex "mediascape" within which coexist the strong specificity of local communication, often enhanced by new and older but reinvented technologies such as the Internet or radio broadcasting, with an increasing presence of transnational conglomerates (Poblete, "Culture"); the development of the social, cultural, and political practice of multiple and complex actors functioning simultaneously on local, regional, national, and global scales (Mato, *Políticas*; Yúdice, *Expediency*); the criminalization of poverty and the blaming of the juvenile victims of a culture of violence, drugs, and exclusion (Hopenhayn, *América*; Reguillo, *Emergencia*.

In all these examples, the nation no longer fully coincides (if it ever did) with its populations, neither socially nor culturally. This fundamental lack of fit produces the need and provides the opportunity for new cartographies of Latin/o America at the time of its globalization. This happens, although not in the same way or to the same degree in the different countries, in both Latin America and the United States. These new maps—which cannot do away with the nation as social, cultural and economic territorialization, but must instead attempt to understand both its transformations and functioning as a space of internal hegemony and relative autonomy, and the new flows of international or transnational interconnection and interdependence—are the potential results of what can be called a new Latin/o Americanism/o.

Suggested Reading

De la Campa, Román. *Latin Americanism*. Minneapolis: University of Minnesota Press, 1999.

Flores, William V., and Rina Benmayor, eds. *Latino Cultural Citizenship: Claiming Identity, Space, and Rights*. Boston: Beacon, 1997.
García Canclini, Néstor. *Diferentes, desiguales y desconectados*. Barcelona: Gedisa, 2005.
Loomba, Ania. *Colonialism/Postcolonialism*. New York: Routledge, 1998.
Poblete, Juan, ed. *Critical Latin American and Latino Studies*. Minneapolis: University of Minnesota Press, 2003.
Quijano, Aníbal. "Colonialidad del poder, eurocentrismo y América Latina." In Lander, *La colonialidad del saber*, 201–46.

Lettered City

JUAN PABLO DABOVE

Ángel Rama (1926–1983) coined the term "lettered city" in the unfinished work of the same name (*La ciudad letrada)*, published posthumously in 1984. The volume, which is a major contribution to Latin American cultural theory, has exerted an enduring influence especially in colonial and nineteenth-century studies. Rama attempted a cultural history of Latin America from 1521 to the mid-twentieth century. The book displays a rare consistency for the field, since it addresses a single topic: the Spanish American lettered "class," its constitution, consolidation, and transformations, its surprising endurance throughout time, the dynamic of its relationship with the colonial and postcolonial metropolis as well as with subaltern groups. At the same time, Rama attempts to construct a productive middle path between epistemology and aesthetics (which Román de la Campa has termed "episthetics").

Rama is considered one of the forerunners of Latin American cultural studies, together with Antônio Cândido, Darcy Ribeiro, Roberto Fernández Retamar, and Antonio Cornejo Polar. However, his practice, in literary and political terms, is firmly placed in the tradition of the postcolonial Latin American essay. While the links between *The Lettered City* and Michel Foucault's notions of episteme and discursive formation are obvious (de la Campa), so too are its parallels with eminent texts of cultural analysis published around the same time, like *Orientalism* (1978) by Edward Said and *Imagined Communities* (1983) by Benedict Anderson. Yet just as important are Rama's links to the Latin American essayists, from Simón Rodríguez to Ezequiel Martínez Estrada and beyond.

"Lettered city" is a hybrid notion that integrates à la Foucault several levels of analysis. On the one hand, it names a *cluster of institutions*. Among these one can mention the branches of the colonial and later national states (the police, the judiciary, the customhouses, the legislature, the county registrars); the corporations devoted to educational, artistic, commercial, and financial matters; the liberal professions (medicine, law, journalism, notaryship), the clergy, political parties, sects, literary groups, and even some guerrilla organizations. According to Rama, all of these institutions have at least one thing in common: the ownership and administration of the technology of the letter. This is the condition for their existence, their ability to function, their power and prestige. Literature occupies a place in this list, of course. But for Rama that place has to be examined from the vantage point of the profound affinities between literature and other institutions based upon the written word—not, as the modern ideology of literature would claim, emphasizing its differences and its assumed epistemological privilege. This affirmation of the difference and privilege of literature is, for Rama, only a recent avatar in the centuries-old history of the lettered city and its internal and external conflicts.

At the same time, lettered city names a *group of individuals* (the *letrados*) that draw a sense of differentiated social identity from belonging to the aforementioned institutions (as in the older term "republic of letters"). One of Rama's achievements is precisely to trace a lineage that runs from the sixteenth-century bureaucrat to the anarchist autodidact of the twentieth century, through the bachelors, cosmopolitan travelers, and positivistic scientists of the nineteenth century.

Finally, lettered city names the numerous *discursive practices* that sustain the hegemony of the aforementioned institutions and individuals. These comprise rituals of inclusion, acknowledgement, or exclusion (graduations, the taking of sacred orders, exams), founding ceremonies, inaugurations, deeds, acts, poet's coronations, criminal sentences, laws, proclamations, sonnets, anthologies, and travelogues. Rama does not analyze these discursive practices exclusively according to their explicit contents, as texts, but as performances intent on the reproduction and perpetuation of the written word as the axis of the social order. This, as Carlos Alonso points out, allows him to cut the Gordian knot in which dependency theory had trapped cultural and literary analysis. For, according to Rama, one should look past the fact that the Spanish American *letrado* imitated or adapted metropolitan models—for example, the anachronistic loyalty to Gongorine, neoclassic, or romantic aesthetics—and rather direct attention to the fact that the *letrado* practice was oriented toward reaffirming its prerogatives as administrator of a technology that was very unequally distributed. Even when it seems that intellectual autonomy crumbles in front of powerful metropolitan models, these often monotonous imitations are highly relevant practices in which a group enacts its differentiated identity, cohesiveness, and imaginary affiliations. This approximation to the dilemma of dependency opened new venues for the analysis of Spanish American culture, thus moving away from the stagnant dichotomy between imitation of metropolitan models and vernacular originality. Furthermore, it revealed the power, relevance, and adaptability of the *letrado* class.

The notion of lettered city has allowed for a new consideration of the ethical challenges that the Spanish American *letrado* faces, a most relevant issue since the mid-1980s, when the rise of testimonial literature seemed to herald a radical change in the evaluation of writing practices that were still linked to literature and the humanities. The link between the written letter and power, as epistemological violence exerted by the *letrado*, is inescapable, and acknowledging that link is the paradoxical starting point of all critical enterprises. It should be equally stressed that for Rama, unlike some of his followers, this did not amount to a condemnation *urbi et orbi* of literature, but rather to a challenge that called for its radical redefinition—and relegitimization.

This semiotic machine has a very precise location: the Spanish American city, simultaneously the creature and the origin of the lettered city. For Rama, the colonial city emerged as a "creation of the human mind." Unlike European cities, formed through the sedimentation of multisecular and multicultural processes, Latin American colonial cities were conceived and planned as cornerstones in the enterprise of expansion of the Iberian empires, where a minority of metropolitan origin dominated vast populations. The colonial city was not organized mainly around the requirements of a self sufficient local economy, but rather around the needs of the imperial economy and administration, in particular the pressing need of *making the empire visible*. This dual need—administrative on the one hand, performative on the other—is responsible for the peculiar checkerboard configuration of the Spanish American city. At the center of the city were (are) the representatives of power and prestige: the cathedral or the church, the viceregal palace or the *cabildo* (later the presidential palace or the mayor's office), the *audiencia* (later the courts), the *montepío* (later the bank). This concentration served the administrative and military needs of the elite. But at the same time, the spatial layout duplicated each family or corporation's place within the colonial hierarchy: the further away from the plaza, the further down on the social ladder. Thus the colonial city (and, to a certain extent, the modern one) had an annular organization. The inner ring coincided with the core of power. The further removed the ring from the core, the more marginalized in the colonial order.

This reduplication, where the visible map of the city mirrors the invisible map of the hierarchy, was a deliberate project. Rama links it to the Early Modern analogical episteme. The reduplication established, from the very start of the incorporation of the continent into the West, the primacy of the letter in its link to power—maps, royal ordinances, acts and protocols, and rituals around which the urban projects would revolve—over colonial "reality." From then on, when this reality did not fit into the *letrado* design, it would be marginalized as subaltern or anomalous. Thus the lettered city, far from being a mere bureaucratic intermediary, legitimated and sustained an empire whose military basis was always fragile. Controlling enormous expanses of land and widely scattered and restive populations, the empire could not have survived without the urban semiotic machine that "performed empire" from the bureau, the pulpit, the church gate, the professor's desk. The *barroco de Indias* is a crucial example of this dynamic.

Rama does not think of the emancipation from Spain and the internecine fights that mushroomed in its aftermath as a terminal crisis of the lettered city. Contrary to the consensus established by nineteenth-century liberal historiography, Rama emphasizes how the criollo *letrados* enjoyed a newfound influence and legitimacy, since the power of last resort did not lie overseas any longer, but rather had been replaced by the *letrados* themselves (or the caudillos with whom many of them were associated). Independence and civil wars had centrifugal effects on many decision-making instances, notably the dissolution of the viceroyalties. But they had a centripetal effect at another level. They eliminated, or displaced, the transatlantic reference that decentered the lettered city. This became, at least ideally, the exclusive instance of sovereignty as origin of the laws and regulations of the new republican order. As minions of the caudillos, as writers of laws and constitutions, as lawyers and judges, as literary writers, the *letrados* found in emancipation a range of opportunities for the expansion and redefinition of lettered culture.

The challenges that emancipation did not pose were later posed by modernization. The successful incorporation of Spanish America into the global capitalist order as defined by the international division of labor toward the mid-nineteenth century caused the growth and accelerated diversification of the population in the cities, and of the productive and administrative infrastructure within them. Because of this, new sectors appeared—social scientists, popular writers—whose lettered practices were barely compatible with traditional ones. On the other hand, the market for cultural goods and the culture industry took a central role in redefining power relations, expectations, and practices within the lettered city. The generalized process of "democratization of the cultural field" spurred by massive literacy campaigns afforded new social sectors access to the technology of the letter. These new sectors, in turn, disputed the lettered elite's epistemological privilege.

Thus the new "anomalous" cultural forms that were appearing or growing—the popular theater, the *folletín criollista*, popular journalism, the mass political party, the radical labor union—were all practices based on a different idea of the role of the written letter and its protocols. Rama's analysis in characterizing these challenges and the ways in which Spanish American *letrados* positioned themselves to them is remarkable. One of these challenges was the appropriation of an oral cultural previously marginalized, with the purpose of reinventing national cultures (and the place of the *letrados* in it), as in *americanismo* and literary *criollismo*. Another was the invention of the "historical" genres (the *tradición* by Ricardo Palma or the *memorialista* novel) that recuperated a vanishing era, or of genres that translated and reterritorialized new realities (like the urban or the travel chronicle).

The Mexican and Uruguayan revolutions that inaugurated the twentieth century were the last avatars of the lettered city, avatars that, if on the one hand they prolonged the prestige of the written word, on the other fostered decisive lines of rupture. Perhaps the most radical attempt at prolonging the impulse of *La ciudad letrada*, since it extends the cultural history that Rama proposes from the vantage point of those fissure lines, is Jean Franco's recent volume *The Decline and Fall of the Lettered City* (2002). We could conceive of this volume as the conclusion that Rama was not able to give to his essay. Franco's volume, which equates the lettered city to literature and the social sciences, studies how, within the context of the Cold War, we witness the lettered city's loss of the epistemological privilege upon which it based its hegemony. Furthermore, we witness the loss of its eminent place as interpreter and guide of the national community.

The notion of lettered city has spawned multiple lines of research. There are, on the one hand, critical-theoretical enterprises that took it upon themselves to extend or to fine-tune Rama's intuitions through case studies that make the patterns of functioning and transformation of the lettered city more precise. Among these we can mention the studies on colonial baroque and the rise of criollo consciousness (*conciencia criolla*), the studies around emancipation literature as continuation-rupture of the lettered paradigms of the eighteenth century, and the studies on literary modernization in Spanish America.

Other lines of research highlight the ways in which the Spanish American lettered city has imagined its "others" (Sommer, *Foundational Fictions*; Dabove), or focus on how the lettered city has addressed modernization (Ramos). A last line of inquiry seeks to define and explore those cultural instances that exceed the lettered city: female or minority writing, graffiti, narco-culture, or globalized digital communities. One example among many is the collective volume *Más allá de la ciudad letrada*, edited by Boris Muñoz and Silvia Spitta (2003).

There have been criticisms of the concept of lettered city. In *Desencuentros*—a book that could not have been conceived in the first place without the precedent of *La ciudad letrada*—Julio Ramos claims that the notions of *letrado* and lettered city unify cultural practices that are not always compatible. This may be so, but Rama's search for a notion that could encompass centuries and a whole hemisphere is precisely what gives his essay its unity of vision and its undeniable strength. It does, however, carry a certain risk of hypostasis and anthropomorphism (throughout this entry, for example, "the lettered city" is referred to as if it were a "being" endowed with self-consciousness and unity of intent).

Other scholars, like Mabel Moraña, indicate that Rama's vision retains a culturalist imprint, found almost everywhere in the tradition of the Latin American national essay. Because of this, Rama does not pay enough attention to the production processes that made the perpetuation of the lettered city possible. Since the privileged analytical category is the binary oral/written word, Rama neglects class, gender, and race—even though the notion of lettered city has been notoriously useful to describe the diglosic cultural dynamic in multiethnic societies. Of course, it is precisely this culturalist emphasis that makes it influential in a post-Marxist, postmodern context, in which culturalism (of a different brand) is back in vogue.

John Charles Chasteen points out that, even though Rama's book aims to be relevant for Latin America in its entirety, it privileges the New Spain and Peruvian contexts, without an adequate discussion of counterexamples taken from the Brazilian context. Furthermore, the section on modernization takes into consideration, almost exclusively, the Río de la Plata case.

Thus Rama displaces the center of gravity of his argumentation toward those cases that better prop up his preexisting hypothesis. Chasteen's critique is valid. However, Rama's selection is not completely arbitrary. New Spain and Peru *were* the centers of the Spanish colonial empire, which was a deliberate enterprise to a degree that the Portuguese empire was not; Buenos Aires and Montevideo *were* the places where modernity at the end of the nineteenth century showed its starkest features.

Perhaps the most radical critique comes from Françoise Perus. Perus rejects the very foundation of Rama's conceptual edifice: the analogical model upon which Rama contemplates the relationship between written word and colonial city as a defining cultural trait. To begin with, she says, Rama does not provide any specific proof to show that *the Iberian world*, as opposed to the French one, participated in this model. Rama quotes (secondhand) Descartes and the *Logic* of Port-Royal, which are quotes of problematic relevance for Spanish America. Further, Rama objectifies "Western rationality," whose very existence was problematic in Iberia with the force and characteristics that Rama gives it.

In any case, even when it is invoked only in order to point to its limitations, the notion of lettered city has deeply informed past and current research.

Suggested Reading

Adorno, Rolena. "La ciudad letrada y los discursos coloniales." *Hispamérica: Revista de Literatura* 16, no. 48 (1987): 3–24.

Alonso, Carlos. "*Rama y sus retoños*: Figuring the Nineteenth Century in Spanish America." *Revista de Estudios Hispánicos* 28, no. 2 (1994): 283–92.

Castro-Gómez, Santiago. "Los vecindarios de La ciudad letrada: Variaciones filosóficas sobre un tema de Ángel Rama." In Moraña, *Ángel Rama y los estudios latinoamericanos*, 123–33.

Chasteen, John Charles. Introduction to Rama, *The Lettered City*, vii–xiv.

Dabove, Juan Pablo. *Nightmares of the Lettered City: Banditry and Literature in Latin America, 1816–1929*. Pittsburgh, Pa.: Pittsburgh Univsersity Press, 2007.

De la Campa, Román. "El desafío inesperado de *La ciudad letrada*." In Moraña, *Ángel Rama y los estudios latinoamericanos*, 29–53.

———. *Latin Americanism*. Minneapolis: University of Minnesota Press, 1999.

Moraña, Mabel. "De *La ciudad letrada* al imaginario nacionalista: Contribuciones de Ángel Rama a la invención de América." In *Políticas de la escritura en América Latina: De la colonia a la modernidad*, 165–73. Caracas: eXcultura, 1997.

Muñoz, Boris, and Silvia Spitta, eds. *Más allá de la ciudad letrada: Crónicas y espacios urbanos*. Pittsburgh, Pa.: Instituto Internacional de Literatura Iberoamericana, 2003.

Perus, Françoise. "¿Qué nos dice hoy *La ciudad letrada* de Ángel Rama?" *Revista Iberoamericana* 71, no. 211 (2005): 363–72.

Ramos, Julio. *Desencuentros de la modernidad en América Latina: Literatura y política en el siglo XIX*. Mexico City: Fondo de cultura económica, 1989.
Remedi, Gustavo. "Ciudad letrada: Ángel Rama y la espacialización del análisis cultural." In Moraña, *Ángel Rama y los estudios latinoamericanos*. 97–122.

Local-Global

EMESHE JUHÁSZ-MININBERG

The binary term "local-global" is widely used to describe the forces that shape the growing interconnectedness on a planetary scale that characterizes contemporary social processes. In the field of cultural studies, the dynamics of local-global relations constitute a significant frame of reference for the analysis of how those connections occur and their effects. While the term poses a challenge to any clear-cut definition because its uses manifest differing and even conflictive meanings, it has provided an epistemologically productive framework for theoretical considerations of the complex forces involved in contemporary social change. Current processes of globalization have altered the space-time dimensions of human experience, eroding the conceptual boundaries that informed the project of Western modernity—especially those associated with the ideas of the nation-state, of collective identities, and of how economic development is shaped. Human activity, however, is still tied to particular geographic locations, and social practices tend to be contextually referred to a "sense of place"—the experience of a particular location to which there may be varying degrees of attachment through everyday life and/or historical memory of collective imaginaries (Martín Barbero). To refer to the local-global aspects of contemporary social processes is to speak both of the dynamics that shape social contacts and interconnections across physical space and of the new elements of social practices associated with those contacts.

The specific dimensions of what is labeled as local or global vary widely. The term "global" is generally not used to refer to the planet as a whole, but instead to the scope of certain practices that tend both to be territorially ample and to play dominant or hegemonizing roles. The word's usage ranges from the realm of ideas and production of knowledge to the more frequently reported development and dissemination of technologies and means of production, consumer goods, and services. "Global" is also used to name a new conceptual space constructed and traversed by a wide array of practices that promote globalizing processes which contribute, among other things, to the destabilization of traditional paradigms of identity. The term "local" is generally used to speak of a specific locality that constitutes the fundamental point of reference for social actors in their everyday experience. It refers to a particular geopolitical space that can be either a nation-state or another social collectivity of greater or lesser size whose conceptual boundaries of identity may or may not coincide with those of a nation-state.

Growing access to high-speed information technologies and the greater ease of movement of peoples across geographic and political boundaries, however, are transforming how actors think of and relate to what is termed the local sphere.

The idea of what the local encompasses is changing as awareness increases of broader spheres of human activity that are labeled as global (García Canclini). The local and the global are neither natural nor discrete entities. Rather, they are relational concepts constructed through diverse practices that result in systems and structures that shape their boundaries. Appadurai remarks that they are thus fundamentally political concepts.

Contemporary social theory stresses the importance of contextualizing the dynamics of global flows, cautioning against approaches that may cast current processes of globalization as independent forces, with a life of their own, irrespective of the social and institutional practices that shape them. What we identify as global tendencies or flows are collectively constructed by communities, of greater or lesser size, in the context of their everyday life experiences. Mignolo, who studies local-global relations from an epistemological perspective, explains that the currents historically shaping global tendencies to this day emerged from local perspectives that spread throughout the globe in the hegemonizing advance of Western modernity. Informed by Quijano's idea of the coloniality of power, Mignolo maintains that it is precisely this type of power relation that has constituted the articulating element between what he calls "global designs" (the hegemonizing projects of modernity) and the "local histories" (how those projects unfold or are manifested in particular locations). Globalizing projects materialize in the local sphere, manifesting themselves variously according to the locality's sociohistorical circumstances.

Calling attention to the importance of making social actors visible within the processes of globalization, Mato remarks that meaning is constructed in the local sphere in the context of everyday life as global flows are adopted and adapted differentially. Moreover, it is at the local level that power struggles and power asymmetries play out concretely. The local and the global spheres coexist in a negotiated relationship, complementary and contradictory, in contemporary social imaginaries informing everyday life and the participation of actors in processes of social change. To speak of the local is to speak of the global and vice versa. Even as new forms of nonterritorial social activity continue to spread throughout the world, especially via the Internet where specific geographical references tend to have less overt relevance, the content and the style in which the actors relate are both associated with the user's geopolitical location and sociohistorical context (Appadurai; García Canclini). The interconnections between the local and the global shape a social geography of power relations that are configured, situated, and differentially related according to particular geopolitical contexts (Mato; Mignolo).

The use of the term local-global follows two general lines of thought that share a common frame of reference in the debate about the cultural effects of current globalization processes, whether they tend toward homogenization, hybridization, or a resignification of traditional forms.

The first line of thought tends to view local dynamics counterposed to global flows in an antagonistic relationship that expresses the conceptual struggle between those flows with a planetary scope and those that have supposedly a much more limited span and, therefore, insufficient capability to resist the impact of the former. This perspective presupposes a lineal and unidirectional hierarchy of power relations in which global flows constitutes an ever-growing and overpowering force fueled by the dynamics of neoliberal capitalism that consume and erase local particularities, thereby contributing to the inexorable homogenization of social structures and relations around the world. Actors involved in the so-called antiglobalization movements who do not question such a label endorse this perspective because they perceive global-scale flows as a significant threat to dynamics within less encompassing spheres/localities. Tending to consider social practices as unidirectional and discrete from one another, this line of thought is fundamentally concerned with the hegemonizing advances of Western cultural systems and practices, which have played a dominant role in globalization processes. This concern, moreover, informs an important debate in current social theory on how the growing social polarization around the world may be attributed in part to the expanding gap between those who have access and are able to participate in global processes and those who are marginalized from them.

Instead of eradicating the distinctions between center and periphery, according to Hannerz, local-global dynamics have created directional flows that further consolidate asymmetries of power. Contemporary social inequalities must be considered in the context of the networks that emerge from local-global contacts (Martín Barbero), which have played a role in the growing social polarization around the planet. These contacts, nevertheless, have also fostered the formation and consolidation of social movements that seek to address the imbalances in those power relations (Mato).

The second line of thought views local-global dynamics as mutually constitutive forces that are simultaneously integrating and disintegrating. A wide variety of social actors share this perspective, including those involved with the so-called antiglobalization movements who resist such a label, stressing instead the ideas of "alter-globalization" and of "another world is possible." The global and the local are not viewed as opposites; rather, they are seen as mutually informing, thus giving place to networks of differential relations depending on the geopolitical context of the actors' practices. Global flows are differentially adopted and adapted depending on the particular locality, thereby generating new modalities in social practices that, in turn, inform social processes of broader scope. Contemporary cultural imaginaries represent not only what is considered to be their "own" but also their relationships with "other" cultures or imaginaries (García Canclini; Mignolo). Growing worldwide interconnectedness has fostered global cultural imaginaries that have not substituted or displaced local imaginaries but have altered traditional boundaries of discourses and practices. The directionality of local-global flows is not readily apparent because the local involves multiple centers of production, mediation, and consumption—especially considering the increased mobility of peoples across geopolitical borders and the speed and ease with which information travels due to the proliferation of information technologies.

Contemporary social processes evince the ambivalent forces that local-global relations prompt as they simultaneously tend to stimulate homogenization and the accentuation of particular differences. This dynamic, which has been conceptualized in various theoretical models, has been hypothesized as a process of hybridization (García Canclini) or "glocalization" (Robertson). Some social analysts have objected, however, that such models gloss over the conflicts and contradictions inherent to globalization processes. There are those who have, therefore, opted to approach such dynamics as an open process of resignification that compels a fundamental rethinking of how to approach the study of contemporary social processes (Mato; Mignolo).

In Latin America, scholarly study of local-global dynamics includes a reflection concerning the systems of production and dissemination of knowledge, and the role that Latin American scholars and activists play in them (Mato; Richard)—a topic that has received less attention in hegemonic circuits. Scholars and activists from Latin America participate in a variety of activities that integrate the region in processes of global scope, thereby constituting a significant presence in diverse transnational circuits and networks. This has created the opportunity for voices "from" the region to construct discourses about Latin America that circulate more broadly in hegemonic circuits (Richard). Yet Latin American scholars and activists face several great intellectual and practical challenges. There is the issue of how the vast diversity of peoples/voices that collectively constitute what is known as Latin America can contribute differentially to the study of globalization processes while also formulating effective models for political action and social change within particular localities (Richard). There is also the need to develop a vocabulary that is contextually referred to the diverse cultural spaces, yet also serves to articulate them as they face common issues.

The question of how to know "from" a particular locality poses a variety of challenges in a world that is increasingly interconnected. The coloniality of power generated around the world through the project of modernity resulted in a historical subalternization of certain types of knowledge. Mignolo, who studies this matter from the perspective of a U.S.-based scholar, remarks that subaltern voices, with their "colonial difference," are contributing in this increasingly interconnected world to the transformation of established value systems regarding the legitimacy of different types of knowledge. He terms this "border thinking," and traces its emergence in the interstices of local-global flows where disjunctures in the universalizing designs of Western hegemony expose the underpinnings of the process of knowledge production, especially as it is informed by historical conditions that are contextually referred to a particular place and time. In contrast to a unified hegemonizing/globalizing narrative, border thinking is shaped as the subaltern perspective constructs and gives voice to diverse imaginaries, pluralizing the points of inquiry and subject matters. According to Mignolo, this may result in the gradual decolonization of current modes of knowledge production and dissemination. Border thinking may thus transform the ways in which we produce knowledge and meaning, and consequently may foster a critical dialogue that ultimately could translate into effective social and political action aimed at creating a future based on greater social justice and equality throughout the world.

Suggested Reading

Appadurai, Arjun. *Modernity at Large: Cultural Dimensions of Globalization*. Minneapolis: University of Minnesota Press, 1996.

García Canclini, Néstor. *La globalización imaginada*. Mexico City: Paidós, 1999.

———. *Hybrid Cultures: Strategies for Entering and Leaving Modernity*. Translated by Christopher L. Chiappari and Silvia L. López. Minneapolis: University of Minnesota Press, 1995.

Hannerz, Ulf. *Transnational Connections: Culture, People, Places*. London: Routledge, 1996.

Martín Barbero, Jesús. "Desencuentros de la socialidad y reencantamientos de la identidad." *Análisis*, no. 29 (2002): 45–62.

Mato, Daniel. "Desfechitizar la globalización: Basta de reduccionismos, apologías y demonizaciones, mostrar la complejidad de las prácticas y los actores." In Mato, *Estudios latinoamericanos*, 147–77.

Mignolo, Walter. *Local Histories/Global Designs: Coloniality, Subaltern Knowledges, and Border Thinking*. Princeton, N.J.: Princeton University Press, 2000.

O'Riordan, Tim, ed. *Globalism, Localism, and Identity: Fresh Perspectives on the Transition to Sustainability*. London: Earthscan, 2001.

Richard, Nelly. "Globalización académica, estudios culturales y crítica latinoamericana." In Mato, *Estudios latinoamericanos*, 185–99.

Robertson, Roland. "Glocalization: Time-Space and Homogeneity-Heterogeneity." In *Global Modernities*, edited by Mike Featherstone, Scott Lash, and Roland Robertson, 25–44. London: Sage, 1995.

Rosenau, James N. *Distant Proximities: Dynamics Beyond Globalization*. Princeton, N.J.: Princeton University Press, 2003.

Memory

MARCELA VALDATA

From ancient Aristotelian and Platonic concepts to contemporary phenomenological, hermeneutic, and/or existentialist postulates, philosophy has always alluded to polarities such as memory-image, memory-remembrance (or recollection), and memory-representation as different ways of dealing with the opposition of the binary memory-oblivion. A remarkable dynamism has been generated around the polarization of the term, which has since the 1960s offered a wide range of meanings and produced, at the same time, new complementary oppositions. It is at the core of works by Paolo Rossi and Paul Ricoeur, among others.

Dealing with memory implies referring to a past that has been forgotten for various reasons. When the past comes back into action, it needs to be articulated to become memory. Several interpretations emerge from this concept, such as, the past as a former time, the past as a structure of truth, and the past as a traumatic experience.

In the field of history, memories are reconstructed as representations of past events. Those who write or narrate history are in charge of these reconstructions through their (conscious or unconscious) selections or representations, and because these are representations of representations, the concept of "historical truth," the truth of the narrated events recovered by the work of the historian's subjective interpretation, is problematized. What is problematic isn't the opposition "objectivity versus subjectivity," but rather the difficulty of intersubjectivity (witness-historian) and the quest for truth. In France this issue came into play in the realm of historiography, and there was no longer an allusion to objective history, but to a history of history.

Works on oral history published since the 1960s in the United States have been crucial in the recovery of individual experiences of the previous decades. In these accounts the topic of gender and the studies of past recollections in traumatic situations have prevailed. Citing Joël Candau in reference to history, but with applicability to all social sciences, it may be said that "history can become an 'object of memory' in the same way that memory can become a historical object." Verónica Zárate Toscano's *Los nobles ante la muerte en México: Actitudes, ceremonias y memoria, 1750–1850*, for example, approaches the ways the nobility of New Spain dealt with death vis-à-vis their everyday practice, value system, and worldview.

The boom of testimonial works evolved into life stories and became the source of studies called "recent history." These represent a different notion of the past, one linked to the idea of memory as today's narration of yesterday's tormented past experience, but in which a future projection that would avoid its repetition is possible. In Tzvetan Todorov's distinction between "literal memory" and "exemplary memory," there is an attempt to separate details and consequences of the events in order to view past experiences as passages toward the present and the future.

The works of Pierre Nora, mainly *Rethinking France = Les lieux de mémoire*, show the link between history and memory. Memory, according to Nora, involves images, people, and facts. He recognizes these "sites of memory" as symbolic places, physical spaces, marks, remains of memory, and proposes that these "sites" have been reduced to "commemorations of patrimonial heritage."

When Nora points out that "modern memory is archival," he leads us to consider the construction of memory sites in Latin America, particularly the archives of repression. These spaces, which today are denominated sites of memory, acquire a functional polyvalence in relation to their past as sites of political persecution, kidnapping, and death and their current transformation into spaces for the reconstruction or recovery of historical memories, legal vindication, and commemoration. Among them we can mention the Police Archives in Paraguay, the Rio de Janeiro Public State Archive of the Department of Political and Social Order in Brazil, the Guatemala National Police Archives, and the Buenos Aires Department of Police Intelligence Archives in Argentina, where research on the logic of repression and extermination by the dictatorships also contributes to the truth trials.

According to Pierre Nora, the relationship between historiography, heritage, politics, and memory sites encourages the development of thematic areas linked to identity, particularly national identity, even though anthropology has normally been the discipline dealing with these topics. Anthropology has developed by operating on the diversity of past recollections, mainly working with preliterate societies that have been traditionally viewed as "societies without history." Past scenes in these societies are transmitted from one generation to the next, vertically from the old to the young, in a context and a time that are specific to each culture. The narratives are conceived as group memory, even when they refer to personal experiences; this might be thought of as a declarative memory, as narrated by witnesses, and whose function is to keep the past alive. The works on memory with preliterate societies refer us to two fundamental aspects: the reproduction of cosmogony and myths, and the resignification of (individual and collective) history, whose gaze is placed in a past that is more highly esteemed than the present. These societies reinforce their oral tradition by devoting their lives to remembering the wealth of their inherited memories.

The place of memory in reference to Latin American anthropological studies may be divided into two analytical categories: identity and representation. In works relating to identity, the use of the term presents a double articulation between what is hidden and what is absent. Anthropological techniques employed in fieldwork have resulted in two types of descriptions: representations and interpretations. The aim to acknowledge cultural diversity sets these studies apart from historical works regarding the search for truth. Among the vast number of Latin American investigations centered on contemporary indigenous issues, we can mention the works of Patricia Medina Melgarejo on the memory of the Yoreme Mayo of Sinaloa, Mexico, which deals with the construction of territoriality. In this work, memory is considered "a process and product built by social relationships and practices, where language and communication have a main role."

In South America, most research on memory has centered on the marks left by ruling dictatorships between 1960 and 1980, and the presence of indigenous voices. Among them, we can mention the studies of Ponciano del Pino on Uchuraccay, Peru, where an Andean farming community murdered eight journalists; we can also cite cases of the disappearances during a power blackout in Ledesma, in northern Argentina, studied in an article by Ludmila da Silva Catela, and of three small communities, Neltume, Liquiñe, and Chihuío, in southern Chile, investigated by Claudio Barrientos, both in the context of political violence (see Pino and Jelin). These studies question testimony as a tool in the search for truth and its relationship to publications whose antecedents we can find in North American cultural research.

These individual memories that include the subjective imprint of witnesses are inexorably framed within social contexts. Maurice Halbwachs has been a key reference in the use of the term "memory." His sociological definition of the notion of collective memory as a concept employed in explaining social phenomena has come to acquire a practical character useful in considering some forms of the past (conscious or unconscious) shared by a collective or a group of individuals. According to this author, individual memory is not opposed to collective memory, but rather the two interconnect.

Since the publication of *Nunca más* in Argentina in the 1980s, testimony has taken center stage in cultural debates about memory. The reports about state terrorism from 1976 to 1983 set in motion the demands for justice for disappeared/murdered victims. The legal proceedings against the military juntas in 1985, and the pardons that followed, led to a multiplicity of testimonies that began to configure different memory sites with the goal of preventing the repetition of these experiences. Written testimonial production by survivors of concentration camps was based on concepts taken from the works of Primo Levi, whose experience in Auschwitz has been a reference for Latin American testimonies. Survival in these liminal situations places the individual within the symbolic gaps of trauma. Dori Laub, a childhood survivor of the Holocaust, speaks of the concern for honesty in the testimony, which is consistent with the need for the recipient to trust what the witness is narrating. Shoshana Felman and Dori Laub claim that this testimony is a genuine imprint of the real, that it allows witnesses to find their own imprint and to readjust to phenomenological reality. Felman distinguishes between truth in discourse and truth in action. The former is the discourse of seduction of power, or an interest group, that makes it believable. In opposition, truth in the act subverts all power and disarms all codes. Laub proposes a parallel between psychoanalytical listening and testimonial listening. Autobiographical testimony, on the other hand, may present the dichotomy between what is reality and what is fiction. It does not entail a search for historical truth: the person emitting the testimony speaks in the first person, although he or she represents a collective seldom enunciated. Singularity is centered within the narration of cultural aspects that can never be identified with the recipient. One such testimony is that of Aurora Arnáiz Amigó, who lost her son and her husband during the Spanish Civil War and went into exile in Mexico. She was able to reconstruct her experience only in conversations with other members of Juventudes Socialistas of the period before the Spanish Civil War. Another paradigmatic example of autobiographical testimony is that of the Guatemalan activist Rigoberta Menchú Tum. Her personal conviction and sense of justice resulted in the government listing her as an enemy and forcing her to flee. Another interesting case is that of Domitila Barrios de Chúngara, a leader of the Bolivian people in resisting oppression. Her goal was to improve the living conditions of the poor in the country, for which she was exiled to Europe.

Latin American literature has been very prolific in the description of the erased or forgotten past. Among the most important works are *La casa y el viento* by the Argentinean Héctor Tizón and *Rumbo al sur deseando el norte* by Ariel Dorfman of Chile, as well as most of the fictional works of Paraguay's Augusto Roa Bastos. The endeavor of the Universidad Nacional de Misiones in Argentina in publishing *Los libros de la memoria* is noteworthy. This collection spans the migratory movements of the nineteenth and early twentieth centuries, and the struggles for social justice, viewed as epic events, and also includes essays written by relatives of disappeared and murdered victims during the most recent Argentine military dictatorship.

In addition, these testimonies are part of the collections of archives and museums, public and private, whose foundational aim has been to organize lost or scattered memory. Among them we can mention Parque por la Paz in Santiago, Chile, located in the former concentration camp Villa Grimaldi, and, in Argentina, the Museo de la Memoria in Rosario, the ESMA Museum (Escuela Mecánica de la Armada) in Buenos Aires, and Mansion Seré in Morón, all former centers of detention, abduction, and death.

Suggested Reading

Calveiro, Pilar. *Desapariciones*. Mexico City: Taurus, 2002.

Candau, Joël. *Antropología de la memoria*. Buenos Aires: Nueva Visión, 2002.

Felman, Shoshana, and Dori Laub, *Testimony: Crises of Witnessing in Literature, Psychoanalysis, and History*. New York: Routledge, 1992.

Halbwachs, Maurice. *La mémoire collective*. Paris: Presses Universitaires de France, 1950. Edited and translated by Lewis A. Coser as *On Collective Memory* (Chicago: University of Chicago Press, 1992).

Jelin, Elizabeth, ed. *Memorias de la represión*. Buenos Aires: Siglo XXI, 2003.

———. *State Repression and the Labors of Memory*. Translated by Judy Rein and Marcial Godoy-Anativia. Minneapolis: University of Minnesota Press, 2003.

Levi, Primo. *Survival in Auschwitz: The Nazi Assault on Humanity*. Translated by Stuart Woolf. New York: Simon & Schuster, 1996.

Medina Malgareno, Patricia. "¿Derechos y políticas de la memoria? Un relato desde el pueblo *yoreme mayo* de Sinaloa, México." Records of the Primer Congreso Latinoamericano de Antropología, "Formas inéditas de la memoria indígena en la construcción de la territorialidad," Rosario, Argentina, July 11–15, 2005.

Nora, Pierre. *Rethinking France = Les lieux de mémoire*. Translated by Mary Trouille. Vol. 1. Chicago: University of Chicago Press, 2001.

Nunca más: Informe de la Comisión Nacional sobre la Desaparición de Personas. Buenos Aires: EUDEBA, 1999.

Pino, Ponciano del, and Elizabeth Jelin, eds. *Luchas locales, comunidades e identidades*. Madrid: Siglo XXI, 2003.

Ricoeur, Paul. *Memory, History, Forgetting*. Translated by Kathleen Blamey and David Pellauer. Chicago: University of Chicago Press, 2004.

Zárate Toscano, Verónica. *Los nobles ante la muerte en México: Actitudes, ceremonias y memoria, 1750–1850*. Mexico City: Colegio de México/Instituto Mora, 2000.

Modernity

SAURABH DUBE

In everyday and academic understandings, being modern and enacting modernity repeatedly appear as a transcending of tradition, as a break with what existed before. Indeed, even those academic, literary, and political discourses that argue for the coexistence of the traditional and the modern do so by treating the two as discrete domains, which are then seen as being variously conjoined (García Canclini, *Hybrid Cultures*). All of this rests on powerful, contending, visceral images of tradition and modernity that have dense worldly, or ontological, attributes. It is important to reconsider these questions, especially by approaching formations of modernity as always particular yet already global.

Abiding Antinomies

For a long time now, formidable oppositions between static, traditional communities and dynamic, modern societies have played an important role in understandings of history and culture. At first, the duality might seem to be little more than an ideological plank of "modernization theory," counterposing (primarily non-Western) tradition with (chiefly Western) modernity. But the antinomy has wider implications and deeper underpinnings (Dube, *Stitches*). It is not only that the duality has animated and articulated other enduring oppositions, such as those between ritual and rationality, myth and history, community and state, magic and the modern, and emotion and reason. It is also that as a lasting legacy of the developmental idea of universal, natural history and an aggrandizing representation of an exclusive, Western modernity, such antinomies have found varied expressions among the distinct subjects that they have named, described, and objectified since at least the eighteenth century (Dube, "Anthropology").

Representations emanating from the European Enlightenment have played a key role here. It has been generally accepted that the period of the Enlightenment was accompanied by ideas and processes of the secularization of Judeo-Christian time (Fabian 26–27, 146–47). In this context, discrete yet overlaying developmental schemes underwrote grand designs of human history, from the rationalist claims of Voltaire and Kant to the historicist frames of Giambattista Vico and Johann Gottfried von Herder.

There was profound contention among such schemas, yet in different ways they each projected developmental blueprints of universal history (Kelley 211–62). Such contrary strains and convergent emphases were bound to the fact, often overlooked, that the Enlightenment was as much historical as philosophical, as much about the rewriting of history as about the rethinking of philosophy. The consequences were limited yet significant. Throughout the nineteenth century but also afterwards Judeo-Christian and Messianic time and temporality did not lose their influence in Western worlds (Moore; Crapanzano). Conversely, by the second half of the nineteenth century, at the very least in the Protestant West, secularized time could acquire a naturalized aura, and developmental thought was distilled (uncertainly and contradictorily, yet potently and powerfully) as historical progress.

It only followed that time came to be increasingly mapped in hierarchical ways to plot peoples and cultures in the movement of history projected as the passage of progress. Frequently articulated by the ur-opposition between the primitive and the civilized, in place here nonetheless was neither a singular Western "self" nor an exclusive non-Western "other." Rather, at play in this terrain were the cultural severalty of Western selves and the historical hierarchies of non-Western otherness. In this scenario, many peoples (for example, Africans, African Americans, and indigenous groups in the Americas and across the world) were still stuck in the stage of barbarism and savagery with few prospects of advancement. Other societies (for example, those of India and China) had reached the ascending steps of civilization, yet lacked the critical foundations of reason. Still other people (chiefly of Western and Northern European stock) had evolved to the higher reaches of humanity through advantages of race and rationality and propensities of history and nationality. Indeed, it was the past and the present of this last set of people, comprising the enlightened European elect, that was seized on and rendered as a looking-glass at large. In this mirror was envisioned the universal history of human destiny—a destiny represented as groups and societies either failing before or rising to the stage of modernity.

The idea of modernity involves a break with the past. Its narrative intimates ruptures with ritual and magic and breaches with enchantment and tradition. Following authoritative understandings (Habermas, *Philosophical Discourse*; Koselleck 3–20), as an epochal concept, modernity has been seen as embodying a distinct and new status from preceding periods, insinuating essentially novel orientations to the past, present, and future.

These are persuasive arguments that carry their own truths, but they also present modernity in rather idealized terms. At the same time, precisely for these reasons, the understandings are acutely representative.

To begin with, authoritative and commonplace understandings of modernity project it as a phenomenon generated purely internally within the West, albeit one that was later variously exported to other parts of humanity. It follows that exactly this measure serves to override the dynamic of the colonizer and the colonized, race and reason, and Enlightenment and empire that underlies modernity as history. These twin procedures announce salient registers of hierarchical mappings of time and space. In both conscious and inadvertent ways, the registers involve two simultaneous measures. Rehearsing the West as modernity, they equally stage modernity "*as* the West" (Mitchell 15).

The idea of modernity as a coming apart from the past rests on the imagination of ruptures within Western history. But such an idea cannot help also turning on the importance of disjunctions of the West with non-Western worlds, whether explicitly or implicitly. On the one hand, the caesura defined by modernity as the new beginning is shifted onto the past, "precisely to the start of modern times" in Europe (Habermas, *Philosophical Discourse* 5). It is ahead of this threshold that the present is seen as being renewed in its vitality and novelty under modernity. On the other hand, exactly when the modern is privileged as the most recent period, the novelty and vitality of modernity confront specters of the "medieval," the "superstitious," the "prophetic," and the "spiritual" meandering in their midst. These spirits are a prior presence *and* an ongoing process. Each attempt to engage them in the present entails marking them as an attribute of the past. My reference is to the ways in which, in dominant representations, the Taliban and Al-Qaeda are simultaneously "coeval" and "medieval"; and the manner in which in pervasive understandings the enchantments today of *los indios* and *lo primitivo* are at once contemporary yet anachronistic.

Subjects of Modernity

But what exactly is modernity? I suggest that modernity needs to be understood as turning on distinct historical processes over the last five centuries. Here are to be found processes entailing, for example, commerce and consumption, reason and science, industry and technology, nation-state and citizen-subject, public spheres and private spaces, and secularized religions and disenchanted knowledges. At the same time, here are to be registered procedures involving empires and colonies, race and genocide, resurgent faiths and reified traditions, disciplinary regimes and subaltern subjects, and magic of the state and enchantments of the modern.

These processes are not subject-less procedures. Rather, they emerge expressed by subjects of modernity, subjects who have engaged and elaborated the stipulations of modernity as history. Here it is patently inadequate to conflate the *subject of modernity* with the *modern subject*. What do I mean by this? Influential discussions and commonplace conceptions of modernity have frequently proceeded by envisioning the phenomenon in the image of the European and Euro-American, also often male, modern subject. In contrast, in speaking of subjects of modernity, I am referring to historical actors who have been active participants in processes of modernity, both *subject to* these processes and also *subjects shaping* these processes.

Over the past few centuries, the subjects of modernity have included, for example, indigenous communities in the Americas under colonial and national rule, peoples of African descent not only on that continent but in different diasporas across the world, and, indeed, subaltern, marginal, and elite women and men in non-Western and Western theaters. In the Latin American instance, the subjects of modernity have consisted not merely of the Westernized, progressive middle classes but of *campesinos*, *indios*, and *trabajadores* that have diversely articulated processes of colony and post-colony.

Time after time, subjects of modernity have revealed that there are different ways of being modern. They have now accessed and now exceeded the determinations of the modern subject, suggesting the need to rethink its exclusivity. Yet subjects of modernity have also betrayed scant regard for the niceties of the modern subject exactly while articulating modernity. Here it bears emphasis that there are other modern subjects besides Western ones. The various modern subjects, in the West and the non-West, are also subjects of modernity, but not all subjects of modernity are modern subjects. All these different subjects have registered within their measures and meanings the formative contradictions, contentions, and contingencies of modernity.

Modernity and Latin America

Intimations of modernity have been long present in Latin America, generally reflected in the image of a reified Europe. The region has itself been envisioned, uneasily yet readily, as part of the Western world, albeit with specific lacks and within particular limits. All of this is a result of dominant mappings and authoritative "metageographies" (Lewis and Wigen), which have split the world into the Occident and the Orient, the East and West, shored up by discourses of Orientalism (Said) and Occidentalism (Coronil, "Beyond Occidentalism"), formidably present in aesthetic and everyday expressions (Paz, *Vislumbres*).

Indeed, in Latin America, as in most of the non-Western world, such blueprints have emerged conjoined with the modern stipulation decreeing that modernity had already happened somewhere else (Morris). If this has generated among Latin American moderns the anxiety of looking unoriginal, it has also led them to a variety of searches for a distinctively national modern, modernism, and modernity, as one poised between the West and the Rest. (Unsurprisingly, diverse "indigenist" and "primitivist" discourses and representations have often played a critical role here.) In early and mid-twentieth-century Mexico, for example, we only need to think of the works and lives not merely of Diego Rivera and Frida Kahlo but also of Los Contemporáneos such as Jorge Cuesta and Salvador Novo. The point is that discussions of modernism—in their simultaneously republican and authoritarian, political and aesthetic, and governmental and everyday avatars—have provided some of the most sustained understandings of narratives of modernity in Latin America (Rama, *La ciudad letrada*; Sommer, *Foundational Fictions*; Ramos, *Desencuentros*; Franco, *Plotting Women*), a tendency that continues into the present (Franco, *Decline and Fall*; González Echevarría). It is against this background, then, that we need to consider three broad sets of recent discussions of modernity in Latin America, which have all put a question mark on facile polarities between prolific modernisms and deficient modernization in the region as expressed by influential authors (Paz, *Ogro*; Cabrujas).

First, considering the relationship between empire and modernity, questions of colonialism have been often understood in Latin America as occupying the locus of a dim and distant past. Against these dominant dispositions, an important body of critical thought on Latin America today (Dussel, *La invención*; Quijano; Lander; Mignolo, *Darker Side*; *Local Histories*) focuses on the subterranean schemes and the overwrought apparitions of the modern and the colonial, joining other key conversations (Chakrabarty, *Provincializing Europe*; Chatterjee). In other words, this corpus critically considers the place and presence of colonial stipulations of knowledge/power within modern provisions of power/knowledge. Consequently, such moves have also held a mirror up to modernity as a deeply ideological project and a primary apparatus of domination—in the past and the present.

Second, in recent years, the notion of the magic of the modern has found interesting articulations, especially in critical anthropology and cultural studies, including of Latin America. An important influence here has been exerted by the ideas of Marx on the fetishism of commodities and capital and the magic of markets and money. In the past, analytical endeavor could subsume such suggestions of Marx to his related emphases on reification and alienation (Taussig, *Devil*). But the newer writings register the interplay between the magical and the modern as more critically constitutive of social worlds (Owen; LiPuma; Meyer and Pels; During). It is in these ways that recent work on Latin America and the Caribbean has provided fresh meanings to discussions of the magic/insanity of capitalism and colonialism (Taussig, *My Cocaine*; *Shamanism*; Price) and of the fetish/reification of state and nation (Coronil, *Magical State*), while related exercises (Taussig, *Defacement*) have moved toward the simultaneous evocation and defacement of power, pointing to the sacred character of modern sovereignty, in order to re-enchant modernity through surrealistic representation and writing, ecstatic thought and theory.

Third and finally, a variety of writings on Latin America (and the Caribbean) have saliently explored critical issues of modernity and its margins. The questions have found multiple expressions of course in a range of scholarship on the region, from discussions of architecture and built form (Fraser; Lejeune) to those of peasant and popular politics (Mallon, *Courage*; Stern, *Battling*; *Remembering*; Thurner), space and territoriality (A. Alonso; Radcliffe), culture and consumption (Yúdice, *Expediency*), and representation and subalternity (Beverley, *Subalternity*; Rodriguez, *Latin American Subaltern Studies*; Rabasa, *Writing Violence*; Bartra, *El salvaje*; G. Williams). At the same time, my point concerns work that has explicitly engaged historical and contemporary terms, textures, and transformations of modernity. In this terrain, the explorations have ranged from influential considerations of the hetero-temporal coordinates of national time-space (García Canclini, *Culturas híbridas*) to those of the mutual articulations and mediations of modernity and nation (Lomnitz-Adler, *Exits*; *Modernidad*; Tenorio-Trillo; Saldaña-Portillo; Overmyer-Velázquez). They have engaged issues of: piety, intimacy, embodiment, and image under entwined regimes of modernity and religion (Lester; Voekel; Bernand and Gruzinski); modernity in its baroque formations (Echeverría) and its vernacular configurations (Rappaport; Coronil, *Magical State*); and, crucially, wide-ranging, acute contradictions and contentions of modernity (Palmié; Fischer; Redfield; D. Scott). Together, here are to be found works focusing on different articulations of modernity as historically grounded and/or culturally expressed, articulations that query a-priori projections and sociological formalism underpinning the category-entity (for such writings in other contexts, see Rofel; Donham; Comaroff and Comaroff; Harootunian; Chakrabarty, *Provincializing Europe*; *Habitations*; Dube, *Stitches*; *Postcolonial Passages*; *Enchantments*). Unsurprisingly, in Latin America and elsewhere, formations and elaborations of modernity are increasingly discussed and debated today as contradictory and contingent processes of culture and power, as checkered and contested histories of meaning and mastery.

Suggested Reading

Asad, Talal. *Genealogies of Religion: Discipline and Reasons of Power in Christianity and Islam*. Baltimore: Johns Hopkins University Press, 1993.

Coronil, Fernando. *The Magical State: Nature, Money, and Modernity in Venezuela*. Chicago: University of Chicago Press, 1997.

Crapanzano, Vincent. *Serving the Word: Literalism in America from the Pulpit to the Bench*. New York: New Press, 2000.

Dube, Saurabh, ed. *Enchantments of Modernity: Empire, Nation, Globalization*. New Delhi/New York: Routledge, 2009.

Dube, Saurabh, Ishita Banerjee-Dube, and Walter D. Mignolo, eds. *Modernidades coloniales: Otros pasados, historias presentes*. Mexico City: Colegio de México, 2004.

Fabian, Johannes. *Time and the Other: How Anthropology Makes Its Object*. New York: Columbia University Press, 1983.

Habermas, Jürgen. *The Philosophical Discourse of Modernity: Twelve Lectures*. Translated by Frederick Lawrence. Cambridge, Mass.: MIT Press, 1987.

Koselleck, Reinhart. *Futures Past: On the Semantics of Historical Time*. Translated by Keith Tribe. Cambridge, Mass.: MIT Press, 1985.

Ramos, Julio. *Desencuentros de la modernidad en América Latina: Literatura y política en siglo XIX*. Mexico City: Fondo de Cultura Económica, 1989.

Rofel, Lisa. *Other Modernities: Gendered Yearnings in China after Socialism*. Berkeley: University of California Press, 1998.

Multiculturalism

DESIRÉE A. MARTÍN (TRANSLATED BY NICHOLAS SANCHEZ)

There is no doubt that multiculturalism as a concept has a very different application in the United States than in Mexico and the rest of Latin America. During the twentieth century, the concept of multiculturalism spread throughout Anglo-Saxon countries such as Canada and the United States, where it continues to be employed as an official national ideology (in the case of Canada) and as an educational and political practice (especially as the root of the civil rights movement in the United States); the term itself remains more frequently used in Anglo-Saxon countries than in the rest of the world. In Canada, for example, the federal government ratified the Canadian Multiculturalism Act, which legalized official bilingualism and multiculturalism in 1971. The Act was integrated into the national constitution in 1982 (Dupont and Lemarchand 309). While in Latin America what has been called "cultural pluralism" by Néstor García Canclini, "heterogeneity" by Antonio Cornejo Polar, "transculturation" by Fernando Ortiz and by Ángel Rama, "hybridity" by Cornejo Polar and by García Canclini, and *mestizaje* is considered an intrinsic part of the nation, in the United States the debate surrounding multiculturalism has been intensely polarizing, creating divisions and pointing to the "separated coexistence of ethnic groups" (García Canclini, *Consumers* 10; see also Aguilar Rivera 13).

Here we have the fundamental dilemma of multiculturalism in the United States and a country like Mexico: the confrontation of views between integration and separatism of culturally diverse nations. As García Canclini and Aguilar Rivera suggest, certain characteristics of multiculturalism today, such as cultural mixture and hybridization, make up the foundational Mexican myth of *mestizaje*. However, in the United States a foundational mythology of hybridity never existed, and the mixture (miscegenation) of distinct races, black and white above all, has historically been considered a weakness at best, if not a total scandal (Cornwell and Stoddard 11–12). In spite of their respective integrationist narratives, both *mestizaje* and multiculturalism tend to produce reductionist and essentialist ideologies and identities. George Yúdice compares *mestizaje* with "Anglo-Saxon conformity," in the sense that both concepts establish normative limits of national identity, effectively excluding diverse racial and regional groups or social classes. But he also indicates that the identitarian system of multiculturalism in the United States, precisely because it privileges the supposed lack of "U.S. normativity"—the idea that there is not only one way of being American—ends up being extremely normative and "North America–centric" (in García Canclini, *Consumers* xxxvii–xxxviii). That is, the normative system of multiculturalism could determine student enrollment in certain classes according to their ethnic origins, or influence our expectations about the conduct of certain groups. Although the mythology of *mestizaje* has been criticized at great length for its implicitly exclusionist and racist characteristics, it would seem that multiculturalism can also be as exclusive as it is inclusive.

Multiculturalism in the United States

Multiculturalism in the United States arises from the conflictive history of the 1960s, and the civil rights movement is related to juridical demands in favor of minority groups for equality in employment and education. The most significant accomplishment of the civil rights movement was undoubtedly the ratification of the Civil Rights Act of 1964, whose Title VI abolished racial segregation in all public schools and institutions of higher education, as it denies federal funds to schools that do not provide unrestricted access to education. Meanwhile, Title VII of the Act mandated equality of employment opportunities, prohibiting employment discrimination on the basis of race, color, religion, ethnic group, sex, or national origin. On the basis of this legislation, the policy of affirmative action was developed, which attempted to remedy the discriminations historically suffered by disadvantaged groups through benefits such as favorable admission policies in schools and universities and student scholarships that promote diversity (Rhoads et al. 197–98). From the end of the 1970s, with the case of University of California vs. Bakke (1978) and the appearance of a strong right-wing politics under the presidencies of Ronald Reagan and George Bush, a violent reaction erupted against affirmative action and equal opportunity programs for employment, housing, and education in general that continues to the current day.

In broader terms, U.S. multiculturalism is characterized by the transition from a monocultural and assimilationist model—which in reality it never was; for example, blacks in the United States were considered completely inassimilable to the nation until the 1940s—to one that is integrationist and resistant to reductionist monoculturalism. Therefore, it can be said that identity and difference form the theoretical frame of multiculturalism and its debates, a frame that becomes the axis that relates the pedagogical structure and politics to the multicultural (Goldberg 12). It is precisely this link between identity and difference, pedagogy and politics that establishes the kinship between multiculturalism and cultural studies in the United States. Cultural studies is at the same time a transdisciplinary academic field and a political project, whose intellectual and political impulse is to challenge and disarticulate hierarchies of power, be they academic, economic, or political. Hence, as Lauren Berlant and Michael Warner affirm, cultural studies proposes to be a space of intellectual activity where multicultural histories can be located that historically have been forgotten or invalidated (108).

Nevertheless, in spite of the possibility that the academic analysis of identity and difference can destabilize broader concepts of national homogeneity or hegemonic identities, there are certain inherent dangers to the theoretical frame of identity and difference. In the first place, according to David Theo Goldberg, identity, which is conceptualized as a link or affinity—undoubtedly affirmative—between members of this or that collectivity, can also exclude subjects who do not belong to the group or whom the group does not allow to enter (12). In the same way, identity can become its own prison, as it tends to determine certain behavioral guidelines or solidarity requirements. Difference, likewise, is as capable of excluding as including, and, as Goldberg argues, there exists a long and violent history of racial, religious, and gender-based exclusions in the name of difference—one has only to think of the Holocaust, or religious fundamentalism of any nature (12–13). In addition, it is imperative to remember that multiculturalism does not necessarily critique or disarticulate power structures, but rather can end up reinforcing them or even being directly co-opted by them, as occurs in so-called "corporate multiculturalism" (Berlant and Warner 115). Under this label we find the implicit defense of "tokenism," or formulism, where, according to Goldberg, the centrist academy and multinational companies celebrate a cultural diversity that corresponds to the principles of philosophical liberalism in general without redistributing power or economic resources at all (7).

Following the warnings of Yúdice, we must contemplate the relativist implications of a multiculturalism that is presumed to be "nonessentialist" and "nonfoundational." That is to say, the insistence on a lack of U.S. normativity tends to impose another type of multicultural normativity which is equally dominant. And this normativity is not necessarily affirmative. The appeal to cultural relativism, with its insistence on a singular truth relative to the group that espouses it, with or without justification or a way of verifying it, can be catastrophic (in García Canclini, *Consumers* 15). The Irish critic David Lloyd indicates that the rhetoric of inclusion and diversity that characterizes the U.S. educational system in general and the university in particular tends to institutionalize a principle of equivalence among all ethnoracial groups—including Anglo-Saxons. The pluralist vision of U.S. culture and history is situated precisely in this principle of equivalence and interchangeability (19). According to Lloyd, the fundamental contradiction of the classroom, in which the minority subject is obliged to forget the way in which she is negated by the subject category through which she is constituted, cannot be vindicated with mere inclusivity, as occurs, for example, in the famous revisions of literary canons (37–38). Berlant and Warner recognize that we still need to theorize a multicultural criticism from the margins that does not reaffirm and duplicate the rhetoric of center and margin (132).

Multiculturalism in Mexico

Daniel Mato insists that concepts like "cultural studies" and related concepts such as multiculturalism should not be translated literally from the Anglo into the Latin American context. In the same way, echoing the warnings of Lloyd and of Berlant and Warner, Hermann Herlinghaus and Mabel Moraña assert that it is necessary to develop "a radical reformulation" of the discussion surrounding modernity in Latin America, in which "it is not enough to assume the margins as a 'theme,' but rather it is necessary to convert the margins into the point of departure for decolonizing thought"—always keeping in mind, of course, that Latin America constitutes a marginal place from a U.S. or European perspective (13, translation ours). If we consider that the perspectives of Mato and of Herlinghaus and Moraña are a challenge to studies *about* Latin America, it would seem that the employment of "Western" concepts such as multiculturalism could reinforce the marginalization of the region. On the other hand, English political scientist Rachel Sieder points out that the application of multiculturalism in Latin America represents nothing less than the defeat of integrationist rhetoric, but void of *mestizaje* or hybridity, in favor of a "politics of difference" based in constitutional reform, politico-juridical legislation, and the right of indigenous self-determination (1–2). It becomes clear that both models of multiculturalism—the model that attempts to proceed *from*, and the other that presumes to be *about* Latin America—look to disarticulate hierarchies of power, but sometimes the debate induces a dialogue of the deaf, dead-ending in mutual incomprehension.

Aguilar Rivera proposes not only to establish a dialogue between multiculturalists in Mexico and the United States, but also to trace out a common history of multiculturalism on both sides of the border. For Aguilar Rivera, multiculturalism is above all a "persuasion" that tries to convince us of "the explicit necessity of the symbolic recognition of minorities" (15, translation ours). Even if this recognition—and the very definition of what constitutes a minority group—takes very different forms in the two countries, Aguilar Rivera prefers to focus on the coincidences rather than the divergences between Mexican and U.S. national experiences. For example, he stresses the similarities between Mexico and the United States in terms of the creation of national identity myths such as *mestizaje* and the melting pot. These myths presuppose different axes of integration, considering that *mestizaje* is a "metaphor of a result," while the melting pot is a "metaphor of transformation," but in the end both look above all to assimilate differences (93).

Nevertheless, in another sense Aguilar Rivera distorts the distinctions between Mexican and U.S. multiculturalism, proclaiming, "The United States is a culturally uniform country that is thought to be diverse, while Mexico is a multicultural country that is presumed to be uniform" (18, translation ours). This declaration is incredible, as it contradicts the dominant rhetoric of integration in both countries—that of mestizo assimilation in Mexico and of racial and cultural harmony in the United States. Here Aguilar Rivera is referring to the presence of groups that do not conform to the myth of *mestizaje*, such as Chinese immigrants and Jewish communities. He also adds that there are certain groups who frankly do not integrate into the Mexican nation for reasons of language, degree of interaction with or isolation from dominant society, and degree of autonomy, such as the Amish, Mennonites, and some Mormon sects. The problem is that Aguilar Rivera confuses ethnoracial difference with national-cultural difference, or uses the two terms interchangeably. That is, as Yúdice suggests, from the Latin American point of view, identity is rooted principally in the nation, while (ethnoracial) U.S. identity politics frequently seems to divide the nation (*Expediency* 59).

Another fundamental axis of multiculturalism in Mexico, and in Latin America in general, is the mass media. The dissemination and consumption of communications media, such as radio, television, film, and the Internet, have perhaps been the principal means of cultural and political integration for multiple and fragmentary sites such as the city, the nation, and the global community. According to García Canclini, the consumption of goods and of the mass media today has replaced the "abstract rules of democracy or collective participation in public spaces" in the creation of citizens (*Consumers* 15). Megacities like Mexico City are spaces that "are reordered multiculturally" through the negotiation of consumption and commercialization. Also, although some communications media in Mexico, such as television and video, have been dominated by conglomerates connected to the state—as has been the case with Televisa—video, radio, and the Internet in particular are key sites of indigenous self-determination and decolonization. Nonetheless, as Jesús Martín Barbero and Ana María Ochoa Gautier warn, multiculturalism implies more than "just giving space to local excluded cultures . . . it also has to do with understanding the manner in which profound stories of identity and memory are recycled in the shifting course of sound and audiovisual aesthetics." And to be truly "multicultural," the consumption and production of goods or mass media must necessarily stop being "mere sums of typified differences and [become] the intersubjective interpellation of the other" (122, translation ours).

Critiques of Multiculturalism

Finally, returning to the problem of the normativity of multiculturalism that Yúdice raises, it is evident that in Latin America it remains necessary to struggle with assimilation or the rejection of multiculturalism as it has been practiced in the United States, rooted in identity and difference. Authors such as García Canclini and Aguilar Rivera do not intend to formulate a nationalist Latin American opposition to this type of multiculturalism, but instead dialogue from a local as well as global Latin American perspective in order to dismantle and reorder the homogenizing tendencies and the appeal to cultural relativism that frequently characterizes multiculturalism in the United States. Meanwhile in the United States, as Lloyd and Berlant and Warner assert, lately the relationship between multiculturalism and globalization has been recognized and more profoundly critiqued.

But if proponents are not to export multiculturalism in a multicultural way, it is necessary to decenter the North American and Anglo-Saxon gaze, and this is perhaps possible only if we first confront the rupture of multiculturalism—that is, the simultaneity of an ideology of cultural plurality and one of homogenization and absolute intolerance. According to Slavoj Žižek, contemporary "postmodern" racism is the symptom of multicultural late capitalism, considering that the other is valorized to the extent that it lacks content from the tolerant "liberal" perspective—take, for example, the proliferation of world music and ethnic cuisine—while alterity or *real* otherness is denounced completely (37). The real difference, the inassimilable type referred to by Aguilar Rivera, is horrifying because it denies the homogenizing impulse behind multiculturalism, according to the French philosopher Alain Badiou (24). In this way, multiculturalism brings a sort of racism "with a distance" that establishes the implicit inferiority of the other by means of the supposed respect for and distance from diverse cultures (Žižek 44). All cultures can be equally valuable, but are interpreted and assimilated from a privileged, universalist reference point that controls the mechanisms of interpretation and knowledge. In this sense, the challenge of multiculturalism in Latin America and the United States perhaps goes further than a careful interrogation of the U.S. gaze versus the Latin American gaze and their respective integrationist and separatist tendencies, even though this is essential. The true challenge is to maintain a reflexive critique of multiculturalism as a confrontation of views between pluralism and homogeneity.

Suggested Reading

Aguilar Rivera, José Antonio. *El sonido y la furia: La persuasión multicultural en México y Estados Unidos*. Mexico City: Taurus, 2004.

Badiou, Alain. *Ethics: An Essay on the Understanding of Evil*. Translated by Peter Hallward. London: Verso, 2001.

Berlant, Lauren, and Michael Warner. "Introduction to 'Critical Multiculturalism.'" In *Multiculturalism: A Critical Reader*, edited by David Theo Goldberg, 107–13. Oxford: Blackwell, 1994.

Cornwell, Grant H., and Eve Walsh Stoddard, eds. *Global Multiculturalism: Comparative Perspectives on Ethnicity, Race, and Nation*. Lanham, Md.: Rowman & Littlefield, 2001.

Dupont, Louis, and Nathalie Lemarchand. "Official Multiculturalism in Canada: Between Virtue and Politics." In Cornwell and Stoddard, *Global Multiculturalism*, 309–36.

García Canclini, Néstor. *Consumers and Citizens: Globalization and Multicultural Conflicts*. Translated by George Yúdice. Minneapolis: University of Minnesota Press, 2001).

Goldberg, David Theo, ed. *Multiculturalism: A Critical Reader*. Oxford: Blackwell, 1994.

Herlinghaus, Hermann, and Mabel Moraña, eds. *Fronteras de la modernidad en América Latina*. Pittsburgh, Pa.: Instituto Internacional de Literatura Iberoamericana, 2003.

Lloyd, David. "Foundations of Diversity: Thinking the University in a Time of Multiculturalism." In *"Culture" and the Problem of the Disciplines*, edited by John Carlos Rowe, 15–44. New York: Columbia University Press, 1998.

Martín Barbero, Jesús, and Ana María Ochoa Gautier. "Políticas de multiculturalidad y desubicaciones de lo popular." In Mato, *Estudios latinoamericanos*, 111–25.

Mato, Daniel, ed. *Estudios latinoamericanos sobre cultura y transformaciones sociales en tiempos de globalización*. Buenos Aires: CLASCO, 2001.

Rhoads, Robert A., Victor Saenz, and Rozana Carducci. "Higher Education Reform as a Social Movement: The Case of Affirmative Action." *Review of Higher Education* 28, no. 2 (2004): 191–220.

Sieder, Rachel, ed. *Multiculturalism in Latin America: Indigenous Rights, Diversity, and Democracy*. New York: Palgrave Macmillan, 2002.

Yúdice, George. *The Expediency of Culture: Uses of Culture in the Global Era*. Durham, N.C.: Duke University Press, 2003.

Žižek, Slavoj. "Multiculturalism, or, the Cultural Logic of Multinational Capitalism." *New Left Review* 1, no. 225 (September–October 1997): 28–51.

Nation

UTE SEYDEL (TRANSLATED BY EDUARDO RABASA)

The term "nation" comes from the Latin *natio*, a derivation of *nascere*. Thus it refers to birth, origin, kinship, relationships, and lineage. During antiquity and the Middle Ages, "nation" designated a community of people born in the same place, though their common origin and lineage did not imply that this group was organized politically. In the High Middle Ages, the term was used to name people who shared a language and a culture, and from the eighteenth century onwards, the idea of nation in Europe served as an instrument against feudalism and autocracy.

The modern-age "nation"—which became dominant under the influence of Enlightenment and liberal ideas—is linked with the foundation of nation-states, and thus implies the existence of a political organization created by a larger social grouping of people who reside in a delineated geographical space with precise borders within which the movement of people, and the exchange of goods and capital, are controlled and restricted. They also share a social organization formed through historical processes.

Since the French Revolution, the creation of nation-states all over the world has been based on the appearance of a social group—generally the bourgeoisie—capable of establishing its hegemony and of defining a political project of self-determination that encompasses all other sectors of the population. Such groups evoke a mythical origin and promise an auspicious future. This evocation of an origin followed by the projection of a common destiny has made the state protection of emerging national capitalism appealing. The need for state protection is seen as offering benefits for all social groups, not only for the private capital of the bourgeoisie. The nation-state is not based only on a consensus regarding economic and political ends or institutional regimen, but it also requires the creation of a sense of cultural unity among people of different ethnicities. This cultural unity is derived from a common spirit and language, and from the fact that members share history, habits and traditions, cultural practices, imaginaries, and literary, cinematographic, and artistic canons, as well as ethical and moral values. The attempt to create or preserve a religious unity within the nation-state has been linked through the centuries to the attempt to disseminate common ethical and moral values. However, it has led to processes of exclusion for those who do not accept the same creed. Given all of these traits, Homi K. Bhabha affirmed that nations are, above all, cultural elaborations, systems of cultural signification and of representation of social life, rather than representations of ways of governing a given social organization ("Introduction" 2–4). The state may try to promote a national history, and high culture, along with totalizing discourses on national identity as something essential that underscores what makes a nation unique. Nevertheless, there is still an instability and a transitory character in this knowledge and a performative and processual construction of identity. Moreover, a variety of meanings of national culture circulate at the same time. The nation, as a cultural elaboration in the Gramscian sense, is an agent of ambivalent narrations that maintains culture in its most productive position insofar as it is a force that subordinates, fragments, disseminates, produces, reproduces, creates, guides and binds, as well as a way to question given meanings (ibid. 3–4).

Institutionalized nationalist discourses hold a pedagogical and ideological value (ibid. 2–3). They purport to be a formal framework for symbolic integration of all members that belong to a group. Women, in their roles as mothers and as teachers, have contributed notably to the dissemination of nationalistic hegemonic discourses, although they were not the ones who formulated them.

For the formation of a national culture it is also essential to have a common history that is conserved and updated in the collective historical memory. Collective memory also informs about consensual forgetting. Nevertheless, the absence or loss of collective memory can lead to serious perturbations in the collective identity of a nation (Le Goff 133). In the places where memory is preserved—monuments, commemorative spaces, school manuals for the teaching of history, holiday calendars, mottos, foundational texts and discourses—the memory of a nation is condensed and crystallized (Nora, *Rethinking France* 7).

While the concept of "nation" alludes to kinship and family ties and not to political ideologies—one is born within a nation in the same way as one is born within a family—nationalism is an ideology. It has been a powerful force in world politics and in the process of the constitution of nation-states since the French Revolution. The creation of nations undermined traditional community structures as they subsumed other identity-formations. Conceiving the nation as a union between the state and the people led to external hostilities with neighboring countries in contraposition to a fictitious ethnic homogeneity within the nation-state. The discourses that proclaimed the importance of ethnically homogeneous nation-states gave rise to ethnic cleansings.

For the populations that had lived under the domination of an imperial foreign force, the foundation of nation-states followed upon successful independence movements. In all the territories of the New World, elites linked the idea of nation from pro-independence discourses of the eighteenth century with the idea of nativism (Chasteen, "Beyond" xv). The criollos (white descendents of Europeans born in the New World) who were the hegemonic groups in Latin America and the Caribbean managed to postulate a political project of self-determination. Thus it was they who ended the colonial regime and took on the positions that were previously held by peninsular authorities, and also worked on national unification.

Lettered culture emerged to record geographic, cultural, social, and historical particularities that distinguished the young Latin American nations from Spain and Portugal, as well as to legitimize their independence, not only political but culturally as well. In addition, by telling love stories and depicting ideal heterosexual couples, the foundational novels of romanticism put national unity above racial and social differences (Sommer, *Foundational Fictions*; Limón).

The independent Latin American states not only faced border wars with neighboring states but also suffered territorial losses due to separatist movements. Also, the political class placed party loyalty above national interests, to the point of seeking alliances with foreign powers, as when Mexican conservatives sought the support of France and Austria and liberals that of the United States. The desire to define and imagine a homogeneous national identity and culture was also in conflict with the existing polyglotism in the Latin American states, with their diverse autochthonous languages. The time-honored idea that language represents a strong mental mechanism, which determines the mentality of its speakers in a decisive way, led to attitudes of contempt toward autochthonous languages and to practices of exclusion and assimilation with regard to indigenous people.

Among the problems faced after their foundation by Latin American nations like Peru, Bolivia, Ecuador, Guatemala, and Mexico with a high percentage of indigenous people, it is worth noting: (1) the indigenous communities' persistent lag in participation in national education systems in general, and Spanish literacy in particular, which have prevented indigenous people from participating in the enunciation of nationalist discourses; (2) the separate legal systems, created in the colonial era and still in place, for criollos and mestizos, on the one hand, and indigenous peoples on the other; (3) an apparent lack of intellectual unity and of shared ethical and moral values; (4) the coexistence of diverse religious practices because of syncretism; (5) the persistence of social and economic inequality along with unequal opportunities for social ascent; (6) the notorious racial heterogeneity of a population, which provoked discriminatory practices by criollos; (7) the existence of alternative economic regimes within indigenous communities, since private property was unthinkable in their cosmovision; (8) the tapestry of memories and a fragmented historical memory inherited from the Conquest and the colony, which mirrored social disintegration and was the "main obstacle for the integration of a nation with a common memory" (Florescano 255, translation ours).

In the twentieth century the official interpretation of history was taught and a strong national culture—movies, muralism, national literature—was created with the support of the state. It was also considered necessary for countries like Mexico to define themselves negatively vis-à-vis the United States by stating that Latin Americans did not wish to be utilitarian, individualist, or Protestant, which illustrates the fact that politics includes both public action and the formation of collective identities based upon contrasts with otherness.

Since today global interdependence strengthens national economies, the policies of protection of national capitalism by the nation-states have been replaced by policies that favor transnational capital (Alarcón et al.). During current times, which are characterized by accelerated processes of globalization and transnational cultural and economic phenomena, the worldwide reemergence of nationalism can be understood only as a part of a long historical process. The vitality and power of nations and nationalism is palpable in a world that globalization has made increasingly interdependent. Nevertheless, globalization processes are accompanied by the eruption of ethnic conflicts and by the resurgence of ethnic consciousness. In Mexico it has led to the rise of *neozapatismo* and the demand for autonomous communities, and in Bolivia to an indigenous movement that has achieved the election of an indigenous president, Evo Morales. According to Anthony D. Smith, the key to understanding nations and nationalism as general phenomena of the modern world lies in the legacy of the diverse historically constituted cultures, as well as ethnic links.

Thanks to the phenomenon of mass migrations and consequent diaspora, borders of the national imaginary have changed and the concept of the nation-state, which assumed a nation's being confined to its geographical limits, has been reformulated. Both national identities and what has been understood as national culture have become more unsteady, fluctuating, and hybrid. In the case of many Latin American states, but particularly Mexico, Cuba, Puerto Rico, and Central American nations, from which millions have migrated to the United States, the imagined community is divided in two parts: one within the nation-state and the other outside national territory in the United States, which together are perceived as a cultural unit but not an administrative or institutional one.

In the sending countries, immigration processes have led to a rethinking of the relationship between the center and the margins of the nation-state, and borders and borderlands are seen as places that produce new codes, discourses, and cultural expressions beyond the preexisting national ones. Any cultural manifestation and production of discourses and cultural goods—movies, literature, performance, plastic arts—in the borderlands can only be analyzed as an ephemeral manifestation that is related to the experiences of crossing/transferring between various norms and cultural codes. The borderlands and the processes that take place within it call into question not only modern metanarratives of the nation and collective identities but also postmodern ones. Even as we speak of hybrid identities, there is a normative and generalizing tendency inherent in this concept. In a time of accelerated social transformations due to immigration, "identity" seems to be an inadequate category that should be substituted by identifications with roles and existing ways of behaving in both national cultures: the sending and the receiving (for instance, Mexico and U.S.) cultures.

Suggested Reading

Alarcón, Norma, Caren Kaplan, and Minoo Moallem. Introduction to *Between Woman and Nation: Nationalisms, Transnational Feminisms, and the State*, edited by Caren Kaplan, Norma Alarcón, and Minoo Moallem, 1–18. Durham, N.C.: Duke University Press, 1999.

Anderson, Benedict, *Imagined Communities: Reflections on the Origin and Spread of Nationalism*, New York, Verso, 1991.

Bhabha, Homi K. "Introduction: Narrating the Nation." In *Nation and Narration*, 1–7. London: Routledge, 1990.
Chasteen, John Charles. Introduction to *Beyond Imagined Communities: Reading and Writing the Nation in Nineteenth Century Latin America*, edited by Sara Castro-Klarén and John Charles Chasteen, ix–xxv. Washington, D.C.: Woodrow Wilson Center Press; Baltimore: Johns Hopkins University Press, 2003.
Florescano, Enrique. *Memoria mexicana: Ensayo sobre la reconstrucción del pasado: Época prehispanica–1821*. Mexico City: Joaquín Mortiz, 1987.
Le Goff, Jacques. *History and Memory*. Translated by Steven Rendall and Elizabeth Claman. New York: Columbia University Press, 1992.
Limón, José E. "Mexicans, Foundational Fictions, and the United States: *Caballero*, a Late Border Romance." In *The Places of History: Regionalism Revisited in Latin America*, edited by Doris Sommer, 236–50. Durham, N.C.: Duke University Press, 1999.
Smith, Anthony D. *Nations and Nationalism in a Global Era*. Oxford: Polity Press, 1995.

Orality

GRACIELA DE GARAY

Among the means of oral communication we find (1) eyewitness testimonials that record verbal statements regarding an event; (2) oral tradition or indirect testimonials passed from generation to generation, by word of mouth, and dependent on collective memory for their conveyance; and (3) oral history defined as a conversational narrative focused on recording, through qualitative interviews, experiences or stories told by witnesses and direct actors on the meaning of lived events rather than the events themselves.

It is worth mentioning that "orality is a notion built from the culture of writing" and, therefore, "in speaking of orality we are in fact within the realm of writing" (Raúl Dorra, quoted in Ostria González, translation ours). According to Walter Ong, writing-oriented ("modern") societies imagine orality as a precarious state that needs to be overcome and assume that progress in primitive forms of sociability means transitioning from orality to writing. From this point of view, orality constitutes a state of cognitive and communicational deficit that impedes traditional cultures from assuring their survival and development. Writing, for example, emerged as a means of power managed by enlightened elites, assuming great importance in Spain's colonial project in the Americas. While it is true that Mayans and Nahuas had developed some form of writing, the knowledge, practice, and control of this writing were limited within hierarchies to a privileged minority. Hence, majorities continued to be functionally oral.

Writing allows verbal forms to be permanently recorded. However, writing cannot do without orality. "Oral expression can exist and mostly has existed without any writing at all, writing never without orality" (Ong 8). According to David R. Olson, writing systems were not created to represent speech but to communicate information, a notion from which emerges the potential analytical capacity of writing. Consequently, orality and writing have their own distinctive qualities, yet it is important to note that for Olson, orality and writing are not opposed to each other. The most highly literate cultures have been, at the same time, the most highly oral cultures (100).

Distinctive Features of Orality and Writing

According to Walter Ong orality is formulary, cumulative, redundant, or verbose and depends on the actual presence of its statement (38–80).

Orality is formulary because it uses mnemonic and rhythmically expressive techniques, such as sayings, as support for memory. These techniques help in setting and processing the data of experience. Orality has no written texts or books to remind us of what we know.

Orality is cumulative in that oral discourse is less dependent on the rules of logic and grammar than on statement contexts—gestures, intonation, volume, pauses, speed, the rhythm of popular speech that accompanies the speaker—that help it to convey meaning. These are hard to reproduce in writing. Writing depends on syntax, the organization of discourse itself. Orality reproduces essential narrative functions, namely the emotional function, the participation of the storyteller; writing tends to eliminate emotion for the sake of objectivity.

Orality is based on repetition to preserve continuity or a line of thought and thus assure its comprehension. Beyond the mind there is nothing to go back to, as the oral statement disappears once it has been pronounced. Hence orality is based on redundancy or repetition of what has just been said to keep the speaker and listener in tune. Oral cultures encourage excess, verbosity, and repetition, known in rhetoric as "copy" and used to lead an audience into responding.

Orality resignifies the meanings of language in the here and now of its enunciation. Oral cultures do not, therefore, produce dictionaries as do written cultures that are interested in polysemic variants.

In other words, oral communication depends on memory for its reproduction. This apparent disadvantage, however, should not be construed as a weakness or loss of the identity of memory. On the contrary, memory should be understood as a discursive process constantly undergoing new formulations and updating meanings. That is why oral traditions vary in different cultural regions, but at the same time share a series of myths that are always undergoing permutation and displacement.

Oral discourse does not require any previous learning, either. It is not based on rigid graphic and grammatical structures; thus its dissemination in other languages is an ongoing process. One might say that oral discourses gain a broad linguistic space as they are passed by word of mouth and from one language to another.

Orality, as a practice of articulating different codes, languages, or registers, records a certain state, a moment or sense of memory. Orality, therefore, is basically self-referential in the sense that it exists only inasmuch as it promotes various representation strategies, and to the extent that the contents to which it refers achieve a pertinent communicative possibility, thanks to the meaning given at the time of enunciation.

Consequently, orality is a deterritorializing means of communication; that is, it is a process leading from the meanings shared by a specific community or culture to a permanent redefinition of daily practices or ritual traditions. This permanent reformulation of orality explains the disappearance of certain traditions and community testimonies and their replacement by new ones.

Why Study Orality?

If one accepts the idea that society is communication, it may be understood that the major problem with social memory is reproducing the social rules that are the basis for its identity. Language is not enough to assure permanent communication of social rules. Thus, certain constructions or social padlocks are required to prevent an infinite process of questioning, a feature of science. In accepting these communications as a premise or basis for further communications, communication continues regardless of any questioning that occurs at a level of individual awareness. The means of communication chosen—orality or written texts—will be, therefore, a determinant for its reproduction. Secrets, mysteries, goodness, revealed truths, and rumors have been some of those social premises that ensure that communication continues and social rules are reproduced. Nonetheless, writing, with its intrinsic analytical possibility, has, over the history of the West, pointed to the difficulty in sustaining those premises or revealed truths that are taken for granted by faith or religion; modern science is the corollary of these interrogations (Chinchilla Pawling 20–21).

It is important to mention, therefore, that the communication frameworks set by each society are related to or depend largely on the vehicle or means of communication by which language is conveyed, namely voice and graphics. Different societies may be characterized as "oral cultures" or "print cultures" depending on the reigning means of communication in any given period of history. Primary orality suggests collectives totally ignorant of writing. Secondary orality represents societies where orality coexists with writing. For instance, in today's high-technology culture, a new orality is maintained over the telephone, radio, television, and other electronic devices that is dependent on writing and print for its existence and performance.

The Term "Orality" in Latin American Studies

Modernity presents different characteristics in the European Western world and in the Latin American world. Experts agree that despite the cultural impact of Western capitalist expansion on Latin American societies, those societies achieved a tangential, even distorted, modernization. Economic, social, political, and cultural changes occurred deficiently and in an unbalanced manner. Economically, the modernizing zeal of lettered elites of a positivistic bent promoted the incorporation of Latin America into the world market as a dependent economy. Socially, they stimulated mass immigration; and politically, they prompted the establishment of liberal regimens with an authoritarian orientation (Grandon Lagunas).

Considering the cultural heterogeneity represented by Latin American societies, it is easy to see why ever since the Conquest a dominated oral (indigenous) culture and a dominant lettered (European) culture have been set against each other. Literacy, Christianization, and colonization introduced a different conceptualization of oral and written discourse practices in the New World. Since then, literate cultures, supported by the colonizing power, have sought to prevail by fostering various modes of interaction between oral and written communication, which leads to the creation of areas with different degrees of literacy and illiteracy (Ostria González).

In order to control deterritorialized and subversive orality, literate cultures imposed a canon transferred from religious and political institutions into literature. The purpose was to regulate and control the power of the word, the power of the beauty of rhetoric. Literate culture's canon was invariably imposed to set limitations, to establish an aesthetic pattern of measurement, and to consolidate an instrument of survival capable of resisting time and reason.

The fact is that modernity in Latin America introduced a Eurocentric vision of the world. This vision, among other things, excluded the orality of indigenous peoples from the literary framework. The lettered city implemented a binary system that divided the earth into two opposing poles. Within this classification, Europe represented modernity and civilization, highly technological and dominated by lettered thinking, while the Americas, on the opposite pole, were the Other, characterized by tradition and barbaric ways. Orality was subsumed and assimilated into the realm of lettered culture. As Peruvian literary critic Antonio Cornejo Polar states, most conquistadores were illiterate and their relationship to books was not much more than superstitious fear. For them books worked as a fetish. This, in and of itself, questions the homogeneity of an alleged civilizing project (Quitián Peña).

Several strata of popular culture in Latin America have managed to develop perfectly effective modes of communication that are expressive of their own reality. According to Pedro Morandé, "incorporating orality by harmonizing it with the book culture" seems to be one of the major issues pending from the viewpoint of the cultural identity of the Latin American peoples (quoted in Ostria González, translation ours).

At any rate, one must distinguish between the full and functional orality of traditional societies and the orality derived from illiteracy resulting from social and economic inequalities in modern literate cultures (Ostria González). Paraphrasing Pierre Bourdieu, at issue is the problem of access to the market of writing competency via schooling. Indeed, education is very closely related to the position agents occupy in the structure of linguistic capital distribution and its relationship to social class (*Ce que parler veut dire* 57–58).

Both orality and writing assume, in addition to conflicts, supplementary and reciprocal influences. On the one hand, orality no longer exists in a pure state anywhere in the Americas and therefore can be studied only in relationship to the hegemonic lettered system. On the other hand, literate forms show hybridization processes with forms of orality, even in those practices considered the most prestigious, such as literary manifestations (Ostria González).

Starting in the 1970s, experts in orality, supported by Walter Ong's hypothesis on orality and writing and Mikhail Bakhtin's theories on the novel, reviewed the Latin American literary tradition, which had treated orality as separate from writing. By then, Latin American literature had already caught the interest of Europeans, who enjoyed its exoticism. The marketing of Third World cultural goods, including literature, culminated in the Latin American literature Boom of the 1970s. Writers turned orality into fiction by simulating a "translation" or passage from dialectic orality into writing. They sought a symbolic restitution so as to redeem the orality of writing, and also to give it legitimacy and make it worthy of entering the great library of cultured Europe. The part of Latin American identity that had been excluded from the European literary canon was recovered via orality. Paradoxically, the effort to import a dimension representing Latin American colloquial speech to the written word did nothing more than strengthen the literate format imposed by the European canon (Montaldo 36).

Latin American literary critics explored the dispute between letter and voice in their fundamental aspects and provided some insights. Antonio Cornejo Polar discussed Eurocentrism in the Hispanic American literary canon and the problems implied by including orality in a lettered framework. On the other hand, Édouard Glissant, from Martinique, claimed that orality was an emblematic element in Caribbean literature that served as a weapon in fighting European hegemony. Ángel Rama offered the concept of transculturation as a means of inclusion of cultures, preferably oral cultures, in the nation-state; as a counterpoint, John Beverley put forward a multicultural proposal that aimed for equality, carried out to its final consequences: an epistemological, cultural, economic, civic-democratic, and specific equality, not an equality of bourgeois affiliation that, in the name of equality, sets inequalities that in fact constitute it as a pattern of power. The concepts expressed by these critics showed the strength of the struggles waged between the written word and voice, between literature and orality, between elites and subalterns, between resistance and domination, between identity and hybridization. To this day, Latin American cultural studies place these issues at the heart of their inquiry.

Suggested Reading

Bourdieu, Pierre. *Ce que parler veut dire: L'économie des échanges linguistiques*. Paris: Fayard, 1982. Translated by Gino Raymond and Matthew Adamson as *Language and Symbolic Power* (Cambridge, Mass.: Harvard University Press, 1991).

Chinchilla Pawling, Perla. *De la compositio loci a la República de las Letras: Predicación jesuita en el siglo XVII novohispano*. Mexico City: Universidad Iberoamericana, 2004.

Dorra, Raúl. *Entre la voz y la letra*. Mexico City: Plaza y Valdés/Universidad de Puebla, 1997.

Gugelberger, Georg M., ed. *The Real Thing: Testimonial Discourse and Latin America*. Durham, N.C.: Duke University Press, 1996.
Lienhard, Martín. *La voz y su huella: Escritura y conflicto étnico-cultural en América Latina, 1492–1988*. Havana: Casa de las Américas, 1990.
Mato, Daniel. *El arte de narrar y la noción de literatura oral: Protopanorama intercultural y problemas epistemológicos*. Caracas: Universidad Central de Venezuela, 1990.
Olson, David R. *The World on Paper: The Conceptual and Cognitive Implications of Writing and Reading*. Cambridge: Cambridge University Press, 1994.
Ong, Walter J. *Orality and Literacy: The Technologizing of the Word*. London: Methuen, 1982.
Ostria González, Mauricio. "Literatura oral, oralidad ficticia." *Estudios Filológicos*, no. 36 (2001): 71–80.
Pachecho, Carlos. *La comarca oral: La ficcionalización de la oralidad cultural en la narrativa cultural latinoamericana contemporánea*. Caracas: Casa de Bello, 1992.
Quitián Peña, Edicsson Esteban. "El conflicto entre letra y voz y los límites de la representación." Bogotá: Pontificia Universidad Javeriana, n.d. www.javeriana.edu.co/Facultades/C_Sociales/especializacion/pdfs/El_conflicto_letra_voz.pdf.
Sarlo, Beatriz. *Tiempo pasado: Cultura de la memoria y giro subjetivo de una discusión*. Mexico City: Siglo XXI, 2005.
Vilches, Lorenzo. *La lectura de la imagen: Prensa, cine, televisión*. Barcelona: Paidós, 1983.

Performance

ANTONIO PRIETO STAMBAUGH

Performance is a concept defying concrete definition, whose multi-semantic nature derives from the many things it expresses in common English speech, such as "acting," "theater play," "execution," and "realization." All in all, performance can be conceived of as a dynamic theoretical approach that moves across disciplines, bringing together apparently disparate subject matters. As an expressive form situated at the interstices between the visual and the performing arts, performance refers to conceptual actions that find their sustenance on the artist's body. For the cultural studies scholar performance—and its allied performativity—are analytical tools well suited to dealing with the various expressive acts involved in a communicative process between the doer and a witness. Drawing from interdisciplinary inquiry, performance is then an innovative concept in both artistic and theoretical terms.

It was not until the 1950s that a new field opened up in which performance as a theoretical concept would thrive as ever more linguists, sociologists, and anthropologists resorted to the metaphors of theatricality and performance to analyze phenomena such as speech, social behavior, and ritual. Among the linguists, one should mention John L. Austin and his pupil John R. Searle, both British scholars who studied language in its performative dimensions—"speech acts"—at the very time of their execution. In this new way of analyzing discourse, communicative competence is as important as the context in which the "performative act" takes place. "Performatives" are, for Austin, transforming action statements, such as the discourse that accompanies a baptism or a wedding ceremony.

From the ranks of sociology, Erving Goffman analyzed the "theatrical" way in which people display themselves in society and interact with others. Though this approach may at first look simplistic, a careful reading of Goffman's work reveals the theoretical key elements that are still in use to analyze social behavior. For example, in his study of social stigma, Goffman developed a careful typology of the different performances displayed by people who are marginalized on account of their physical appearance, disability, social class, gender, or race, as well as the performative attitudes of those who interact with the marginalized subject.

Another innovative approach in its time was the one followed by Richard Bauman, Dell Hymes, and others within linguistic anthropology who established the methodological criteria necessary to examine the performative dimensions of ritual. One could analyze, for example, the actions of a healer carrying out a "spiritual cleansing," taking into account the existing relationships between words and the bodily techniques employed, the strategies to involve the patient and the accompanying people, and the time-space framework of the ritual. Such an analysis would make it possible to identify all the elements that lend sociocultural relevance to the act, as well as those allowing the participants to perceive it as a healing one.

From the field of anthropology, Victor Turner studied how, in ritual systems, performance can contribute to maintaining the established order (official rituals) and/or help to parody, critique, and subvert it at the same time, as happens with carnivals or political demonstrations. According to this author, social conflicts are structured very much the way drama is, with their well-defined rupture, crisis, transition, and resolution (or separation) phases, following the tripartite structure of classical Greek theater. Turner dedicated a major part of his work to the study of ritual processes such as rites of passage, pilgrimages, and initiation rites in different societies, and identified in them a liminal anti-structure that creates, so to speak, a "parenthesis" or "exception zone" in the system, governed as it is by the dominant social structure. It is in this liminal space that the *communitas* (a concept taken from Durkheim) becomes possible—that is, the feeling of solidarity between participants who are normally separated by social-status conventions. However, such a space is momentary, and its subversive potential is subjected to the temporary character of ritual, which must come to an end in order to reinstate participants to the dominant social structure, sometimes with a different status, as happens with initiation (*Dramas* 201–2).

Richard Schechner, whose main contribution is to have established a connection between the above-mentioned disciplines and the world of theater studies, adopted some of Turner's ideas. One of the main figures of the theatrical avant-garde of the 1960s and 1970s, Schechner became interested in nurturing his practice with the knowledge coming from disciplines outside the realm of theater, such as ethnology and anthropology. In 1977, Schechner met Turner, and each became immediately fascinated with the other's field of research: while Turner was interested in theatricality as a tool for a more dynamic approach to ethnographic studies, Schechner was captivated by the possibilities offered by anthropology to the study of performative phenomena.

Schechner argues that performance studies can examine virtually any human activity, from ritual to play through sports, popular entertainment, stage arts, everyday acting, social ceremonies, class and gender roles, and even the relations of the body with the media and the Internet. And the list can be expanded to add the study of inanimate objects which, even though they are not a performance, they can be analyzed *as* a performance, inasmuch as they are the product of a creative action and interact with those who make them and those who use them and/or see them. The catalog of possible approaches is then widened to include objects such as religious images, torture instruments, mannequins, toys, weapons, food—the list is endless. In each and every case, what matters is not so much the "reading" or the study of an object in itself, but its "behavior"—its performative dimension. We can imagine how the performativity of a votive offering, a national flag, or a business logo would be analyzed from the perspective of the ritual, political, and economic actions they generate. The theoretical and institutional trajectory of performance studies is lucidly expounded from a Latin-American perspective by Diana Taylor in the first chapter of her 2003 book *The Archive and the Repertoire: Performing Cultural Memory in the Americas.*

Toward the end of the 1980s, performance studies—like cultural studies—incorporated the paradigms derived from poststructuralism, postmodernism, and gender studies. In the 1990s the analytical scope opened up even more to encompass postcolonial and queer studies as well. In this context, the performative aspect of social phenomena has been analyzed in the social construction of class, race and gender identities, the simulacra and theatrical exercises of power in postindustrial society (Baudrillard; García Canclini), and the subversive possibilities of performance art (Schneider; Muñoz).

Key to the analysis of the performative dimension of gender is Judith Butler, for whom identity is not an abstract category but a performance that is ruled by social institutions. Such a statement has political implications, inasmuch as it reveals society's coercive strategies to subject people to arbitrary norms of conduct. Butler suggests that the quasi-ritual reiteration of social codes resembles a series of citation acts that never really reproduce the "original text." It is in this gap—between the norm and its iteration—that a slippage is produced, enabling a departure from the established code (*Bodies* 122–24).

The work of Butler constitutes a radical revision of the premises of Austin, Turner, and Schechner (see McKenzie). While the last two value the liminal and transgressive power of performance, this, for Butler, is mostly a dominant and punitive form of power, even though her analysis paves the way for a deconstruction—and subversion—of performative acts.

At the institutional level, the field of performance studies has earned legitimacy within the Anglo-Saxon academic world, leading to the foundation of a series of university departments in the 1980s. Though slow and tentative, the trajectory of performance in Latin America has borne interesting fruits. In the specific case of Mexico, performance studies was introduced at the beginning of the 1980s by a series of conferences by Richard Schechner at the Universidad Nacional Autónoma de México (UNAM) and the contacts he established with Mexican scholars such as Gabriel Weisz. In 1982, Weisz and Óscar Zorrilla summoned an interdisciplinary group of scientists and theater people from UNAM to found the Ethno-Dramatic Research Seminar, whose goal was to study the ritual origins of theater. Years later, Weisz published *El juego viviente*, a small but ambitious book that sought to establish the foundations of what the author defined as a theory of representation. In it Weisz analyses the relationships between body and perception in recreational activities associated with the ritual and the toy.

It was not until the year 2000 that performance studies began to be promoted systematically in Latin America through the interventions of the Hemispheric Institute of Performance and Politics in several countries. Headed by Diana Taylor of New York University, this body has established official venues in Mexico, Brazil, Peru, and Argentina, where it organizes itinerant meetings bringing together researchers, artists, and activists in a debate about everything pertaining to performance and its manifestations across the continent. In Mexico, the Hemispheric Institute founded a regional center in the town of San Cristóbal de Las Casas, Chiapas, in association with the Maya women's theater group FOMMA (Fortaleza de la Mujer Maya).

In 2002 the University of Guadalajara included performance studies in its Master of Sciences in Music program, with orientation toward ethnomusicology, under the direction of Arturo Chamorro, of the University Center for the Arts, Design, and Architecture. Chamorro, a disciple of Richard Bauman, incorporates performance theory with rigor in his studies on musical traditions in western Mexico. Recently the Universidad Veracruzana has also included performance studies in its graduate program in performing arts.

In Peru, performance theory has been applied in the anthropological works of Gisela Cánepa and Luis Millones, among others. Fundamental to Cánepa's work is the relationship between the actor's body and the context in which the acting takes place. She maintains that the embodied experience of performance underlines the indeterminate and subjective character of the cultural fact. In this sense, performance studies is a good ally for the reflexive critique in which anthropology has entered as of the early 1990s, moving away from the construction of the "subject matter" to enquire instead into culture as a dialogical process (18).

Though, as we have just pointed out, performance studies as a paradigm is beginning to be applied in several academic works throughout Latin America, it has not yet acquired general acceptance in the region, nor have specific analytical tools for the Latin American context been developed. However, the work of the above-mentioned researchers is opening up the field, and it is to be expected that performance will yield new ways of analyzing cultural processes in the region.

Suggested Reading

Bauman, Richard. *Verbal Art as Performance*. Newbury, Mass.: Rowland House, 1977.

Cánepa Koch, Gisela, ed. *Identidades representadas: Performance, experiencia y memoria en los Andes*. Lima: Pontificia Universidad Católica del Perú, 2001.

Carlson, Marvin. *Performance: A Critical Introduction*. New York: Routledge, 1996.
Chamorro, Arturo, and María Guadalupe Rivera, eds. *Música, ritual y performance*. Guadalajara: Universidad de Guadalajara, 1999.
Goffman, Erving. *Stigma: Notes on the Management of Spoiled Identity*. Englewood Cliffs, N.J.: Prentice-Hall, 1963.
McKenzie, Jon. "Genre Trouble: (The) Butler Did It." In *The Ends of Performance*, edited by Peggy Phelan and Jill Lane, 217–35. New York: New York University Press, 1998.
Muñoz, José Esteban. *Disidentifications: Queers of Color and the Performance of Politics*. Minneapolis: University of Minnesotta Press, 1999.
Prieto Stambaugh, Antonio. "Los estudios del performance: Una propuesta de simulacro crítico." *Citru.doc Cuadernos de investigación teatral*, no. 1 (November 2005): 52–61. performancelogia.blogspot.com/2007/07/los-estudios-del-performance-una.html.
Schechner, Richard. *Performance Studies: An Introduction*. London: Routledge, 2002.
Schneider, Rebecca. *The Explicit Body in Performance*. London: Routledge, 1997.
Taylor, Diana. *The Archive and the Repertoire: Performing Cultural Memory in the Americas*. Durham, N.C.: Duke University Press, 2003.
Turner, Victor. *The Anthropology of Performance*. New York: Performance Arts Journal Press, 1988.
Weisz, Gabriel. *El juego viviente: Indagación sobre las partes ocultas del objeto lúdico*. Mexico City: Siglo XXI, 1986.

Postcolonialism

JOSÉ RABASA

Postcolonialism is among the terms most debated in Latin American cultural studies since the mid-1980s. The reason lies partly in its manufacture in the English language but partly in historical differences. There has been a misunderstanding in both instances. Latin American criticism has questioned the applicability of postcolonialism when considering that the object of study and the postcolonial realities in African, Asian, and Oceanic countries have little in common with Latin America, given that the majority of Latin American countries achieved their independence at the beginning of the nineteenth century, precisely at the time when the imperial projects in Africa, Asia, and Oceania were consolidated. With respect to the English language, it has been seen with suspicion that postcolonial studies have been incorporated from the North American academy and to a lesser degree from the British. Paradoxically, one of the themes most rigorously treated in postcolonial studies is the exportation and translation of ideas created in the former imperial metropolis. Observe that the "post" does not indicate a moment in which colonialism has been surpassed, but rather the consciousness of colonial continuities and legacies even centuries after the political independences.

Though we may date the origin of postcolonial studies to Edward Said's 1978 book *Orientalism*, the new postcolonial reality, in both its historical and its intellectual character, had its origin in anticolonial discourses that accompanied the new independent nations after World War II. The work of Albert Memmi, Aimé Césaire, Amilcar Cabral, C. L. R. James, and Frantz Fanon, just to name the field's most important precursors, anticipated the criticism that emerged in the 1980s in England and the United States. We must keep in mind that these critics had a productive reception in Latin America in the years that followed the Cuban Revolution in 1959. It would be an error, however, to forget the antecedents and contributions of Latin American intellectuals of the magnitude of José Carlos Mariátegui, who in the 1920s had already laid out the necessity to reflect on the place of indigenous cultures in struggles of Marxist inspiration. In contrast to intellectuals intimately bound to national liberation struggles, the criticism of the 1980s was for the most part within the academy; nevertheless, both generations concerned themselves with the continuities of colonial pasts in postcolonial presents. Accordingly, the project has been of a decolonization of culture and academic knowledge.

The conference "Europe and Its Others" at the University of Essex in 1984 constituted a first moment in which the postcolonial project was laid out in an academic setting. Among its participants were Edward Said, Gayatri Spivak, Homi Bhabha, Peter Hulme, Talal Asad, and, in the area of Latin American cultural studies, Gordon Brotherston, Doris Sommer, and José Rabasa. The proceedings of the conference collected the first formulation of texts that have come to be considered foundational of postcolonial studies, texts that have exerted a profound influence in a broad range of academic disciplines. Another entry to this dictionary examines the project of subaltern studies, whose contributions could very well be understood from within postcolonial studies. The distinction between postcolonial studies and subaltern studies is *academic*, in that frequently we find the same authors writing in one or the other modality, even within the same essay; the objective here is to indicate that such a distinction can be tenuous, if not arbitrary.

Today in the context of Latin America one speaks of postcolonial moments to refer to the emergence of states after the wars of independence.

Even though this denomination seems transparent, we must insist, however, that this periodization lacks rigor. To speak of the postcolonial as a historical moment lends itself to equivocation and criticism that remind us that although the countries in the so-called Third World have achieved their formal independence from the former metropolis, socioeconomic and cultural realities frequently reproduce colonial structures under the modality of neocolonialism. One must make a distinction between postcolonialism understood as historical moment (whether the one corresponding to the formal independence of the nineteenth or of the twentieth century) and the decolonizing articulations of postcolonial critique. In the case of Latin America the most common argument was that the consolidated elites after the wars of independence constituted internal colonialisms that subjected Indian and black populations to processes of marginalization and exclusion from full citizenship. The term "postcolonial" carries in the state of "post" the shadows and specters of colonial pasts. To reflect on the postcolonial, no longer as a moment posterior to the formal independences, implies becoming conscious that colonial continuities entail inevitable linguistic, cultural, and political legacies.

The postcolonial critique of the 1980s set out to transform academic knowledge. Said's concept of orientalism had global effects on studies of Africa, Asia, and Oceania. One would no longer be able to think without being fully conscious of the imperialist origins directly or indirectly imbricated in colonialism, not only in the context of the former metropolis but also in the exportation of its paradigms to countries like Mexico, where the history of the centers for the study of Africa and Asia remains to be written. The concept of orientalism has also proved useful for conceptualizing aspects of Latin American culture that accompany internal colonialisms. But beyond formulations explicitly "orientalist," Said's book offers us an approximation to the exercise of power in colonial discourses.

Said's novelty resided in his juxtaposing the thinking of Michel Foucault, Antonio Gramsci, and Frantz Fanon, which allowed him to conceive of orientalism no longer as an ideology that could be surpassed by an unmasking, but rather as a set of practices and *dispositifs* that structure the world for a hegemonic appropriation. The postcolonial problematic in Latin America includes both North American imperialism and the colonial past that dates back to the sixteenth century. Beyond a resistance to the cultural, political, and economic influx from the United States, the postcolonial problematic forces us to conceive of hegemony in the interior of the Spanish language and the cultural habits of the criollos, in the incorporation of pre-Columbian indigenous cultures into the nationalist projects, and in the veiled racisms that reproduce the servitude of contemporary Indians—ultimately, in teleologies of Marxist inspiration that consign Indian cultures to a past without a future. This doesn't mean that postcolonial critique is anti-Marxist, but that it offers Marxists conceptions critical of Stalinist orthodoxy.

In this regard one may view the Zapatista movement of the end of the twentieth century (consider the communiqués drafted in the aftermath of the uprising of the Ejército Zapatista de Liberación Nacional in 1994) as postcolonial inasmuch as its political and cultural articulations assume full consciousness of the need to include, or, better stated, to think of social transformation projects from indigenous spaces. It is surely not a question of reducing the Zapatista project to Said's critique of orientalism, but of tracing a practice in which the objective of a decolonization of knowledge has as much if not more validity. *Zapatismo* clearly is not an academic practice, but this doesn't keep it from holding lessons for those who theorize about Latin America from the academy (Mignolo, "Zapatistas' Theoretical Revolution"; Rabasa, "Of Zapatismo"). But before mentioning a few instances of Latin American postcolonialism, we must examine the concept of *epistemic violence* as it has been developed by Gayatri Spivak.

In "Can the Subaltern Speak?" Spivak offers a coherent and rigorous formulation of epistemic violence. As the title of her essay suggests, Spivak explores the limits of the representation of the subaltern: one exercises epistemic violence with evaluative criteria that exclude knowledge by subaltern groups and privilege the intellectual mediations without which subaltern speech remains unintelligible. If Spivak's answer is negative, we must observe that she writes against the claim that the communication of subaltern knowledge is direct and transparent. Indeed, in her essay the negative response has as much importance as her insistence that "in seeking to learn to speak to (rather than listen to or speak for) the historically muted subject of the subaltern woman, the postcolonial intellectual *systematically* 'unlearns' privilege" (295).

In the context of Latin American cultural studies, the question of subaltern speech has influenced the conceptualizations of and debates on the testimonial genre. Spivak's essay has also resonated among those who study the forms by means of which colonial historiography exercises an epistemic violence by constituting indigenous cultures under the rubric of superstition and idolatry, and thereby denying the indigenous historian any expression of a historical criterion that doesn't subordinate itself to the categories of Western history (Rabasa, "Beyond Representation?").

In their most basic formulation, colonizing processes mark the passage to history inasmuch as incorporation into the Roman Catholic Church is defined as entering universal history. This doesn't mean that the missionaries and Spanish bureaucrats were so dim-witted that they couldn't recognize writing and memory in indigenous cultures that manifest a historical sense, but that indigenous memory is historical insofar as it is constituted *for* the formation of a colonial order. Cartographies, genealogies, and annals, to name only those genres most characteristic of indigenous history, assume a historical character for the clarification of the place of indigenous cultures within the colonial order. The postcolonial perspective that gives form to the concept of epistemic violence allows us to also understand how Indians use colonial historical categories to create their own spaces and to negotiate a place within the administration and structures of colonial power. This observation would apparently contradict Spivak's negative on subaltern speech in that one assumes agency in Indians' appropriation of European historical concepts. Nevertheless, in turning to one's own history (in Spanish *historia propia*, both in the sense of property and of propriety), one loses the indigenous sense of memory and temporality. One must observe that the concept of subalternity is always relative to the reigning structures of power.

The question of the applicability of postcolonial theory to Latin American culture lacks importance once we consider that it is in its inapplicability that we find the most productive results (Beverley; Mignolo; Rodríguez). It is never a question of a servile application of postcolonial theory, but of creating spaces for debate in which one would become conscious of differences, which in turn would lead us to a deeper understanding of the specific Latin American nature of its colonial history. The zeal to deny the relevance of postcolonial theory has led to the extreme of denying that in Latin America—and in particular in Mexico—there ever was a colonizing process. There is an assumption that there never was a Spanish imperialism, and there is a preference for speaking of the viceroyalty instead of the colonial period. Consequently the tendency is to ignore the debates and the production of rigorous theory regarding the legitimacy of Spanish dominion in the Americas in the sixteenth century, which comes down to the legitimacy of the usurpation of the sovereignty of the indigenous peoples.

In Mexico, one must cite *De dominio infidelium et iusto bello* by the

Augustinian Alonso de la Vera Cruz. Vera Cruz's treatise consists of the lectures he delivered for the inauguration of the University of Mexico in 1553–54. An approximation to Vera Cruz's work from postcolonial theory would lead us to the paradox that the postcolonial question has its origins in Mexico in the sixteenth century, perhaps in the first moment of the Spanish invasion and indigenous resistance. Vera Cruz's text—one should also mention the work of Bartolomé de las Casas—lays out the necessity to create a just and equitable colonial order, in which wealth would have to be redistributed for the promotion of the common good. For Vera Cruz corrupt indigenous leaders who sell communal lands without consulting their communities are as problematic as the Spaniards who buy them or appropriate them by exercising terror. In becoming conscious that the exercise of colonial power is not a matter of a mere binary schema that opposes the colonizer to the colonized resides the depth of postcolonial theory that in the case of Mexico dates back to the colony.

The relationship with postcolonial theory must be understood as a two-way street in which Asian, African, and Oceanic critics would learn something about the implementation of colonialism, the debates on imperialism, and the practices of resistance and insurgency in Latin America. These debates and dialogues have already taken place in both subaltern studies and postcolonial theory (Ashcroft, Griffiths, and Tiffin; Rodríguez; Lowe and Lloyd). In the European context the work of David Lloyd on Ireland is particularly relevant for a reflection on the national-popular in national liberation struggles. These conversations have led to joint publications in Spanish and English. The circulation of texts does not lack irony, as when we find Argentine intellectuals from Tucumán at a congress in Pittsburgh learning about conversations with and translations of Indian intellectuals conducted in La Paz, Bolivia (Rivera Cusicanqui and Barragán; Kaliman, "Cómo reconstruir"). Observe that these conversations have taken place directly between India and Bolivia without the intervention of the North American academy. It is fitting to end the present entry with this geopolitical indication, not to deny the power that can be exerted from the United States when its academics export intellectual paradigms to Latin America, but to underscore that the circulation of discourses flows as much from South to North as from South to South. The work of intellectuals at other latitudes has had an important impact on the definition of Latin American cultural studies, but the value of the conversations has resided above all in the debate and the articulation of differences.

Suggested Reading

Ashcroft, Bill, Gareth Griffiths, and Helen Tiffin, eds. 2nd ed. *The Post-colonial Studies Reader.* New York: Routledge, 2006.

Chakrabarty, Dipesh. *Provincializing Europe: Postcolonial Thought and Historical Difference.* Princeton, N.J.: Princeton University Press, 2000.

Lowe, Lisa, and David Lloyd, eds. *The Politics of Culture in the Shadow of Capital.* Durham, N.C. Duke University Press, 1997.

Mignolo, Walter. *Local Histories/Global Designs: Coloniality, Subaltern Knowledges, and Border Thinking.* Princeton, N.J.: Princeton University Press, 2000.

Rivera Cusicanqui, Silvia, and Rossana Barragán, eds. *Debates post coloniales: Una introducción a los estudios de la subalternidad.* Translated by Raquel Gutiérrez et al. La Paz: Historias/Aruwiri/SEPHIS, 1997.

Rodríguez, Ileana, ed. *Convergencia de tiempos: Estudios subalternos/contextos latinoamericanos estado, cultura, subalternidad.* Amsterdam: Rodopi, 2001.

Spivak, Gayatri Chakravorty. *A Critique of Postcolonial Reason: Toward a History of the Vanishing Present.* Cambridge, Mass.: Harvard University Press, 1999.

Toro, Alfonso de, and Fernando de Toro. *El debate de la postcolonialidad en América Latina: Una modernidad periférica o cambio de paradigma en el pensamiento latinoamericano.* Madrid: Iberoamericana; Frankfurt am Main: Vervuert, 1999.

Postmemory

MÓNICA SZURMUK

The term "postmemory" originates within the field of memory studies in the United States toward the end of the 1980s to account for the experience of the generation of the children of Holocaust survivors, but it has already been used to explain the perdurability of trauma in other contexts. It was coined by Marianne Hirsch to define

> a powerful and very particular form of memory precisely because its connection to its object or source is mediated not through recollection but through an imaginative investment and creation. This is not to say that memory itself is unmediated, but that it is more directly connected to the past. Postmemory characterizes the experience of those who grow up dominated by narratives that preceded their birth, whose own belated stories are evacuated by the stories of the previous generation shaped by traumatic events that can be neither understood nor recreated. I have developed this notion in relation to

> children of Holocaust survivors, but I believe it may usefully describe other second-generation memories of cultural or collective traumatic events and experiences. (22)

The daughter of Holocaust survivors who emigrated to the United States soon after the end of World War II, Hirsch was already a full professor and an expert in the field of French literature and feminism when she became interested in the experience of the "second generation." The shift in Hirsch's career is paradigmatic of a cultural turn in literary and historical studies in the United States in the 1980s when the inclusion of the personal came to be encouraged, and scholars increasingly featured their own experiences in their academic writing. This coincided with a growing interest in the genres of the personal such as oral history, testimony, memoir, and autobiography, and with a diversification and democratization of the objects of study. Hirsch, for her part, expanded her corpus to include photography, film, cartoons, and the visual arts.

Andreas Huyssen has eloquently described the process whereby the privilege of the future that was a hallmark of modernity was replaced by a discourse about the past that dominates contemporary culture and is evidenced not only by the interest in memory as an academic endeavor but also in the explosion of rememoration, the discourses about the past in popular culture, the popularization of museums, and the proliferation of cultural products about the past including television programs and films. Postmemory stretches this phenomena even more creating a space of commemoration and memorialization that has no concrete link with the original traumatic experience.

In *At Memory's Edge*, James Young wonders how people can remember events they have not experienced directly. Young differentiates between "Remember" and "remember" to mark the difference between lived experience and the recall of narratives and images that one did not experience and that are more remote in time. This latter way of remembering is, according to Young, vicarious. He submits that intergenerational effects of certain events can be transmitted culturally and leave a mark on an entire society. From this perspective, for example, American society as a whole can be considered a postmemorial Holocaust society via its experience of the Holocaust as a mediatic sociocultural phenomenon through photography, cinema, art, and television.

Like the studies of memory, those of postmemory accompany processes of decolonization, and posttraumatic events, and hence are key to the debates about human rights violations in Central and South America, the end of apartheid in South Africa, and the civil rights movement in the United States. According to Argentinean sociologist Elizabeth Jelin, "Discussion of contemporary memories can rarely be done from outside the scenario where struggles are taking place. The researcher cannot avoid being involved, incorporating his or her subjectivity, experience, beliefs, and emotions" (xvi).

The term "postmemory" has been embraced by specialists devoted to the study of trauma, memory, and conflict from interdisciplinary or transdisciplinary perspectives in the United States and Europe. At the heart of the postmemory debate is the conceptualization of cultural memory that, according to Mieke Bal, has "displaced and subsumed the discourses of individual (psychological) memory and of social memory" (vii). Critics who use the term "postmemory" argue that there are specific characteristics of the experience of generations marked by a trauma they did not live through that cannot be explained successfully with the term "memory." Unlike memory, which is directly connected to the past, and which can be used to describe all types of experiences, postmemory deals solely with traumatic events whose emotional perdurability marks the generations that follow those who experienced the events. In the case of traumatic experiences, therefore, the term "memory" is used to refer to the experience and the ensuing cultural production by its victims, witnesses, or perpetrators, while "postmemory" focuses on the cultural registers produced by those who grew up in the shadow of those memories. They may be direct descendents of the victims, witnesses, or perpetrators, or they may have grown up in societies traversed by trauma but not have experienced it firsthand. For example, in the case of the young people born in Argentina during the 1970s, postmemory can be used not only to analyze the production of the filmmakers Natalia Bruschtein, Albertina Carri, and María Inés Roqué, daughters of disappeared activists, but also to describe the discourse of young people who did not have direct experiences of repression in their families, the focus of Susana Kaiser's *Postmemories of Terror*.

The use of the term "postmemory" has, then, extended well beyond Holocaust studies. In the United States there is research on the experiences of slavery and segregation. The concept has been utilized to describe postcolonial trauma in Africa, the Caribbean, and Southeast Asia. Some scholars have used it to talk about geographical spaces with multiple collective memories such as the case of Palestine/Israel, and India/Pakistan. It has been used to describe the Armenian genocide at the hands of the Turks, and to analyze photography and personal items that depict immigrant experiences.

In Latin America, postmemory has been used to analyze the experience of Holocaust survivors (Spitzer; Szurmuk; Waldman), to study cultural productions of the children of the disappeared (Arruti; Forcinito; Nouzeilles), and to examine the experiences of the generation born during the dictatorship (Kaiser). Francine A'ness uses postmemory as intersubjective remembrance to refer to memorial practices in Peru, and also to the organization of committees of truth in the Andes. The methodological usefulness of the term "postmemory" is more evident in the analysis of visual products, as becomes clear in the recent work on Marcelo Brodsky's installations and on the Argentinean film *Garage Olimpo*. There have also been interesting community oral history projects that appeal to postmemory for the reconstruction of immigrant experiences, such as the study of the Ukrainian community of Berisso in Argentina by Daniel James and Mirta Zaida Lobato.

Surprisingly for a term that has not had much circulation in Latin America (the books by Hirsch and Young have not yet been translated into Spanish or Portuguese), it has already been criticized adamantly by Argentinean cultural critic Beatriz Sarlo, who considers the use of postmemory a theoretical gesture "more wide-reaching than necessary" (*Tiempo pasado* 152, translation ours). Why, she wonders, coin a new term whose meaning would occupy the same semantic space as "remembrance" or "memory"? She argues that all memory of the past is mediated and vicarious, and furthermore takes to task the subjective aspects of postmemory. Sarlo's critique is included within a wider attack on what she calls the "subjective turn"—that is, the space granted to the subjective and personal within academic research through the popularization of oral history and testimony that, according to Sarlo, depoliticize memory.

A case that serves Sarlo in exemplifying her ideas is the debate surrounding the film *Los rubios*, directed by Albertina Carri, a daughter of *desaparecidos* who uses this first film to explore her relationship with her parents. Employing experimental techniques, Carri reconstructs the history of the disappearance of her parents and delves into how she articulates subjectivity in their absence. This film, without a doubt, is an exercise in postmemory, which we can claim, with Young, does not attempt a historical reconstruction, but rather a simulation of loss (92). Subsequent debates challenged Carri's subject position in the film, accusing her of being narcissistic and apolitical, and arguing that the political has to be articulated either from the strictly political and collective or through creative fictionalization. Sarlo feels that literature or experimental art, or academic texts, are the most adequate cultural responses to deal with traumatic recent memory; testimonial accounts only serve as archival sources to be weighed against other sources, or as juridical evidence.

Postmemory as a critical term used to study and understand traumatic experiences of the twentieth century has already gained a space within European and North American cultural studies. As a twentieth-century phenomenon that exemplifies the efforts to account for an ever-growing corpus of cultural productions, it is a term that has inspired new ways of conceiving the relationship between culture, society, and subjectivity. It remains to be seen whether this concept will be adopted or rejected in Latin America, whether it will demonstrate its usefulness for the debates on memory, mourning, and the articulation of the future in traumatic recent experiences such as state terrorism in the 1970s and 1980s, massive uprootings of indigenous populations, and migration.

Suggested Reading

A'ness, Francine. "Resisting Amnesia: Yuyachkani, Performance, and the Postwar Reconstruction of Peru." *Theater Journal* 56, no. 3 (2004): 395–414.

Arruti, Nerea. "Tracing the Past: Marcelo Brodsky's Photography as Memory Art." *Paragraph* 30, no. 1 (2007): 101–20.

Bal, Mieke, Jonathan Crewe, and Leo Spitzer, eds. *Acts of Memory: Cultural Recall in the Present.* Hanover, N.H.: University Press of New England, 1999.

Bruschtein, Natalia. *Encontrando a Víctor.* Mexico City: Centro de Capacitación Cinematográfica, 2005.

Carri, Albertina. *Los rubios.* Documentary film, 2003.

Forcinito, Ana. "Narración, testimonio y memorias sobrevivientes: Hacia la posmemoria en la posdictadura uruguaya." *Letras Femeninas* 32, no. 2 (2006): 197–220.

Hirsch, Marianne. *Family Frames: Photography, Narrative and Postmemory.* Cambridge, Mass.: Harvard University Press, 1997.

Huyssen, Andreas. *After the Great Divide: Modernism, Mass Culture, Postmodernism.* Bloomington: Indiana University Press, 1986.

James, Daniel, and Mirta Zaida Lobato. "Family Photos, Oral Narratives, and Identity Formation: The Ukranians of Berisso." *Hispanic American Historical Review* 84, no. 1 (2004): 5–36.

Jelin, Elizabeth. *Los trabajos de la memoria.* Buenos Aires: Siglo XXI, 2002.

Kaiser, Susana. *Postmemories of Terror: A New Generation Copes with the Legacies of the "Dirty War."* New York: Palgrave MacMillan, 2005.

Nouzeilles, Gabriela. "Postmemory Cinema and the Future of the Past in Albertina Carri's *Los rubios.*" *Journal of Latin American Cultural Studies* 14, no. 3 (2005): 263–78.

Roqué, María Inés. *Papá Iván*. Dramatic film. Mexico City: Centro de Capacitación Cinematográfica, 2004.

Sarlo, Beatriz. *Tiempo pasado: Cultura de la memoria y giro subjetivo de una discusión*. Mexico City: Siglo XXI, 2005.

Spiegelman, Art. *Maus: A Survivor's Tale*. New York: Pantheon, 1986.

Szurmuk, Mónica. "Usos de la postmemoria: *Lenta biografía* de Sergio Chejfec." In *Memoria y ciudadanía*, edited by Ileana Rodríguez and Mónica Szurmuk, 311–21. Santiago, Chile: Cuarto Propio, 2008.

Waldman, Gilda. "Postmemoria: Una primera aproximación." In *Memorias (in)cógnitas, contiendas en la historia*, edited by Maya Aguiluz Ibargüen and Gilda Waldman M., 387–403. Mexico City: Universidad Nacional Autónoma de México, 2007.

Young, James E. *At Memory's Edge: After-Images of the Holocaust in Contemporary Art and Architecture*. New Haven, Conn.: Yale University Press, 2002.

Postmodernity

SANDRA LORENZANO (TRANSLATED BY LAURA KANOST)

From this heterogeneous and multiple territory that is Latin America, a territory marked by inequality, violence, and injustice, thought on the relationship between modernity and postmodernity transcends the limits of theoretical, academic discourse, entering the space of the political. Knowledges in tension seek to apprehend reality—social, aesthetic, analytical—so as to decenter the hegemonic subject. Discourse constructed on the periphery recycles bits and pieces of voices from the metropolis and adds them to its own voice, thus inventing a path of its own.

By way of an unfinished modernizing project and a postmodernity whose installation is incomplete, the Latin American critical space seeks its own image in the "shattered mirror" of modernity's failed consolidation (Brunner, *Un espejo trizado*). This reflection is nothing new: "The fact that the different stages of modernity . . . have not succeeded in taking place among us, except as modernity in crisis, makes the current debate about a postmodern sensibility a sort of longstanding experience in the Latin American chronicle" (Casullo 95, translation ours). The discussion alludes to our own "reality," as well as to the status that we are assigned within the market of production and knowledge exchange. To think, then, about the relationship between modernity and postmodernity is to restage a vindication that claims the periphery as a privileged space of enunciation, rereading agreements, figures, and tensions in order to construct, from them, a discourse that is fragmented, not in error but in response to the horror of an exclusionary authorized/authoritarian totality.

Consequently, some refer to a "postmodernism *avant la lettre*" or to a "peripheral modernity" regarding the cultural heterogeneity of Latin America. In this sense, and as proposed by Nelly Richard, one of the primary protagonists of the debate, "Postmodernity is not what follows modernity in linear terms . . . but rather the conjunctural pretext for its rereading via the suspicion that historically weighs on the cognitive and instrumental articulations of its universal design" ("Latinoamérica" 16, translation ours). In order to enter this area of reflection it is necessary to begin with a brief analysis of modernity, considering that both modernity and postmodernity are complex and irregular concepts.

We might begin by thinking of modernity as the legacy of the rationalist Enlightenment project of the eighteenth century. It is, then, a "particular condition of history" (Casullo, Forster, and Kaufman 10) arising from the awareness of living at a special moment in which the triumph of reason expressed in scientific discoveries, technological advances, and industrialization would guarantee a destiny of progress for humanity. These terms—reason and progress—form the nucleus of modernity. The new historical period is also evident in the awareness that the world is above all the representation that we make of it. This new way of understanding that embraces the self, the world, and nature emerges in the breakdown of religious representations of the world. The place formerly occupied by God comes to be occupied by Reason. We can observe a long historical process crystallizing in the so-called Age of Enlightenment; it is at this point that the Enlightenment project will systematize the great paradigms of modernity.

There are three spheres that organize knowledge in the rational Enlightenment project: the *cognitive sphere* corresponding to science; the *normative sphere*, site of ethical and moral questions; and the *expressive sphere*, ruled by art and aesthetics. All three converge upon the ideal of progress. That is, modernity points toward the future as the space of realization of these three spheres; it is in this sense a hopeful process, one that imbues history with meaning.

Jürgen Habermas reclaims modernity as a project of reason. Modernity constitutes a global vision of the world, self, and reality, organized into four fundamental projects: an *emancipatory project* that consists of the secularization of knowledge and culture; an *expansive project* seeking to extend the knowledge and possession of nature; a *renovating project* that implies pursuing permanent improvement and innovation; and a *democratizing project* linked above all to education and the diffusion of knowledge (García Canclini, *Hybrid Cultures* 12).

Modernity faced one of its worst crises in the mid-twentieth century: Auschwitz. Here the Enlightenment showed its "dark" side, as analyzed by, among others, Theodor Adorno and Max Horkheimer in *Dialectic of Enlightenment*. World War II ushered in a stage of skepticism and criticism of the defining idea of modernity as an emancipatory project, a stage marked by the questioning of its foundational metanarratives: democracy, revolution, progress.

The contemporary world faced a panorama of crises that would bring about the breakdown of the modern project (Casullo, Forster, and Kaufman 196). The most significant crises included reformulations of: the capitalist system, the welfare state, the society of work, bourgeois forms of politics, and historical subjectivity. Meanwhile, the era brought a rampant neoliberalism accompanied by economic globalization and cultural internationalization (R. Ortiz) that tended to homogenize realities, subjects, messages, receptors, images, and desires in accordance with the market. According to Jean-François Lyotard, these crises caused the rupture in modernity and the emergence of postmodernity, accompanied by the ascendency of simulacra, consumption, hedonism, and disillusionment.

In a playful yet schematic way, the following outline proposed by Ihab Hassan gives a quite accurate idea of the principal differences between the two concepts:

Modernism	Postmodernism
Form (conjunctive, closed)	Antiform (disjunctive, open)
Purpose	Play
Design	Chance
Hierarchy	Anarchy
Art object/Finished work	Process/Performance/Happening
Presence	Absence
Centering	Dispersal
Genre/Boundary	Text/Intertext
Root/Depth	Rhizome/Surface

But it is also the postmodern gaze that has witnessed the emergence on the scene of everything that was veiled or canceled by the hegemonic rational subject. Those who had been excluded from the modern project have made their appearance, calling into question the masculine-heterosexual-Western-white-rational human being of modernity; new forms of political participation have developed; strong artistic proposals with innovative languages have appeared; creative borders have been transgressed. In sum, this conglomerate of elements changes what we have come to call postmodernity, and what surely implies a change in the contemporary sensibility, into a collage that is complex, contradictory, and ambiguous in many ways.

The term "postmodernity" ("postmodernism," "postmodern condition," "late capitalism," "postindustrial era") was first used in the field of literary criticism by Irving Howe and Harry Levin, in the late 1950s, to refer to the decadence of the modernist movement. In the 1960s it was used by critics such as Leslie Fiedler and Ihab Hassan, although without agreement on the meaning of the term. In the 1970s the usage became widespread, first in reference to architecture, and later to dance, theater, painting, film, and music. This notion was taken up again by Julia Kristeva and Jean-François Lyotard in France, and by Jürgen Habermas in Germany (Huyssen, "Guía"). "Early in the 1980s, the constellation of modernism-postmodernism in the arts and modernity-postmodernity in social theory had become one of the most contested spaces in Western intellectual life" ("Guía" 234, translation ours).

It is important to consider that reflections on postmodernity are not the same in the field of sociology and the history of ideas as in aesthetics; nor do they refer in a homogeneous way to their own problematic: "In cultural politics today a basic opposition exists between a postmodernism which seeks to deconstruct modernism and resist the status quo and a postmodernism which repudiates the former to celebrate the latter: a postmodernism of resistance and a postmodernism of reaction" (Foster xi–xii). Accordingly it makes sense that the new and often exciting projects in the field of aesthetics and the struggles of minorities in society coexist, in the same "postmodern scene," with neoconservative plans heralding the end of ideologies and the triumph of the market.

Within this panorama, Habermas, for example, advocates a new critical appropriation of the modernist project, in opposition to a conservative antimodernism. The German philosopher attempts to recover the emancipatory potential of reason, differentiating himself from those who confuse reason with domination, and from this point he elaborates a defense of enlightened modernity.

Another fundamental author in the debate, Jean-François Lyotard, believes that postmodernity signals the end of master narratives—that is, the metanarratives of modernity and their explicatory capacity. In *The Postmodern Condition* Lyotard analyzes the transformations of enlightened thought at the threshold of the informatization of societies. Fredric Jameson, in contrast, considers postmodern aesthetic forms in close relation to the globalization of the market. With the commodification of art bringing creative expression to banalization, superficiality, and pastiche, postmodernity would represent the "cultural logic of late capitalism."

Also indispensable in discussions on modernity-postmodernity is the work of Andreas Huyssen, who rejects binary oppositions and proposes recovering the political potential and the complexity of both projects. One of the elements that he takes into account in the contemporary scene is the presence of new technologies—media, culture of image—principally in the development of aesthetic proposals, which breaks with the Adornian notions of high culture and popular culture. Huyssen analyzes the links of continuity and criticism established with the projects of the historical avant-gardes. Thus, postmodernism in art can be understood in a sense similar to that in the avant-gardes as it confronts the traditional artistic institution of classical modernism. In an almost paradoxical way, thinking about tradition—following the vanguards, which rejected all tradition—allows a break with the permanent demand for innovation into which modern art had fallen. While rethinking tradition and the relationship between art and life, new attention is directed to the voices coming from outside Western institutionalized art.

It should be pointed out that the experiments conducted by postmodernism do not yield homogeneous results, but rather are transformed into, "on the one hand, the emergence of a culture of eclecticism, an amply affirmative postmodernism that abandons all critical claims, all negations and transgressions; and, on the other hand, an alternative postmodernism that defined criticism, resistance and transgression of the *status quo*, not in modernist or vanguardist terms, but in line with the political changes occurring within contemporary culture" (Huyssen, "Guía" 237, translation ours).

Viewed in the light of the modernity-postmodernity relationship, contemporary art implies abandoning the facile notion of "everything goes"—an oversimplification of certain readings on postmodernism—in order to enter a complex territory that revalues voices and proposals that had been excluded from the modern concept of art, such as industrial forms or mass culture or, as mentioned above, expressions of "othernesses" (women, native peoples, gays). In formal terms, while it is difficult to generalize about these projects without banalizing, we can observe a tendency to blur the borders between different artistic genres, as well as the deliberate use of the "quotation" through intertextuality or collage. Postmodern pastiche is thus also dialogue with the past, and therefore memory (this element has become a space of resistance in places like Latin America). It looks not toward the future, as modern art does, but toward a past made current through irony and re-creation. On the one hand, it is a celebration of the decline of the power of rationalism, and on the other, it is a diverse array of expressions of disillusionment covering a broad ideological spectrum. The mix of kitsch and erudition, fragmentation, irreverence, the opposition to the search for meanings beyond the work itself, the fetishization of commodities, and superficiality as an aesthetic language would be some of the characteristics of postmodern works. However, this list seeks not to exhaust but rather to open up the possibilities of a space in which the loss of the utopias of modernity does not always diminish the political potential of artistic quests.

Modernity and postmodernity cannot be read as phases within a temporal logic "but as problems of reading and rereading—retrospective and introspective—of the vocabularies (in crisis) of the configuration of subject/reason/history/progress" (Richard, "Latinoamérica," translation ours). In this sense, we can take "*Latin American* advantage" of what postmodernity signifies as fissures in the authority of central thought.

Reflection on Latin American modernity—culturally discontinuous, socially unequal, politically incomplete as it is—is obliged, in this new historical scene, to fold back upon itself, to debate its old paradigms and to revise the principles that have sustained it over the centuries. It involves taking a step back from the "static-essentialist and political-pragmatic premises" (Herlinghaus and Walters) and recognizing the identity of the continent as a complex whole made up of unstable systems that are heterogeneous and mutable.

Some Latin American theorists prefer the concept of "peripheral modernity" over that of "postmodernity" as a way of conceptualizing the contradictions between the modern projects and the historical backwardness of the region; it would be a way to reconsider—without abandoning the frame of rationality or the four central projects of modernity and its fundamental political commitment—the discrepancies between cultural modernity and social modernization that have developed as a result: in the same geographic space, the most destitute live alongside elites who have access to the most sophisticated of communications and technologies; alongside traditional cultural manifestations is mass media consumption that spans social classes; as historical political forms decline, social movements of a different nature gain momentum, their specific demands clearly transcending party lines. These are just a few examples of a panorama that extends beyond the dichotomies that have characterized modernity, such as highbrow/popular and rural/urban. How, for example, can we analyze the phenomenon of Mexican or Central American rural indigenous peoples who move to the United States and become bilingual in English and their mother tongue, bypassing Spanish altogether? Or the emergence of new social actors with unconventional demands and forms of struggle actors like Madres de Plaza de Mayo and Movimiento de los Sin Tierra? How can we understand post-avant-garde artistic production, in many cases already incorporated into the international mainstream, in the context of sky-high illiteracy rates? The concepts of modernity and postmodernity do not allow us to consider these realities, in that their use seeks to homogenize heterogeneity, or forget differences, limiting discussions to urban and lettered sectors; in this respect, they are insufficient and therefore not very productive in thinking about Latin American reality. Once again we are faced with the need to imagine possible responses and conceptual frameworks and not attempt to impose concepts coined by "hegemonic epistemes."

Certainly, the experiences of modernity are varied and changeable throughout the region. The intersection and interaction between popular culture, mass culture, and "high culture" characteristic of Latin American culture gave rise to a concept of "hybridity" (García Canclini, *Hybrid Cultures*) that has proved to be especially productive for thought on Latin American reality since the 1990s. This notion allows us to analyze the tense relationship that is established between the unfinished Latin American modernity and the phenomena characteristic of postmodernity; it offers tools for reading, through theory, the tense everyday point of contact that joins transnational economic neoliberalism and a deterritorialized culture of consumption with local forces, resignified ancestral traditions, and "premodern" spaces. This proposal does not abandon the frame of enlightened rationality, but rather complicates it, taking into account new scenarios.

There is definitely a consensus among the principal theorists about the "premodern-modern-postmodern conglomerate" that Latin American culture has become, although their ways of dealing with this reality may not always be similar (consider the reflections of José Joaquín Brunner, Jesús

Martín Barbero, Beatriz Sarlo, Nicolás Casullo, Carlos Monsiváis, John Beverley, Renato Ortiz, Walter Mignolo, and Nelly Richard, among others). In her analysis of Latin American postmodernity, Richard writes: "A mixture of *modes* (doubt in philosophy, parody and simulacrum in aesthetics, deconstruction in critical theory, skepticism in politics, relativism in ethics, syncretism in culture) and fashions (*modas*) (pastiche and citation in architecture, post-Marxist disenchantment, narcissist play and cool detachment, neutral eclecticism in cultural taste, and bland pluralism in social values, etc.)" ("Cultural Peripheries" 156). This "mixture" is also an example of the depoliticization that characterizes a certain concept of postmodernity in hegemonic countries, becoming in Latin America a space of subversion of the rationalist project through the insertion of "other" voices, "minority" voices that until now have been silenced: indigenous peoples, women, gays and lesbians.

It is in this context that the disciplines—communications, sociology, art theory, literary criticism, anthropology—have seen their boundaries blurred and consequently been forced to rethink their own relevance as well as the configuration of their traditional objects of study. Inter- and transdisciplinarity are not academic fads, but rather are demanded by the contemporary scene.

The proposals of Richard Hoggart, Raymond Williams, Stuart Hall, and other thinkers based in England in the 1970s, attempted primarily through literary studies, to reject the rigidity of the institutionalization of knowledge, via Marxism and certain elements of critical theory, to incorporate the problems of popular and media culture into the reflection being done in universities. To this legacy will be added a variety of discourses generated as much in academia—central and peripheral—as in all kinds of artistic, media, and cultural practices, forming, in a sense, the foundation for Latin American thought in studies of culture at the present moment. Through cultural studies, as well as through the revision of traditional disciplines, perhaps a more productive discussion of the modernity/postmodernity tension can be initiated, thereby enriching reflections on Latin American culture. The new studies about culture—will they be counterhegemonic or not? From the vantage point of these lines, we're betting that they will be.

Suggested Reading

Baudrillard, Jean. *Simulacra and Simulation*. Translated by Sheila Faria Glaser. Ann Arbor: University of Michigan, 1994.

Beverley, John, Michael Aronna, and José Oviedo, eds. *The Postmodernism Debate in Latin America*. Durham, N.C.: Duke University Press, 1995.
Casullo, Nicolás, ed. *El debate modernidad-posmodernidad*. Buenos Aires: Retórica, 2004.
García Canclini, Néstor. *Hybrid Cultures: Strategies for Entering and Leaving Modernity*. Translated by Christopher L. Chiappari and Silvia L. López. Minneapolis: University of Minnesota Press, 1995.
Habermas, Jürgen. "Modernity—An Incomplete Project." In *The Anti-Aesthetic: Essays on Postmodern Culture*, edited by Hal Foster, 3–16. Minneapolis: University of Minnesota, 1983.
Herlinghaus, Hermann, and Monika Walters, eds. *Posmodernidad en la periferia: Enfoques latinoamericanos de la nueva teoría cultural*. Berlin: Langer, 1994.
Huyssen, Andreas. *After the Great Divide: Modernism, Mass Culture, Postmodernism*. Bloomington: Indiana University Press, 1986.
Jameson, Fredric. *Postmodernism and Cultural Theories: Lectures in China* (Houxiandaizhuyi he Wenhualilun). Xi'an: Shaanxi Teachers University, 1987.
———. *Postmodernism, or, The Cultural Logic of Late Capitalism*. Durham, N.C.: Duke University Press, 1991.
Lyotard, Jean-François. *The Postmodern Condition: A Report on Knowledge*. Translated by Geoff Bennington and Brian Massumi. Minneapolis: University of Minnesota Press, 1984.
———. *The Postmodern Explained: Correspondence, 1982–1985*. Edited by Julian Pefanis and Morgan Thomas. Translated by Don Barry et al. Minneapolis: University of Minnesota Press, 1993.
Picó, Josep, ed. *Modernidad y postmodernidad*. Madrid: Alianza, 1988.
Richard, Nelly. *La estratificación de los márgenes: Sobre arte, cultura y políticas*. Santiago, Chile: Francisco Zegers, 1989.
Vattimo, Gianni, et al. *En torno a la posmodernidad*. Barcelona: Anthropos, 1994.

Postnationalism

CLAUDIA SADOWSKI-SMITH

The term "postnationalism" became popular throughout the 1990s to emphasize the declining role of the nation-state for the organization of social life, human activity, and academic inquiry in the age of globalization. Academic accounts of postnationalism come from a variety of disciplines, including political science, anthropology, sociology, and literary and cultural studies. Left-leaning and utopian in direction, many of these discourses view globalization as a process that erodes national borders and increases the potential to free marginalized ethnic groups from oppression by state and national forms.

Postnationalism especially celebrates minority and immigrant experiences of diaspora in First World countries and the increase in cultural productions about such experiences. Postnationalist discourses often emphasize that a growing number of racialized and immigrant communities maintain or reestablish ties with the countries or regions of origin from which they have been displaced. As they exhibit multiple loyalties, move between regions, and often become conduits for the increased flow of money, goods, information, images, and ideas across national boundaries, members of diaspora undermine state-sponsored nationalisms by defying a central aspect of state power—to define, discipline, control, and regulate all kinds of populations, whether in movement or in residence. Postnationalist discourses often diagnose increases in these transnational practices as manifestations of the declining role of the nation-state by collapsing its potential decline as an object of *emotional* investment with declarations about its decreasing role as a *political* entity.

Almost simultaneously with its surge in popularity, the rhetoric of postnationalism was critiqued for relying on questionable premises about a fundamental antagonism between transnational processes and the nation-state system. In fact, private corporations and nation-states have not been opposed to each other, but have collaborated in creating the very conditions and infrastructures of globality, such as financial, cultural, consumer, and labor markets that operate on a global scale. As members of free trade agreements and global caretaking institutions, nation-states have abdicated their sovereignty over certain kinds of cross-border movements. They have also decreased their proactive role in using social policy and other programs for immediate national development needs by encouraging domestic and international policies of deregulation, privatization, economic restructuring, and structural adjustment. Meanwhile, the neoliberal removal of barriers to free trade has allowed international trade and financial institutions as well as corporations to increasingly operate beyond the control of nation-states.

Despite their left-leaning direction, discourses celebrating the rise of diasporic citizenship practices and the demise of state-sponsored nationalisms thus tend to perpetuate the currently dominant neoliberal rhetoric that views globalization and nation-states as two separate and opposed entities to promote minimal state intervention into the operations of private corporations. Postnationalist celebrations of diaspora, for example, simply describe the global shifting and breaching of political boundaries by labor migrants who move in response to the pressures of global corporate restructuring and thus produce different notions of belonging than those traditionally associated with the nation-state (A. Ong). Much recent scholarship has also demonstrated that postnationalist expectations about the declining importance of state-sponsored forms of nationalism have been overstated. Nation-states have persisted in managing differential forms of access to civil, economic, and social citizenship rights, while traditional and dual forms of citizenship have continued to dominate anticipated postnationalist models (Bloemraad; P. James).

It may be instructive to look at the origin of postnationalist discourses in U.S. popular and academic discourses to understand their antistatist direction. For U.S. American studies scholars, who explore U.S. culture, postnationalist perspectives have promised an escape from the field's problematic nationalist origins. In many of its manifestations, American studies initially attempted to construct narratives of national development and identity that markedly differed from what were believed to be the United States' exclusively European origins, while also, ironically, perpetuating the belief that the country is dominated by a uniformly European-descended citizenry. (Exemplified by the work of scholars like R. W. B. Lewis, Perry Miller, and Leo Marx, the "myth and symbol school" came to replace the earlier, more narrowly defined focus on the American past with an interdisciplinary venture, combining methods of intellectual history, literary criticism, political theory, sociology, and cultural anthropology. In the 1950s Cold War climate, several American studies programs were created through the support of U.S. corporations and foundations. The American Studies Association also emerged at the time). In this sense, U.S. American studies have reinscribed assumptions about the United States' internal homogeneity and about the country's exceptionalist status in the world, particularly its difference from European countries and European forms of imperialism.

In a 1998 essay titled "Post-Nationalism, Globalism, and the New American Studies" (an essay later expanded into the introduction to *Post-Nationalist American Studies*), John Carlos Rowe highlighted postnationalism as a way to move American studies beyond narratives of U.S. "national character" and beyond the field's imperialist appropriation of the term "America." As a solution, Rowe proposes two postnationalist narratives, one focusing on the United States' internal diversity and a broader geopolitical lens that recognizes the "multicultural and multilingual histories of other nations in the hemisphere" (called "the Americas"). Both of these perspectives are modeled after Chicana/o studies' emphasis on points of historical, geographical, and linguistic contact between two or more communities (Rowe, "Post-Nationalism" 13). In addition to highlighting the recognition of the United States' internal diversity and its role in the hemisphere, Rowe follows the lead of other U.S. Americanists, most prominently Jane Desmond and Virginia Domínguez, who have called for the recognition of work about the United States by international scholars. Rowe argues specifically for the inclusion of scholarship that has characterized processes of globalization in other parts of the world as a form of "Americanization." He believes that, taken together, an internally comparative focus, a hemispheric model, and a global lens will produce "an understanding of the United States in the comparative contexts of Western hemispheric and, finally, global study" (21).

While Rowe's proposal masterfully summarizes ways to enlarge the focus on the United States, also in 1998 Frederick Buell articulated a powerful critique of one version of Rowe's postnationalism. Buell characterizes the focus on the United States' internal diversity as a "recovery narrative" that rewrites U.S. nationalism in postnationalist form rather than thoroughly challenging traditional models of nationhood. Narratives of internal diversity, writes Buell, have moved the United States beyond an initial rejection of globalization as a threat to U.S. internal traditions and U.S. global dominance. As a form of national consensus, multiculturalism has instead served corporate agendas that view U.S. postnationalist identity as the precursor of a new international order and in this sense commodify such an identity for use in domestic and international markets. Buell thus shows how multiculturalist discourses, which have emerged from the progressive focus on U.S. race and ethnicity, have ended up coming close to promoting U.S. paradigms to the rest of the globe in the realm of popular culture and media.

The recent emergence of empire studies has begun to correct some of the assumptions underlying postnationalist discourses within American studies by focusing on the role of the U.S. nation-state as an empire in addition to its function as nationalist mythmaker. Empire studies highlight manifestations of U.S. imperialism, both in relation to the country's internal population and to territories outside U.S. borders. As Amy Kaplan has shown, the United States' role as an empire that dates back to the 1863 Monroe Doctrine and U.S. interest in expansion into the Pacific and the Caribbean has long been ignored because prevailing notions of American exceptionalism have characterized the United States as a nation separate from European imperial powers. The belief in American exceptionalism has also put in place an artificial divide between continental expansion in the area of Manifest Destiny and the annexation of overseas territory as well as other manifestations of empire like trade and investment, the involvement in foreign markets, and the establishment of overseas military bases.

Besides dominating popular culture worldwide, the United States has also inscribed its economic and political domination over the hemisphere in the North American Free Trade Agreement and its proposed hemispheric extension. NAFTA has foremost created dependent sites of production in Mexican border areas, intensifying the development of *one* of Mexico's economies while the country as a whole is still faced with chronic unemployment, with millions subsisting on part-time work or struggling in the "informal" economy, and with wages declining in absolute and relative terms. The persistence and deepening of such hemispheric inequalities make it unlikely that U.S. postnationalist discourses, which are grounded in multicultural rhetoric and a celebration of the U.S. nation-state's demise, will find parallels south of the border.

In Latin America, while the term has not been as widely used, "postnationalism" has often functioned as a utopian designation for anticolonial discourses that critique U.S. dominance of the hemisphere. These discourses draw on the anticolonial histories of individual state-sponsored nationalisms and/or on calls to pan–Latin American solidarity in the face of United States imperialism that date back to the Spanish-American War. The war produced a wave of hemispheric consciousness exemplified in José Martí's anti-imperialist writings. Similarly, Mexican state-sponsored forms of nationalism that arose in the aftermath of the Mexican Revolution took on anticolonial overtones. Exemplified in José Vasconcelos's emphasis on Mexican identity as a form of *mestizaje,* concepts of Mexican identity were based on a strong dualism between the Anglo-Saxon Protestant and the Ibero-American Catholic world. The insistence on a Mexican identity that was shaped by the mixture of European and pre-Columbian cultures also set itself in direct opposition to notions of U.S. nationhood that have largely dismissed the influence of indigenous peoples.

In contemporary Latin American discourses of postnationalism, the nation-state (rather than state-sponsored forms of nationalism) often figures as a yet unfulfilled project through which it may be possible to articulate public interests and protect natural resources in the face of transnational corporate expansion, massive external debt, and U.S. foreign policy. Néstor García Canclini, for example, has argued that Mexico's membership in NAFTA and the European trade agreements with Mercosur countries make those two Latin American regions the ones primarily affected by the inter-American and Euro-American categories. He has highlighted the potentially positive effects of protectionist cultural policies, based on the collective efforts of various Latin American nation-states, for promoting greater Latin American self-expression on a global and regional level. And Roger Bartra has used the term "postnationalism" to signify the potential for popular democratic renewal that might emerge from Mexico's profound political crisis. Bartra explicitly cautions his international readers that "when I point out the need to overcome cultural unease, I am not proposing as a cure an integration of the Anglo-American world parallel to the economic agreements on free trade with the United States and Canada" (63).

While Latin American discourses of postnationalism thus differ from the U.S. emphasis on hybrid forms of citizenship, it will become increasingly important to establish intersections between the two approaches. Several tenets underlying postnationalist thought will help reform various academic fields of study and perhaps provide interdisciplinary links among them. Debra Castillo, for example, has recently argued that, in the manner of U.S. American studies, Spanish needs to become a "postnational" field held together by a focus on the language in which a work of literature is written rather than by the "imaginary consolidation of national literatures" (195). Besides expanding academic disciplines, we will also need comparative accounts of postnationalism throughout the globe that consider the persistent dominance of the United States. The U.S. postnationalist emphasis on diversity and extra-statal forms of citizenship have also helped conceal the United States' role in modeling the further decline of public services and safety nets, and the growths in societal inequality within and among nations that characterize neoliberal forms of globalization everywhere. Latin American thinkers not only appear to recognize these manifestations more clearly, but also critique them by emphasizing the nation-state as a potential vehicle for the protection of its citizenry and as a guarantor of sovereignty. What U.S. postnationalist discourses have identified as the crisis of the nation-state may simply signal growing contradictions between the increasing transnationalization of capital and the persistence of the state system as the exclusive political pattern in the world.

Suggested Reading

Bartra, Roger. "The Malinche's Revenge: Toward a Postnational Identity." In *Blood, Ink, and Culture: Miseries and Splendors of the Post-Mexican Condition*, translated by Mark Alan Healey, 61–64. Durham, N.C.: Duke University Press, 2002.

Bloemraad, Irene. "Who Claims Dual Citizenship? The Limits of Postnationalism, the Possibilitites of Transnationalism, and the Persistence of Traditional Citizenship." *International Migration Review* 38, no. 2 (Summer 2004): 389–426.

Buell, Frederick. "Nationalist Postnationalism: Globalist Discourse in Contemporary American Culture." *American Quarterly* 50, no. 3 (1998): 548–91.

Castillo, Debra A. *Redreaming America: Toward a Bilingual American Culture*. Albany: State University of New York Press, 2005.

Desmond, Jane C., and Domínguez, Virginia R. "Resituating American Studies in a Critical Internationalism." *American Quarterly* 48, no. 3 (1998): 475–90.

Gilman, Susan. "The New, Newest Thing: Have American Studies Gone Imperial?" *American Literary History* 17, no. 1 (2005): 196–214.

James, Paul. "Relating Global Tensions: Modern Tribalism and Postmodern Nationalism." *Communal/Plural: Journal of Transnational and Crosscultural Studies* 9, no. 1 (April 2001): 11–31.

Kaplan, Amy, and Donald E. Pease, eds. *Cultures of United States Imperialism*. Durham: Duke University Press, 1993.

Rocha Valencia, Alberto. *Configuración política de un mundo nuevo: Dimensiones políticas de lo global, lo supraregional, lo posnacional y lo local*. Guadalajara: Universidad de Guadalajara, 2003.

Rowe, John Carlos, ed. "Post-Nationalism, Globalism, and the New American Studies." *Cultural Critique* 40 (Fall 1999): 11–28.

———. *Post-Nationalist American Studies*. Berkeley: University of California Press, 2000.

Power

MARÍA INÉS GARCÍA CANAL (TRANSLATED BY MATTHEW RUSSELL)

Beginning in the 1980s, the term "power" began to acquire a new and singular importance in the analysis of the social and cultural problems of Latin America; it was the initial moment of the reception, discussion, criticism, and debate in Latin America regarding the work of the French philosopher Michel Foucault. His conception of power, developed from a series of archaeological and genealogical studies, made possible the fluid use, characterization, and analysis of this concept beyond the forms that had been employed until that time. This put into doubt the symbiosis between *power* and the *state* and its *apparatuses*, and caused, at the same time, an expansion of its use to the entire social structure.

Power, from this perspective, appears as a constant presence in the social realm, always acting, and in permanent tension. A fundamental characteristic of Foucault's proposal is that there is no exteriority of the subject in relation to power; the subject is always connected to it, and it therefore makes itself present in the actions and efficacy of the subject. In "The Subject and Power" Foucault writes that "what defines a relationship of power is that it is a mode of action which does not act directly and immediately on others. Instead it acts upon their actions: an action upon an action, on existing actions or on those which may arise in the present or the future" (220)—that is, a form of action not only over bodies but also over proposed meanings, affirmed significations, valorized images, and desires projected onto the future.

Power is strength and connection. It is a relation of forces. It is force in relation to other forces, a performing energy that covers the entire social field from one end to the other. It is not one single form (the state); rather, it expresses itself in all relationships. It cannot be understood as a simple repression: not only does it prohibit, it also incites and arouses, seduces, induces, facilitates; it hinders, expands, and limits.

This enunciation called into question a range of theoretical schools that, until that moment, had treated the issue: it placed doubt on the liberal conception of political power, which sees power as a right that the subject possesses and can transfer, dispose of, or cede either partially or completely; it confronted, in turn, the Marxist conception in which the fundamental role of power is to maintain and reproduce systems of production and class domination. It also placed under its critical eye the mode of conceiving of power as a repressing mechanism. It denied, at the same time, the attempt to apprehend power through the notion of representation: power is not constructed through will, whether individual or collective, nor does it derive from the interests or the intentions of individuals or groups; it is constructed and functions through multiple forces that cover the entire social field, without ever appearing in an independent form, and it is decipherable only from within these multiple relations that crisscross the social field.

Nor can power be equated with the figure of the master, since that would imply a reductive vision in which processes of power are mere legal prohibitions. This concept—which allows for power to be contemplated only in negative terms, and its workings only through language—is present in certain ethnological studies that center their analyses on prohibitions of alliance; it is also found in the psychoanalytical postures having to do with mechanisms of repression. Power, then, is converted into an emblematic instance of negation, as an interdiction or a repression that inevitably subjectifies. From the perspective of the execution of power, a "great absolute subject" appears, whether real, imaginary, or juridical, which prohibits or suppresses: the sovereignty of the father, the monarch, the tyrant, the general will. From the perspective of those over whom power is exercised, it also tends to subjectify, as it seeks to determine the point at which the subject accepts the prohibition, at which the subject says yes or no to power, which assumes that the subject renounces individual rights, the terms of the social contract, or else indicates the subject's voluntary subjugation for love of the master.

Power, as relationships of forces in continuous imbalance and tension, transforms the social space into a complex framework of relationships with its two poles: the exercising of power at one end and, at the other, the most diverse forms of resistance. Resistance is a constitutive element of power understood as a relation of force, and it transmits movement and creativity to the space in which it is played out.

Power relations observed from the perspective of their capacity for execution may take two different paths, though these may occur in tandem in a given space and time. On the one hand, they conform to an anatomo-politics directed particularly at the body of the subject, with an individualizing quality, whose technique is discipline; and, on the other hand, they produce a bio-politics directed at large populations, whose technique is governmentality.

Discipline exerts itself on bodies; it consists of imposing tasks or codes of conduct on a series of individuals. This results in a political anatomy that distributes bodies within a finite space, assigning a rhythm to these subjects' temporality as well as their body language under a regime of uninterrupted control and strict vigilance. Discipline is transformed, in Western modernity, into the privileged technique of the practice of power, whose objective is to efficiently individualize subjects in such a way as to achieve, with the greatest possible effectiveness, their homogenization, to make them subjects of normality.

Governability, in turn, consists of negotiating and controlling the lives of a large number of individuals (population) within an extensive and demarcated space (territory). It functions through a group of institutions, procedures, analyses, reflections, calculations, and tactics that permit the execution of power over a determined population. This system, whose fundamental knowledge is based on political economy, and whose tools are primarily mechanisms of security and the technologies of governance, then produces specific governing apparatuses, while developing a series of knowledges.

In the analysis of power relations it is necessary to examine not only the aforementioned regimes—the ensemble of enunciations emitted in a society at a given moment—but also their visibility, as the production of a perceptive field that distributes the clear and the obscure, the opaque and the transparent, the seen and the unseen, provoking the world of evidences. In this way, the multiple power relations of a determined social field, discursive or not, interwoven and in continuous movement, tension, and confrontation, make up the specific devices and mechanisms of strategic manipulation of the forces in a given domain.

The key term of the notion of power, which links it to the urgency of political action and makes it indispensable to cultural studies, is resistance. Resistance involves multiple forms and creative, multiplied responses to the subject converted into the vital energy that circulates through the entire society, making its existence possible. Resistance takes the form of an intervention in the social realm by subjects. It attempts to break existing norms, with their acquired certainties. It is always unexpected, inopportune, out-of-date; it therefore establishes a play on time; it is a present action against the present and against all perpetuated forms of the past in function of a time to come.

From this resistance, time makes its appearance, transmitting movement to the clash of forces and inscribing power into temporality. In this way, power relations forge their own history, encounter their own singular and never definitive forms that are always in motion and confrontation, always framed by a given space and time.

The notion of resistance, as a constitutive element of power, appears as a key term in research in Latin America (see Rodríguez, *Latin American Subaltern Studies Reader*; Mato, *Estudios y otras prácticas*; Quijano; Ludmer, "Las tretas"). The objective of these investigations is the study of subaltern groups, popular classes, migrations and diasporas, social, cultural, and artistic movements, as well as gender studies and those studies relating to the reception and consumption of cultural goods, and to the configuration and functioning of diverse institutions, especially the family. The analysis makes its appearance from the subject's capacity (real or virtual) to resist in the context of the quotidian in such a way that case studies that involve fieldwork cannot leave aside the description, analysis, and interpretation of the concrete forms that their respective power relations assume.

Resistance can assume three general characteristic forms. The subject may resist external assault by opposing it with a contrary force that is similar to the one exercised over the subject and that takes the form of negation. Resistance may also assume an affirmative character while transforming itself into an intervening force capable of affecting its surroundings. Or it may take another form: the relation of the subject to itself; it is a way for the subject to affect itself in a continual clash, dialogue, pact, agreement, and struggle between the parts that constitute its interiority.

The analysis of power is not the search for formal structures with universal value, but instead can only be carried out through historical investigation, through the search for forms of working order, quotidian tasks, its decomposition, ruptures, and discontinuities, the production of its mechanisms and technologies, always inscribed in a given space and with its own historicity.

The notion of resistance was taken up by cultural studies beginning with the perspective launched by Michel de Certeau (*Practice*) of centering his analysis on the quotidian practices of supposedly passive subjects in the face of discipline. Certeau's intention is to show the operating logic of practices that constitute "tactics of consumption," denominated as anti-discipline: popular procedures that play on the mechanisms of surveillance and discipline in order to break free of them, "ways of doing," minuscule procedures not privileged by history that execute their actions hidden within the mesh of instituted technologies.

Power seen in a positive light—as the producer of subjects, bodies, knowledges, and discourses—was critically taken up at the end of the twentieth century from various theoretical perspectives. Deconstructionist feminism, most notably the work of Judith Butler in *Bodies That Matter*, considers that the subject, the body, sex, and sexuality are effects of a power dynamic and of a discursive order, within both reiterative and referential practice by means of which discourse produces effects (performativity). Postcolonial studies, focused on the notion of bio-power, criticizes, from a Foucauldian perspective, Eurocentrism, revealed in modernity's insistent spatialization of time (Bhabha), in its silencing of colonial societies, and in imperial powers (Stoler). The notions of bio-power and governability have opened new perspectives of analysis and reflection, such as those that refer to societies of control (Hardt and Negri), naked life (Agamben), racism and postcolonial societies, and subaltern subjects (Dube, *Sujetos subalternos*).

Suggested Reading

Calveiro Garrido, Pilar. *Redes familiares de sumisión y resistencia.* Mexico City: Universidad Ciudad de México, 2003.

Certeau, Michel de. *The Practice of Everyday Life.* Translated by Steven F. Rendall. Berkeley: University of California Press, 1984.

Dube, Saurabh. *Sujetos subalternos: Capítulos de una historia antropológica.* Translated from the German by Franco and Ari Bartra. Mexico City: Colegio de México, 2001.

Foucault, Michel. *Discipline and Punish: The Birth of the Prison.* Translated by Alan Sheridan. New York: Pantheon, 1977.

———. *Dits et écrits (1954–1988).* 4 vols. Paris: Gallimard, 1994.

———. "The Subject and Power." In *Michel Foucault: Beyond Structuralism and Hermeneutics,* edited by Hubert Dreyfus and Paul Rabinow, 208–26. Chicago: University of Chicago Press, 1982.

García Canal, María Inés. *Foucault y el poder.* Mexico City: Universidad Autónoma Metropolitana–Xoxhimilco, 2002.

Hardt, Michael, and Antonio Negri. *Empire.* Cambridge, Mass.: Harvard University Press, 2000.

Stoler, Ann Laura. *Race and the Education of Desire: Foucault's "History of Sexuality" and the Colonial Order of Things.* Durham, N.C.: Duke University Press, 1995.

Public Sphere

ALEJANDRO MONSIVÁIS (TRANSLATED BY EDUARDO RABASA)

The public sphere is a space for discussion and collective deliberation, open to the voluntary participation of any person. By abiding to norms of inclusion, deliberation, and publicity, this concept interweaves naturally with many ideals of modernity. In particular, it contributes to the formulation, at the normative level, of the possibility of a convergence between rationality and political action. The public sphere is thus conceived as the space where citizens discuss matters of collective interest and where courses of political action that the community as a whole will undertake are defined and implemented.

Such a notion holds a powerful appeal. However, the strength of its attraction is equaled by the difficulties it faces in materializing. A model that seeks the coincidence of political participation and public reasoning seems incompatible with the contemporary world. In fact, the public sphere model may be founded on a simplified conception of the relation between private and public. Such a vision takes for granted that the state and civil society form an organic unit. There is no difference between the legislator and the citizen, social participation is political participation, and the private space is a realm in which kinship and affective relationships are closely linked to economic imperatives. A conception of this sort may be valid for societies with little differentiation—for example, classical Greece—but for a society that locates itself within the metaphor of a complex network that extends throughout the entire planet, such a conception is unproductive and naïve.

The incompatibility of the classical model of the public sphere with the geometry of modern societies has been acknowledged even by its own supporters. Hannah Arendt considered that modernity transformed once and for all the republican model of public space into a matter of history. In the same spirit, Jürgen Habermas (*The Structural Transformation*) showed that the emerging of the modern state bureaucracy, mass society, and culture industries led to the decline of the model of public opinion that was closest to the classical ideal: the bourgeois public sphere that reached its climax in Western Europe during the eighteenth century. This interpretation coincides with the criticisms expressed by such thinkers as Carl Schmitt and Niklas Luhmann, who rejected the possibility that a social space of communication transcends the irreducibility of political antagonisms, or its capability of holding up against the increasing differentiation of social systems.

The aspiration to rescue the notion of public sphere, if it persists, must overcome yet another obstacle: the political consequences of the normative assumptions of the classical model. In the republican view of public sphere, the notions of "community" and "common good" decorate a homogeneous, consensual, and closed image of society. This same posture embodies a masculine and belligerent vision of citizenship. Virtuous citizens are not only those interested in the common good; they are also those who will shed their blood for their community. Even with a liberal twist, this model of public sphere cannot account for the counterpublics (Fraser)—spaces in which subaltern identities and moral views are expressed.

Given these considerations, how may the renewed interest in the concept of public sphere in contemporary social theory be explained? An answer may be found in the fact that the norms of inclusion, deliberation, and publicity are still important for some strands of critical theory. The concept of public sphere that emerged toward the end of the twentieth century is not tied to concrete spatial localizations—the public plaza or, say, parliament. Instead, the understanding of the public space is metaphorical: it is a virtual space composed of an amorphous framework of conversations and discussions. Due to the technological resources provided by the mass media, communication is no longer linked to concrete spatial-temporal scenarios (Thompson). The visibility introduced by the media extends to every space in which social interactions occur. Virtual resources introduced by the Internet have led to a transformation in the conventional understanding of the public spaces of communication (Dean). It has resulted in not only an expansion in the possibilities of access and scope of conversations and their content, but also an opening of spaces of discursive and identity experimentation. Flow, instability, and mobility are all properties that strengthen the endurance and influence of virtual publics.

The impulse provided by virtual technologies has renewed the ideals of public space. But the question of the political importance of emerging publics remains open. How is it possible to revitalize the idea of a democratic public sphere? In principle, the emergence of any publicity space is linked with the mere possibility of the existence of social actions coordinated through communication. To reach a minimal understanding requires that interlocutors state the codes that regulate communication up front. When discussing the coordination of actions based upon agreements, the motivations and goals should be explicitly justified. Then, communicative interaction generates a form of social relation constituted by the possibility of scrutiny and the demands for a justification. Public opinion—an opinion that anyone who is interested can access—is turned into *public-political* opinion when the matter of the discussion is the normative bases of social and political cooperation, the courses of political action, and the legitimacy of procedures and outcomes.

In contemporary societies, the emergence and sustainability of the public sphere depend upon associative dynamics having a relative autonomy with regard to market imperatives and political-administrative power. In this sense, Cohen and Arato have pointed out the need to protect the rights of freedom, association, communication, and expression to ensure associative autonomy and noncoerced public debate. Along the same lines, in *Between Facts and Norms,* Habermas manages to reconcile the normative principles of publicity, communication, and democratic legitimacy with the functional differentiation of social systems. According to Habermas, the public sphere is the metaphorical space where an anonymous, decentralized, and fluid opinion constitutes the communicative power that is to be transformed, through democratic procedures, into legitimate legal resolutions and state power. In this way, Habermas gives continuity to the aspirations of the critical theory of articulating democratic participation along with the exercise of public reasoning in increasingly complex societies. However, as many critics have pointed out, the reconciliation of the normative edge of critical theory with the systemic and functional demands of current societies occurs in such a way that the result is a pretty conventional model. One wonders where the radical potential of a democracy dependent upon public opinion influencing legislative processes stands.

A revalorization—post-Habermasian, so to speak—of the concept of public sphere has been made by the supporters of deliberative democracy. Deliberative theorists argue that the concept of the public sphere is associated with the expectation of multiplying the spaces of political justification, symbolic contestation, and democratic coordination. To begin with, public reasoning doesn't need to follow a rationalist model of argumentation; it can rest on a wide variety of rhetorical resources—narratives, testimonies, and emotional expressions (I. Young).

On the other hand, inasmuch as deliberative dynamics are based on diverse associative expressions and discursive contentions (Dryzek), they are linked to networks of influence and social communication that transcend conventional structures of governance and go beyond state and regional frontiers. Indeed, the function of discourses in the public sphere is not limited to exerting an influence on the direction of political power; they also may strengthen the democratic norms and practices within society itself.

Deliberative theorists have also become interested in the political and cultural consequences of diverse publics that either emerge in specific situations or are localized in special sectors of the state or society, such as "minipublics" (Fung). Included in the category of "minipublic" is a wide variety of formats of participation and social discussion: educational forums whose purpose is to promote deliberation, units of consulting and advising, mechanisms of citizenship participation in the implementation and evaluation of public policies, decentralized public administration organisms that are run by citizen councils, among others. Because of its varied scope, they represent plural instances in which politics and public deliberation may converge to offer effective solutions to problems of collective coordination.

Studies in Latin America have made innovative contributions to the development of the concept of public sphere. In the field of political philosophy, Nora Rabotnikof explicitly underlines the tensions in contemporary political thought associated with the possibility of imagining a "common place"—a space that, resting on the principle of publicity, would be capable of conferring rationality on the exercise of power and politics. In the same way, on the level of historical investigation, the concept of public sphere has allowed the highlighting of the emergence of spaces of free association and expression during the construction of nation-states in Latin America. Many studies have registered the circumstances associated with the development of freedom of the press, the media, and diverse forms of association in Latin American countries during the nineteenth and twentieth centuries.

One of the fields in which theoretical reflection and empiric research have been particularly productive is that concerning the relationship between public space and the recent trend of democratization in Latin American. For instance, a work by Leonardo Avritzer shows how the emergence of diverse "participating publics" introduced institutional innovations of a deliberative nature and dislocated some of the bases of authoritarianism in several countries—a collective and undifferentiated conception of the "people," the colonization and manipulation by the state of the sphere of associative practices, and the hybridization between public and private. Other studies (see, for example, Olvera) have underscored the importance of associative dynamics and discursive disputes in the public sphere and their impact on the institutional development of Latin American polities. Among the unresolved issues on an agenda of sociocultural investigation of public spaces we find the conditions under which public discourses emerge, the mechanisms of circulation that these discourses generate, and the ways in which they participate in the definition of current symbolic codes.

Suggested Reading

Arendt, Hannah. *The Human Condition*. Chicago: University of Chicago Press, 1958.

Avritzer, Leonardo. *Democracy and the Public Space in Latin America*. Princeton, N.J.: Princeton University Press, 2002.

Cohen, Jean L., and Andrew Arato. *Civil Society and Political Theory*. Cambridge, Mass.: MIT Press, 1992.

Dean, Jodi. "Cybersalons and Civil Society: Rethinking the Public Sphere in Transnational Technoculture." *Public Culture* 13, no. 2 (2001): 243–65.

Fraser, Nancy. "Rethinking the Public Sphere: A Contribution to the Critique of Actually Existing Democracy." In *Habermas and the Public Sphere*, edited by Craig Calhoun, 109–41. Cambridge, Mass.: MIT Press, 1992.

Fung, Archon. "Recipes for Public Spheres: Eight Institutional Design Choices and Their Consequences." *Journal of Political Philosophy* 11, no. 3 (2003): 338–67.

Habermas, Jürgen. *Between Facts and Norms: Contributions to a Discourse Theory of Law and Democracy*. Translated by William Rehg. Cambridge, Mass.: MIT Press, 1996.

———. *The Structural Transformation of the Public Sphere: An Inquiry into a Category of*

Bourgeois Society. Translated by Thomas Burger with Frederick Lawrence. Cambridge, Mass.: MIT Press, 1989.

Olvera, Alberto J., ed. *Sociedad civil, esfera pública y democratización en América Latina: Mexico*. Mexico City: Fondo de Cultura Económica, 2003.

Rabotnikof, Nora. *En busca de un lugar común: El espacio público en la teoría política contemporánea*. Mexico City: Instituto de Investigaciones Filosóficas, UNAM, 2005.

Queer Theory

ROBERT MCKEE IRWIN

The word "queer" has been employed since the early twentieth century to refer to homosexuality, or more precisely to sexual heterodoxy in all its possibilities (Chauncey 15–16). In contexts in which more explicit terms would be too scandalous, "queer" has served as a useful code word. In the sometimes puritanical United States in the early twentieth century, where the sexualized meaning of the word originated, the term assumed a derogatory tone reflective of the discomfort evoked by sexual questions in general, and by sexual diversity in particular. "Queer" signaled sexual abnormality, difference, and perversion, and its usage implied repulsion.

Around 1990, the term took on new life during an era of activism by groups protesting the lack of attention paid by the U.S. government to the AIDS epidemic. As many of the country's most visible political and religious leaders were poised to let those with AIDS die simply because they were different (queer) and therefore "immoral," activists, including a newly formed radical group called Queer Nation, staged actions questioning the ethical criteria that determined "normalcy." Queer Nation also reacted against an essentialism endemic to both AIDS activism and gay rights organizing in general, which tended to define themselves through fixed identities and a hetero/homo binary. The most visible gay identity among militants had always been that of white middle-class men, leaving groups of other races, income levels, and gender identities marginalized within activist organizations. Members of Queer Nation insisted on rejecting binary identities—man/woman, hetero/homo, masculine/feminine, active/passive—instead assuming and emphasizing more fluid and varied subjectivities. The queers of Queer Nation proudly and inclusively strove to represent all categories of the sexually marginalized, heterodox, unconventional, and abnormal. They appropriated the word "queer," empowering themselves with a concept that had until then been used against them, converting its meaning into a positive descriptor of sexual heterodoxy, indeed celebrating difference, rejecting identity politics as conformist, and making sexual diversity visible. Queer Nation did not last long as an active organization, but its impact was significant, both in popular culture and in the academy.

Its objectives, in effect, provoked a great deal of academic interest. What had until that time been known as "gay and lesbian studies" was a product of the gay activism of the 1960s and 1970s of pioneering homosexuals whose curiosity concerning themes of sexuality, almost always articulated in the binary terms of hetero/homo, frequently complicated their professional lives, given the institutional homophobia of the academy, and found little legitimacy in universities or related institutions such as academic publishers and fellowship-granting foundations. Indeed, many of the earliest studies on questions of sexual diversity in world history; biographies of queer artists, scientists, political leaders; anthropological investigations on sexual behaviors; and aesthetic analyses of homoerotic works of art or literature were realized outside the academy, and published by nonacademic publishers.

The urgency of the AIDS crisis and the militancy that it generated were key in challenging the academic status quo. Questions that had previously been hidden within the "closet" of private life suddenly became visible. Many academics who identified as liberal were made to face their own homophobia upon learning of the homosexuality of their colleagues, students, and neighbors. But at the very moment that gay and lesbian studies began to find acceptance—for example, through its institutionalization in such daringly innovative programs as those of the Center for Lesbian and Gay Studies of the City University of New York—they were attacked from within. The concept of queerness promoted by Queer Nation led to a deconstruction of the intellectual underpinnings of the project of gay and lesbian studies, most particularly the notion of fixed sexual identity and binary categories of sexuality.

The year 1990, roughly the height of Queer Nation's activism, saw the publication of two books whose arguments coincided in important ways with the questioning of sexual identity politics of the activists. One came from the field of literary criticism: Eve Kosofsky Sedgwick's *Epistemology of the Closet*. Its author, a professor of English literature, had already gained attention with a previous book, *Between Men*, for its use of the provocative notion of the "homosocial" to interrogate various categories of relationships of male bonding that could often be very close, without (necessarily) being sexual. In *Between Men*, Sedgwick identified significant implications of homoeroticism in contexts that appeared on the surface to be heterosexual or even homophobic.

In *Epistemology*, Sedgwick continued with her deconstructive critical reading of binary notions of sexuality in English and U.S. literature, finding various contradictions in their meanings. On the one hand, it appears that there are only two categories of sexual desire and sexual identity: hetero and homo. However, if this were the case, the notion of "homosexual panic" would not exist. Homosexual panic refers to the reaction of a heterosexual man to the threat of homosexuality brought on by his becoming too close to a homosexual man, a reaction that might often take the form of homophobic violence. This fear of "contagion" of an encroaching but external homosexuality is indicative of a second notion generally shared in the same (English and U.S.) cultures, that of the existence of a continuum of varying degrees of sexual desire and identity that ranges from one extreme of absolute heterosexuality to another of exclusive homosexuality, with infinite intermediary gradations.

Aside from highlighting the fundamental contradiction in these basic notions of sexuality, upon analyzing the metaphor of the "closet," a slang expression that refers to the (essential and real) homosexual life hidden beneath a (visible but feigned) heterosexual façade, Sedgwick deconstructs a lengthy list of fundamental concepts of Anglophone culture that are conceived of through binary oppositions—masculine/feminine, hetero/homo, public/private—many of which have little to do directly with sexual identity. Sedgwick thus signals how sexual diversity, and the homophobia it provokes, profoundly marks everyday life for everyone, if not through active desires and assumed identities, then through repressions, fears, and hatreds. Queerness, for Sedgwick—although still not articulated using this terminology—was a problem that implied a need to deconstruct Anglophone culture as a whole. Subsequent to Sedgwick, the practice of "queer reading," that is, the interrogation of the apparently orthodox from a perspective that recognizes that queerness is likely lurking anywhere, became immensely popular, especially in literature departments of the Anglophone academy.

The other highly influential book published in 1990 was more of a theoretical interrogation of notions of gender identity that brought feminist theory, philosophy, and psychoanalysis to bear on gender-oriented identity politics. The author of *Gender Trouble*, Judith Butler, carried out a deconstruction of the concept of gender by way of a meticulous juxtaposing of lines of thinking from multiple fields, including those of psychoanalysts Sigmund Freud and Melanie Klein, feminists Simone de Beauvoir and Julia Kristeva, historian and philosopher Michel Foucault, and anthropologist Claude Levi-Strauss, ending with a provocative reading of a forgotten study by a U.S. anthropologist of a much less elevated stature than any of these figures, and whose marginalization may well have been due to the controversial nature of her work. The book in question, *Mother Camp: Female Impersonators in America*, which studied the way of life of drag queens active in urban nightclubs in the United States, was first published in 1972 by Esther Newton. Butler, upon rereading the account of these transvestites, identified a patently artificial articulation of gender (masculinity/femininity) not as an essential or biologically founded aspect of the subject, nor as a mere ideological construction absorbed through education, but as a "performance," an act of representation learned subconsciously or realized consciously by the subject. This performative aspect of gender also caused a stir, as it broke with eternal debates on determinism versus constructionism and held important implications for identity politics.

Another of Butler's books, *Bodies That Matter* (1993), followed the same deconstructionist line but took on more consciously the concept of queerness, reiterating, for example, that the lack of a biological essence that predetermines identity (and refutation of any scheme that would insist on basing identity upon the binary categories of man/woman and heterosexual/homosexual) does not mean that bodies have no influence on the roles subjects assume (thus the book's title). It also does not make it impossible or even necessarily imprudent to form communities or social movements based on shared needs or objectives defined in terms of essentialist identity categories. Identity politics, which assumes a constellation of political desires shared by a community with the same fixed identity, had been jolted into crisis, as the notion of homosexuality was, from this perspective, just as problematic as that of heterosexuality. Nonetheless, Butler argued that it can sometimes be expedient to assume positions aligned with a false shared identity, in an act of "phantasmatic" identification, in order to form a community of subjects with shared interests so as to be able to struggle together for change. Queerness thus maintains its power to unite not only homosexuals but also individuals of diverse sexual identities and desires: bisexuals, transgenders, sadomasochists, intersexuals, and all others who do not fit neatly into the reductive categories prescribed by the unwritten codes of "heteronormativity," the normative force aimed at universalizing heterosexual orthodoxy, which has been a fundamental aspect of many religions, nation-building projects, and branches of the sciences (Warner xxi).

The visibility of AIDS activists, the resonance of the books of Sedgwick and Butler and others, and a new public presence of sexual diversity, most particularly in such mass media as movies, television, and music videos, incited an explosion of intellectual curiosity, which manifested itself in conferences and symposia, new courses and workshops, and a boom in academic articles and books, now published by prestigious academic publishers and journals, for example *GLQ: A Journal of Lesbian and Gay Studies*. From within various disciplines, scholars began to assiduously investigate issues of sexuality, and they did so from this new "queer" angle: they studied institutions from their margins; they questioned both the abnormal and the normal, but from their exclusions. Cultural studies, with its inherent interdisciplinarity, its focus on both elite and popular and mass media cultural expression, and its underlying political objectives, has found the project of queer studies falling unofficially under its rubric in the Anglophone academy.

In recent years, the legitimacy that both queer studies within the academy and queer identities in mainstream culture have gained has led to a political agenda focused upon further consolidating this legitimacy—gays in the military, gay marriage, gay adoption—leading contemporary critics to insist upon queer theory as a practice of rupture of and not conformance to norms, thus challenging what has been deemed the discourse of "homonormativity," or of homosexuality becoming just one more minority identity to be assimilated and absorbed into the mainstream (Duggan).

Despite a persistent institutional machismo and resulting homophobia both within the Latin American academy and among Latin Americanists in other countries, a few pioneers such as the Argentine Néstor Perlongher (*O negócio do michê: Prostitução viril em São Paulo*, 1987) began to carry out studies on themes related to sexual diversity before they became acceptable within such institutional spaces. Indeed, the political repression of the 1970s was built upon a generalized ideology of intense homophobia that reacted with arbitrary violence to any expression of a nonnormative or nonreproductive sexuality (this was the case not only in right-wing military dictatorships but also, for example, in communist Cuba). Even with the gradual rise of gay activism, gay culture, and gay community in some Latin American cities in the 1980s, it was nearly impossible to obtain academic support for research or publication on these kinds of topics in Latin America. Thus many of the first Latin American publications that took up perspectives of queer theory were produced either by activists (Jáuregui), by activist scholars at great personal and professional risk (Mott), by activist scholars obtaining significant support abroad (Mogrovejo), or by scholars working from "safe" spaces within the U.S. academy (Salessi; Quiroga; Arroyo).

In the English-speaking academy, in the field of Latin American literary studies, the publication in 1995 of the critical anthology *¿Entiendes? Queer Readings, Hispanic Writings*, edited by Hispanists Emilie Bergmann and Paul Julian Smith, who compiled sixteen critical essays on questions of sexuality in cultural production (principally literature) of Hispanophone cultures, was something of a watershed. This and other similar books, among them Balderston and Guy's *Sex and Sexuality in Latin America* (1997) and Molloy and Irwin's *Hispanisms and Homosexualities* (1998), applied queer readings to an ever greater variety of genres of cultural texts: literature, autobiography, film, television, ethnography, epistles.

By the 1990s, Latin American scholars, too, began to engage increasingly in research on themes related to sexual diversity. Some of these works analyzed aspects of contemporary culture—the openly queer expression of writers and artists, strategies of resistance against homophobia, the devastating effects of AIDS, among many others—putting traditions of literary criticism in dialogue with sociology, anthropology, and psychoanalysis. Social science studies, such as that of Perlongher, researched sexual behaviors and identities, gender constructs, structures of community, and performances of gender roles. Other studies focused on the past, teasing out queer histories both by reinterpreting the artistic or literary production of known closeted homosexuals and their "mundo soslayado," or world of furtive glances (a term that Carlos Monsiváis applies to the life of queer Mexican poet Salvador Novo), and also by discovering nonheteronormative aspects of even such apparently homophobic institutions as the literary canon, national culture, politics, and sports. On the one hand, critics have studied the most obviously queer aspects of Latin American culture—the lives and works of Cuban "queer" poets (Sierra Madero), "queer" participation in the Mexican public sphere (Marquet), the work of pioneering "queer" activists in Brazil (Trevisan)—in order to legitimate their status as a topic of intellectual inquiry; on the other hand, their research has gone "beyond carnival" (*Beyond Carnival* is the title of a multifaceted study of Brazilian cultural history by historian James Green), deconstructing the most homophobic works of cultural production or institutions, or reinterpreting those that appear to be the least queer, such as macho nationalism, in order to demonstrate the ubiquity of queerness and the impossibility of definitively separating the orthodox from the heterodox. These studies outed some well-known figures, sometimes inciting emotional discussions—for example, on the poet Gabriela Mistral in Chile (Fiol-Matta). Of great influence on these scholars was the work of Michel Foucault, most particularly his *History of Sexuality*, in which he proposed "the discursive hypothesis," arguing that discourse that attempts to repress ends up producing what it seeks to erase. This theory made it possible to seek out sexual diversity even in those cultures least open to sexual freedom and has been applied repeatedly to Latin America.

While it is true that many distinguished Latin American scholars continue to exhibit disdain toward gender and sexuality studies (Molloy, "La flexión"), spaces dedicated to these areas of research have opened up, among them the Programa Universitario de Estudios de Género of the Universidad Nacional Autónoma de México and the independent Área Queer NorOeste Argentino. Indeed, Latin America's burgeoning graduate programs in cultural studies have begun to take on queer studies as an important area of inquiry. Latin American queer criticism, which is published in specialized journals such as *Debate Feminista* in Mexico, and with a certain regularity in more broadly defined cultural studies journals such as *Revista de Estudios Sociales* in Colombia or *Comunicaçaõ, Mídia e Consumo* in Brazil, and informs provocative works and sometimes highly visible public interventions by writers and performers such as the Chilean Pedro Lemebel and the Mexico-based team of Jesusa Rodríguez and her Argentine-born partner Liliana Felipe, has quickly made inroads within the Latin American academy. Still, only recently, despite the rhetoric of "diversity" expounded by critics informed by queer theory and that of social justice articulated by specialists in postcolonial studies, have these two schools been brought into productive dialogue through analysis of issues of sexuality in contexts outside the mainstream of national cultures, or of considerations of sexuality in tandem with interrogations on social class or race. Nonetheless, queer themes are becoming more and more prevalent among thesis topics in Latin American cultural studies, a new dynamism driven less by an effort on the part of cultural studies faculty than by student demand generated by students' own activist agendas. Indeed, public debates and legal inroads on such issues as gay marriage or legally recognized civil unions in Argentina, Brazil, Colombia, Mexico, Uruguay, and Ecuador have brought issues of sexual heterodoxy to the fore, and ensure that they will remain prominent in Latin American cultural studies for years to come.

Suggested Reading

Butler, Judith. *Bodies That Matter: On the Discursive Limits of "Sex."* New York: Routledge, 1993.

———. *Gender Trouble: Feminism and the Subversion of Identity*. New York: Routledge, 1990.

Chauncey, George. *Gay New York: Gender, Urban Culture, and the Makings of the Gay Male World, 1890–1940*. New York: Basic Books, 1994.

Duggan, Lisa. "The New Homonormativity: The Sexual Politics of Neoliberalism." In *Materializing Democracy: Toward a Revitalized Cultural Politics*, edited by Russ Castronovo and Dana D. Nelson, 175–94. Durham, N.C.: Duke University Press, 2002.

Foucault, Michel. *The History of Sexuality*. Translated by Robert Hurley. 3 vols. New York: Pantheon, 1978–86.

Molloy, Sylvia. "La flexión del género en el texto cultural latinoamericano." *Revista de Crítica Cultural*, no. 21 (2004): 54–56.

Monsiváis, Carlos. *Salvador Novo: Lo marginal en el centro*. Mexico City: Era, 2000.

Santiago, Silviano. "The Wily Homosexual (First—And Necessarily Hasty—Notes)." In *Queer Globalizations: Citizenship and the Afterlife of Colonialism*, edited by Arnaldo Cruz Malavé and Martin F. Manalansan IV, translated by Robert McKee Irwin and Arnaldo Cruz Malavé, 13–19. New York: New York University Press, 2002.

Sedgwick, Eve Kosofsky. *Between Men: English Literature and Male Homosocial Desire*. New York: Columbia University Press, 1985.

———. *Epistemology of the Closet*. Berkeley: University of California Press, 1990.

Warner, Michael, ed. *Fear of a Queer Planet: Queer Politics and Social Theory*. Minneapolis: University of Minnesota Press, 1993.

Race/Ethnicity

EDUARDO RESTREPO (TRANSLATED BY ARTURO VARGAS)

In the approach to cultural studies that traces its roots to Birmingham and the Centre for Contemporary Cultural Studies (CCCS), the problematics of race appeared at the end of the 1970s. Stuart Hall and Paul Gilroy are the two most notable figures in this approach to cultural studies, which has since focused its attention on aspects related to race and ethnicity. On the whole, the elaborations of race and ethnicity developed in this context stemmed from challenges to economicist reductionism, which is peculiar to "vulgar materialism," and to its opposing view, discursive reductionism, which is associated with certain textualist movements.

The challenge to economicist reductionism consists of a departure from the different theoretical framings that had subsumed the analyses of race and ethnicity into a simple reflection of class or economic aspects; it was argued that race and ethnicity were relatively autonomous with respect to other components of social formation in general, and that they were irreducible to economic aspects in particular. This challenge to economicist reductionism, however, did not signify that this approach to cultural studies would adhere to those more extreme sociologically oriented movements that rejected any relationship between race or ethnicity and the material conditions of economic production and moreover disregarded class relations within a given social formation. According to such movements, race and ethnicity were autonomous social phenomena, comprehensible in their own terms. That is to say, race and ethnicity constituted a particular case of social relationships, whether in the establishment of differences and hierarchies within a particular society or in the juxtaposition (generally by force) of different social orders. Although this approach to cultural studies concurred with these sociological movements in not considering race and ethnicity simply as derivatives of economic aspects, it differed from those extreme views that flatly rejected any economic conditioning whatsoever. The categories of "articulation" and "overdetermination," imbued in the works of Laclau and Althusser, offered theoretical inputs to this approach to cultural studies so that it might elaborate theories of social totality and determination that took into account the material conditions of existence of social formations while circumventing the problems peculiar to "vulgar materialism" and economicism (Hall, "Race").

In its elaborations of race and ethnicity, this approach to cultural studies has also questioned discursivist reductionism. This reductionism derives from an overinterpretation of the "discursive turn" that considers race and ethnicity reducible to the discourses that constitute them. Although this approach to cultural studies is squarely in agreement with the affirmation that social reality in general, and race and ethnicity in particular, are discursively constituted, it distances itself from those who thereby conclude that discourse is the foundation of intelligibility to which everything social can be reduced. This approach to cultural studies does not consider the discursive dimension of race and ethnicity to be merely an aggregate that in due course integrates formerly constituted nondiscursive relationships and practices. Consequently, this approach is not limited to a discursive analysis, nor does it fail to recognize the relevance of the nondiscursive dimensions of any practice or relationship in a particular social formation. Less still does this approach concur with those movements that reduce what is discursive to a formalist conceptualization of language, while treating race and ethnicity as either systems of social classification, concepts that are "good to think about," or systems of the exchange of signs.

In addition to challenging economicist and discursivist reductionisms, this approach to cultural studies underscores the historicity of race and ethnicity. In other words, it argues that race and ethnicity are historically and contextually constituted (Hall, "Problem"). Rather than fixed and immutable entities that are found in every time and place, race and ethnicity are products of concrete historical conditions, and they vary in substance from one social formation to another. Consequently, this premise of historicity signifies challenges to both biologistic and culturalist essentialisms. This approach to cultural studies questions biologistic essentialism which supposes the idea that race may be a biological reality and would therefore be an expression of "human nature." Contrary to biologistic essentialism, this approach to cultural studies concurs with a preponderance of contemporary academic opinion in its supposition that the idea of race as a biological entity traces its origins to the European colonial expansion with its Eurocentric topologies and hierarchizations of human beings and of nature in general. Although this notion of race as a biological entity has been refuted by the biological sciences since the middle of the last century, the idea has persisted in various forms in the collective imaginary and as common sense, prescribing an interweaving of practices of differentiation, regulation, normalization, exclusion, and control. These multiple and changeable practices, relationships, and representations, which constitute race as if it were a biological entity within a particular social formation, are examined from the perspective of this approach to cultural studies.

Along the same lines, the historicism of this approach to cultural studies also questions culturalist essentialism. According to culturalist essentialist thinking, ethnicity and race appear as expressions of a few primary cultural features that are preserved as immutable throughout history. This vision could not be more distant from that of cultural studies, which does not explain ethnicity and race as resulting from isolations and emanations of primary cultural nuclei that are rooted in a supposed collective unconscious. Instead, cultural studies treats ethnicity and race as resulting from interactions that are situated historically in contexts of power relationships constituent of groups, identities, and particular subjects.

The distinction between the two categories is another aspect to consider in the elaboration of race and ethnicity in the view of cultural studies associated with Birmingham, and especially with the work of Stuart Hall. Although he analytically distinguishes ethnicity from race, Hall believes that there are analogies and superpositions between these two categories. Generally speaking, in Hall's view, ethnicity is a concept that has been associated with a social location (the language of place) and articulated by means of "cultural features" ("Question"). Race, on the other hand, has been related to discrimination, employing somatic characteristics that operate as racial diacritics ("Conclusion" 222–23).

Nonetheless, Hall transcends this simple opposition between race and ethnicity, further noting that although "biological racism" utilizes corporal characteristics as diacritics of race, these characteristics connote social and cultural differences. In the last few decades, this notion of race has been displaced by an explicitly cultural concept. More extreme notions of biological race, expressed in eugenics, social Darwinism, and fascism, "have been replaced by *cultural* definitions of race, which allow race to play a significant role in discourses about the nation and national identity" ("Question" 618). This displacement of racial thought from somatically based racism toward a culturally based form is represented in Paul Gilroy's concept of "cultural racism" (*There Ain't*).

As far as Hall is concerned, in ethnicity "the articulation of difference with Nature (biology and the genetic) is present, but displaced *through kinship and intermarriage*" ("Conclusion" 223). In Hall's view, these discourses of ethnicities and races (biologically or culturally sutured) are strongly interrelated, even if they constitute distinguishable systems of discursive practices and subjectivities that divide and classify the social world with its specific histories and its modes of operation. Despite their particularities, these discourses constitute two registers of racism: biological racism and cultural differentialism ("Conclusion" 223).

Racism inscribes ineluctable and naturalized differences and hierarchies onto a social formation: "Racism, of course, operates by constructing impassable symbolic boundaries between racially constituted categories, and its typically binary system of representation constantly marks and attempts to fix and naturalize the difference between belongingness and otherness" (Hall, "New Ethnicities" 445). Racism should be understood as a type of practice whose specificity refers to the ineluctable naturalization of the segregation, separation, and hierarchization of difference: "Racism is a structure of discourse and representation that tries to expel the Other symbolically—blot it out, put it over there in the Third World, at the margin" (Hall, "Ethnicity" 16). Racism must be analyzed as a series of practices more or less institutionalized in specific social formations. The deployment of these practices guarantees the inscription of relationships of inequality, asymmetry, and exclusion onto the social and individual body. Having established this, as he did with notions of race and ethnicity, Hall emphasizes the plurality and historicity of racism, arguing for the existence of a plurality of racisms rather than one sole racism.

In Latin America, there are multiple elaborations of race and ethnicity that can clearly be considered in dialogue with cultural studies. Among the most relevant are the work of Claudia Briones in Argentina with her conceptualization of "aboriginality," that of Marisol de la Cadena concerning the "indigenous mestizos" of Peru, and, focusing on the coloniality of power, the body of work associated with the doctorate in cultural studies at the Universidad Andina Simón Bolívar (UASB) in Quito, coordinated by Catherine Walsh.

Briones proposes transcending the increasingly sterile debates anchored in discussions about decontextualized semantics, which tend to presume the given character of categories such as "ethnic group" or "race." In Briones's view, it becomes theoretically and methodologically important to emphasize a *pragmatics of social uses* that is linked to specific historical contexts (257). In this regard, Briones suggests that the notion of "aboriginality" be explored as an analytical alternative in the context of a political economy of cultural (difference) production (242–43). Accordingly, "aboriginality" may be understood from a processual and relational perspective with two focal points: the coproduction of others (marked-different) and us (unmarked-different), and their inscription onto a social framework of exclusions and inclusions that belong to the dialectics of the permanent reproduction and contestation of hegemony and subalternity.

For her part, Marisol de la Cadena has been working from the perspective of a historicization of the notions of *mestizaje* that have operated at different times in the twentieth century in Peru and elsewhere in Latin America. Her analyses of the discourses and practices of local articulations of *mestizaje* and Indianness have shown how cultural features such as education, manner of dress, and urbanity serve as racial diacritics, making "race" a category that can invoke either the sphere of culture or that of biology. De la Cadena suggests a methodology of radical contextualism and historicization, employing "dialogism as epistemological mode to explore the multiple meanings inscribed in the genealogy of the identity label 'mestizo,' and its related political ideology, *mestizaje*" ("Are Mestizos Hybrid?" 262).

Finally, also significant is the body of work affiliated with the doctorate in cultural studies from UASB because of its novel approach to race and ethnicity as viewed from the intellectual and political project of modernity/coloniality (Walsh, *Pensamiento*). Working from the elaboration of an "other" mode of thought that questions Eurocentric foundations of modernity and Western knowledge, this approach demonstrates how racial thought has played a key role in constituting coloniality. Consequently, it seeks to intervene in the very terms from which the geopolitics of modern/colonial knowledge operates, casting away the racial thought that subalternizes other experiences, selves, and knowledges. To that end, indigenous and Afrodescendent social movements are articulated from a standpoint of colonial difference, offering alternatives to modernity and providing epistemic, ontological, and existential stratagems geared toward decoloniality.

Inspired in part by cultural studies in Latin America, an equally copious body of work has been advanced to address race and ethnicity with a focus on Afrodescendent populations. Research by Livio Sansone concentrating on Brazil, Jean Rahier on Ecuador, Kevin Yelvington on the Caribbean, and Peter Wade on Colombia addresses the relationships between representations of power and ethnic/racial alterity that operate in constructs of blackness, nation, and diaspora. For example, Sansone demonstrates the different racial articulations in Brazil and in "black culture," taking into account the impacts of the global circulation of images and objects. Consequently, this work highlights the analytical importance of the influences of transnational networks in local racial articulations. Based on Stuart Hall's notion of representation, Rahier's detailed discursive and visual analysis of an Ecuadorian magazine illustrates the different tropes of hegemonic racial thought concerning blackness. Rahier's study therefore constitutes an interesting illustration of what can be achieved methodologically with a discursive and visual analysis in race/ethnicity studies. In one of his articles, Yelvington introduces a relevant challenge to the notion of diaspora, which tends to be taken for granted rather than be subject to an historical examination of how it is, or is not, constituted in concrete terms and in highly specific situations, as exemplified in his case study of the reaction in the Caribbean to the Italian invasion of Ethiopia. Finally, Wade presents one of the most complete studies of racial dynamics in the regional inscriptions of race and in the nation-building project demonstrating the imbrications between the notions of race, *mestizaje*, and difference. Combining ethnography and document analysis, Wade underscores the significance of thinking relationally and contextually about the formation of racial differences and hierarchies.

Suggested Reading

Briones, Claudia. *La alteridad del "cuarto mundo": Una deconstrucción antropológica de la diferencia*. Buenos Aires: Ediciones del Sol, 1998.

De la Cadena, Marisol. "Are Mestizos Hybrids? The Conceptual Politics of Andean Identities." *Journal of Latin American Studies* 37 (2005): 259–84.

———. *Indigenous Mestizos: The Politics of Race and Culture in Cuzco, Peru, 1919–1991*. Durham, N.C.: Duke University Press, 2000.

Gilroy, Paul. *"There Ain't No Black in the Union Jack": The Cultural Politics of Race and Nation*. Chicago: University of Chicago Press, 1991.

Hall, Stuart. "Conclusion: The Multi-Cultural Question." In *Un/settled Multiculturalisms: Diasporas, Entanglements, "Transruptions,"* edited by Barnor Hesse, 209–41. London: Zed, 2000.

———. "The Question of Cultural Identity." In *Modernity: An Introduction to Modern Societies*, edited by Stuart Hall, David Held, Don Hubert, and Kenneth Thompson, 596–634. Cambridge: Polity Press, 1995.

———. "Race, Articulation, and Societies Structured in Dominance." In *Sociological Theories: Race and Colonialism*, 305–45. Paris: UNESCO, 1980.

Morley, David, and Kuan-Hsing Chen, eds. *Stuart Hall: Critical Dialogues in Cultural Studies*. London: Routledge, 1996.

Rahier, Jean. "'Mami, ¿qué será lo que quiere el negro?': Representaciones racistas en la revista *Vistazo*, 1957–1991." In *Ecuador racista: Imágenes e identidades*, edited by Emma Cervone and Fredy Rivera, 73–110. Quito: FLACSO, 1999.

Sansone, Livio. *Blackness without Ethnicity: Constructing Race in Brazil*. New York: Palgrave Macmillan, 2003.

———. *From Africa to Afro: Use and Abuse of Africa in Brazil*. Amsterdam: SEPHIS; Dakar: Codesria, 1999.

Wade, Peter. *Blackness and Race Mixture: The Dynamics of Racial Identiy in Colombia*. Baltimore: Johns Hopkins University Press, 1993.

———. *Music, Race, and Nation: Música tropical in Colombia*. Chicago: University of Chicago Press, 2000.

Walsh, Catherine, ed. *Estudios culturales latinoamericanos: Retos desde y sobre la región andina*. Quito: Universidad Andina Simón Bolivar/Abya-Yala, 2003.

———. *Pensamiento crítico y matriz (de)colonial: Reflexiones latinoamericanas*. Quito: Universidad Andina Simón Bolivar/Abya-Yala, 2005.

Yelvington, Kevin. "Dislocando la diáspora: La reacción al conflicto italo-etíope en el Caribe, 1935–1941." *Estudios Migratorios Latinoamericanos* 17, no. 52 (2003): 555–76.

Representation

FELIPE VICTORIANO AND CLAUDIA DARRIGRANDI
(TRANSLATED BY ROBERT WEIS)

In the most basic sense, representation is the result of a cognitive act that produces a sign or a symbol that serves as the "double" of the supposed "reality" or the "original." In other words, representation occurs through a process of perception and interpretation of a referent, the represented object. In the word "representation," the prefix "re" indicates a new presentation of what has already been presented. To re-present is to *present again*, to *put in the present something that is no longer here now*, to reconstitute it through re-presentation. In one sense, then, intrinsic to representation is a certain temporal disparity that marks the distance between the two moments implied in the very structure of re-presentation: as if something were being presented for the second time. In another sense, the prefix "re" also supposes an iteration, a repetition, another placement, which, unlike the temporal distance, indicates a sort of artificiality. Representation, then, is an event through which something is repeated, re-produced in the present, and, therefore, reconstituted artificially in and by its representation.

Both meanings coexist in the word "representation" and have a relationship with the essence or the pre-essence of things. Representation makes or allows things to come back to the present (where to represent is to return to presence), whether by making things or letting things come back to the present (where represent might make possible the return of a presence), or by presenting them again in the form of a double, an image, an idea, a thought, or, more precisely, through a "representative"—something or someone meant to substitute or stand in for another.

Representations have been the object of study in diverse disciplines. In the humanities and social sciences, they are linked to the study of society and culture. On the one hand, representation designates fundamental codes of culture, symbolic constellations meant to order social discourses and practices: images that produce subjects that participate in determined cultures and epochs. On the other hand, the gesture of articulating epochs through "representations" implies that a *representational idea about representations* governs the representation—the *ensemble of images that are the representation* of a culture, a mentality, an essential order of things. These images not only possess the virtue of representing historical epochs and holding the state of composition of an era; for scholars of culture, they are also objects of representation in the sense that they too can be represented.

Representation, then, constitutes the structure of comprehension—a "worldview," mentality, or historical perception—through which the subject perceives the world. This structure of comprehension is expressed in language, which "represents" the subject's very act of cognition. Hence, representation carries meanings that are materialized through written, visual, sonorous, corporal, or other types of language. Representations are generally part of a system of social and cultural practices that involve a real or imaginary referent, or even a representation. They can be agents endowed with certain ideologies that produce the representation in a specific historical-social context. Finally, they can be receptors that perceive or interpret such a representation in the act of reception. In cultural studies, the concept of representation is the consequence of a series of mediated practices that produce meaning, or multiple meanings, that are not necessarily true or false. This, in turn, suggests a constructedness in which subjects are implicated.

Forms of representation have varied through time and space, and each discipline has certain specifications regarding what constitutes a representation. In literature, representation is closely related to genres—poetry, narrative fiction, drama, essay, chronicle—and to literary currents that predispose the reader to expect a certain type of representation. For instance, Georg Lukács considered the realistic novel to be a narrative expression that represented reality satisfactorily. In theater, plays are defined as synonyms of representation and have been viewed as a mirror of reality, a function that became more pronounced in bourgeois theater. Even though they follow the same dramatic text, each representation is a unique and ephemeral act.

In the field of history, the function of representing the reality of the past differs from that of literature. History's positivistic search for objectivity meant that historical representations sprang from written sources, documents that attested to and scientifically validated a historical truth. Poststructuralism, postmodernism, and postcolonialism, however, have transformed contemporary historiographical methodologies and parameters of objectivity, and now the past acquires meaning through its representations.

In politics, representation refers to the process through which citizens delegate their will and interests to a representative, meant to substitute for them in the arena of large collective decisions. In this case, the political representative occupies the place of citizens through a series of procedures authorized from the public sphere within so-called "representative democracies."

In their origin, social and cultural representations have been the constant object of study because they were considered to be a medium by which to accede to a "truth," an "essence," or a "reality." Nonetheless, the possibility of achieving knowledge of this "essence," as well was the very definition of this "truth/reality," has been at the center of the debate around representation since antiquity.

There are three main general theories within the study of representation: the mimetic, the intentionalist, and the constructivist (Hall, *Representation* 24–26). According to Greek philosophy, mimesis was the process through which written or visual language imitated nature. Language fulfilled the function of imitating a truth that existed in the outside world. However, Plato posited that, given the existence of an immutable truth independent of men, art was an imitation of nature and could only approach the exterior forms of things, which were more closely related to the representation of an ideal.

The intentionalist theory supposes that the producer of a representation uses language to impose a unique meaning of the world or of the represented object. This theory assumes an absence of communication with social surroundings. However, it is difficult to conceive of representation as carrying the unique and exclusive meaning of the agent who produces it. The final overarching theory that Stuart Hall mentions in relation to representations is constructivism. It postulates that neither things, nor the outside world, nor those who use language can grant or endow a unique and invariable meaning to language. Rather, the meaning of the outside world is constructed through representational systems (Hall, *Representation* 25).

The work of Ferdinand de Saussure (1857–1913) in linguistics related the construction of meaning to language, which he defined as a system of signs. In Saussure's terms, language is part of a structure where the sign (in this case, the word) is formed by the concept or idea expressed by a sound or an icon (signified) and the acoustic image (signifier). The outside world acquires meaning only through contrast with other elements within a structure: the study of the relationship between the sign and its referent (the object represented by the sign, or what the word denotes) provides meaning or sense. That is, within a structure, every sign is a representation.

Many intellectuals followed Saussure's model; indeed, structuralism became a dominant theoretical framework of the mid-twentieth century. The most salient structuralist intellectuals—Roland Barthes, Jacques Derrida, Michel Foucault, and Jacques Lacan—also became its critics and developed poststructuralism.

In the formative process of structuralist theory, semiotics widened the field of study to include anything that could be read as a text: everyday activities, works of art, advertisements, photographs. It therefore encompassed popular expressions previously disregarded within the study of culture. Semiotics indeed includes any object or cultural expression that operates as language and communicates sense or meaning. Unlike Saussure, Barthes incorporated the reading of representations (signs) and their meanings into a second structure of signification. Consequently, semiotics not only studied the denotative—that is, the sign in relation to its referent and its signifier—but also the same sign within a broader structure that connects it to other themes and meanings. In Barthes' terms, this second level of analysis is connotative and linked to ideology.

Michel Foucault went beyond the study of representation as a mere linguistic act and incorporated it into discursive analysis. Discourse is a way of representing knowledge related to a particular topic at a particular historical moment. At the same time, discourse produces knowledge; that is, the representational practice becomes a medium for the production of knowledge through language. If, for structuralism, meaning was constructed from the relationship between the sign and the referent, for Foucault, meaning is constructed within discourse and its practices. To summarize his view, outside discourse, nothing has sense or meaning; even the subject loses autonomy and can be constituted only within discourse and the discursive practices of a determined place and time.

Poststructuralism, then, posited that no objective representation is possible, that all representation is a subjective construction. The consensus of historians affiliated with poststructuralism problematized historiography's practice. Since poststructuralism holds that it is impossible to accede to the past directly—that is, in an unmediated manner—a debate arose around the degree to which a historical narrative could be an objective representation. Perhaps the most interesting polemic around representation, led by Hayden White, questioned the very foundations of history as an academic discipline. White points out that history and literature share the same manner of narration; they differ only in their referent: the veridical event and the imagination, respectively. The representational practices of what is supposed to be historical ("real") and of the literary ("fiction") operate in the same fashion. Historical and fictional narratives draw on the same tropes.

In conclusion, before structuralism, representation was understood as an objective referent. Today representation is understood as an ideological, cultural, social construction (which is also a representation). The outside world acquires meaning through the representation that can be made of it. An image, a movie, a political demonstration, a book, a song, all these cultural products are understood as representations inserted into representational practices. Generally speaking, without delving into the differences that underlie the academic practices of scholars affiliated with cultural studies, representation is studied through modes of representation (the subject or subjects who produce the representation, the theoretical forms and frameworks to which they subscribe, the aesthetic and ideological options that underlie the act of representing), practices of representation, and representational systems.

In Latin America, debates around representation have focused on key problems regarding representation as a means to accede to and produce knowledge. Subaltern studies have questioned hegemonic discourses that constitute a representational practice that appropriates the "other" as an object of representation. Who has the right to speak for others? To what degree is the intellectual capable of representing? The publication of *Me llamo Rigoberta Menchú y así me nació la conciencia* provoked debates around the capacity of *testimonio* to represent minority subjects, and the possibility of treating it as a literary genre distinct from oral history or autobiography. Something similar has happened in history. As members of the intellectual elite who endeavor to speak for the powerless, historians write the history of a subaltern group within their own ideological framework and thus impose their own cultural codes.

A second key problem in the debate regarding representation in Latin America emerged from the so-called postdictatorship studies in the 1990s. Postdictatorship studies sought to enter the space of "disputed representations" that began with the democratizing process. The debate sought to position the concept of "historical memory" within a political context that attempted to symbolically efface the social wound inflicted by the dictatorships of Argentina (1976–83), Brazil (1964–85), Uruguay (1973–85), and Chile (1973–90), to name the most salient cases. Indeed, the term "postdictatorship"—unlike "democratic transition" from political science jargon—

caused the state of composition of the era to be inflected by the sinister prefix affixed to the noun (Richard, *Cultural Residues* 7).

The postdictatorship debate's ability to politically articulate its critical discourse stemmed from a renewal of critical strategies that intervened in the new democratic contexts and revealed the image of transparency and stability that the new democratic state wished to preserve in its transition to neoliberalism. For Beatriz Sarlo, this transition was symptomatically expressed in academia by the move from "intellectual" to "expert" (*Escenas* 148). It implied not only a radical shift in the realm of culture from politics to the market but also an erasure of the political violence unleashed by the dictatorship. Above all, the postdictatorship debate aimed to generate critical practice that, through the mobilization of certain symbolic resources, would preserve the social memory of the dictatorship and reveal the strategies of exclusion that this memory suffered. Hence, the debate provoked by the postdictatorship produced a radical change in critical language, a "lexical attention" (Avelar 175) through which the experiences and subjectivities that suffered, and continue to suffer, the total and absolute exclusion from social representation and the savage force that executed this exclusion could be articulated.

As we see, this debate hinges on a "politics of representation." At stake are critical spaces—alternatives to the hegemonic structure that projects "the order of things"—and, even more so, the very persistence of the system, its *autopoietic* capacity. The triumph of the system is the triumph over representations that give continuity to time, that re-produce it. "The order of things" is the result of a hegemonic act capable of asserting itself as an authorized vision of the world, an image that condenses the cultural specificity of an era. The perceptive regime of the world, therefore, is a strategic and political problem, especially today when images and discourses have achieved unprecedented technological extension with the exponential development of so-called information and communication technology.

Suggested Reading

Avelar, Idelber. "La práctica de la tortura y la historia de la verdad." In *Pensar en/la postdictadura*, edited by Nelly Richard and Alberto Moreiras, 175–96. Santiago, Chile: Cuarto Propio, 2001.

Barthes, Roland. *Mythologies*. Translated by Annette Lavers. London: Jonathan Cape, 1972.

Gugelberger, Georg M. *The Real Thing: Testimonial Discourse and Latin America*. Durham, N.C.: Duke University Press, 1996.

Hall, Stuart, ed. *Representation: Cultural Representations and Signifying Practices*. London: Sage, 1997.

Lanzmann, Claude. "The Obscenity of Understanding: An Evening with Claude Lanzmann." In *Trauma: Explorations in Memory*, edited by Cathy Caruth, 200–220. Baltimore: Johns Hopkins University Press, 1995.
Masiello, Francine. *The Art of Transition: Latin American Culture and Neoliberal Crisis.* Durham, N.C.: Duke University Press, 2001.
White, Hayden. *Metahistory: The Historical Imagination in Nineteenth-Century Europe.* Baltimore: Johns Hopkins University Press, 1973.

Subalternisms

ILEANA RODRÍGUEZ (TRANSLATED BY MAGALÍ RABASA)

Toward the end of the twentieth century, the term "subaltern" was introduced by a group of scholars in India, who founded a celebrated Subaltern Studies Group. However, the genealogy of the term can be traced back to Antonio Gramsci, the first to use it in its theoretical sense to refer to the relationship between hegemony (government by consent) and dominance (government by force). For Gramsci, subaltern is a concept used in the collective sense, as in a "subaltern group." Particularly evident in the Italian context, a subaltern group is one that remains unconscious of its strength and potential for political development, and therefore does not escape the primitivist stage, by which he means the nexus between free trade ideology and theoretical syndicalism. The subaltern group cannot become a dominant group or develop beyond the economic corporativist stage (to the hegemonic-political one), because in the syndicalist context, the autonomy of the subaltern group is sacrificed to the intellectual hegemony of the dominant class. For Gramsci, the idea of the autonomy of the subaltern group is only one aspect of liberal free trade theory, but he uses this to develop various concepts that are central to his political theory, including hegemony (which must include awareness of the interests and tendencies of those over whom it is exerted), free trade and syndicalism, and the relation that these bear to civil society and politics, considering the final concept to be a transcendence of the first.

Ranajit Guha borrows the Gramscian concept, uses it to reread Indian history and historiography, and proposes a new way of looking at the relationship between hegemony and dominance. Guha expands the *Concise Oxford Dictionary* definition of subaltern, "of inferior rank," to encompass "the general attribute of subordination in South Asian society whether this is expressed in terms of class, caste, age, gender, office or otherwise" (Guha and Spivak 35). Importing concepts formed in European contexts to other regions has often incited polemics (commonly referenced as the debate about traveling theories), but this importation makes sense if Italy is understood as a suitable case study for theorizing the unequal effects of capitalist development. In addition, the fruits of redeploying this concept are readily seen in the radical changes made to history and historiography that occur when read from the subaltern, a practice Guha calls "reading in reverse" or "against the grain." These changes occurred not only in the disciplinary sense by examining hegemony and dominance through the lens of colonization and postcolonialization, but also by calling into question the very exercise of dominance as they make visible the expectations that dominance carries for the subaltern groups over which it is exerted.

Two definitions of subalternity typify the use by subsequent generations. In reference to Asian subalternism, Gyan Prakash maintains that we should understand subalternity as an abstraction used to identify the intractability that surfaces inside the dominant system—it signifies that which the dominant discourse cannot appropriate completely, an otherness that resists containment. But precisely because dominance fails to appropriate the radical incommensurability of the subaltern, it registers only the recalcitrant presence of subalternity, records impressions of that which it cannot contain; it never captures subalternity itself, which can be rescued by the subalternist scholar. Quite simply, I wish to suggest that subalternity erupts within the system of dominance and marks its limits from within, that its externality to dominant systems of knowledge and power surfaces inside the system of dominance, but only as an intimation, as a trace of that which eludes the dominant discourse. It is this partial, incomplete, distorted existence that separates the subaltern from the elite. This means that the subaltern poses counterhegemonic possibilities not as inviolable otherness from the outside but from within the functioning of power, forcing contradictions and dislocations in the dominant discourse and providing sources of an immanent critique (288).

In reference to Latin American subalternism, Gareth Williams states:

> Subalternity is . . . the name for the multifarious points of excess within the national and postnational histories of Latin American developmentalism. It is the limit at which hegemonic narratives and dominant modes of social and intellectual (re)production encounter their points of radical unworkability. As a result it brings hegemonic

> thought (and in Latin America this invariably means hegemonic criollo thought) face to face with imminent ruin. And by doing this it keeps alive the demand for reflection and for a sustained politics of culture. (10–11)

There are other ways of understanding subalternity; for example, Juan Zevallos considers that "immigrants have a subaltern position. The subalternity of Andean immigrants lies in the fact that the majority completely lack—or else experience a minimal standard of—work, housing, food, and education to achieve basic human well-being" (368). For Walter Mignolo, "the idea of 'subalternity' is not simply a question of the dominance of certain social groups over others, but rather it has broader global repercussions, in the interstate system analyzed by Guha and [Aníbal] Quijano" ("Colonialidad" 179). Subalternity connects local histories and global structures of dominance, which is what constitutes the coloniality of power. It is used as a metaphor for the limits or negations of knowledge identified as Western, dominant, or hegemonic, that which Enlightenment reason cannot explain. On the other hand, the subaltern is a social position that affects the body of the oppressed, and/or the condition that generates the coloniality of power at all levels and in all colonial situations that structure interstate power. Subaltern is, then, the concept that spans the field of subaltern studies through these multiple articulations.

Latin American Subaltern Studies

After the defeat of the Sandinistas in the 1990 Nicaraguan presidential elections, a group of intellectuals concerned with the global political situation and the politics of academic institutions met in Washington, D.C. It was a moment of significant paradigm shifts, and for this reason the proposal was to discuss the project undertaken by the South Asian Subaltern Studies Group. They shared the belief that subaltern studies could be productive for Latin Americanists. The group was composed of John Beverley, Robert Carr, José Rabasa, Javier Sanjinés, Patricia Seed, and Ileana Rodríguez. Other social scientists and cultural critics were invited to participate, and though they did not attend the meeting, some, including Norma Alarcón and Mónica Szurmuk, signed the original manifesto.

Following the Asian subalternists, the group became a democratic collective whose academic project was to continue the legacy of politically committed intellectual labor. The Latin Americanists found particularly useful the South Asian group's proposal of a "new humanism," defined by the existence of social consciousness combined with theoretical tenacity and commitment, and an academic militancy. Their desire was to express a postrevolutionary solidarity with the sufferings of the poor, in a period in which the collapse of socialism had made that attitude unpopular and doubtful. Like the South Asian collective, the Latin American subalternists were profoundly dissatisfied with the absence of the poor in their own history. Nevertheless, while the Asian subalternists were critiquing the liberal postcolonial state and the nationalist and anticolonialist movements coming from the left, the Latin Americanists were critiquing the leftist states and the party organizations for their liberalism.

The majority of the founding members of the group had had formational political experiences: some with the Sandinista Revolution, others with the Jamaican government of Michael Manley, the Mexican guerrillas and student movement, or solidarity movements in the United States. They were all active participants in disciplinary debates about gender and ethnicity. Coming from Marxism, they were uncomfortable with the "triumphant multiculturalism" that paid little attention to the decentralization of wealth and the democratization of political power. Later the group was extended, and the first to be invited were Walter Mignolo, María Milagros López, and Michael Clark. At their 1996 conference in Puerto Rico, Sara Castro-Klarén, Fernando Coronil, Gareth Williams, John Kraniauskas, Alberto Moreiras, Abdul Mustafa, Marcia Stephenson, and María Josefina Saldaña joined the group. The last conference was held at Duke in 1998. The group collectively produced a series of publications that defined the field of Latin American subaltern studies, including the monograph special issue of *Boundary 2* edited by Beverley et al. and published as *The Postmodernism Debate in Latin America* (1993); the *Latin American Subaltern Studies Reader* (2001) and *Convergencia de Tiempos* (2001), edited by Rodríguez; *LASA Forum* 33, no. 2 (2002); and *Dispositio/n* 25, no. 52 (2005), edited by Gustavo Verdesio.

The specific use of the term became tangible in discussions that considered, first, the current meaning of subaltern studies and its various trajectories; second, the relationship between Latin American studies and South Asian subaltern studies; third, the relationship between the state, culture, and subalternity. The contributions from these debates are (1) to demonstrate how the aporias of knowledge that present the theoretical agenda of subaltern studies are reproduced in all areas: those of knowledge, theory, politics, the state, and globalization; (2) to discuss the dualistic dynamic from which Western thought articulates its knowledge, and demonstrate through analysis that the same logic that constructs the relationship between elite and subaltern can be productive for understanding the relationship between local and global, state and society, particularities and universalisms; (3) to diagnose the impasse that exists within the humanistic knowledge of high modernity. The theoretical work of subalternism is dedicated to examining the articulation of the logics of hegemony; its fieldwork, to understanding the social practices of the subaltern; its cultural work, to the analysis of the everyday, of solidarity, and of stigmas; its work on the indigenous question, to the exploration of issues of multiculturalism, the difference between social practice and hermeneutics, and the debate on postcoloniality.

For Walter Mignolo, subalternism means the possibility of establishing a theoretical connection to different peripheries affected by the coloniality of power, of crossing borders and putting affinities in dialogue, adding nuances to the central discussion. His points of debate are the recuperation of continental historical specificities, the recognition of the work of Latin Americans on the coloniality of power, and the revelation of the fact that modernity does not begin in the nineteenth century, but rather in the sixteenth (*Darker Side*).

For Florencia Mallon, the appeal of subaltern studies is that the proposal comes from intellectuals in the Third World, and it offers the possibility of dialogue across regions, within which she insists there must be attention to specific contexts. She warns of the dangers of borrowing and offers a reflection on the disciplines themselves. She questions the deconstructionist view in subalternism, suggesting that this approach undoes the central assumptions of the political purpose of the group, such as that which concerns itself with the autonomy of subaltern practices in relation to elite culture (*Peasant and Nation*).

John Beverley posits the impossibility of thinking the subaltern from *any* position of power. The subaltern is an evanescent subject that escapes representation. The subaltern is, therefore, a heuristic apparatus that reveals the aporias of hegemonic thought (*Subalternidad).*

María Josefina Saldaña proposes an elite/subaltern reading of popular fronts that are caught between opposing forces. Given this polarization, popular fronts must mediate and make undesirable choices for the forces they represent, as in the case of the Nicaraguan Sandinista Front that she studies. She suggests that the popular fronts must be dissolved as fronts so that some component of the group might enter the party system, and serve as connecting coalitions that enable the transition of power.

Alberto Moreiras refers to subaltern studies in relation to the discussion about the global and the local, the particular and the universal. Like Žižek, he proposes that "each pole of an antagonism is inherent to its opposite" ("Hegemonía" 71). From there we derive the notion of double articulation or double reading that "allows subalternists to commit themselves simultaneously and distinctly with radical negativity and strategic positivity" (77).

José Rabasa reveals how the need to inhabit multiple worlds is a characteristic of subaltern spaces and discourses; how the coexistence of different worlds in subaltern discourses implies an unenlightening enlightenment; and how all postulates of a dominant system or ideology ultimately constitute illusions of perception. He proposes that subaltern studies are theoretical unlearnings, as, for example, in the case of Subcomandante Marcos and the *ladinos* in the Lacandon Jungle. Thinking in one language is not the same as thinking in another; writing is not the same as painting.

Javier Sanjinés considers ethnic representation in Bolivia and ways of thinking about the national ethnic question in terms of the ways the lettered and intellectual classes (elites) relate the European to the autochthonous Indian, mestizo, criollo, and *cholo* (subaltern). While mestizo and *cholo* are not likely to be confused, mestizo and criollo are often merged. Unthinking, unreading, and negotiating are the methods he suggests. The most fundamental question is the "representation of the autochthonous." Is the gaze always from above, or is a subaltern gaze possible? The former is classic, while the latter is baroque and carnivalesque.

María Milagros López articulates the relation between intellectual and subaltern, citizenship and governability. She speaks of "post-work" society—in Puerto Rico half of the adult population is structurally unemployed—and of the ungovernability that is predicated on an opaque subject, lacking common interests, situated beyond communicative rationality. López proposes rethinking insurgency in terms of persuasion, and by extension the invention of pleasure as a form of justice. Pleasure is one of the sites from which rebellion is possible. López opposes ideas such as alienation, false consciousness, and class that do not mitigate human suffering. Alienation—as the only way subjectivity is conceived—and revolution and negation are elite modes of looking from above, and are tactics of subalternization. In post-work society we must look from the optic of marginality, of drug addiction, of a history without a future, of greasy foods, of the market that pleases.

Subalternist works clearly demonstrate that the integration of the subaltern is impossible, that the mandate of the elites is to maintain hegemony, which means producing and reproducing the constitutive heterogeneities of a world in which the "lag-time" of Homi Bhabha, divergent modernities, and incongruous temporalities predominate. But does this mean that the work of subalternists must be limited to identifying the contradictions of modernity? Is a return to some premodern utopia possible? Is subalternism also caught in the dialectic of the elites, of asking questions from above—from modernity, development, capitalism, socialism, hegemonies, the state, civil society, or the coloniality of power—with regard to how to see, think, and even feel the subaltern? What are the spaces from which to think subalternity? From what position can we think a society that is radically heterogeneous and egalitarian? From what location can we organize a form of thought and life that is not that of the heterogeneity of the ghettos? These are a few of the challenges of subaltern studies.

Suggested Reading

Beverley, John. *Subalternity and Representation: Arguments in Cultural Theory*. Durham, N.C.: Duke University Press, 1999.

Gramsci, Antonio. *A Gramsci Reader: Selected Writings, 1916–1935*. London: Lawrence and Wishart, 1988.

Guha, Ranajit. "Dominance without Hegemony and Its Historiography." *Subaltern Studies* 6 (1989): 210–309.

———. *Elementary Aspects of Peasant Insurgency in Colonial India*. Delhi: Oxford University Press, 1983.

Guha, Ranajit, and Gayatri Chakravorty Spivak, eds. *Selected Subaltern Studies*. Oxford: Oxford University Press, 1988.

Latin American Subaltern Studies Group. "Founding Statement." In Beverley, Aronna, and Oviedo, *Postmodernism Debate*, 135–46.

Mignolo, Walter. "Colonialidad del poder y subalternidad." In Rodríguez, *Convergencia de tiempos*, 155–84.

Moreiras, Alberto. "Hegemonía y subalteridad." In Rodríguez, *Convergencia de tiempos*, 91–102.

Prakash, Gyan. "The Impossibility of Subaltern History." In Rodríguez, *Convergencia de tiempos*, 61–70.

Rodríguez, Ileana, ed. *Convergencia de tiempos: Estudios subalternos/contextos latinoamericanos estado, cultura, subalternidad*. Amsterdam: Rodopi, 2001.

Spivak, Gayatri Chakravorty. *The Spivak Reader*. Edited by Donna Landry and Gerald MacLean. New York: Routledge, 1996.

Verdesio, Gustavo, ed. "Latin American Subaltern Studies Revisited." Special issue, *Dispositio* 25, no. 52 (2005).

Williams, Gareth. *The Other Side of the Popular: Neoliberalism and Subalternity in Latin America*. Durham, N.C.: Duke University Press, 2002.

Zevallos, Juan. "Baile, comida y música en la construcción de una identidad cultural subalterna andina en el exilio norteamericano." In Rodríguez, *Convergencia de tiempos*, 365–80.

Subjectivities

VALERIA AÑÓN (TRANSLATED BY KRISTEN WARE)

The question of the subject and the formation of subjectivities is a longstanding concern; a theoretical, philosophical, and epistemological problem, it unites subjectivity, identity, and otherness in attempts at totalizing definitions. Articulated in the humanist tradition, in Enlightenment reasoning, and in the experience of modernity (as an "incomplete project" or as a universal achievement, always from an occidental and ethnocentric perspective), the subject—and its reflexive projection, subjectivity—has been defined as a "modern subject," accurate and unambiguous, and with (apparently) distinguishable limits that can be verified within the paradigm that gives it shape and theoretical legitimacy.

The poststructuralist perspective and debates on postmodernity and postcolonialism disrupt these assumptions by posing a non-affirmative view of subjectivities—indeed, by calling into question the very idea of "subject" and its capacity for signification. In that sense, reflection on displaced and heterogeneous subjectivities that elude reductionist definition is connected both to the Latin American essay genre of the first half of the twentieth century and to the literary criticism and cultural sociology that began early on to foreground the peculiar experience of the region. As Gayatri Spivak shows, however,

> some of the most radical criticism coming out of the West in the eighties was the result of an interested desire to conserve the subject of the West, or the West as Subject. The theory of pluralized "subject-effects" often provided a cover for this subject of knowledge. Although the history of Europe as Subject was narrativized by the law, political economy, and ideology of the West, this concealed Subject pretended it had "no geo-political determinations." The much-publicized critique of the sovereign subject thus actually inaugurated a Subject. ("History" 248)

This problem, which exceeds the debates and disciplinary limits of cultural studies, has also been one of the field's central concerns since its earliest manifestations. As early as his 1957 *Uses of Literacy*, Richard Hoggart alluded to the question of popular subjectivities by establishing an identifying definition from a binary us/them position that would also define one of the modes of self-denomination and recognition. This conceptualization—indebted, however, to a certain self-identity/otherness dichotomy that constitutes as much the logocentric episteme as the critical and literary archive with which Hoggart works—nevertheless presents the advantage of viewing subjectivity as a notion (and perception) construed in discourse *and* in practice. Likewise, it calls attention to those ways of speaking that function as signs of identification and difference, emphasizing what is active in these uses. This non-complacent (though not devoid of nostalgia) conceptualization of popular subjectivities is especially echoed in the work of Stuart Hall, who revives and amplifies this problem ("Notes"). Hall is particularly persistent in his rereadings of the Marxist categories of "class" and "culture" as well as in his reasoning that the structured ways of conceiving of (popular) subjectivity elude conflict, resistance, negotiation, and acceptance, concepts that are always linked to hegemonic discourses and the experience of inequality. This manifestation of cultural studies views subjectivity in heterogeneous, plural, nonautonomous terms—that is to say, in a relational way. In subsequent works, subjectivities are primarily conceived of as diffuse or in constant redefinition, linked as much to ethnicity as to displacements and migrations (Hall and du Gay).

This point, crucial in the definition of "subjectivity" as a category, links cultural studies with the postcolonial perspective. Thus, since the mid-1970s, the ideas of a subjectivity "out of place" (Said, *Out of Place*), of an "in-between place in Latin American discourse" (Santiago, *Entrelugar*), and of a "heterogeneous subject" (Cornejo Polar, *Escribir*) have been established concepts in academic discussions of different—though not completely dissimilar—theoretical traditions. Definitively, in different cultural fields one must take into account subjectivities between worlds, subjectivities with constantly shifting definitions and anchoring of senses. Clearly, this admits reflection on migration and territorial movement in the context of globalization, but it also especially leads to a way of conceiving of the subject that does not permit essentialist or immanent positions.

In the tradition of Latin American thinking, colonial studies has privileged the problem of the construction of new subjectivities (unpublished, conflictive, changing) from the experience of the Conquest and the subsequent colonial order. Making use of the distance that separates investigator from object of study, these studies capitalize on the radical otherness one faces in colonial texts and connected reflections on the subject with reevaluations of the notions of discourse, text, context, author, style, and genre. In this context, taking into account the proposals of Homi Bhabha ("The Other") and Peter Hulme, taken up again by Rolena Adorno, a definition of the "colonial subject" emerges, a definition linked to enunciation theory, to discursive analysis, and to a "dense description" of texts (Geertz), which considers the cultural and social fabric in which the texts are formed. The notion of the "colonial subject," then, frames the colonized and the colonizer and defines, in a privileged way, a situation of enunciation that stages both the perception of otherness and the inequality of access to (textual) spaces faced by the enunciator. If indeed these studies emerge from a binary conception of identity and otherness—much like that adhered to in the sixteenth century—the detailed analysis of letters, chronicles, records, geographical descriptions, and all types of legal, juridical, and historical texts reveals discursive (and cultural) fabrics in which subjectivity is formed in a complex and changing way, sometimes among different texts and sometimes within a single text. In this sense, colonial texts stage subjects in territorial and textual displacement, illuminating a zone of cleavage in the production of subjectivities that is continuous as much with previous imagery as with the ruptures of established orders and the constitution of new ones.

Also from colonial studies Walter Mignolo proposes an analysis of "speaking subjects" and their social roles, that is to say, those aspects that make speaking, "which brings with it social roles (who is in the position to say what) and forms of inscription (what is the materiality in which speech acts are inscribed)" ("Decires," translation ours). The different textualities shape and update multiple modes of speaking subjectivity, interlacing speaking modalities: "being able to speak" is closely linked to "knowing how to speak," as many chronicles inform readers in their prologues, dedications, and letters. These social roles, inscribed in discourse, also show the effort of colonial subjects to organize new modes of identity in an early colonial order, an order in permanent reaccommodation. In this effort, colonized subjects propose a synthesis of social positions in agreement with indigenous worldviews in which implication predominates over explanation (Johansson), inclusion over difference (León Portilla, "Imágenes"), and synthesis over separation. These strategies for perceiving the other, functional and of tremendous possibility for adaptation in the first moments of the "fractal, post-Conquest societies" (Bernand and Gruzinski), benefited, however, from the limited effectiveness of resistance to the inequality (both practical and symbolic) imposed by the colonial order (Klor de Alva). These modes of subjectivity, marked by conflict, dissidence, negotiation, and loss, represent the initial diachronic definition of migratory or displaced subjects, of subjects out of place or "in between places" (*nepantla*).

The first of these ideas—that of subjects out of place—refers to postcolonial studies as they were proposed by Edward Said, as well as to their Latin American inflections. Focusing on just one of the best-known texts, it should be remembered that the term "orientalism" has multiple articulations and defines as much an "invention," an image of the other, an imagery, as a discursive way of configuring the world, which is closely related to imperialist expansion (*Orientalism*). With this premise in mind, Said recognizes the ways in which discourses configure subjectivities and situate the other in an otherness that is as much exoticism as myth, and the difference and inequality in which the imperialist project is legitimized. Among his many contributions, Said reformulates the notion of the "canon" by commenting on occidental (Anglophone) culture's conception of other cultures and its always ethnocentric mechanisms of discursive construction of identities. His critical reading and methodological commitment recover a tradition that combines the occidental perspective with other archives to articulate the conception of the intellectual as a subject "out of place" (*Out of Place*). This extemporality, this displaced subject, functions as a condition of possibility and metaphor for the production of knowledge, capitalizing on or producing a distance that permits a reading of the object as something more than what is implied by its obvious meanings or canonical uses. In contrast to the binary perspectives with which the Enlightenment has conceived of difference, Said argues for approaching the other using the other culture's knowledge, a logic that proposes a complex articulation between the symbolic and the social.

Interlaced with this reading and with the proposals of subaltern studies—as they are proposed by Ranajit Guha, for example—is the definition of the subaltern subject. This appears, then, with "multiple articulations" (Rodríguez, in "Subalternisms" above): understood in the context of conflict (Guha, Preface), as a metaphor of the impossibility of knowing and of saying (Moreiras, *Exhaustion*), and as a space, both textual and symbolic but also material, from which to understand the coloniality of knowledge and power (Mignolo, *Local Histories*). The issue of the subaltern subject also points to the eternal cultural studies question regarding the speech of the subaltern posed, though from different theoretical, disciplinary, and epistemological agendas, by Michel de Certeau in *Culture in the Plural* and by Gayatri Spivak in "Can the Subaltern Speak?"

The second idea turns to the tradition of the Latin American essay, a genre with which cultural studies is linked and dialogues, and from which it benefits. In the first half of the twentieth century, the problem of the definition of subjectivities manifested itself in the interpretive essay (Weinberg) and in textual inscriptions that sought to configure a Latin American identity that was especially problematic considering its cultural mix and heterogeneity. These essays—among which figure the works of Ezequiel Martínez Estrada, José Vasconcelos, Alfonso Reyes, and Pedro Henríquez Ureña—still, however, conceived of subjectivity in an all-encompassing way and sought a space that synthesized and harmonized contradictions, as represented by, for example, terms such as *mestizaje*. From the 1970s on, these perspectives were revised, especially in literary criticism, wherein the search for such a harmonizing space was questioned and an approach that illuminated conflicts and contradictions was called for. In this context, one of the most lucid critical voices is that of the Peruvian Antonio Cornejo Polar. In a diachronic proposal for the analysis of literary and cultural objects, Cornejo Polar considers chronicles from the conquest of Peru together with all of Peruvian literature from a perspective that sees in multiplicity and conflict its primary articulation. He proposes, then, the category of "enunciatory heterogeneity," by which he means a series of principally literary discourses marked by distinct conceptions and filiations. These discourses are produced by the tension inherent in Latin American societies and have as their beginning the conquest of the Americas as a historical moment of complex and dissimilar relationships between subjects, societies, and worldviews. If, as Octavio Paz showed in his analysis of the work of Sor Juana (*Sor Juana*), the modern perception of subjectivity is indeed linked to the romantic *I* that implies as much an "overload of sentiment" as the possibility of self-reflection and autonomy, then what is found in Latin American culture is "a complex, disperse, and multiform subject" (Cornejo Polar, *Escribir*), conceived along a diachronic axis that includes (but also exceeds) the Enlightenment. Therefore, reading representations and discourses also implies analyzing the ways in which the heterogeneous subject is configured in them, presenting evident contradictions.

This complex notion of subjectivity, strongly linked to the Latin American experience, is accentuated and complicated by the concept of the "migrant subject" to which Cornejo Polar alludes in his final works. As Raúl Bueno shows, "the concomitant idea is that this concept is the result of the natural evolution of his thoughts on the category of heterogeneity. Properly viewed, this consists of the incorporation of heterogeneity in the subject itself as a consequence of the act of migrating. The subject, thus, is then *internally* heterogeneous" (173, translation ours). The experience of displacements, migrations, and journeys that constitutes the very genesis of the region's history from the moment Columbus landed at the island of Guanahaní acquires a central function in the definition of subjectivities, especially in the context of the large-scale population movements of the twentieth century. This perspective (which is also the product of a certain autobiographical experience in terms of displacement toward the U.S. academy) accentuates even more the heterogeneity and conflict of the subject, perceptible in discourses of multiple natures, all with a common underlying axis of strangeness, change, and the experience of *being* in a different language, and of returning to one's native language (to one's native worldview) in a reflexive way. In this way, a discourse that is "radically off-center in that it is constructed around axes that are various, asymmetrical, and in some ways incompatible and contradictory in a non-dialectical way" (Cornejo Polar, "Una heterogeneidad" 843, translation ours) is constructed from a tension that seeks not resolution but lucidity and criticism.

Finally, it is worth calling attention to another form of narration and construction of subjectivities that links cultural studies to aesthetic and literary proposals. As regards new modes of subjectivity structured by way of the experience of Latin American megalopolises of the second half of the twentieth century, cultural studies has included aesthetic proposals linked to the definition of a popular subject, for example, as seen in Latin American chronicles from the last thirty years of the past century. If all chronicles emphasize the subjectivity and the singularity of the chronicler, this *locus* of enunciation becomes doubly problematic in cases in which the object is popular culture, constituting, then, a "frontier text" that is part of a series of "narratives in crisis" (Reguillo, "Textos" 62), a crisis concomitant with the reformulation of the concepts of nation, identity and modernity, among others. The contemporary urban chronicle (of the second half of the twentieth century at least) emerges as part of a social change linked to the increase in displacements and to urban phenomena of incessant demographic growth (García Canclini, *Imaginarios*), and assumes the form of the popular story so as to tell tales of everyday life with the support of melodrama (Martín Barbero, *Communication*). This is possible given that the narrative voice, in addition to not being univocal, also permits the use of irony and humor along with the textual strategies of montage, collage, and the superimposition of speakers, constituting a popular subjectivity that interweaves processes of modernization, grammars and imageries taken from the culture industry, and retooled traditions. The chronicle narrates, then, those subjects that have been excluded from larger theories of society. The ideas of Pedro Lemebel in Chile, Edgardo Rodríguez Juliá in Puerto Rico, and Elena Poniatowska and Carlos Monsiváis in Mexico, to name but a few, make use of this genre and this tradition to narrate new forms of subjectivity—and new forms of agglomeration, multitude, and citizenship—and to create, from an intellectual perspective, a vision that is not exclusive but rather inclusive, placing, in this way, "the marginal at the center" (Monsiváis, *Entrada*).

Beyond these different emphases, what the notion of subjectivity calls into question (and disputes), among many other things, is the viability of its definition and its demarcation—indeed, the possibility of knowledge itself beyond the opacity and incompleteness that defines representation. In Latin America, to speak of subjectivities is to allude to conflicts, inequalities, resistances, and also negotiations, always framed in the material conditions of practices and discourses. The notion of subjectivity in cultural studies obliges both a reevaluation of the occidental, logocentric tradition and a revival of the debate, both cultural and political, regarding the accessibility to material and symbolic goods in the hardly encouraging setting of Latin America at the beginning of the new century.

Suggested Reading

Adorno, Rolena. "El sujeto colonial y la construcción cultural de la alteridad." *Revista de Crítica Literaria Latinoamericana* 14, no. 28 (1988): 55–68.

Bernand, Carmen, and Serge Gruzinski. *Historia del nuevo mundo: Del descubrimiento a la conquista: La experiencia europea, 1492–1550*. Translated by María Antonia Neira Bigorra. Mexico City: Fondo de Cultura Económica, 1996.

Bhabha, Homi K. "The Other Question: Difference, Discrimination and the Discourse of Colonialism." In *Literature, Politics, and Theory*, edited by Francis Barker, Peter Hulme, Margaret Iversen, and Diane Loxley, 148–72. London: Methuen, 1986.

Bueno, Raúl. "Sujeto heterogéneo y migrante: Constitución de una categoría de estudios culturales." *Revista de crítica literaria latinoamericana* 25, no. 50 (1999): 173–94.

Certeau, Michel de. *Culture in the Plural*. Translated by Tom Conley. Minneapolis: University of Minnesota Press, 1997.

García Canclini, Néstor. *Imaginarios urbanos*. Buenos Aires: EUDEBA, 1998.

Geertz, Clifford. *The Interpretation of Cultures*. New York: Basic Books, 1974.

Guha, Ranajit. Preface to *Selected Subaltern Studies*, edited by Ranajit Guha and Gayatri Spivak, 35–36. Delhi: Oxford University Press, 1988.

Hall, Stuart, and Paul du Gay, eds. *Questions of Cultural Identity*. London: Sage, 1996.

Mignolo, Walter. "Decires fuera de lugar: Sujetos dicentes, roles sociales y formas de inscripción." *Revista de Crítica Literaria Latinoamericana* 21, no. 41 (1995): 9–32.

Said, Edward W. *Out of Place: A Memoir*. New York: Random House, 1999.
———. *The World, the Text, and the Critic*. Cambridge, Mass.: Harvard University Press, 1983.
Spivak, Gayatri Chakravorty. "History." In *A Critique of Postcolonial Reason*, 198–311.

Text

HORACIO LEGRÁS

The notion of text that is employed today in the humanities and the social sciences springs from two main sources: semiology and philology. Since the eighteenth century, philology has emphasized the importance of language in the formation of human cultures. Philologically driven theories put national languages, folklore, and popular traditions at the center of humanistic concerns. Semiology, on the other hand, emerged as part of the pioneering work of Ferdinand de Saussure. Modeled after linguistic studies, semiology conceives the totality of culture and society to be organized in terms of codes, messages, and discrete units such as "signifiers." The two approaches have, however, marked differences. In the philological tradition, meaning and ideology are very important. Semiology focuses instead on the transhistorical and transideological nature of communication. This latter attitude is well exemplified by structuralism, an offspring of Saussure's semiological concerns. Finally, there are approaches that combine the two tendencies. In the work of Mikhail Bakhtin language is both a structuring principle of society and at the same time the place where popular meanings and intentions are inscribed.

The full-fledged introduction of *textuality* as an analytical tool produced a truly revolutionary change in the way culture was conceived. To better understand the nature of this impact, a brief etymological parenthesis may be useful. The word "text" comes from the Latin *texere*, to weave, via its participle *textum*, woven, used as a noun to mean textile; it was used in that sense for at least two thousand years. This graphic representation of the text as textile captures better than any other both the problems and the promises of *textuality* as an analytical tool for the study of culture. The etymology suggests a continuous and unlimited totality. Its porous body does not recognize preestablished frontiers. The different discourses that compose the great text of culture traverse different realms and institutions without being subjected to their laws, but retain instead (although not without some contamination) a logic of their own. As human beings, we always live in some intersection of that texture.

It is not by chance that the popularization of this notion of text and the emergence of a conception of culture that could be understood in terms of textual logic coincided with a vast intellectual reevaluation of the humanities and the social sciences in the 1960s and 1970s. In this context, and especially in France, the notion of text became entangled in a vast interdisciplinary dialogue that included disciplines as diverse as philosophy, anthropology, semiology, communications, psychoanalysis, and literary studies. Often structuralism, a doctrine that favors the understanding of the social and the cultural as a systemic-textual totality, served as the lingua franca for these different realms.

In retrospect, Roland Barthes' essay "From Work to Text" can be identified as a key moment in the rising awareness that textuality does not simply describe a literary quality, but provides a fundamental model for the study of contemporary society and culture. Barthes' starting point is the differentiation between text and literary work. The literary work, the French critic explains, is a closed concept, inextricably linked to the figure of the author, a figure that traditional literary criticism had used as an explanatory instance for the meaning of the work. However, as any experience of reading (and more specifically of rereading) shows, the literary experience is not constituted by a singular meaning. A constitutive polysemy lies at the root of any literary text. Barthes goes further. He not only proposes that some discourses traverse different works of a single author, making the notion of a unitary work problematic; he states that the same can be said of works that belong to different authors and even of works that pertain to completely different registers. Barthes offers a synthesis of his notion of text under a striking image: while the work occupies a space in a library, the text is a methodological field that traverses several works, putting their imaginary identity in question.

This tension between work and text finds an important antecedent in the influential theorization of Mikhail Bakhtin introduced in France by Julia Kristeva with the publication of *Sēmeiōtikē* in 1969. The notion that Kristeva elicits from the Bakhtinian corpus is that of intertext. Like Barthes' text, the Bakhtinian intertext is not restricted to the realm of the literary or aesthetics. It is rather a system of solidarities that traverses different social spheres and that problematizes the assumption that an author is fully responsible for the content of his/her creation. Creation itself is often a misnomer in Bakhtin. The writer is rather the purveyor of language. In his book *Rabelais and His World*, Bakhtin explains how one of the defining features in the evolution of the modern European novel is the ability to incorporate all kinds of verbal genres—popular sayings, professional languages, songs. The novel form is for Bakhtin the paradigmatic example of text, in that it offers (as medieval carnival did) a space for the intertwining of different discourses, levels of language, modalities of speech, all of them translating different forms of conceiving the world. This Bakhtinian notion of text would acquire paramount importance in the conformation of cultural studies despite the misgivings of many cultural analysts regarding Bakhtin's rendering of the democratic potentialities of medieval carnival. Bakhtin's analysis made it possible to distinguish different ideological tonalities and layers at the levels of form and circulation, with relative independence of their content. His celebrated emphasis on parody is one of those instances in which the stress on the function of language outstrips the importance of meaning.

The introduction of the textual mode in cultural analysis did not just unveil unsuspected solidarities among different discursive realms. It also produced the idea that the text as a text has a different logic, so to speak. Some linguists and semiologists promoted the study of textual grammars in the 1980s. Particularly notable were the works of Teun van Dijk, M. A. K. Halliday, and Rugaiya Hasan, and the pioneering theorization of Jan Firbas on the dynamics of narrative. But it was up to two other discourses, psychoanalysis and deconstruction, to make important inroads into the question of how a text works. The textual mode of signification, according to a psychoanalytic approach, must recognize that meaning is always overdetermined (the notion appears illustrated in Freud's *Interpretation of Dreams*). This overdetermination should not be confused with ambiguity, which is far more common at the level of the sentence or the word. While lexical ambiguity can be alleviated by appealing to glosses, the referent, or the dictionary, textual overdetermination is inherent to the textual event itself. Often, an attempt to fix the meaning of the text ends up triggering the proliferation of meaning rather than its stabilization. In the 1970s Louis Althusser applied this model of signification to Marxist analysis, initiating a prolific line of research that would have a great impact on the constitution of cultural studies.

The contribution of deconstruction lies in showing how any textual typology is always already assaulted and even constituted by elements that the type is supposed to have excluded. In "Plato's Pharmacy" (*Dissemination*),

Derrida shows how Plato systematically invokes mythical lore in his work *Phaedrus* despite the fact that for Plato himself the founding act of philosophy lies in the expulsion of myth as an explanatory principle. Derrida's emphasis on dissemination and overdetermination soon elicited the question of how a stable textual meaning could be produced at all. In this regard, we have to notice that the notion of discourse, a notion close to but distinct from that of text, often works as a supplement of the textual in a way that guarantees a tenuous consistency to the textual. This is so because while the text is a field—as Barthes said—a discourse is tied to a series of ideas, practices, or propositions that facilitate its identification against the background of a widespread textuality. As for cultural analysis at large, we often see the two notions sharing the burden of analytical work.

In the field of Latin American studies, there are several important examples of how the combined notions of text and discourse have helped disclose new areas of analysis and research. Two important examples can be found in the works of Beatriz Sarlo (*El imperio de los sentimientos*) and Adolfo Prieto (*El discurso criollista en la formación de la Argentina moderna*). The notion of discourse becomes especially pertinent when the textuality is of an oral nature. In his book *Buscando un Inca*, the Peruvian historian Alberto Flores Galindo invokes the notion of an "Andean utopia" to trace a popular history of political thinking that traverses (but is not confused with) the whole institutional history of Peruvian politics. The well-known expression "versión de los vencidos," which refers to an indigenous worldview coded in songs and testimonies of the surviving Mesoamerican elite, was used by authors like Miguel León Portilla to (re)construct an alternative discourse to that of the Spanish conquistadores, offering thus a minimum consistency to a verbal tradition of resistance in the region.

Textuality and Visual Culture

Since at least the 1970s (and as a matter of fact much earlier, as we will see) the notion of text has made important inroads in the terrain of visual analysis—art criticism, photography, film. A semiological and textual approach to the visual realm rests on the proposition that this register, traditionally associated with the mimetic and hence with the regulation of meaning in terms of evidence, is in fact the product of a complex codification. In the 1970s many studies showed how Western photography and painting are organized following the order of textual literacy. We see (read) from left to right and from above to below. This structure of reading images explains that the protagonist of a photo (or a photogram in a film) appears either at the center or the center right of the frame. As different studies have shown, the seemingly simple act of seeing is indeed the product of a long educational process. Especially significant in this area are the studies of John Berger and Norman Bryson. The discovery of the codified character of visual reproduction and reception invited the creation of concepts such as "visual literacy." The question remains whether visual literacy is something other than a metaphor—that is, whether it is indeed possible to find in it enough elements to ground a textual theory of the image.

The area in which semiological and textual approaches have proved most fruitful is film studies. The introduction of semio-textual approaches to film appeared in the Russian formalist school, and more fundamentally in the works of Iuri Tinianov, Samuel Eichelbaum, and Viktor Shklovsky. Closer to our times, authors such as Christian Metz, Raymond Bellour, and Marie-Claire Ropars have ably applied linguistics and semiological tools to the analysis of film. Still the justification and productivity of applying textual strategies to film remains contested. As John Mowitt has pointed out, the introduction of textualist approaches to film produced some but not all of the benefits that the same strategy produced in the study of literary texts. The use of textual categories in authors like Metz and Bellour has been criticized for making the notion of text itself, rather than the phenomenon of film, the center of analysis. Often the complexity of film is reduced to better accommodate textual categories. Some critics have remarked that the notion of text deployed in film studies was perhaps too influenced by the work of Barthes and the Tel Quel collective. This intellectual debt to the French linguistic avant-garde may have prevented the emergence of a properly visual theory of the filmic text.

Textual analyses of film proceed, as a rule, through two main strategies. The first strategy sees film itself as text despite the fact that the figure of the author (and consequently of directorial style) is problematic in a production that is intrinsically industrial. This first approach confronts a series of difficult questions: Can we say that the different elements that enter into the composition of a film—lighting, camera angle, wardrobe, acting—are intertwined in the same way that different linguistic registers concur in a novel? Aren't these minimal components of the film mutually irreducible? It is true of course that camera angle, lighting, or acting appears articulated in a film. But can their form of articulation justify the word "textual" to refer to it? Or is it better to look for another concept to name the totality produced by them? In brief, the question that hovers over a textual analysis of film is: What is exactly textual in a film and how can textuality be produced from a set of mutually heterogeneous elements?

The second strategy under which the notion of text enters into film analysis is the postulation of an autonomous and properly visual equivalent to the literary notion of text. Iconography—which means, literally, image-writing—can be seen as the forerunner of this historical codification of visual meaning. While iconography is widely popular among students of plastic arts, it is not clear how an iconography of film (certain meanings attached to certain images independently of their context) can be established. A phenomenon easier to apply in film is intertextuality. As an example, the aesthetic of Emilio Fernández's films is, despite their often acclaimed Mexicanness, a result of his interest in the work of Sergei Eisenstein. But Eisenstein seems to have influenced Fernández only through the "translation" of Eisenstein's style as reproduced in the work of Emilio Gómez Muriel and Fred Zinnemann in *Redes* (*The Wave*, 1936). Finally, several of Eisenstein's compositions that were rescued by Muriel-Zinnemann and later by Fernández come in fact from the work of Mexican artist José Clemente Orozco, many of whose formal solutions are incorporated verbatim in Eisenstein's *¡Qué Viva México!*

Predicaments of Textual Models in Sociocultural Analysis

Despite the fact that some authors, like John Frow and Meaghan Morris, have seen the incorporation of the notion of text into cultural analysis as the founding event of cultural studies, analyzing culture in terms of text is not without important risks. For some authors, the notion of text is alien to one of the main concerns of cultural studies: that of bringing political criticism of society back into the academic agenda. Jacques Derrida's famous but also infamous "there is nothing outside the text" stirred a lot of controversy and put some practitioners of cultural studies at odds with textual strategies of analysis. Many critics did not realize that Derrida's proposition translated a materialist credo, forbidding analysis founded in elements extrinsic to the textual realm itself (the author, for instance). The same critics also read this proposition as a form of methodological solipsism inherent to the notion of the textual. This charge is more difficult to shrug off. All we have been saying about the text confirms the textual logic as a labyrinth whose threads surpass our subjective ability to master the textual horizon within which we live. Living within the text means among other things the impossibility of fathoming its outside. If the totality of culture is a text and the analyst him/herself is caught in its web, is a valid (or objective) analysis of social totalities possible? As we can see, the notion of text draws a long arc. After having initially served the expansion of the critical function, it seems now to contribute to the occlusion of the same critical function, as it has turned into a tool that cannot exceed the epistemological horizon that it itself has built.

Some authors have attempted to salvage the notion of the textual from this criticism by proposing a difference between text and system. The system—which we imagine as a system of power—mimics a textual logic but restricts its play to a series of "legitimate" articulations. Authors like Ernesto Laclau and Slavoj Žižek have attempted to reintroduce the textual into the systemic. This reintroduction amounts to proposing an element of undecidability at the heart of the system. The undecidability is not seen as an accident but actually as the (textual) condition of possibility of any systemic functioning. This movement, which has endowed notions such as "contingency" and "strategy" with its current visibility in the contemporary vocabulary of critical theory, has not really solved the tensions between system and text. As a matter of fact, one of the main results of this tension was the splitting of hegemony (a deeply textual notion in an author like Laclau) into a good hegemony (identified with democracy and even radical democracy) and a bad hegemony (identified with the stagnation of social mechanisms of reform).

A second and related objection has to do with the connotations that the notion of text seems to introduce into cultural analysis. In *Emancipation(s)*, Ernesto Laclau proposes a vision of social totality in terms of a chain of signifiers united by their common adhesion to a utopian moment incarnated in the figure of the "empty signifier." This image elicits the question of what happens to all the elements that are left outside the chain. Even if we assume a chain capable of including all possible elements—an absurd presupposition in both practical and theoretical terms—the problem arises of how this chain reflects or translates social tensions and confrontations. The Laclaudian chain attempts to contain both good and bad hegemony, but his schema leaves open the possibility that bad hegemony (the representation that power offers of the totality that it dominates) can swallow up the contestatory possibilities of good hegemony.

In this light, it is interesting to ponder Ángel Rama's ambiguous attitude toward the textualization of the social that he proposes in *La ciudad letrada*. For Rama, a founding instance in the textualization of the social happens during the baroque period of colonial Mexico. Rama saw the baroque as a complex grammar whose discrete units were made of speeches, theater plays, paintings, sculptures, music, dances, and colors. However, even when clearly sustaining his theory of the textualization of the social, Rama remains attentive to a world outside the textual network established by the collusion of intellectual and state functions.

In the field of Latin American cultural studies, the search for a critical standpoint within the domain of culture-as-text has promoted the notions of heterogeneity (developed by the Peruvian critic Antonio Cornejo Polar) and subalternity (adopted into Latin Americanism from its inaugural appearance in South Asian studies). Subaltern studies interrogates the modalities that police access to representation, especially in the case of representations of socially marginalized subjects. Central to subaltern studies' engagement with social analysis is the conviction that any form that facilitates representation—the nation, the market, literature, history—simultaneously draws up a system of exclusions. It is this exclusion that becomes salient for the subalternist perspective. Often the influence of subaltern studies pairs up with that of postcolonial criticism. Such is the case of Bolivian critics Silvia Rivera Cusicanqui and Rossana Barragán, who successfully employed the notion of subalternity in the study of Andean culture. Productive engagements with both subaltern studies and textual strategies of historical analysis can be found in the work of a number of contemporary Latin Americanists. Two outstanding cases are those of Steve Stern's *Secret History of Gender* and Florencia Mallon's *Peasant and Nation*.

Cornejo Polar's notion of heterogeneity is as famous as it is elusive. A way to understand what Cornejo Polar means by heterogeneity is to compare the concept to the Bakhtinian notion of the carnivalization of meaning. Even when stressing the widespread and multiform poliphony of the Renaissance, Bakhtin always assumed the existence of a common ground undergirding the variety of linguistic and textual expressions. Such a ground was provided by a Christian sensibility which was sometimes respected but often parodied by medieval popular culture. In the case of Latin America, and especially in areas of dense indigenous population such as the Andes, we are faced with an equally variegated array of linguistic traditions, verbal formulas, and popular wisdom codified in songs, sayings, and proverbs. But this linguistic wealth is seldom integrated into a more general textuality, in part because they come from cultural (textual) spaces so heterogenous that they cannot find a common ground even in such general notions as literature and culture. When they are indeed put in dialogue, the result appears difficult to read (works of José María Arguedas) or even unintelligible (Gamaliel Churata's *El pez de oro*). Heterogeneity names this problem of the absence of a common ground that will allow different productions to meet in a common structure that is simultaneously able to respect the system of their differences.

This type of impossibility forms the kernel of some outstanding literary experiments in Latin America. In the case of Paraguay, Augusto Roa Bastos gives the name of "the absent text" to the Guaraní oral tradition. Despite being a bilingual writer and knowing both the history and the culture of the Guaraní people in depth, Roa Bastos finds it impossible to represent the complex nature of oral Guaraní culture in his literature. As in the case of heterogeneity, Roa Bastos's work alerts us about the limits of the cultural experience in Latin America. These limits are at once unsurpassable (the virtual Guaraní voice is irretrievable) and yet constitutive of culture (the impossibility of recovering the Guaraní voice is the quintessential Paraguayan cultural experience).

This tension between cases of happy incorporation of differences into a textual totality on the one hand (Bakhtin) and resounding failures to accomplish that synthesis on the other (Cornejo Polar, Roa Bastos) should alert us to the limitations inherent in the notion of text, especially in its dependency on an alphabetic and phonocentric imaginary. Jacques Derrida has shown how alphabetic writing is intimately linked to the long humanist tradition that culminates in the emergence of modern liberalism and the theory of the sovereignty of the individual—a tradition that the notion of text puts into crisis. But now the question arises of how the textualist model can negotiate its influence with other textualities like pre-Columbian ways of writing, the Andean quipu, or Mesoamerican codices. Many scholars of these traditions (Elizabeth Hill Boone, Walter Mignolo, Joanne Rappaport, James Lockhart) have questioned the pertinence of notions such as writing to describe indigenous ways of coding. In these cases, the relationship between written code and social code, the acts of reading and the preservation of meaning, seems to articulate itself following a logic that is incommensurable with the Western tradition, where the notion of text originates. Even in those instances in which the alphabetic text dominates indigenous expression, as in the case of land titles that multiplied in sixteenth-century Mexico or in the work of colonial chroniclers like Alvaro Tezozómoc or Domingo Chimalpahin, the reader often runs up against forms of intertextuality extraneous to the combination of discourses described in the works of authors like Barthes, Bakhtin, or Derrida. In these chroniclers it is not uncommon to see the introduction of a second discourse that unexpectedly interrupts the flow of information and then disappears without leaving any trace of its presence in the dominant text. Martin Lienhard calls this procedure "montage" to better underscore its compositional value.

These examples should suffice to alert us to the fact that intertextual relationships and hence the concept of text itself are less universal than we might assume. While the discoveries of textual analysis are of obvious importance for any cultural analysis, they may show some limitations when put to work on the most recalcitrantly heterogenous regions of the Americas.

Suggested Readings

Bakhtin, Mikhail. *Rabelais and His World.* Bloomington: Indiana University Press, 1984.

Barthes, Roland. *The Rustle of Language*. Translated by Richard Howard. New York: Hill and Wang, 1986.

Bellour, Raymond. *The Analysis of Film.* Translated by Constance Penley. Bloomington: Indiana University Press, 2000.

Berger, John. *Ways of Seeing.* New York: Penguin, 1972.

Boone, Elizabeth Hill, and Walter Mignolo D., eds. *Writing Without Words: Alternative Literacies in Mesoamerica and the Andes*. Durham, N.C.: Duke University Press, 1996.

Bryson, Norman. *Vision and Painting: The Logic of the Gaze.* New Haven, Conn.: Yale University Press, 1983.

Cornejo Polar, Antonio. "El indigenismo andino." In *América Latina: Palavra, literatura e cultura*, edited by Ana Pizarro, 719–38. São Paulo: UNICAMP, 1994.

Derrida, Jacques. *Dissemination.* Translated by Barbara Johnson. Chicago: Chicago University Press, 1981.

Foucault, Michel. *The Order of Things.* New York: Pantheon, 1971.

Lockhart, James. *The Nahuas After the Conquest.* Stanford, Calif.: Stanford University Press, 1992.

Metz, Christian. *Language and Cinema.* Translated by Donna Jean Umiker-Sebeok. The Hague: Mouton, 1974.

Mowitt, John. *Text: The Genealogy of an Antidisciplinary Object.* Durham, N.C.: Duke University Press, 1992.

Rama, Ángel. *La ciudad letrada.* Hanover, N.H.: Ediciones del Norte, 1984. Translated by John Charles Chasteen as *The Lettered City* (Durham, N.C.: Duke University Press, 1996).

Ropars-Wuilleumier, Marie-Claire. *Écramiques: Le film du texte.* Lille: Presses Universitaires de Lille, 1990.

———. *Le texte divisé: Essai sur l'écriture filmique.* Paris: Presses Universitaires de France, 1981.

Transculturation

LILIANA WEINBERG (TRANSLATED BY SHARADA BALACHANDRAN-ORIHUELA)

The neologism "transculturation" was coined by the Cuban academic Fernando Ortiz, who employs the term in the well-known essay *Cuban Counterpoint: Tobacco and Sugar* to refer to a form of cultural contact that, far from being a unilateral and unidirectional relationship between a hegemonic or dominant donor culture and a subordinated or dominated receptive culture, is instead thought of as a creative interaction between the different cultural entities that meet, which results in processes of selection, interaction, and transformation. This creative interaction gives rise to a new generation, a new cultural entity, that comprises elements from both.

Ortiz contrasts his neologism with the term "acculturation":

> *Acculturation* is used to describe the process of transition from one culture to another, and its manifold social repercussions. . . . I have chosen the word *transculturation* to express the highly varied phenomena that have come about in Cuba as a result of the extremely complex transmutations of culture that have taken place here, and without a knowledge of which it is impossible to understand the evolution of the Cuban folk, either in the economic or in the institutional, legal, ethical, religious, artistic, linguistic, psychological, sexual, or other aspects of its life. (98)

Ortiz interprets the processes of transculturation of distinct groups that suffered a complex phenomenon of uprooting from their original culture, as the dual process of clash and readjustment:

> I am of the opinion that the word *transculturation* better expresses the different phases of the process of transition from one culture to another because this does not consist merely in acquiring another culture, which is what the English word *acculturation* really implies, but the process also necessarily involves the loss or uprooting of a previous culture, which could be defined as a deculturation. In addition it carries the idea of the consequent creation of new cultural phenomena, which could be called neoculturation. . . . the result of every union of cultures is similar to that of the reproductive process

> between individuals: the offspring always has something of both parents but is always different from each of them. (102–3)

While these terms were at first used to interpret uniquely Cuban historical and cultural phenomena, and the *complexity* of doing so, the concept would soon be extensive and broadly applicable to distinct processes of cultural encounter in asymmetrical conditions: more specifically those triggered by the introduction of a colonial relationship, which give shape to what Mary Louise Pratt calls "contact zones." Among the many characteristics associated with the process of transculturation are dynamism, historicity, complexity, creativity, situationality, and diversity in forms, levels, and periods of interrelation. Transculturation is always heterogeneous and asymmetrical, and is a process that anticipates the differential gains and losses that stem from placing different cultural groups in contact, since it produces a tension that does not allow for the abolition of asymmetry or difference. The process of transculturation is one that always presupposes a creative, resignifying, and refunctionalizing dynamic.

The strength and vitality of the concept are remarkable. Originally coined in the 1940s and corresponding to a historical period in which scholarly work turned to the interpretation of national life (José Carlos Mariátegui; Ezequiel Martínez Estrada; Gilberto Freyre), it was soon reappropriated with interest by Latin American essayists (Picón Salas) and was to insert itself definitively, beginning with the 1960s and 1970s, in discussions of disciplinary standardization in which anthropology and the social sciences, as well as literary theory and criticism, would have to rethink it (Aguirre Beltrán; Rama). "Transculturation" would also be a building block in the large explicative categories of cultural processes specific to Latin America and the Caribbean, as would such terms as *mestizaje*, "hybridity," and "heterogeneity."

The term allows Ortiz to observe the phenomenon from the perspective of large historical, economic, and social processes, as well as a more limited perspective that examines the birth of the processes of encounter and exchange in certain sectors and zones specific to a particular society: like those that represent the "low life" of the port zones where a more intense type of meeting of cultures transpired, or the particular music and food practices that emerge from contact zones.

The process of "transculturation" is proposed as an alternative to its racist or racialist antecedents, and is seen as overcoming unidirectional, deterministic, and mechanical approaches to the description of cultural encounters. The new concept is not at odds with that of *mestizaje*—or *mestizamiento*, as Ortiz phrases it—nor is it emancipated of all positivistic tendencies, but rather integrates the two as part of a broader explanatory pattern. As noted by the scholar Fernando Coronil in the introduction to *Cuban Counterpoint*, "the concept of 'transculturation' is used to apprehend at once the destructive and constructive moments in histories affected by colonialism and imperialism. Through his critical valorization of popular creativity, Ortiz shows how the social spaces where people are coerced to labor and live are also made habitable by them" (xv).

There are many reasons why this concept has become prominent in cultural studies and the dialogue between different academic traditions. Firstly, it is a concept coined from Latin America and the Caribbean, by a Cuban author devoted to studying phenomena peculiar to his country and whose writings would also join in discussions of the history and culture of that nation. It is also an important qualitative leap from the scholarship dedicated to thinking of the nation from a homogenizing vision that flattens the different social groups that make up a national entity. With regard to the interpretation of the processes focused in a particular nation, transculturation paradoxically leads to the discovery of processes that overcome and cross national boundaries, and places them in the context of transnational regional processes, or within phenomena that can only be understood on a global scale—such is the articulation of their relationship with the colonial economy. Soon Ortiz would become part of the larger discussion of American (Franz Boas) and European (Bronislaw Malinowski) anthropology, transcending his local environment to enter the field of Anglo-Saxon anthropological debate. It is significant then, that there soon would appear a critical commentary on the use of the term by the Mexican anthropologist Gonzalo Aguirre Beltrán, who in *El proceso de aculturación* expressed a preference for the term "acculturation." As Enrico Mario Santí has shown, these debates go far beyond mere preference for either term, since below the surface of these debates lies the relationship between the anthropologist and power ("Prólogo," *Contrapunteo cubano*).

Finally, overcoming racial and racist overtones of other concepts such as "mixing" or *mestizaje*, the longevity of the concept was made clear as it passed through several decades of discussion and debate by critical thinkers of the sixties and seventies, which linked the term to colonialism or dependency, for example, to arrive later and become a key term in discussions related to cultural studies. This term gives visibility to the ways in which "subordinated or marginal groups select and invent from materials transmitted to them by a dominant or metropolitan culture," so that, "while subjugated peoples cannot readily control what emanates from the dominant culture, they do determine to varying extents what they absorb into their own, and what they use it for"; while the imperial metropolis tends to see itself as determinant of the periphery, it is often blind to the ways in which it is determined by the periphery (Pratt 6).

Rama's Narrative Transculturation

The very flexibility of the concept used to address issues as varied as the economic and social, as well as the historical and literary, allowed for its quick adoption and discussion in different academic circuits, from the anthropological to the literary, first in Latin America and later in the United States, mainly stemming from the consolidation of cultural studies and postcolonial studies. Ángel Rama incorporated the term in the title of one of his best-known texts: *Transculturación narrativa en América Latina* (1982), a work that constitutes an important precedent to cultural studies and new ways of studying literary and symbolic production. Rama translates the concept to the field of literary studies and uses it as a key to understanding processes that link literature, history, and culture. He considers the phenomena of transculturation as part of a broad and complex process that includes the possibility of "losses, selections, rediscovery and additions," concurrent operations that "are all resolved within an overall restructuring of the cultural system, which is the highest creative function fulfilled in transculturating process" (39, translation ours). Rama pays attention to possibilities not addressed by Ortiz, and emphasizes active processes of cultural selection as well as creative processes under which we can consider questions relative to "language" and "form," incorporating concepts of "regional and class based subculture" into literary analysis. According to Rama, "literary works do not fall outside the scope of culture, but are, rather, its culmination, and insofar as these cultures are secular and multidirectional inventions, the writer is a producer who labors with the works of countless others" (19, translation ours).

As Alicia Ríos notes, Rama's neologism openly problematizes the relationship between modernity and tradition, while at the same time overcoming the critical-mythical model in such a way that the author is aligned with the counterhegemonic potential of regional and local cultures ("Traditions" 30). Rama redesigned the cultural map from colonial times onwards in order to underscore the domination that subjugated diverse literary and cultural systems of various regions. He focuses his study of literature and

Latin American cultures on three basic concepts: originality, independence, and representation. Rama raises the possibility of focusing on the process of narrative transculturation as an alternative to the paradigms of modernization, regionalism, or the avant-garde to better understand Latin American cultural history.

The concept of transculturation is one of the most representative forms of the ways in which a conversation between the seminal Latin American interpretive essays, pioneering works of anthropology on the region, and cultural and postcolonial studies has been articulated. It also represents one of the characteristic ways in which our intellectual elites have thought of the popular—addressing issues such as asymmetry and, intuitively, subalternity—and even of their own place as producers of knowledge on the horizon of heterogeneous formations and national cultures.

Of particular importance is the figure of Antonio Cornejo Polar, who in "*Mestizaje*, Transculturation, Heterogeneity" wondered in the early 1990s whether the concept of "transculturation" corresponds to an epistemological term ultimately distinguishable from the concept of *mestizaje*, or whether in fact *mestizaje* is not a part of transculturation. In his words:

> My first question-proposal consists of arguing whether the category of *transculturation*—either the Fernando Ortiz and Angel Rama versions or any other version—is the theoretical device that offers a reasonably epistemological base to the concept (which I consider mostly intuitive) of *mestizaje*, or involves, on the contrary, a distinct epistemological proposal. Although I have used this category many times, I believe it is the former case. *Transculturation* would imply, in the long run, the construction of a syncretic plane that finally incorporates in a more or less unproblematical totality (in spite of the conflictive character of the process) two or more languages, two or more ethnic identities, two or more aesthetic codes and historical experiences. (117)

In those same years, Garcia Canclini's concept of "hybridity" also came to represent a position vis-à-vis other concepts and categories in understanding Latin America's cultural processes. As he noted years later, "If we want to go beyond liberating cultural analysis of its own fundamentalist identitarian tropes, then we must situate hybridization within another network of concepts: for example, contradiction, mestizaje, syncretism, transculturation, and creolization" ("Noticias recientes," translation ours).

There is a wide range of scholarship tied to new critical currents, particularly cultural studies and postcolonial studies, and a new generation of literary studies linked to these scholarly currents seen in works by Pratt, Silvia Spitta, Román de la Campa, and Mabel Moraña, who have rethought the concept.

There are also several revisions that allow a critical overview of the various studies that the concept of transculturation "revisited" has occasioned. For example, in 2000 Silvia Nagy-Zekmi reviews the concept from the vantage point of postcolonial theory to focus on authors who emphasize "the interaction and reciprocal influences on modes of representation and cultural practices of different kinds in the metropolis and former colonies that are produced in so-called 'contact zones'" (194, translation ours). The author recuperates the creative nature of the phenomenon, and uses the tenets of Homi Bhabha to reinterpret it as "a creative praxis that deconstructs the conceptual apparatus of modernity" (197).

Reread today in light of the processes of globalization and transnationalization, new regionalisms and nationalisms, amid the debates on modernity and postmodernity, the concept has received renewed attention from fields as diverse as poststructuralism, gender studies, and postcolonial studies. It continues to attract the attention of intellectual communities from Latin America but also the United States, including Latin American scholars living in the United States, who have made the notion of transculturation a new bridge between different intellectual traditions and a way of drawing forth new genealogies of thought. Such is the case, for example, of the preliminary studies that Coronil and Santí devoted to Ortiz's essay.

The same applies to "The Conflict in Transculturation" by Alberto Moreiras, who posits that just as there is no capitalism without primitive accumulation, there is "no Latin-American culture without transculturation." Thus, transculturation underpins the history of the Americas because it constitutes "the very violence of culture," in such a way that it is the explanation behind any kind of historical explanation: "Transculturation is the reason for cultural reason—at the same time culture's principle of sufficient reason and its abyss" (129).

Suggested Reading

Cornejo Polar, Antonio. "Mestizaje, transculturación, heterogeneidad." In *Asedios a la heterogeneidad cultural: Libro de homenaje a Antonio Cornejo Polar*, edited by José Antonio Mazzotti and U. Juan Zevallos Aguilar, 54–56. Philadelphia: Asociación Internacional de Peruanistas, 1996. Translated by Christopher Dennis as "*Mestizaje*, Transculturation, Heterogeneity," in Sarto, Ríos, and Trigo, *Latin American Cultural Studies Reader*, 116–19.

García Canclini, Néstor. "Noticias recientes sobre la hibridación." In *Revista Transcultural de Música* 7 (2003). www.sibetrans.com/trans/trans7/canclini.htm.

Moreiras, Alberto. "The Conflict in Transculturation." In *Literary Cultures of Latin America: A Comparative* History, edited by Mario J. Valdés and Djelal Kadir, 3: 129–37. New York: Oxford University Press, 2004.

Nagy-Zekmi, Silvia. "Ángel Rama y su ensayística transcultural(izadora) como autobiografía en clave crítica." *Cuadernos Americanos*, no. 81 (2000): 193–202.

Ortiz, Fernando. *Cuban Counterpoint: Tobacco and Sugar*. Translated by Harriet de Onís. Durham, N.C.: Duke University Press: 1995.

Pratt, Mary Louise. *Imperial Eyes: Travel Writing and Transculturation*. London: Routledge, 1992.

Rama, Ángel. *Transculturación narrativa en América Latina*. Mexico City: Siglo XXI, 1982.

Ríos, Alicia. "Traditions and Fractures in Latin American Cultural Studies." In Sarto, Ríos, and Trigo, *Latin American Cultural Studies Reader*, 15–34.

Sobrevilla, David. "Transculturación y heterogeneidad: Avatares de dos categorías literarias en América Latina." *Revista de Crítica Literaria Latinoamericana* 27, no. 54 (2001): 21–33.

Trigo, Abril. "The 1990s: Practices and Polemics within Latin American Cultural Studies." In Sarto, Ríos, and Trigo, *Latin American Cultural Studies Reader*, 347–73.

Tropicália

CHRISTOPHER DUNN

Tropicália (or Tropicalismo) is generally understood as a late 1960s movement in popular music, although recent scholarly and curatorial work has attempted to contextualize tropicalist music in relation to contemporaneous manifestations in visual art, theater, cinema, fiction, and fashion. In this reading, Tropicália should be seen as a cultural "moment" involving dialogue among artists of several fields, without any unified program of action (Süssekind). The genesis of the name provides some insight into the confluence of interests and aesthetic proposals during that time. The name Tropicália was first invented by visual artist Hélio Oiticica for an art installation shown at the 1967 group exhibit Nova Objetividade Brasileira. At the suggestion of filmmaker Luiz Carlos Barreto, singer-songwriter Caetano Veloso appropriated the name for a recently composed song without having even seen Oiticica's work. Frederico Coelho has proposed a useful distinction between Tropicália as a cultural moment and *tropicalismo musical* as a movement, complete with an album-manifesto that sought to change the field of Brazilian popular music (Coelho). Yet tropicalist musicians themselves usually prefer to speak of Tropicália to describe the movement, as a way to distance themselves from the modernist succession of "isms."

Tropicália was a response to the rise of an authoritarian military regime (1964–85), which entered its most draconian phase in 1968, mostly in response to the emergence of an urban guerrilla movement. It expressed the crisis of a middle-class urban youth who passed through adolescence during a hopeful period of democratic rule and modernization in the late 1950s, were politically energized by socialist and anti-imperialist movements in the early 1960s, and became young adults just as a U.S.-backed authoritarian military regime took power in 1964. This sense of despair and disorientation among left-wing artists was captured by Glauber Rocha's 1967 film *Terra em Transe*, which depicted the demise of traditional populist politics and the rise of authoritarian rule. With references to Portuguese colonial conquest, the brutal suppression of disenfranchised peasants, the cynical machinations of national elites allied with multinational capital, and the crisis of progressive nationalist intellectuals, the film allegorized the failure of a democratic modernity in Brazil (Xavier). Although not a tropicalist film per se, *Terra em transe* profoundly influenced artists subsequently identified with the movement.

Tropicália is most closely associated with a group of musicians from the northeastern state of Bahia, including Caetano Veloso, Gal Costa, Gilberto Gil, and Tom Zé, who first performed together in Salvador in 1964. The tropicalist musicians were influenced by the early phase of bossa nova, a new style of samba developed by guitarist-singer João Gilberto, composer-pianist Antônio Carlos Jobim, modernist poet Vinícius de Moraes, and several other artists from the middle- and upper-class Zona Sul of Rio. In the mid-1960s, the *grupo baiano* migrated south, first to Rio de Janeiro and then to São Paulo, where they made contact with the concrete poets and members of the Música Nova avant-garde, most notably the composer-arranger Rogério Duprat. They also began working with a trio of young rock musicians, Arnaldo and Sérgio Baptista and Rita Lee, who formed the core of the band Os Mutantes, which developed a highly original approach to rock.

The *grupo baiano* gained national attention in 1967–69 in several televised music festivals broadcast from São Paulo and Rio, while releasing a series of solo albums and one collective concept album, *Tropicália, ou Panis et Circensis* (1968). At that time there was considerable tension between proponents of rock 'n' roll, known as the Jovem Guarda, and post–bossa nova artists, identified with the tag MPB (Música Popular Brasileira), who sought to defend the tradition of Brazilian song. MPB artists tended to associate rock and electric instruments with U.S. cultural imperialism. While Jovem Guarda artists showed little interest in themes of social and political protest, the MPB camp regarded popular music as a potent arm of protest against the military dictatorship.

The tropicalists identified with MPB, but they also sought to develop the tradition of Brazilian song in dialogue with international trends in pop, rock, and soul. At the same time, they sought to recuperate, sometimes with ironic distance, pre–bossa nova Brazilian song, as well as Spanish American genres like bolero and mambo, which their own generation and social milieu considered passé. This embrace of kitsch was ambiguous and multivalent. On the one hand, it represented a sincere gesture to recognize the cultural importance of outmoded artists. On the other, it subtly lampooned, through parody and ironic citation, conservative cultural values that had underwritten the rise of authoritarian rule. Veloso's "Tropicália" exalted Carmen Miranda, the internationally famous samba singer who had fallen out of favor with Brazilian critics when she pursued a successful film career in Hollywood in the 1940s. Veloso later compared this gesture to Andy Warhol's renditions of Campbell's soup cans in the way that it recycled with equal doses of irony and reverence an internationally famous icon of popular culture. A similar gesture is evident in Veloso's "Lindonéia," a melodramatic bolero that narrates the life of an anonymous working-class woman depicted in a 1966 portrait by Rubens Gerchman, a work that drew heavily on the aesthetics of kitsch.

To varying degrees, most tropicalists saw themselves as heirs to Oswald de Andrade, a key figure of the modernist avant-garde in Brazil who mobilized a group of artists around the idea of cultural cannibalism, or *antropofagia,* which was inspired by Enlightenment-era chronicles of ritual cannibalism among Brazilian natives. His "Manifesto Antropófago" (1928) proposed a critique of the Catholic, patriarchal legacy of Portuguese colonialism, while expressing a will to "devour" and, in a sense, "Brazilianize" cultural practices and ideas from Europe and the United States. Oswaldian *antropofagia* may be regarded as a "heterogeneous discourse" (Cornejo Polar) that had more to do with the desires of cosmopolitan intellectuals than with the symbolic universe of Brazilian Indians. It was a modernist strategy for interpreting and mobilizing the cultural legacy of "internal others" vis-à-vis dominant Eurocentric narratives.

In the 1960s, Oswaldian *antropofagia* was revived by proponents of *poesia concreta,* most notably the brothers Augusto and Haroldo de Campos, who positioned their own literary movement as a mid-century avant-garde. The Oswaldian turn in Brazilian culture functioned on several levels: it served as a way to critique essentialist forms of cultural nationalism, injected a dose of satiric humor into left-wing cultural discourse, reaffirmed the imperative of formal experimentation, and revived allegory as a strategy for representing the impasses and contradictions of modern Brazil. In a 1968 interview with Augusto de Campos, Veloso declared that Tropicália was a form of *neo-antropofagismo* (Campos).

Oswaldian poetics were developed most vigorously by José Celso Martinez Corrêa (known as Zé Celso), the founder and director of the Teatro Oficina in São Paulo. In 1967 the Teatro Oficina staged a landmark production of *O rei da vela,* written in 1933 by Oswald de Andrade. The play tells the story of a loan shark who runs a side business selling candles, a multivalent symbol for death (used in funerary rites), underdevelopment (used in the absence of electric lights), and sexual domination (given its phallic shape). *O rei da vela* caustically satirized the vulgar machinations of upstart bourgeois capitalists and the pathetic foibles of decadent aristocrats, who are all ultimately beholden to an American investor. Conceiving it as "guerrilla theater," Zé Celso staged *O rei da vela* as a ritual of "miseducation" and "demystification" meant to provoke his mostly left-wing middle-class audience.

Following Néstor Garcia Canclini in *Culturas híbridas*, we may say that tropicalist aesthetics were fundamentally "hybrid" in that they frequently undermined or relativized entrenched notions of erudite and popular, traditional and modern, and national and foreign. Zé Celso's productions drew from Brechtian epic theater and Artaudian theater of cruelty, but also from circus performance and lowbrow *teatro de revista* from Rio de Janeiro. Oiticica positioned popular culture at the very center of his project to develop a distinctly Brazilian avant-garde within the tradition of constructivism. Tropicalist musicians mixed pop music from Brazil, the United States, and Europe with experimental music of the São Paulo avant-garde. The Veloso-Gil song "Batmacumba" combined references to Batman, rock 'n' roll, and Afro-Brazilian religion, yet it also appropriated techniques from concrete poetry. The mythologies of mass culture—Hollywood stars, comic book superheroes, pop music icons—figured into experimental literature. José Agrippino de Paula's 1967 novel *Panamérica,* which has been interpreted as a "pop-tropicalist" work (Hoisel), featured larger-than-life characters like Che Guevara, Marilyn Monroe, Burt Lancaster, Cary Grant, and

John Wayne cast in a Hollywood megaproduction based on epic stories from the Bible.

This mixture and juxtaposition of heterogeneous references and registers in Tropicália was a response to dramatic transformations of urban life under military rule. The regime pursued a program of conservative modernization based on capitalist growth, industrialization, and the expansion of mass media, while restricting political rights and suppressing the labor movement. The effects of conservative modernization were complex. It contributed to national integration through a strong central government and a greatly enhanced system of mass communication, but it also exacerbated social inequalities and regional disparities.

The stark contrast between modernity and underdevelopment was allegorized in works such as Oiticica's *Tropicália,* which beckoned participants to enter and experience sensorially. It featured two structures, called *penetráveis,* which were reminiscent of the precarious architecture of the urban favelas. In the larger structure spectators would make their way through a dark passage until they reached a functioning television set, which at that time was a symbol of modern technology and mass communication. In a similar fashion, some of the most important tropicalist songs, like "Tropicália" (Veloso), "Geléia Geral" (Gil-Neto), and "Parque Industrial" (Tom Zé), juxtaposed signs of underdevelopment with references to high techology, industrial modernization, and mass communication. The inventory of images and references in these songs brings to mind what García Canclini called "multitemporal heterogeneity"—the simultaneous presence of different temporalities.

Critics of Tropicália, such as Roberto Schwarz, regarded the simultaneity of "archaic" and "modern" temporalities as a contradiction to be resolved dialectically. In Schwarz's view, the tropicalist allegory merely rendered these contrasts as humorous, absurd aberrations. Neil Larsen extended Schwarz's critique of Tropicália to the field of cultural studies, especially the work of García Canclini, arguing that both failed to advance emancipatory social ends. For other critics, like Celso Favaretto, the tropicalist allegory maintained its critical edge precisely because it refused dialectical resolution, thereby generating a fragmentary and indeterminate image of Brazil. Although initially criticized by left-wing artists and intellectuals, especially those affiliated with the Brazilian Communist Party, Tropicália eventually aroused the suspicions of the regime. Several tropicalist artists, including Veloso, Gil, and Zé Celso, were arrested and exiled during the late 1960s and early 1970s.

Suggested Reading

Basualdo, Carlos, ed. *Tropicália: A Revolution in Brazilian Culture.* São Paulo: Cosac Naify, 2005.

Calado, Carlos. *Tropicália: A história de um revolução musical.* São Paulo: Editora 34, 1997.

Campos, Augusto de, et al. *Balanço da bossa e outras bossas.* 2nd ed. São Paulo: Perspectiva, 1974.

Coelho, Frederico, and Sérgio Cohn, eds. *Tropicália.* Rio de Janeiro: Beco de Azougue, 2008.

Dunn, Christopher. *Brutality Garden: Tropicália and the Emergence of a Brazilian Counterculture.* Chapel Hill: University of North Carolina Press, 2001.

Favaretto, Celso. *Tropicália: Alegoria, Alegria.* São Paulo, Editora Ateliê, 1996.

Schwarz, Roberto. "Culture and Politics in Brazil, 1964–1969." In *Misplaced Ideas*, 126–59.

Veloso, Caetano. *Tropical Truth: A Story of Music and Revolution in Brazil.* Translated by Isabel de Sena. New York: Knopf, 2002.

Violence

MARTA CABRERA

"Violence," from the Latin *violentia* (vehemence, impetuousness), appears at the end of the Middle Ages to describe the exercise of physical force against a person. Though it is generally understood with some sense of certainty, "violence" is a notoriously difficult term to define with a universally applicable definition. The concept, in fact, has only expanded from its medieval connotation in response to theoretical needs. Paul Heelas, for example, makes a comparative analysis of notions of violence in various societies from a radically contextualist stance. From a temporal perspective, John Keane stresses the historicity of the term, as well as its relentlessly expanding usages. Certainly, neither Heelas's contextualism nor Keane's historicization exhausts the possibilities of signification of the term, but both help to delineate the contours of a vision of violence that stems from culture. Given this cultural character, Keane suggests that the term be treated as an *ideal-type*, as a selection of some aspects of reality that are never found in their pure form.

From a genealogical standpoint, violence appears as a concept in classical philosophy, staged in its symbolic forms in Greek tragedy and associated with the irrational, reappearing at the end of the eighteenth century in the work of Hegel, and then theorized by Georges Sorel and later by Marx and Engels. In the writings of these last, violence appears as a necessary element in attaining political goals embodied in social and historical change. Sorel would take violence beyond the level of the instrumental to make it a key factor in the transformation of revolutionary consciousness (a point that Slavoj Žižek takes up more recently in *Revolution*). Sorel's influence on other theorists such as Walter Benjamin and Georg Lukács is evident; for both, the relationship between the violence required to overthrow bourgeois institutions and legality was problematic. For Hannah Arendt in *On Violence*, similarly, revolution was possible without violence.

With the advent of decolonization and the minority movements of the 1960s, new perspectives theorizing violence appeared. In this context, Frantz Fanon would adapt the Marxist take on violence with regard to the relationship between First and Third World in *Black Skin, White Masks* (1952) and *The Wretched of the Earth* (1961). In these projects the colonial classes assume the role of the bourgeoisie, and the peasants of the colonies that of the proletariat. The role of violence here is to help the colonized achieve revolutionary consciousness through confrontation with their oppressors.

In modernity, violence is increasingly linked to rationalization and instrumentality (Horkheimer and Adorno; Foucault; Deleuze), mediated by institutions and exerted by bureaucratic actors (who fill out forms, press buttons, keep statistics); it is at the root of the industrialized massacres of the last century. The cases analyzed by Michel Foucault in *Discipline and Punish*, in which subjects' bodies are deliberately confined against their will in the name of the improvement of discipline, where violence is privatized (removed from the public domain) and sanitized and hidden behind the walls of a prison or a hospital or a nursing home, also fall into this category.

For Raymond Williams, violence reflects contemporary ideas and values including aggressive behavior, vehement conduct, violations against property or dignity, and the use or threat of physical force, as well as the dramatic performance of any of these elements (*Keywords*). David Riches, on the other hand, argues that violence is a social resource—both action and imagery culturally situated, it can be practical or symbolic, visible or invisible (in the case of witchcraft, for example), physical or emotional, and can come from an individual or society. For Pierre Bourdieu the range of social events that qualify as violence is so broad that it might include any act resulting in distress (*Outline*), to the point of reaching, for example, Johan Galtung's definition, which includes all that can be avoided and that impedes the personal fulfillment of a human being ("Violence"). This *symbolic violence*, contained in the hegemonic practices of everyday life, is key, in the opinion of feminist and subalternist critique, in articulating relations of domination and subordination.

The concept of symbolic violence has similarities with Galtung's *structural violence*, where there are no actors but rather social structures that discriminate and exploit. The concept of *cultural violence*, also Galtung's, then refers to the legitimization of such structures through their symbolic mechanisms nestled in "religion and ideology, language and art, empirical science and formal science (logic, mathematics)" ("Cultural Violence" 291). This particular dimension of legitimization of a particular form of violence with both epistemic and material consequences relates as well to the notion of *epistemic violence* developed by Gayatri Spivak in her essay "Can the Subaltern Speak?" In this text Spivak argues that epistemic violence results from the silencing of the subaltern in postcolonial discourse by both colonial and patriarchal power. Building on this discussion, as well as on the work of Beatriz González Stephan, Santiago Castro Gómez suggests that Latin America was well acquainted with these processes. There, the social sciences, politics, and such institutions as schools, hospitals, the law, and the constitutions jointly built devices to create ideal models of subjectivity as well as its Others. This system, the modern/colonial world-system, has a geopolitical dimension and needs also to be contemplated from the perspective of *longue durée* (Braudel; Wallerstein) and positioned largely on the notion of coloniality of power (Quijano).

Contemporary forms of violence arising from the context of advanced globalization and erosion of state power offer a field of analysis from a cultural perspective. Though macro-approaches were privileged during the Cold War at the expense of internal dynamics—seen as mere reflections of the confrontation between superpowers—other categories of violence along with other forms of analysis have emerged more recently.

For example, notions like the "clash of civilizations" (Huntington) and the "new wars" (Kaldor)—characterized by the breakdown of boundaries between revolutionary struggle, organized crime, and human rights violations—have appeared as frameworks for analysis, and other lines of conflict have been identified, such as religious, ethnic, and nationalist tensions and, more recently, terrorism. This enlarged perspective of the phenomenon implies referring to superimposed forms of violence rather than to a single violence.

In this context, explanations of political violence have yielded to other forms of analysis that focus on symbolic or expressive manifestations such as pain or cruelty, which link the senses to representations of violence. Thus the field of analysis of violence has been reconfigured as a result of the emergence of new movements and players with new perceptions and possibilities for intervention, along with the need for interdisciplinary perspectives—given the limitations of the disciplines of the social sciences to account for such a multifaceted phenomenon.

For Coronil and Skurski, the body becomes the intersection between individuality and collectivity. Assertions of power aimed at communities are inscribed and occur through the body, the place where history ultimately takes place (290). This perspective has been productive in the analysis of some contemporary cases where the body (and its destruction) is central (Aretxaga; Feldman). In the case of Colombia, for example, Maria Victoria Uribe's and Elsa Blair's work on the phenomenon of massacres exposes them as a mise-en-scène imbued with meaning, where it is not enough to kill the other, but becomes essential to reveal their suffering and their final destruction through the mutilation and subsequent manipulation of their body parts. From this point of view, violence can be seen as a form of communication, as a "social text" (Castillejo) that combines two fundamental factors: on the one hand, the visibility and sensuality of the violent act, and on the other, its intelligibility across multiple cultural contexts (Riches).

State violence, by contrast, produced obvious consequences that are both physical (deaths, disappearances, torture) and psychological (fear, anxiety). Although the tortured, maimed body is not displayed, symbolic violence is added to physical violence precisely through the invisibilization of the body and by the lack of public knowledge regarding its final fate. In this (phantom) public sphere where there are no bodies, only terror and absence, mourning must be transferred to the private sphere, depriving individuals and the community of fundamental rituals. Beatriz Sarlo describes how the "politics of the Argentine dictatorship" ("Política" 104) privatized the public sphere and depoliticized social life, which is why the response of artists and intellectuals, though marked by fear, still tried to represent this context as well as to articulate a "critique of the present" (34)—a term associated with Raymond Williams's structures of feeling. In the case of Chile, the so-called Escena de Avanzada articulated a series of informal experimental artistic and literary practices identified with opposition to dictatorship and restoration of democracy. In the words of Nelly Richard, and in a manner similar to that expressed by Sarlo: "Under such conditions of surveillance and censorship, artistic-cultural production becomes the substitute field—displaced and compensatory—that allows what is forbidden by official discourse to relocate in indirect figurations" ("La Escena" 104, translation ours).

In Latin America, however, organized violence and micro-violence (Salazar) coexist with forms of state violence or violence derived from situations of armed conflict. This testifies to the deterioration of the social pact due to a multitude of transnational actors—paramilitaries, gangs, guerrilla groups, drug traffickers—who install regimes of paralegality in the interstices left by the neoliberal Latin American state (Reguillo, "La construcción"). The urban environment in Latin America has become the main forum for experiencing violence, and it needs to be *narrated*—that is, mediated by stories and the mass media (García Canclini, *Consumers*). These stories largely articulate a widespread sense of insecurity, of fear as "individually experienced, socially constructed, and culturally shared" (Reguillo, "La construcción" 189, translation ours). Fear responds to perceptions of unavoidable violence, of danger, that, although linked to the individual, are socially produced through notions of risk and threat that generate a standardized response; they are thus "everyday experiences that point to the urban feeling of widespread helplessness and the risk of paralysis or the pursuit of repressive mechanisms capable of controlling the disorder" (Rotker 16–17, translation ours). A connected issue arises, that of the visibility of violence, in which the mass media plays a double role: it exposes social conflicts that reveal undesirable facets of the state, and it produces an informative agenda based on crime, thus stigmatizing certain subjects or sectors while favoring policies of security. Fear becomes a central feature of the mediatic narration of violence through the production of an unmanageable, irrational environment (Martín Barbero, "La ciudad").

This analytical perspective is based on the studies on "moral panic" by Stuart Hall and the Glasgow University Media Group (Hall et al., *Policing*), according to which the media reproduce dominant institutional relations, reinforcing and mobilizing social forces against individuals or groups that allegedly threaten established values at a particular moment. Thus the mass media produce "criminal subjects"—often marginal subjects—through processes of information selection and discursive strategies that operate as social control mechanisms. For Reguillo, the overexposure of "current" violence runs parallel to the invisibilization of structural violence as a result of the lack of historical perspective and/or political context, producing a perceived need "to discipline" a society reduced to the category of passive victim ("La construcción).

In violent contexts there are consequences not only of this form of mediation but of the penetration of fear in daily life: Firstly, the articulation of collective national stories is hindered and replaced by discontinuous and fragmented narrations. Secondly, the creation of public spaces for dialogue and debate is stalled, as are commemorations as places for collective mourning and political pedagogy.

Suggested Reading

Blair, Elsa. "Mucha sangre y poco sentido: La masacre: Por un análisis antropológico de la violencia." *Boletín de Antropología* 18, no. 35 (2004): 164–84.

Castro Gómez, Santiago. "Ciencias sociales, violencia epistémico y el problema de la 'invención del otro.'" In Lander, *La colonialidad del saber*, 145–61.

Coronil, Fernando, and Julie Skurski. "Dismembering and Remembering the Nation: The Semantics of Political Violence in Venezuela." *Comparative Studies in Society and History* 33 (1991): 288–337.

García Canclini, Néstor. *Consumers and Citizens: Globalization and Multicultural Conflicts*. Translated by George Yúdice. Minneapolis: University of Minnesota Press, 2001.

Martín Barbero, Jesús. "La ciudad: Entre medios y miedos." In Rotker, *Ciudadanías del miedo*, 29–35.

Quijano, Aníbal. "Colonialidad del poder, cultura y conocimiento en América Latin." In *Pensar (en) los intersticios: Teoría y práctica de la crítica poscolonial*, edited by Santiago Castro-Gómez, Oscar Guardiola-Rivera, and Carmen Millán de Benavides, 99–109. Bogotá: CEJA, 1999.

Reguillo, Rossana. "La construcción social del miedo: Narrativas y prácticas urbanas." In Rotker, *Ciudadanías del miedo*, 185–202.

Richard, Nelly. "La Escena de Avanzada y su contexto histórico-social." In *Copiar el Edén: Arte reciente en Chile = Copying Eden: Recent Art in Chile*, edited by Gerardo Mosquera. Santiago: Puro Chile, 2006: 103–19.

Rotker, Susana. *Ciudadanías del miedo*. Caracas: Nueva Sociedad, 2000.

Sarlo, Beatriz. "Política, ideología y figuración literaria." In *Ficción y política: La narrativa argentina durante el proceso militar*, edited by Daniel Balderston et al., 30–59. Buenos Aires: Alianza, 1987.

Uribe, María Victoria. *Matar, rematar y contramatar: Las masacres de la violencia en el Tolima, 1948–1964*. Bogotá: Cinep, 1996.

General Bibliography

Acuña, Rodolfo. *Occupied America: A History of Chicanos*. New York: Harper & Row, 1972.

Adorno, Rolena. "La ciudad letrada y los discursos coloniales." *Hispamérica: Revista de Literatura* 16, no. 48 (1987): 3–24.

———. "El sujeto colonial y la construcción cultural de la alteridad." *Revista de Crítica Literaria Latinoamericana* 14, no. 28 (1988): 55–68.

Adorno, Theodor W. "Cultural Criticism and Society." Translated by Samuel and Shierry Weber. In *The Adorno Reader*, edited by Brian O'Connor, 195–210. Oxford: Blackwell, 2000.

———. *See also* Horkheimer, Max, and Theodor W. Adorno.

Agamben, Giorgio. *Homo Sacer: Sovereign Power and Bare Life*. Translated by Daniel Heller-Roazen. Stanford, Calif.:Stanford University Press, 1998.

Agosti, Héctor Pablo. *Ideología y cultura*. Buenos Aires: Asociación Héctor P. Agosti, 2005.

Aguilar, Miguel Ángel, Adrián de Garay, and José Hernández Prado, eds. *Simpatía por el rock: Industria, cultura y sociedad*. Mexico City: Universidad Autónoma Metropolitana–Azcapotzalco, 1993.

Aguilar Rivera, José Antonio. *El sonido y la furia: La persuasión multicultural en México y Estados Unidos*. Mexico City: Taurus, 2004.

Aguirre Beltrán, Gonzalo. *El proceso de aculturación*. Mexico City: Universidad Nacional Autónoma de México, 1957.

Ainslie, Ricardo C. "Cultural Mourning, Immigration, and Engagement: Vignettes from the Mexican Experience." In *The New Immigration: An Interdisciplinary Reader*, edited by Marcelo M. Suárez-Orozco, Carola Suárez-Orozco, and Desirée Baolian Qin, 207–16. New York: Routledge, 2005.

Alarcón, Norma. *Chicana Critical Issues*. Berkeley, Calif.: Third Woman Press, 1993.

Alarcón, Norma, Caren Kaplan, and Minoo Moallem. Introduction to *Between Woman and Nation: Nationalisms, Transnational Feminisms, and the State*, edited by Caren Kaplan, Norma Alarcón, and Minoo Moallem, 1–18. Durham, N.C.: Duke University Press, 1999.

Alonso, Ana María. "Territorializing the Nation and 'Integrating the Indian': 'Mestizaje' in Mexican Official Discourses and Public Culture." In Hansen and Steputtat, *Sovereign Bodies*, 39–60.

Alonso, Carlos. "*Rama y sus retoños*: Figuring the Nineteenth Century in Spanish America." *Revista de Estudios Hispánicos* 28, no. 2 (1994): 283–92.

Altamirano, Carlos. *Términos críticos de la sociología de la cultura*. Buenos Aires: Paidós, 2002.

Althusser, Louis. *Lenin and Philosophy, and Other Essays*. Translated by Ben Brewster. London: New Left, 1971.

Anderson, Benedict. *Imagined Communities: Reflections on the Origins and Spread of Nationalism*. London: Verso, 1993.

Anderson, Perry. "Modernity and Revolution." *New Left Review* 1, no. 144 (March–April 1984): 96–113.

Andrade, Oswald de. "Anthropophagite Manifesto." Translated by Adriano Pedrosa and Veronica Cordeiro. *XXIV Bienal de São Paulo: Núcleo Histórico: Antropofagia e Histórias de canibalismo*. Vol. 1. São Paulo: Fundacion Bienal, 1998. 536-39.

———. "Cannibalist Manifesto." Translated by Leslie Bary. *Latin American Literary Review* 19, no. 38 (1991): 38–43.

———. "Manifiesto antropofago." In *Obras Escogidas*, 65–72. Caracas: Biblioteca Ayacucho, 1981.

Anzaldúa, Gloria. *Borderlands/La Frontera: The New Mestiza*. San Francisco: Aunt Lute Books, 1987.

Aparicio, Frances R. *Listening to Salsa: Gender, Latin Popular Music, and Puerto Rican Cultures*. Hanover, N.H.: University Press of New England, 1998.

Appadurai, Arjun, ed. *Globalization*. Durham, N.C.: Duke University Press, 2001.

———. *Modernity at Large: Cultural Dimensions of Globalization*. Minneapolis: University of Minnesota Press, 1996.

———. "Sovereignty Without Territoriality: Notes for a Postnational Geography." *Public Culture* 8 (1996): 40–57.

Arendt, Hannah. *The Human Condition*. Chicago: University of Chicago Press, 1958.

———. *On Violence*. New York: Harcourt, Brace & World, 1969.

Aretxaga, Begoña. *Shattering Silence: Women, Nationalism, and Political Subjectivity in Northern Ireland*. Princeton, N.J.: Princeton University Press, 1997.

Arguedas, José María. *Los ríos profundos*. Buenos Aires: Losada, 1957.

Aricó, José. *Mariátegui y los orígenes del marxismo latinoamericano*. Mexico City: Pasado y Presente/Siglo XXI, 1978.

Arnold, Matthew. *Culture and Anarchy*. 1869. New Haven, Conn.: Yale University Press, 1994.

Arroyo, Jossianna. *Travestismos culturales: Literatura y etnografía en Cuba y Brasil*. Pittsburgh, Pa.: Instituto Internacional de Literatura Iberoamericana, 2003.

Asad, Talal, ed. *Anthropology and the Colonial Encounter*. New York: Humanities Press, 1973.

———. *Genealogies of Religion: Discipline and Reasons of Power in Christianity and Islam*. Baltimore: Johns Hopkins University Press, 1993.

Augé, Marc. *Non-places: Introduction to an Anthropology of Supermodernity*. Translated by John Howe. London: Verso, 1995.

Austin, J. L. *How to Do Things with Words*. Oxford: Clarendon, 1962.

Badiou, Alain. *Ethics: An Essay on the Understanding of Evil*. Translated by Peter Hallward. London: Verso, 2001.

Balderston, Daniel, and Donna J. Guy, eds. *Sex and Sexuality in Latin America*. New York: New York University Press, 1997.

Barbosa, Heloisa Gonçalves, and Lia Whyler. "Brazilian Tradition." In *Routledge Encyclopedia of Translation Studies*, edited by Mona Baker, 326–32. London: Routledge, 1998.

Barker, Chris, and Dariusz Galasiński, eds. *Cultural Studies and Discourse Analysis: A Dialogue on Language and Identity*. London: Sage, 2001.

Barrios de Chungara, Domitila, with Moema Viezzer. "*Si me permiten hablar . . .*": *Testimonio de Domitila, una mujer de las minas de Bolivia*. Mexico City: Siglo XXI, 1978.

Barthes, Roland. "The Death of the Author." In *The Rustle of Language*, 49–55.

———. *Elements of Semiology*. Translated by Annette Lavers and Colin Smith. London: Jonathan Cape, 1967.

———. "From Work to Text." In *The Rustle of Language*, 56–64.

———. *A Lover's Discourse: Fragments*. Translated by Richard Howard. New York: Hill and Wang, 1978.

———. *Mythologies*. Translated by Annette Lavers. London: Jonathan Cape, 1972.

———. *The Rustle of Language*. Translated by Richard Howard. New York: Hill and Wang, 1986.

Bartra, Roger. *El salvaje en el espejo*. Mexico City: UNAM/Era, 1992. Translated by Carl T. Berrisford as *Wild Men in the Looking Glass: The Mythic Origins of European Otherness* (Ann Arbor: University of Michigan Press, 1994).

Baudrillard, Jean. *Simulacra and Simulation*. Translated by Sheila Faria Glaser. Ann Arbor: University of Michigan Press, 1994.

Beauvoir, Simone de. *The Second Sex*. Translated by H. M. Parshley. New York: Knopf, 1953.

Bell, Daniel. *The End of Ideology: On the Exhaustion of Political Ideas in the Fifties*. Rev. ed. New York.: Collier, 1961.

Bello, Andrés. *Obras*. Caracas: Academia Venezuela, 1989.

Bellour, Raymond. *The Analysis of Film*. Translated by Constance Penley. Bloomington: Indiana University Press, 2000.

Beltrán, Luis Ramiro. "Communication and Cultural Domination: USA–Latin American Case." *Media Asia* 5 (1978): 183–92.

Benjamin, Walter. *Angelus Novus*. Berlin: Suhrkamp, 1988.

———. *Illuminations*. Edited by Hannah Arendt. Translated by Harry Zohn. New York: Harcourt, Brace & World, 1968.

———. *Selected Writings*. Vol. 1, *1913–1926*. Edited by Marcus Bullock and Michael W. Jennings. Cambridge, Mass.: Belknap, 2004.

———. "Theses on the Philosophy of History." In *Illuminations*, 253–64.

———. *The Work of Art in the Age of Its Technical Reproducibility, and Other Writings on Media*. Edited by Michael W. Jennings, Brigid Doherty, and Thomas Y. Levin. Translated by Edmund Jephcott et al. Cambridge, Mass.: Belknap, 2008.

Bergmann, Emilie L., and Paul Julian Smith, eds. *¿Entiendes? Queer Readings, Hispanic Writings*. Durham, N.C.: Duke University Press, 1995.

Bernand, Carmen, and Serge Gruzinski. *Historia del Nuevo Mundo: Del descubrimiento a la conquista: La experiencia europea, 1492–1550*. Translated by María Antonia Neira Bigorra. Mexico City: Fondo de Cultura Económica, 1996. Originally published as *Histoire du Nouveau Monde* (Paris: Fayard, 1991).

Beverley, John. *Against Literature*. Minneapolis: University of Minnesota Press, 1993.

———. "The Im/Possibility of Politics: Subalternity, Modernity, Hegemony." In Rodríguez, *Latin American Subaltern Studies Reader*, 47–63.

———. "La persistencia del subalterno." *Revista Iberoamericana* 69, no. 203 (2003): 335–42.

———. "Postcriptum." In Moraña, *Nuevas perspectivas desde/sobre América Latina*, 579–88.

———. "Siete aproximaciones al 'problema indígena.'" In Moraña, *Indigenismo hacia el fin del milenio*, 243–83.

———. *Subalternity and Representation: Arguments in Cultural Theory*. Durham, N.C.: Duke University Press, 1999.

Beverley, John, Michael Aronna, and José Oviedo, eds. *The Postmodernism Debate in Latin America*. Durham, N.C.: Duke University Press, 1995.

Bhabha, Homi K. *The Location of Culture*. London: Routledge, 1994.

———. "The Other Question: Difference, Discrimination and the Discourse of Colonialism." In *Literature, Politics, and Theory*, edited by Francis Barker, Peter Hulme, Margaret Iversen, and Diane Loxley, 148–72. London: Methuen, 1986.

Bonfil Batalla, Guillermo. *México profundo: Una civilización negada*. 1987. Mexico City: Grijalbo/Consejo Nacional para la Cultura y las Artes, 1990.

Boone, Elizabeth Hill, and Walter Mignolo. *Writing Without Words: Alternative Literacies in Mesoamerica and the Andes*. Durham, N.C.: Duke University Press, 1996.

Borges, Jorge Luis. *Ficciones*. 1944. Madrid: Alianza, 2002.

———. *Selected Poems*. Edited by Alexander Coleman. New York: Viking, 1999.

Bourdieu, Pierre. *Ce que parler veut dire: L'économie des échanges linguistiques*. Paris: Fayard, 1982.

———. *Distinction: A Social Critique of the Judgement of Taste*. Translated by Richard Nice. Cambridge, Mass.: Harvard University Press, 1984.

———. *Language and Symbolic Power*. Translated by Gino Raymond and Matthew Adamson. Cambridge, Mass.: Harvard University Press, 1991.

———. *Outline of a Theory of Practice*. Translated by Richard Nice. Cambridge: Cambridge University Press, 1977.

———. *The Rules of Art: Genesis and Structure of the Literary Field*. Translated by Susan Emanuel. Stanford, Calif.: Stanford University Press, 1996.

———. *Sociology in Question*. Translated by Richard Nice. London: Sage, 1993.

Braudel, Fernand. *The Mediterranean and the Mediterranean World in the Age of Philip II*. Translated by Siân Reynolds. 2 vols. New York: Harper & Row, 1972–73.

Brunner, José Joaquín. *Un espejo trizado: Ensayos sobre cultura y políticas culturales*. Santiago, Chile: FLACSO, 1988.

———. *Globalización cultural y posmodernidad*. Santiago, Chile: Fondo de Cultura Económica, 1998.

Bryson, Norman. *Tradition and Desire: From David to Delacroix*. Cambridge: Cambridge University Press, 1984.

Butler, Judith. *Bodies That Matter: On the Discursive Limits of "Sex."* New York: Routledge, 1993.

———. *Gender Trouble: Feminism and the Subversion of Identity*. New York: Routledge, 1990.

Cabrujas, José Ignacio. "El Estado del disimulo." In *Heterodoxia y estado: 5 respuestas*, 7–35. Caracas: COPRE, 1987.

Calveiro Garrido, Pilar. *Desapariciones*. Mexico City: Taurus, 2002.

———. *Redes familiares de sumisión y resistencia*. Mexico City: Universidad Ciudad de México, 2003.

Cândido, Antônio. *Crítica radical*. Translated by Márgara Russotto. Caracas: Biblioteca Ayacucho, 1991.

———. *Varios escritos*. São Paulo: Duas Cidades, 1970.

Carri, Albertina. *Los rubios*. Documentary film, 2003. Distributed by Women Make Movies.

Casas, Bartolomé de las. *Brevísima Relación de la Destrucción de las Indias*. 1552. Madrid: Cátedra, 1982.

Castells, Manuel. *La cuestión urbana*. Mexico City: Siglo XXI, 1973.

Castillejo, Alejandro. *Poética de lo otro: Antropología de la guerra, la soledad y exilio interno en Colombia*. Bogotá: Conciencias-ICANH, 2000.

Castillo, Debra A., and María Socorro Tabuenca Córdoba, eds. *Border Women: Writing from La Frontera*. Minneapolis: University of Minnesota Press, 2002.

Castro Gómez, Santiago. "Althusser, los estudios culturales y el concepto de ideología." *Revista Iberoamericana* 64, no. 193 (2000): 737–51.

———. "Los vecindarios de *La ciudad letrada*: Variaciones filosóficas sobre un tema de Ángel Rama." In Moraña, *Ángel Rama y los estudios latinoamericanos*, 123–33.

Castro Gómez, Santiago, and Eduardo Mendieta, eds. *Teorías sin disciplina: Latinoamericanismo, poscolonialidad y globalización en debate*. Mexico City: Miguel Ángel Porrúa, 1998. www.ensayistas.org/critica/teoria/castro/richard.htm.

Castro-Klarén, Sara, ed. *Narrativa femenina en América Latina: Prácticas y perspectivas teóricas = Latin American Women's Narrative: Practices and Theoretical Perspectives*. Madrid: Iberoamericana; Frankfurt am Main: Vervuert, 2003.

Castro Ricalde, Maricruz, Laura Cázares Hernández, and Gloria Prado Garduño, eds. *Escrituras en contraste: Femenino, masculino en la literatura mexicana del siglo XX*. Mexico City: Aldus/Universidad Autónoma Metropolitana- Iztapalapa, 2004.

Casullo, Nicolás, ed. *El debate modernidad-posmodernidad*. Buenos Aires: Retórica, 2004.

———. "Posmodernidad de los orígenes." *Nuevo Texto Crítico* 3, no. 6 (1990): 95–104.

Casullo, Nicolás, Ricardo Forster, and Alejandro Kaufman. *Itinerarios de la modernidad: Corrientes del pensamiento y tradiciones intelectuales desde la ilustración hasta la posmodernidad*. Buenos Aires: EUDEBA, 1999.

Cella, Susana, ed. *Dominios de la literatura: Acerca del canon*. Buenos Aires: Losada, 1998.

Certeau, Michel de. *Culture in the Plural*. Edited by Luce Giard. Translated by Tom Conley. Minneapolis: University of Minnesota Press, 1997.

———. *The Practice of Everyday Life*. Translated by Steven Rendall. Berkeley: University of California Press, 1984.

Cervantes Barba, Cecilia. "Política cultural y ¿nuevos movimientos culturales en México?" Paper presented at the Latin American Studies Association conference, Las Vegas, October 8, 2004.

Césaire, Aimé. *Discourse on Colonialism*. Translated by Joan Pinkham. New York: MR, 1972.

Chakrabarty, Dipesh. *Habitations of Modernity: Essays in the Wake of Subaltern Studies*. Chicago: University of Chicago Press, 2002.

———. *Provincializing Europe: Postcolonial Thought and Historical Difference*. Princeton, N.J.: Princeton University Press, 2000.

Chang Rodríguez, Raquel. "La trayectoria intelectual de Antonio Cornejo Polar." *Revista de Crítica Literaria Latinoamericana* 25, no. 50 (1999): 15–19.

Chasteen, John Charles. Introduction to *Beyond Imagined Communities: Reading and Writing the Nation in Nineteenth Century Latin America*, edited by Sara Castro-Klarén and John Charles Chasteen, ix–xxv. Washington: Woodrow Wilson Center Press; Baltimore: Johns Hopkins University Press, 2003.

———. Introduction to Rama, *The Lettered City*, vii–xiv.

Chatterjee, Partha. *The Nation and Its Fragments: Colonial and Postcolonial Histories.* Princeton, N.J.: Princeton University Press, 1993.

Chaturvedi, Vinayak, ed. *Mapping Subaltern Studies and the Postcolonial.* New York: Verso, 2000.

Chomsky, Noam. *Year 501: The Conquest Continues.* Boston: South End, 1993.

Cixous, Hélène. "The Laugh of the Medusa." Translated by Keith Cohen and Paula Cohen. *Signs* 1, no. 4 (1976): 875–93.

Clark, Michael. "Twenty Preliminary Propositions for a Critical History of International Statecraft in Haiti." In Rodríguez, *Latin American Subaltern Studies Reader*, 241–59.

Clifford, James. *Routes: Travel and Translation in the Late Twentieth Century.* Cambridge, Mass.: Harvard University Press, 1997.

Cocco, Giuseppe. "Antropofagias, racismos y acciones afirmativas." Translated by Gisela Daza. *Nómadas*, no. 30 (2009): 50–65.

Coelho, Frederico. "A formação de um tropicalista: Um breve estudo da coluna 'Música Popular' de Torquato Neto." *Estudos Históricos* 2, no. 30 (2002): 129–46.

Comaroff, John, and Jean Comaroff. *Of Revelation and Revolution: The Dialectics of Modernity on the South African Frontier.* 2 vols. Chicago: University of Chicago Press, 1997.

Cornejo Polar, Antonio. *Escribir en el aire: Ensayo sobre la heterogeneidad socio-cultural en las literaturas andinas.* Lima: Horizonte, 1994.

———. "Una heterogeneidad no dialéctica: Sujeto y discurso migrante en el Perú moderno." *Revista iberoamericana* 62, nos. 176–77 (1996): 837–44.

———. "El indigenismo andino." In *América Latina: Palavra, literatura e cultura*, edited by Ana Pizarro, 719–38. São Paulo: UNICAMP, 1994.

———. "El indigenismo y las literaturas heterogéneas: Su doble estatuto socio-cultural." *Revista de Crítica Literaria Latinoamericana* 4, nos. 7–8 (1978): 7–21.

———. "Mestizaje e hibridez: Los riesgos de las metáforas." *Revista de Crítica Literaria Latinoamericana* 24, no. 47 (1998): 7–11.

———. "Mestizaje, transculturación, heterogeneidad." In *Asedios a la heterogeneidad cultural: Libro de homenaje a Antonio Cornejo Polar*, edited by José Antonio Mazzotti and U. Juan Zevallos Aguilar, 54–56. Philadelphia: Asociación Internacional de Peruanistas, 1996.

Coronil, Fernando. "Beyond Occidentalism: Toward Nonimperial Geohistorical Categories." *Cultural Anthropology* 11, no. 1 (1996): 52–87.

———. "Introduction to the Duke University Press Edition." In F. Ortiz, *Cuban Counterpoint*, lx–lvi.

———. *The Magical State: Nature, Money, and Modernity in Venezuela.* Chicago: University of Chicago Press, 1997.

Cortázar, Julio. *Rayuela.* Buenos Aires: Sudamericana, 1963.

Crapanzano, Vincent. *Serving the Word: Literalism in America from the Pulpit to the Bench.* New York: New Press, 2000.

Cueva, Agustín. *Literatura y conciencia histórica en América Latina.* 1977. Quito: Planeta, 1993.

D'Allemand, Patricia. *Latin American Cultural Criticism: Re-Interpreting a Continent*. Lewiston, N.Y.: Edwin Mellon Press, 2000.

Davis, Mike. *Magical Urbanism: Latinos Reinvent the US City*. London: Verso, 2000.

De Genova, Nicholas. "Migrant 'Illegality' and Deportability in Everyday Life." *Annual Review of Anthropology*, no. 31 (2002): 419–47.

De la Cadena, Marisol. "Are Mestizos Hybrids? The Conceptual Politics of Andean Identities." *Journal of Latin American Studies* 37 (2005): 259–84.

———. *Indigenous Mestizos: The Politics of Race and Culture in Cuzco, Peru, 1919–1991*. Durham, N.C.: Duke University Press, 2000.

De la Campa, Román. "El desafío inesperado de *La ciudad letrada*." In Moraña, *Ángel Rama y los estudios latinoamericanos*, 29–53.

———. *Latin Americanism*. Minneapolis: University of Minnesota Press, 1999.

———. "Magical Realism: A Genre for the Times?" *Canadian Review of Hispanic Studies*, Summer 1999, 103–18.

Deleuze, Gilles. *The Logic of Sense*. Translated by Mark Lester with Charles Stivale. New York: Columbia University Press, 1990.

Deleuze, Gilles, and Félix Guattari. *Anti-Oedipus*. Vol. 1 of *Capitalism and Schizophrenia*. Translated by Robert Hurley, Mark Seem, and Helen R. Lane. New York: Viking, 1977.

———. *Rhizome: Introduction*. Paris: Minuit, 1976.

———. *A Thousand Plateaus*. Vol. 2 of *Capitalism and Schizophrenia*. Translated by Brian Massumi. Minneapolis: University of Minnesota Press, 1987.

Derrida, Jacques. "Différance." In *Margins of Philosophy*, 1–27. Translated by Alan Bass. Chicago: University of Chicago Press, 1982.

———. *Dissemination*. Translated by Barbara Johnson. Chicago: University of Chicago Press, 1981.

———. "Marx and Sons." In *Ghostly Demarcations: A Symposium on Jacques Derrida's "Specters of Marx,"* edited by Michael Sprinker, 235–54. London: Verso/NLB, 1999.

———. *Of Grammatology*. Translated by Gayatri Chakravorty Spivak. Baltimore: Johns Hopkins University Press, 1976.

———. "Plato's Pharmacy." In *Dissemination*, 61–171.

———. *Specters of Marx: The State of the Debt, the Work of Mourning, and the New International*. Translated by Peggy Kamuf. New York: Routledge, 1994.

Díaz Bordenave, Juan E. *Communication and Rural Development*. Paris: UNESCO, 1977.

Donham, Donald L. *Marxist Modern: An Ethnographic History of the Ethiopian Revolution*. Berkeley: University of California Press, 1999.

Donoso, José. *El lugar sin límites*. 1966. Mexico City: Alfaguara, 1995.

Dorfman, Ariel. *Heading South, Looking North: A Bilingual Journey*. New York: Farrar, Straus & Giroux, 1998. Translated by the author from the original English as *Rumbo al sur, deseando el norte: Un romance en dos lenguas* (Buenos Aires: Planeta, 1998).

Dorfman, Ariel, and Armand Mattelart. *Para leer al Pato Donald*. Valparaíso, Chile: Ediciones Universitarias de Valparaíso, 1971. Translated by David Kunzle as *How to Read Donald Duck: Imperialist Ideology in the Disney Comic* (New York: International General, 1975).

Dorra, Raúl. *Entre la voz y la letra*. Mexico City: Plaza y Valdés/Universidad de Puebla, 1997.

———. "¿Grafocentrismo o fonocentrismo? Perspectivas para un estudio de la oralidad."

In *Memorias: Jornadas andinas de literatura latinoamericana*, edited by Ricardo J. Kaliman, 1: 56–73. Tucumán, Argentina: Universidad Nacional de Tucumán, 1997.

Dryzek, John. *Deliberative Democracy and Beyond: Liberals, Critics, Contestations*. Oxford: Oxford University Press, 2000.

Duany, Jorge. *The Puerto Rican Nation on the Move: Identities on the Island and in the United States*. Chapel Hill: University of North Carolina Press, 2002.

Dube, Saurabh. "Anthropology, History, Historical Anthropology." In *Historical Anthropology*, 1–74.

———, ed. *Enchantments of Modernity: Empire, Nation, Globalization*. New Delhi/New York: Routledge, 2007.

———, ed. *Historical Anthropology*. New Delhi/New York: Oxford University Press, 2007.

———. "Introduction: Enchantments of Modernity." *South Atlantic Quarterly* 101, no. 4 (Fall 2002): 729–55.

———, ed. *Postcolonial Passages: Contemporary History-Writing on India*. New Delhi/New York: Oxford University Press, 2004.

———. *Stitches on Time: Colonial Textures and Postcolonial Tangles*. Durham, N.C.: Duke University Press, 2004.

———. *Sujetos subalternos: Capítulos de una historia antropológica*. Translated from the German by Franco and Ari Bartra. Mexico City: Colegio de México, 2001.

Dube, Saurabh, Ishita Banerjee-Dube, and Walter D. Mignolo, eds. *Modernidades coloniales: Otros pasados, historias presentes*. Mexico City: Colegio de México, 2004.

Dunn, Christopher. *Brutality Garden: Tropicália and the Emergence of a Brazilian Counterculture*. Chapel Hill: University of North Carolina Press, 2001.

Dupont, Louis, and Nathalie Lemarchand. "Official Multiculturalism in Canada: Between Virtue and Politics." In *Global Multiculturalism*, edited by Grant H. Cornwell and Eve Walsh Stoddard, 309–36. Lanham, Md.: Rowman & Littlefield, 2001.

Durand, Jorge, and Douglas S. Massey. *Clandestinos: Migración México–Estados Unidos en los albores del siglo XXI*. Mexico City: Miguel Ángel Porrúa, 2003.

Durham, Meenakshi Gigi, and Douglas M. Kellner, eds. *Media and Cultural Studies: Keyworks*. Rev. ed. Malden, Mass.: Blackwell, 2006.

During, Simon. *Modern Enchantments: The Cultural Power of Secular Magic*. Cambridge, Mass.: Harvard University Press, 2002.

Durkheim, Emile. *The Elementary Forms of Religious Life*. Translated by Karen E. Fields. New York: Free Press, 1995.

Dussel, Enrique. *Ética de la liberación en la edad de la globalización y la exclusión*. 2nd ed. Madrid: Trotta, 1998.

———. *The Invention of the Americas: Eclipse of "the Other" and the Myth of Modernity*. Translated by Michael D. Barber. New York: Continuum, 1995.

———. "Sistema mundo y 'transmodernidad.'" In Dube, Banerjee-Dube, and Mignolo, *Modernidades coloniales*, 201–26.

Eagleton, Terry. *Ideology: An Introduction*. London: Verso, 1991.

Echeverría, Bolivar. *La modernidad de lo barroco*. Mexico City: Universidad Autónoma Metropolitana/Era, 1998.

Ejército Zapatista de Liberación Nacional. "Al Congreso Nacional Indígena: El dolor nos une y nos hace uno." palabra.ezln.org.mx/comunicados/2001/2001_03_04.htm.

Eliot, T. S. *Selected Essays*. 3rd ed. London: Faber, 1972.

Esteinou Madrid, Javier. *La comunicación y la cultura nacionales en los tiempos del libre comercio*. Mexico City: Fundación Manuel Buendía, 1993.

Fabian, Johannes. *Time and the Other: How Anthropology Makes Its Object*. New York: Columbia University Press, 1983.

Fanon, Frantz. *Black Skin, White Masks*. Translated by Charles Lam Markmann. New York: Grove Press, 1967.

———. *The Wretched of the Earth*. Translated by Constance Farrington. New York: Grove Press, 1965.

Fausto, Boris. *História do Brasil*. São Paulo: Edusp/Fundação para o Desenvolvimento da Educação, 1994.

Fausto-Sterling, Anne. "The Five Sexes: Why Male and Female Are Not Enough." *The Sciences*, March–April 1993, 20–24.

Feldman, Allen. *Formations of Violence: The Narrative of the Body and Political Terror in Northern Ireland*. Chicago: University of Chicago Press, 1991.

Felman, Shoshana, and Dori Laub. *Testimony: Crises of Witnessing in Literature, Psychoanalysis, and History*. New York: Routledge, 1992.

Fernández Retamar, Roberto. *Calibán: Apuntes sobre la cultura en nuestra América*. Mexico City: Diógenes, 1971.

———. *Para una teoría de la literatura hispanoamericana*. 2nd ed. Mexico City: Nuestro Tiempo, 1977.

Ferreira de Almeida, Maria Cândida. "'Só a antropofagia nos une.'" In Mato, *Estudios y otras prácticas*, 121–32.

Fiedler, Leslie. "Cross the Border—Close the Gap." 1969. In *A New Fiedler Reader*, 270–94. Amherst, N.Y.: Prometheus, 1999.

Fiol-Matta, Licia. *A Queer Mother for the Nation: The State and Gabriela Mistral*. Minneapolis: University of Minnesota Press, 2002.

Fischer, Sibylle. *Modernity Disavowed: Haiti and the Cultures of Slavery in the Age of Revolution*. Durham, N.C.: Duke University Press, 2004.

Flores, Juan. "The Diaspora Strikes Back: Reflections on Cultural Remittances." *NACLA Report on the Americas* 39, no. 3 (2005): 21–25.

———. *From Bomba to Hip-Hop: Puerto Rican Culture and Latino Identity*. New York: Columbia University Press, 2000.

Flores, William V., and Rina Benmayor, eds. *Latino Cultural Citizenship: Claiming Identity, Space, and Rights*. Boston: Beacon Press, 1997.

Florescano, Enrique. *Memoria mexicana: Ensayo sobre la reconstrucción del pasado: Época prehispanica–1821*. Mexico City: Joaquín Mortiz, 1987.

Flores Galindo, Alberto. *Buscando un Inca: Identidad y utopía en los Andes*. Havana: Casa de las Americas, 1986.

Foster, Hal, ed. *The Anti-Aesthetic: Essays on Postmodern Culture*. Seattle: Bay Press, 1983.

———. "Postmodernism: A Preface." In *The Anti-Aesthetic*, ix–xvi.

Foucault, Michel. *Abnormal: Lectures at the Collège de France, 1974–75*. Translated by Graham Burchell. New York: Picador, 2003.

———. *The Archaeology of Knowledge*. Translated by A. M. Sheridan Smith. New York: Pantheon, 1972.

———. *Discipline and Punish: The Birth of the Prison*. Translated by Alan Sheridan. New York: Pantheon, 1977.

———. *Dits et écrits (1954–1988)*. 4 vols. Paris: Gallimard, 1994.

———. *The History of Sexuality*. Translated by Robert Hurley. 3 vols. New York: Pantheon, 1978–86.

———. *L'ordre du discours*. Paris: Gallimard, 1971.

———. *The Order of Things: An Archaeology of the Human Sciences*. New York: Pantheon, 1971.

———. *Society Must Be Defended: Lectures at the Collège de France, 1974–75*. Translated by David Macey. New York: Picador, 2003.

———. "The Subject and Power." In *Michel Foucault: Beyond Structuralism and Hermeneutics*, edited by Hubert Dreyfus and Paul Rabinow, 208–26. Chicago: University of Chicago Press, 1982.

Fox, Jonathan. "Reframing Mexican Migration as a Multi-Ethnic Process." *Latino Studies* 4, nos. 1–2 (Spring–Summer 2006): 39–61.

Franco, Jean. *Critical Passions: Selected Essays*. Durham, N.C.: Duke University Press, 1999.

———. *The Decline and Fall of the Lettered City: Latin America in the Cold War*. Cambridge, Mass.: Harvard University Press, 2002.

———. *Plotting Women: Gender and Representation in Mexico*. New York: Columbia University Press, 1989.

———. "Policía de frontera." In *Mapas culturales para América Latina: Culturas híbridas, no simultaneidad, modernidad periférica*, edited by Sarah de Mojica, 55–60. Berlin: WVB, 2000.

Fraser, Valerie. *Building the New World: Studies in the Modern Architecture of Latin America, 1930–1960*. London: Verso, 2000.

Freud, Sigmund. *The Interpretation of Dreams*. Translated by James Strachey. London: Allen & Unwin, 1954.

———. "Mourning and Melancholia." In *The Standard Edition of the Complete Psychological Works of Sigmund Freud*, translated by James Strachey, 14: 239–60. London: Hogarth Press, 1953–74.

———. *Three Essays on the Theory of Sexuality*. Translated by James Strachey. London: Hogarth Press, 1962.

Freyre, Gilberto. *The Masters and the Slaves (Casa-grande & senzala): A Study in the Development of Brazilian Civilization*. Translated by Samuel Putnam. Rev. ed. New York: Knopf, 1956.

Frow, John. *Genre*. London: Routledge, 2006.

Fuentes, Carlos. *La muerte de Artemio Cruz*. Mexico City: Fondo de Cultura Económica, 1962.

Fuenzalida, Valerio, and María Elena Hermosilla, with Paula Edwards. *Visiones y ambiciones del televidente: Estudios de recepción televisiva*. Santiago, Chile: Ceneca, 1989.

Galtung, Johan. "Cultural Violence." *Journal of Peace Research* 27, no. 3 (1990): 291–305.

———. *Peace by Peaceful Means: Peace and Conflict, Development and Civilization*. Oslo: International Peace Research Institute; London: Sage, 1996.

———. "Violence, Peace, and Peace Research." *Journal of Peace Research* 6, no. 3 (1969): 167–91.

Garber, Marjorie. *Vested Interests: Cross Dressing and Cultural Anxiety*. New York: Routledge, 1992.

García Canal, María Inés. *Foucault y el poder*. Mexico City: Universidad Autónoma Metropolitana–Xoxhimilco, 2002.

García Canclini, Néstor. *Consumers and Citizens: Globalization and Multicultural Conflicts*. Translated by George Yúdice. Minneapolis: University of Minnesota Press, 2001.

———, ed. *El consumo cultural en México*. Mexico City: Consejo Nacional para la Cultura y las Artes/Grijalbo, 1993.

———, ed. *Cultura y comunicación en la ciudad de México*. 2 vols. Mexico City: Grijalbo, 1998.

———. *Las culturas populares en el capitalismo*. Mexico City: Nueva Imagen, 1982. Translated by Lidia Lozano as *Transforming Modernity: Popular Culture in Mexico* (Austin: University of Texas Press, 1993).

———. "Culture and Power: The State of Research." *Media, Culture, and Society* 10, no. 4 (1988):467–97.

———. *Desigualdad cultural y poder simbólico: La sociología de Pierre Bourdieu*. Córdoba, Spain: Instituto Nacional de Antropología e Historia/Escuela Nacional de Antropología e Historia, 1986.

———. *Diferentes, desiguales y desconectados: Mapas de la interculturalidad*. Barcelona: Gedisa, 2004.

———. "La épica de la globalización y el melodrama de la interculturalidad." In Moraña, *Nuevas perspectivas desde/sobre América Latina*, 35–47.

———. *La globalización imaginada*. Mexico City: Paidós, 1999.

———. *Hybrid Cultures: Strategies for Entering and Leaving Modernity*. Translated by Christopher L. Chiappari and Silvia L. López. Minneapolis: University of Minnesota Press, 1995.

———. *Latinoamericanos buscando lugar en este siglo*. Buenos Aires: Paidós, 2002.

———. "Ni folklórico ni masivo: ¿Qué es lo popular?" *Dialogos de la comunicación*, no. 17 (June 1987): 6–11. www.infoamerica.org/documentos_pdf/garcia_canclini1.pdf.

———. "Noticias recientes sobre hibridación." *Revista Transcultural de Música/Transcultural Music Review* 7 (December 2003).www.sibetrans.com/trans/trans7/canclini.htm.

García Espinosa, Julio. "For an Imperfect Cinema." Translated by Julianne Burton. In *New Latin American Cinema*, edited by Michael T. Martin, 1: 71–82. Detroit: Wayne State University Press, 1997.

García Márquez, Gabriel. *Cien años de soledad*. Buenos Aires: Sudamericana, 1967.

Geertz, Clifford. *The Interpretation of Cultures: Selected Essays*. New York: Basic Books, 1973.

Gilroy, Paul. *The Black Atlantic: Modernity and Double Consciousness*. Cambridge, Mass.: Harvard University Press, 1993.

———. *"There Ain't No Black in the Union Jack": The Cultural Politics of Race and Nation*. Chicago: University of Chicago Press, 1991.

Glantz, Margo. *La lengua en la mano*. Mexico City: Premià, 1983.

Glissant, Édouard. *Caribbean Discourse: Selected Essays*. Translated by J. Michael Dash. Charlottesville: University Press of Virginia, 1989.

Goffman, Erving. *Frame Analysis: An Essay on the Organization of Experience*. Cambridge, Mass.: Harvard University Press, 1974.

———. *The Presentation of Self in Everyday Life*. Garden City, N.Y.: Doubleday, 1959.

———. *Stigma: Notes on the Management of Spoiled Identity*. Englewood Cliffs, N.J.: Prentice-Hall, 1963.

Goldberg, David Theo, ed. *Multiculturalism: A Critical Reader*. Oxford: Blackwell, 1994.

González, Patricia Elena, and Eliana Ortega, eds. *La sartén por el mango: Encuentro de escritoras latinoamericanas*. Santo Domingo: Huracán, 1985.

González Echevarría, Roberto. *Myth and Archive: A Theory of Latin American Narrative*. Cambridge: Cambridge University Press, 1990.

González Stephan, Beatriz, ed. *Cultura y tercer mundo*. Caracas: Nueva sociedad, 1996.

Graham, Richard, ed. *The Idea of Race in Latin America, 1870–1940*. Austin: University of Texas Press, 1990.

Gramsci, Antonio. *A Gramsci Reader: Selected Writings, 1916–1935*. Edited by David Forgacs. London: Lawrence and Wishart, 1988.

Grandon Lagunas, Olga. "Gabriela Mistral y la identidad tensionada de nuestra modernidad." *Acta Literaria*, no. 30 (2005): 81–96.

Grimson, Alejandro. *Relatos de la diferencia y la igualdad: Los bolivianos en Buenos Aires*. Buenos Aires: EUDEBA, 1999.

Gugelberger, Georg M., ed. *The Real Thing: Testimonial Discourse and Latin America*. Durham, N.C.: Duke University Press, 1996.

Guha, Ranajit. *Dominance without Hegemony: History and Power in Colonial India*. Cambridge, Mass.: Harvard University Press, 1997.

———. "Dominance without Hegemony and Its Historiography." *Subaltern Studies* 6 (1989): 210–309.

———. *Elementary Aspects of Peasant Insurgency in Colonial India*. Delhi: Oxford University Press, 1983.

———. Introduction to *A Subaltern Studies Reader, 1986–1995*, ix–xxii. Minneapolis: University of Minnesota Press, 1997.

Guha, Ranajit, and Gayatri Chakravorty Spivak, eds. *Selected Subaltern Studies*. Oxford: Oxford University Press, 1988.

Guillory, John. *Cultural Capital: The Problem of Literary Canon Formation*. Chicago: University of Chicago Press, 1993.

Gutiérrez de Velasco, Luzelena, Gloria Prado, and Ana Rosa Domenella, eds. *De pesares y alegrías: Escritoras latinoamericanas y caribeñas contemporáneas*. Mexico City: Colegio de México/Universidad Autónoma Metropolitana–Iztapalapa, 1999.

Gutiérrez Estupiñán, Raquel. *Una introducción a la teoría literaria*. Puebla, Mexico: Benemérita Universidad Autónoma de Puebla, 2004.

Habermas, Jürgen. *Between Facts and Norms: Contributions to a Discourse Theory of Law and Democracy*. Translated by William Rehg. Cambridge, Mass.: MIT Press, 1996.

———. "Modernity—An Incomplete Project." In Foster, *The Anti-Aesthetic*, 3–16.

———. *The Philosophical Discourse of Modernity: Twelve Lectures*. Translated by Frederick Lawrence. Cambridge, Mass.: MIT Press, 1987.

———. *The Structural Transformation of the Public Sphere: An Inquiry into a Category of Bourgeois Society*. Translated by Thomas Burger with Frederick Lawrence. Cambridge, Mass.: MIT Press, 1989.

Hall, Stuart. "Conclusion: The Multi-Cultural Question." In *Un/settled Multiculturalisms: Diasporas, Entanglements, "Transruptions,"* edited by Barnor Hesse, 209–41. London: Zed, 2000.

———. "Cultural Studies and Its Theoretical Legacies." In Morley and Chen, *Stuart Hall*, 262–76.
———. "Encoding/Decoding." In Durham and Kellner, *Media and Cultural Studies*, 163–73.
———. "Ethnicity: Identity and Difference." *Radical America* 23, no. 4 (1989): 9–20.
———. "New Ethnicities." In Morley and Chen, *Stuart Hall*, 441–49.
———. "Notes on the Deconstruction of 'the Popular.'" In *People's History and Socialist Theory*, edited by Raphael Samuel, 227–40. London: Routledge & Kegan Paul, 1981.
———. "The Problem of Ideology: Marxism Without Guarantees." In Morley and Chen, *Stuart Hall*, 25–46.
———. "The Question of Cultural Identity." In *Modernity: An Introduction to Modern Societies*, edited by Stuart Hall, David Held, Don Hubert, and Kenneth Thompson, 596–634. Cambridge: Polity Press, 1995.
———. "Race, Articulation, and Societies Structured in Dominance." In *Sociological Theories: Race and Colonialism*, 305–45. Paris: UNESCO, 1980.
———, ed. *Representation: Cultural Representations and Signifying Practices*. London: Sage, 1997.
———. "When Was the Postcolonial? Thinking at the Limit." In *The Post-colonial Question: Common Skies, Divided Horizons*, edited by Iain Chambers and Lidia Curti, 242–60. New York: Routledge, 1996.
Hall, S., C. Critcher, T. Jefferson, J. Clarke, and B. Roberts. *Policing the Crisis: Mugging, the State, and Law and Order*. London: Macmillan, 1978.
Hall, Stuart, and Paul du Gay, eds. *Questions of Cultural Identity*. London: Sage, 1996.
Hansen, Thomas Blom, and Finn Steputtat, eds. *Sovereign Bodies: Citizens, Migrants, and States in the Postcolonial World*. Princeton, N.J.: Princeton University Press, 2005.
Haraway, Donna J. "A Cyborg Manifesto: Science, Technology, and Socialist-Feminism in the Late 20th Century." In *Simians, Cyborgs, and Women: The Reinvention of Nature*, 149–82. New York: Routledge, 1990.
Hardt, Michael, and Antonio Negri. *Empire*. Cambridge, Mass.: Harvard University Press, 2000.
Harootunian, Harry. *Overcome by Modernity: History, Culture, and Community in Interwar Japan*. Princeton, N.J.: Princeton University Press, 2000.
Hart, Stephen, and Richard Young, eds. *Contemporary Latin American Cultural Studies*. London: Hodder Arnold, 2003.
Hassan, Ihab. *The Dismemberment of Orpheus: Toward a Postmodern Literature*. New York: Oxford University Press, 1971.
Heelas, Paul. "Anthropology, Violence and Catharsis." In *Aggression and Violence*, edited by Peter Marsh and Anne Campbell, 48–61. Oxford: Blackwell, 1982.
Henríquez Ureña, Pedro. *La utopía de América*. Caracas: Biblioteca Ayacucho, 1978.
Herlinghaus, Hermann, and Mabel Moraña, eds. *Fronteras de la modernidad en América Latina*. Pittsburgh, Pa.: Instituto Internacional de Literatura Iberoamericana, 2003.
Herlinghaus, Hermann, and Monika Walters, eds. *Posmodernidad en la periferia: Enfoques latinoamericanos de la nueva teoría cultural*. Berlin: Langer, 1994.
Hirsch, Marianne. *Family Frames: Photography, Narrative and Postmemory*. Cambridge, Mass.: Harvard University Press, 1997.
Hoggart, Richard. *The Uses of Literacy: Aspects of Working-Class Life with Special References to Publications and Entertainments*. London: Chatto and Windus, 1957.

Hoisel, Evelina. *Supercaos: Estilhaços de cultura em "Panamerica" e "Nações Unidas."* Rio de Janeiro: Civilização Brasileira, 1980.
hooks, bell. *Ain't I a Woman: Black Women and Feminism*. Boston: South End Press, 1981.
Hopenhayn, Martín. *América Latina: Desigual y descentrada*. Buenos Aires: Norma, 2005.
———. *Ni apocalípticos ni integrados*. Santiago, Chile: Fondo de Cultura Económica, 1994.
Horkheimer, Max, and Theodor W. Adorno. *Dialectic of Enlightenment*. Translated by John Cumming. New York: Herder and Herder, 1972.
Hulme, Peter. *Colonial Encounters: Europe and the Native Caribbean, 1492–1797*. London: Methuen, 1986.
Huntington, Samuel P. *The Clash of Civilizations and the Remaking of World Order*. New York: Simon & Schuster, 1996.
Huyssen, Andreas. *After the Great Divide: Modernism, Mass Culture, Postmodernism*. Bloomington: Indiana University Press, 1986.
———. "Guía del posmodernismo." In Casullo, *El debate modernidad-posmodernidad*, 266–318.
Hymes, Dell. *"In Vain I Tried to Tell You": Essays in Native American Ethnopoetics*. Philadelphia: University of Pennsylvania Press, 1981.
Irwin, Robert McKee. *Mexican Masculinities*. Minneapolis: University of Minnesota Press, 2003.
Irigary, Luce. *This Sex Which Is Not One*. Translated by Catherine Porter with Carolyn Burke. Ithaca, N.Y.: Cornell University Press, 1985.
James, C. L. R. *The Black Jacobins: Toussaint L'Ouverture and the San Domingo Revolution*. 2nd ed. New York: Vintage, 1963.
James, Paul. "Relating Global Tensions: Modern Tribalism and Postmodern Nationalism." *Communal/Plural: Journal of Transnational and Crosscultural Studies* 9, no. 1 (April 2001): 11–31.
Jameson, Fredric. *The Political Unconscious: Narrative as a Socially Symbolic Act*. Ithaca, N.Y.: Cornell University Press, 1981.
———. *Postmodernism, or, The Cultural Logic of Late Capitalism*. Durham, N.C.: Duke University Press, 1991.
———. "Sobre los 'estudios culturales.'" In Jameson and Žižek, *Estudios culturales*, 69–136.
Jameson, Fredric, and Slavoj Žižek. *Estudios culturales: Reflexiones sobre el multiculturalismo*. Buenos Aires: Paidós, 1998.
Jáuregui, Carlos. *La homosexualidad en Argentina*. Buenos Aires: Tarso, 1987.
Jelin, Elizabeth. *State Repression and the Labors of Memory*. Translated by Judy Rein and Marcial Godoy-Anativia. Minneapolis: University of Minnesota Press, 2003.
Jitrik, Noé. *Producción literaria y producción social*. Buenos Aires: Sudamericana, 1975.
Johansson, Patrick. *La palabra de los aztecas*. Mexico City: Trillas, 1993.
Johnson, Randal. "Film Policy in Latin America." In *Film Policy: International, National, and Regional Perspectives*, edited by Albert Moran, 128–47. London: Routledge, 1996.
Kaiser, Susana. *Postmemories of Terror: A New Generation Copes with the Legacies of the "Dirty War."* New York: Palgrave MacMillan, 2005.
Kaldor, Mary. *New and Old Wars: Organized Violence in a Global Era*. Cambridge: Polity Press, 1999.
Kaliman, Ricardo J. "¿Cómo reconstruir la conciencia de los subalternos?" In Rodríguez, *Convergencia de tiempos*, 103–15.

———., comp. *Memorias de JALLA Tucumán 1995*. Tucumán, Argentina: Universidad Nacional de Tucumán, 1997.

Kant, Immanuel. *Critique of Practical Reason, and Other Writings in Moral Philosophy*. Translated by Lewis White Beck. Chicago: University of Chicago Press, 1949.

Kaplún, Mario. *La pedagogía de la comunicación*. Madrid: Ediciones de la Torre, 1998.

Keane, John. *Violence and Democracy*. New York: Cambridge University Press, 2004.

Kelley, Donald R. *Faces of History: Historical Inquiry from Herodotus to Herder*. New Haven, Conn.: Yale University Press, 1998.

Klor de Alva, J. Jorge. "El discurso nahua y la apropiación de lo europeo." In León Portilla et al., *De palabra y obra en el Nuevo Mundo*, 1: 339–68.

Koselleck, Reinhart. *Futures Past: On the Semantics of Historical Time*. Translated by Keith Tribe. Cambridge, Mass.: MIT Press, 1985.

Kraniauskas, John. "Critical Closeness: The Chronicle-Essays of Carlos Monsiváis." In *Mexican Postcards*, by Carlos Monsiváis, ix–xxii. London: Verso, 1997.

Kristeva, Julia. *Powers of Horror: An Essay on Abjection*. Translated by Leon S. Roudiez. New York: Columbia University Press, 1982.

———. *Sēmeiōtikē: Recherches pour une sémanalyse*. Paris: Seuil, 1969. Translated by Thomas Gora, Alice Jardine, and Leon S. Roudiez as *Desire in Language: A Semiotic Approach to Literature and Art* (Oxford: Blackwell, 1980).

Lacan, Jacques. *Écrits: The First Complete Edition in English*. Translated by Bruce Fink with Héloïse Fink and Russell Grigg. New York: Norton, 2006.

Laclau, Ernesto. *Emancipation(s)*. New York: Verso, 1996.

———. *On Populist Reason*. London: Verso, 2005.

Laclau, Ernesto, and Chantal Mouffe. *Hegemony and Socialist Strategy: Towards a Radical Democratic Politics*. Translated by Winston Moore and Paul Cammack. London: Verso, 1984.

Lamas, Marta. *Feminismo: Transmisiones y retransmisiones*. Mexico City: Taurus, 2006.

Lander, Edgardo, ed. *La colonialidad del saber: Eurocentrismo y ciencas sociales: Perspectivas latinoamericanas*. Buenos Aires: Consejo Latinoamericano de Ciencias Sociales, 2000.

Larraín, Jorge. *Identity and Modernity in Latin America*. Cambridge: Polity Press; Malden, Mass.: Blackwell, 2000.

Larsen, Neil. "Brazilian Critical Theory and the Question of Cultural Studies." In *Reading North by South: On Latin American Literature, Culture, and Politics*. Minneapolis: University of Minnesota Press, 1995.

———. *Determinations: Essays on Theory, Narrative, and Nation in the Americas*. London: Verso, 2001.

Latin American Subaltern Studies Group. "Founding Statement." In Beverley, Aronna, and Oviedo, *Postmodernism Debate in Latin America*, 135–46.

Lejeune, Jean-François. *Cruelty and Utopia: Cities and Landscapes of Latin America*. Princeton, N.J.: Princeton Architectural Press, 2005.

Lemebel, Pedro. *Tengo miedo torero*. Santiago: Planeta Chilena, 2001.

Lenin, Vladimir Il'ich. *Imperialism, the Highest Stage of Capitalism*. New York: International Publishers, 1933.

Lenkersdorf, Carlos. "El mundo del nosotros." In *Lecciones de Extranjería*, edited by Esther Cohen and Ana María Martínez de la Escalera, 147–53. Mexico City: Siglo XXI, 2002.

León Portilla, Miguel. "Imágenes de los otros en Mesoamérica antes del encuentro." In León Portilla et al., *De palabra y obra en el Nuevo Mundo*, 1: 35–54.

———. *El reverso de la conquista: Relaciones aztecas, mayas e incas*. Mexico City: Joaquín Mortiz, 1964.

León Portilla, Miguel, Manuel Gutiérrez Estévez, Gary H. Gossen, and J. Jorge Klor de Alva, eds. *De palabra y obra en el Nuevo Mundo*. 4 vols. Madrid: Siglo XXI, 1992.

Lester, Rebecca J. *Jesus in Our Wombs: Embodying Modernity in a Mexican Convent*. Berkeley: University of California Press, 2005.

Levi-Strauss, Claude. *The Raw and the Cooked*. Translated by John and Doreen Weightman. New York: Harper & Row, 1969.

Levin, Harry. "What Was Modernism?" 1960. In *Refractions*, 271–95. New York: Oxford University Press, 1966.

Levinas, Emmanuel. *Totality and Infinity*. Translated by Alphonso Lingis. Pittsburgh, Pa.: Duquesne University Press, 1969.

Lewis, Martin W., and Kären E. Wigen. *The Myth of Continents: A Critique of Metageography*. Berkeley: University of California Press, 1997.

Lewis, R. W. B. *The American Adam: Innocence, Tragedy, and Tradition in the Nineteenth Century*. Chicago: University of Chicago Press, 1955.

Lienhard, Martin. *La voz y su huella: Escritura y conflicto étnico-cultural en América Latina, 1492–1988*. Havana: Casa de las Américas, 1990.

LiPuma, Edward. *Encompassing Others: The Magic of Modernity in Melanesia*. Ann Arbor: University of Michigan Press, 2001.

Lloyd, David. *Anomalous States: Irish Writing and the Post-Colonial Moment*. Durham, N.C.: Duke University Press, 1993.

———. "Foundations of Diversity: Thinking the University in a Time of Multiculturalism." In *"Culture" and the Problem of the Disciplines*, edited by John Carlos Rowe, 15–44. New York: Columbia University Press, 1998.

Lomnitz-Adler, Claudio. *Exits from the Labyrinth: Culture and Ideology in the Mexican National Space*. Berkeley: University of California Press, 1993.

———. *Modernidad indiana: Nueve ensayos sobre nación y mediación en México*. Mexico City: Planeta, 1999.

López, Ana M. "Tears and Desire: Women and Melodrama in the 'Old' Mexican Cinema." In *Mediating Two Worlds: Cinematic Encounters in the Americas*, edited by John King, Ana M. López, and Manuel Alvarado, 147–63. London: BFI, 1993.

López, María Milagros. "Solidarity as Event, Communism as Personal Practice, and Disencounters in the Politics of Desire." In Rodríguez, *Latin American Subaltern Studies Reader*, 64–80.

López González, Aralia, Amelia Malagamba Ansótegui, and Elena Urrutia, eds. *Mujer y literatura mexicana y chicana: Culturas en contacto*. 2 vols. Mexico City: Colegio de México; Tijuana: Colegio de la Frontera Norte, 1988–90.

Lorenzano, Sandra. *Escrituras de sobrevivencia: Narrativa argentina y dictadura*. Mexico City: Universidad Autónoma Metropolitana–Iztapalapa/Beatriz Viterbo/Miguel Ángel Porrúa, 2001.

Lotman, Yuri. "Para la construcción de una teoría de la interacción de las culturas (el aspecto semiótico)." *Criterios*, no. 32 (1994): 117–30.

Lowe, Lisa, and David Lloyd, eds. *The Politics of Culture in the Shadow of Capital*. Durham, N.C.: Duke University Press, 1997.

Lozano, José Carlos. "Del imperialismo cultural a la audiencia activa: Aportes teóricos recientes." *Comunicación y sociedad*, nos. 10–11 (September–April 1991): 85–106. www.allbusiness.com/sector-61-educational-services/133876-1.html.

Ludmer, Josefina, ed. *Las culturas de fin de siglo en América Latina*. Rosario, Argentina: Beatriz Viterbo, 1994.

———. "Las tretas del débil." In González and Ortega, *La sartén por el mango*, 47–54. www.isabelmonzon.com.ar/ludmer.htm.

Luhmann, Niklas. *Social systems*. Translated by John Bednarz Jr. with Dirk Baecker. Stanford, Calif.: Stanford University Press, 1995.

Lukács, György, et al. *Realismo: Mito, doctrina o tendencia histórica?* Buenos Aires: Tiempo Contemporáneo, 1969.

Lyotard, Jean-François. *The Postmodern Condition: A Report on Knowledge*. Translated by Geoff Bennington and Brian Massumi. Minneapolis: University of Minnesota Press, 1984.

———. *The Postmodern Explained: Correspondence, 1982–1985*. Edited by Julian Pefanis and Morgan Thomas. Translated by Don Barry et al. Minneapolis: University of Minnesota Press, 1993.

MacGregor, José Antonio. "El promotor cultural del nuevo siglo." *Sol de Aire* (Instituto Coahuilense de Cultura), no. 3 (2002).

Macherey, Pierre. *A Theory of Literary Production*. Translated by Geoffrey Wall. London: Routledge, 1978.

Malinowski, Bronislaw. *Estudios de psicología primitiva: El complejo de Edipo*. Buenos Aires: Paidós, 1963.

Mallon, Florencia E. *Courage Tastes of Blood: The Mapuche Community of Nicolás Ailío and the Chilean State, 1906–2001*. Durham, N.C.: Duke University Press, 2005.

———. *Peasant and Nation: The Making of Postcolonial Mexico and Peru*. Berkeley: University of California Press, 1995.

Mariátegui, José Carlos. *Siete ensayos de interpretación de la realidad peruana*. Lima: Amauta, 1928.

Marquet, Antonio. *El crepúsculo de heterolandia: Mester de jotería*. Mexico City: Universidad Autónoma Metropolitana, 2006.

Martí, José. *Obras completas*. 28 vols. Havana: Editorial Nacional de Cuba, 1963–73.

Martín Barbero, Jesús. *Communication, Culture and Hegemony: From the Media to Mediations*. Translated by Elizabeth Fox and Robert A. White. London: Sage, 1993.

———. "Desencuentros de la socialidad y reencantamientos de la identidad." *Análisis*, no. 29 (2002): 45–62.

Martín Barbero, Jesús, and Ana María Ochoa Gautier. "Políticas de multiculturalidad y desubicaciones de lo popular." In Mato, *Estudios latinoamericanos*, 111–25.

Martínez Estrada, Ezequiel. *Radiografía de la pampa*. Buenos Aires: Losada, 1968.

Martínez San Miguel, Yolanda. *Caribe Two Ways: Cultura de la migración en el Caribe insular hispánico*. San Juan: Callejón, 2003.

Marx, Karl, and Friedrich Engels. *Die deutsche Ideologie: Werke*. 3 vols. Berlin: Dietz, 1971. Translated by S. Ryazanskaya as *The German Ideology* (Moscow: Progress Publishers, 1964).

Marx, Leo. *The Machine in the Garden: Technology and the Pastoral Ideal in America.* New York: Oxford University Press, 1964.

Mato, Daniel. *El arte de narrar y la noción de literatura oral: Protopanorama intercultural y problemas epistemológicos.* Caracas: Universidad Central de Venezuela, 1990.

———. "Desfechitizar la globalización: Basta de reduccionismos, apologías y demonizaciones, mostrar la complejidad de las prácticas y los actores." In *Estudios latinoamericanos*, 147–77.

———, ed. *Estudios latinoamericanos sobre cultura y transformaciones sociales en tiempos de globalización.* Buenos Aires: CLASCO, 2001.

———, ed. *Estudios y otras prácticas intelectuales latinoamericanas en cultura y poder.* Caracas: CLACSO/CEAP/FACES, 2002.

———. *Políticas de economía, ambiente y sociedad en tiempos de globalización.* Caracas: FACES, 2005.

Mattelart, Armand. *Mapping World Communication: War, Progress, Culture.* Translated by Susan Emanuel and James A. Cohen. Minneapolis: University of Minnesota Press, 1994.

Mattelart, Armand, and Michèle Mattelart. "La recepción: El retorno al sujeto." *Diálogos de la comunicación*, no. 30 (1991): 10–17.

Melo, José Marques de. *As telenovelas da Globo: Produção e exportação.* São Paulo: Summus, 1988.

Memmi, Albert. *The Colonizer and the Colonized.* Translated by Howard Greenfeld. New York: Orion, 1965.

Menchú Tum, Rigoberta, with Elisabeth Burgos Debray. *Me llamo Rigoberta Menchú y así me nació la conciencia.* Havana: Casa de las Américas, 1983.

Meyer, Birgit, and Peter Pels, eds. *Magic and Modernity: Interfaces of Revelation and Concealment.* Stanford, Calif.: Stanford University Press, 2003.

Mignolo, Walter. "Colonialidad del poder y subalternidad." In Rodríguez, *Convergencia de tiempos*, 155–83.

———. *The Darker Side of the Renaissance: Literacy, Territoriality, and Colonization.* Ann Arbor: University of Michigan Press, 1995.

———. "Decires fuera de lugar: Sujetos dicentes, roles sociales y formas de inscripción." *Revista de Crítica Literaria Latinoamericana* 21, no. 41 (1995): 9–32.

———. "Entre el canon y el corpus." *Nuevo Texto Crítico* 7, nos. 14–15 (1995): 23–36.

———. *Local Histories/Global Designs: Coloniality, Subaltern Knowledges, and Border Thinking.* Princeton, N.J.: Princeton University Press, 2000.

———. "The Zapatistas' Theoretical Revolution: Its Historial, Ethical, and Political Consequences." *Review* 25, no. 3 (2002): 245–75.

Miller, Perry, ed. *The American Transcendentalists, Their Prose and Poetry.* Garden City, N.Y.: Doubleday, 1957.

Mitchell, Timothy. "The Stage of Modernity." In *Questions of Modernity*, 1–34. Minneapolis: University of Minnesota Press, 2000.

Mogrovejo, Norma. *Un amor que se atrevió a decir su nombre: La lucha de las lesbianas y su relación con los movimientos homosexual y feminista en América Latina.* Mexico City: Plaza y Valdés, 2000.

Molloy, Sylvia. "La flexión del género en el texto cultural latinoamericano." *Revista de Crítica Cultural*, no. 21 (2000): 54–56.

Molloy, Sylvia, and Robert McKee Irwin, eds. *Hispanisms and Homosexualities*. Durham, N.C.: Duke University Press, 1998.

Money, John, and Anke A. Ehrhardt. *Man & Woman, Boy & Girl: The Differentiation and Dimorphism of Gender Identity from Conception to Maturity*. Baltimore: Johns Hopkins University Press, 1972.

Monsiváis, Carlos. *Aires de familia*. Barcelona: Anagrama, 2000.

———. "De la cultura mexicana en vísperas del Tratado de Libre Comercio." In *La educación y la cultura ante el Tratado de Libre Comercio*, edited by Gilberto Guevara Niebla and Néstor García Canclini, 190–209. Mexico City: Nueva Imagen, 1992.

———. *Entrada libre: Crónicas de la sociedad que se organiza*. Mexico City: Era, 1987.

———. *Los rituales del caos*. 2nd ed. Mexico City: Era, 2001.

———. "¿Tantos millones de hombres no hablaremos inglés? (La cultura norteamericana y México)." In *Simbiosis de culturas: Los inmigrantes y su cultura en México*, edited by Guillermo Bonfil Batalla, 500–513. Mexico City: Consejo Nacional para la Cultura y las Artes/Fondo de Cultura Económica, 1993.

Monsiváis, Carlos, and Carlos Bonfil. *A través del espejo: El cine mexicano y su público*. Mexico City: El Milagro, 1994.

Montaldo, Graciela. "Culturas críticas: La extensión de un campo." *Iberoamérica* 4, no. 16 (2004): 35–47.

Moore, R. Laurence. *Touchdown Jesus: The Mixing of Sacred and Secular in American History.* Louisville, Ky.: Westminster John Knox Press, 2003.

Moraga, Cherríe, and Gloria Anzaldúa, eds. *This Bridge Called My Back.* Watertown, Mass.: Persephone, 1981.

Moraña, Mabel, ed. *Ángel Rama y los estudios latinoamericanos*. Pittsburgh, Pa.: Instituto Internacional de Literatura Iberoamericana, 1997.

———. "De *La ciudad letrada* al imaginario nacionalista: Contribuciones de Ángel Rama a la invención de América." In *Políticas de la escritura en América Latina: De la Colonia a la Modernidad*, 165–73. Caracas: eXcultura, 1997.

———. "Ideología de la transculturación." In *Ángel Rama y los estudios latinoamericanos*, 137–46.

———, ed. *Indigenismo hacia el fin del milenio: Homenaje a Antonio Cornejo-Polar*. Pittsburgh, Pa.: Instituto Internacional de Literatura Iberoamericana, 1998.

———. *Nuevas perspectivas desde/sobre América Latina: El desafío de los estudios culturales*. Santiago, Chile: Cuarto Propio, 2000.

———. *Viaje al silencio: Exploraciones del discurso barroco*. Mexico City: Universidad Nacional Autónoma de México, 1998.

Moraña, Mabel, and María Rosa Olivera Williams, eds. *El salto de Minerva: Intelectuales, género y estado en América Latina*. Madrid: Iberoamericana/Vervuert, 2005.

Moreiras, Alberto. "The Conflict in Transculturation." In *Literary Cultures of Latin America: A Comparative History*, edited by Mario J. Valdés and Djelal Kadir, 3: 129–37. Oxford: Oxford University Press, 2004.

———. *The Exhaustion of Difference: The Politics of Latin American Cultural Studies*. Durham, N.C.: Duke University Press, 2001.

———. "Hegemonía y subalteridad." In Rodríguez, *Convergencia de tiempos*, 71–90.

Morin, Edgar. *Cinema, or, The Imaginary Man*. Translated by Lorraine Mortimer. Minneapolis: University of Minnesota Press, 2005.

———. *L'esprit du temps: Essai sur la culture de masse.* 2 vols. Paris: Grasset, 1962–75.

Morley, David, and Kuan-Hsing Chen, eds. *Stuart Hall: Critical Dialogues in Cultural Studies.* London: Routledge, 1996.

Morris, Meaghan. "Metamorphoses at Sydney Tower." *New Formations* 11 (Summer 1990): 5–18.

Mott, Luiz. *O lesbianismo no Brasil.* Porto Alegre: Mercado Aberto, 1987.

Muñoz, José Esteban. *Disidentifications: Queers of Color and the Performance of Politics.* Minneapolis: University of Minnesota Press, 1999.

Mustafa, Abdul-Karim. "Questions of Strategy as an Abstract Minimum: Subalternity and Us." In Rodríguez, *Latin American Subaltern Studies Reader*, 211–25.

Nagy-Zekmi, Silvia. "Ángel Rama y su ensayística transcultural(izadora) como autobiografía en clave crítica." *Cuadernos Americanos*, no. 81 (2000): 193–202.

Nietzsche, Friedrich. "On Truth and Lying in an Extra-Moral Sense." In *Literary Theory: An Anthology*, edited by Julie Rivkin and Michael Ryan, 2nd ed., 262–65. London: Blackwell, 2004. .

Nivón Bolán, Eduardo. "Cultura e integración económica: México a siete años del Tratado de Libre Comercio." *Pensar Iberoamérica*, no. 2 (October 2002–January 2003). www.campus-oei.org/pensariberoamerica/ric02a02.htm.

Nora, Pierre. *Rethinking France = Les lieux de mémoire.* Translated by Mary Trouille. Vol. 1. Chicago: University of Chicago Press, 2001.

Nunca más: Informe de la Comisión Nacional sobre la Desaparición de Personas. Buenos Aires: EUDEBA, 1999.

Ong, Aihwa. *Flexible Citizenship: The Cultural Logics of Transnationality.* Durham, N.C.: Duke University Press, 1999.

Ong, Walter J. *Orality and Literacy: The Technologizing of the Word.* London: Methuen, 1982.

Orozco Gómez, Guillermo. "La audiencia frente a la pantalla: Una exploración del proceso de recepción televisiva." *Diálogos de la comunicación*, no. 30 (July 1991): 55–62.

———. *Televisión, audiencias y educación.* Buenos Aires: Norma, 2001.

Ortiz, Fernando. *Cuban Counterpoint: Tobacco and Sugar.* Translated by Harriet de Onís. Durham, N.C.: Duke University Press, 1995.

Ortiz, Renato. "Diversidad cultural y cosmopolitismo." In Moraña, *Nuevas perspectivas desde/sobre América Latina*, 43–53.

———. *A moderna cultura brasileira.* São Paulo: Editora Brasilense, 1988.

———. *Mundialização e cultura.* São Paulo: Brasiliense, 1994. Translated by Elsa Noya as *Mundialización y cultura* (Buenos Aires: Alianza: 1997).

Overmyer-Velázquez, Mark. *Visions of the Emerald City: Modernity, Tradition, and the Formation of Porfirian Oaxaca, Mexico.* Durham, N.C.: Duke University Press, 2006.

Owen, Alex. *The Place of Enchantment: British Occultism and the Culture of the Modern.* Chicago: University of Chicago Press, 2004.

Palmié, Stephan. *Wizards and Scientists: Explorations in Afro-Cuban Modernity and Tradition.* Durham, N.C.: Duke University Press, 2002.

Passel, Jeffrey S., and Roberto Suro. *Rise, Peak and Decline: Trends in U.S. Immigration, 1992–2004.* Washington, D.C.: Pew Hispanic Center, 2005.

Pasquali, Antonio. *Comunicación y cultura de masas: La masificación de la cultura por medios audiovisuales en las regiones subdesarrolladas*. Caracas: Universidad Central de Venezuela, 1963.

Pasternac, Nora, Ana Rosa Domenella, and Luzelena Gutiérrez de Velasco, eds. *Escribir la infancia: Narradoras mexicanas contemporáneas*. Mexico City: Colegio de México, 1996.

Paz, Octavio. *Los hijos del limo*. Barcelona: Seix Barral, 1974.

———. *El laberinto de la soledad*. Mexico City: Fondo de Cultura Económica, 1950.

———. *El ogro filantrópico: Historia y política, 1971–1978*. Mexico City: Joaquín Mortiz, 1979.

———. "The Power of Ancient Mexican Art." *New York Review of Books*, December 6, 1990.

———. *Sor Juana Inés de la Cruz, o, Las trampas de la fe*. Mexico City: Fondo de Cultura Económica, 1982.

———. *Vislumbres de la India*. Barcelona: Seix Barral, 1995.

Pérez Firmat, Gustavo. *Life on the Hyphen: The Cuban-American Way*. Austin: University of Texas Press, 1994.

Perlongher, Néstor. *El negocio del deseo: La prostitución masculina en San Pablo*. Translated by Moira Irigoyen. Buenos Aires: Paidós, 1999.

Perrone, Charles A. *Masters of Contemporary Brazilian Song: MPB, 1965–1985*. Austin: University of Texas Press, 1989.

Picón Salas, Mariano. *De la conquista a la independencia: Tres siglos de historia cultural hispanoamericana*. Mexico City: Fondo de Cultura Económica, 1944.

Piedras, Ernesto. *¿Cuánto vale la cultura? La contribución económica de las industrias protegidas por el derecho de autor en México*. Mexico City: Consejo Nacional para la Cultura y las Artes, 2004.

Pizarro, Ana, ed. *La literatura latinoamericana como proceso*. Buenos Aires: Centro Editor de América Latina, 1985.

Poblete, Juan, ed. *Critical Latin American and Latino Studies*. Minneapolis: University of Minnesota Press, 2003.

———. "Culture, Neoliberalism, and Citizen Communication: The Case of Radio Tierra in Chile." *Global Media and Communication* 2, no. 3 (2006): 315–33.

Poniatowska, Elena. *Hasta no verte, Jesús mío*. Mexico City: Era, 1969.

———. *La noche de Tlatelolco: Testimonios de historia oral*. Mexico City: Era, 1971.

Porchia, Antonio. *Voices*. Translated by W. S. Merwin. Chicago: Big Table, 1969.

Portantiero, Juan Carlos, and Miguel Murmis. *Estudios sobre los orígenes del peronismo*. Buenos Aires: Siglo XXI, 1971.

Pozuelo Yvancos, José María, and Rosa María Aradra Sánchez. *Teoría del canon y literatura española*. Madrid: Cátedra, 2000.

Prada Alcoreza, Raúl. *Territorialidad*. La Paz: Punto Cero, 1996.

Prakash, Gyan, ed. *After Colonialism: Imperial Histories and Postcolonial Displacements*. Princeton, N.J.: Princeton University Press, 1995.

———. "La imposibilidad de la historia subalterna." In Rodríguez, *Convergencia de tiempos*, 61–70.

Pratt, Mary Louise. *Imperial Eyes: Travel Writing and Transculturation*. London: Routledge, 1992.

Preminger, Alex, and T. V. F. Brogan, eds. *The New Princeton Encyclopedia of Poetry and Poetics*. Princeton, N.J.: Princeton University Press, 1993.

Price, Richard. *The Convict and the Colonel: A Story of Colonialism and Resistance in the Caribbean*. Boston: Beacon Press, 1998.

Prieto, Adolfo. *El discurso criollista en la formación de la Argentina moderna*. Buenos Aires: Sudamericana, 1988.

Prieto Stambaugh, Antonio. "Los estudios del performance: Una propuesta de simulacro crítico." *Citru.doc Cuadernos de investigación teatral*, no. 1 (November 2005): 52–61. performancelogia.blogspot.com/2007/07/los-estudios-del-performance-una.html.

———. "Performance transfronterizo como subversión de la identidad: los (des)encuentros chicano-chilangos." In *Hacia otra historia del arte mexicano: Disolvencias (1960–2000)*, edited by Issa Benítez Dueñas, 21–59. Mexico City: Consejo Nacional para la Cultura y las Artes, 2004.

Quijano, Aníbal. "Colonialidad del poder, eurocentrismo y América Latina." In Lander, *La colonialidad del saber*, 201–46.

Quiroga, José. *Tropics of Desire: Interventions from Queer Latino America*. New York: New York University Press, 2000.

Rabasa, José. "Beyond Representation? The Impossibility of the Local (Notes on Subaltern Studies in Light of a Rebellion in Tepoztlán, Morelos)." In Rodríguez, *Latin American Subaltern Studies Reader*, 191–210.

———. "Of Zapatismo: Reflections on the Folkloric and the Impossible in a Subaltern Revolution." In Lowe and Lloyd, *Politics of Culture*, 399–431.

———. *Writing Violence on the Northern Frontier: The Historiography of Sixteenth-Century New Mexico and Florida and the Legacy of Conquest*. Durham, N.C.: Duke University Press, 2000.

Radcliffe, Sarah A. "Imagining the State as a Space: Territoriality and the Formation of the State in Ecuador." In Hansen and Stepputat, *States of Imagination*, 123–45.

Rama, Ángel. *La ciudad letrada*. Hanover, N.H.: Ediciones del Norte, 1984. Translated by John Charles Chasteen as *The Lettered City* (Durham, N.C.: Duke University Press, 1996).

———. *Transculturación narrativa en América Latina*. Mexico City: Siglo XXI, 1982.

Ramos, Julio. *Desencuentros de la modernidad en América Latina: Literatura y política en el siglo XIX*. Mexico City: Fondo de Cultura Económica, 1989.

———. *Paradojas de la letra*. Caracas: eXcultura, 1996.

Rappaport, Joanne. *Intercultural Utopias: Public Intellectuals, Cultural Experimentation, and Ethnic Pluralism in Colombia*. Durham, N.C.: Duke University Press, 2005.

Redfield, Peter. *Space in the Tropics: From Convicts to Rockets in French Guiana*. Berkeley: University of California Press, 2000.

Reguillo, Rossana. *Emergencia de culturas juveniles*. Buenos Aires: Norma, 2000.

———. "Pensar el mundo en y desde América Latina: Desafío intercultural y políticas de representación." *Diálogos de la Comunicación*, no. 65 (2002): 61–71.

———. "Textos fronterizos: La crónica, una escritura a la intemperie." *Diálogos de la Comunicación*, no. 58 (August 2000): 68–62.

Remedi, Gustavo. "Ciudad letrada: Ángel Rama y la espacialización del análisis cultural." In Moraña, *Ángel Rama y los estudios latinoamericanos*, 97–122.

———. "Production of Local Public Spheres: Community Radio Stations." In Sarto, Ríos, and Trigo, *Latin American Cultural Studies Reader*, 513–34.

Reyes, Alfonso. *Visión de Anáhuac (1519)*. Madrid: Índice, 1923.

Reyes Matta, Fernando. *Estrategia imperialista y medios de comunicación: Nuevo orden informativo y enseñanza de la comunicación*. Mexico City: Universidad Nacional Autónoma de México, 1979.

Ribeiro, Darcy. *Las Américas y la civilización: Proceso de formación y causas del desarrollo desigual de los pueblos americanos*. Caracas: Biblioteca Ayacucho, 1992.

Richard, Nelly, ed. "La crítica: Revistas literarias, académicas y culturales." Special issue, *Revista de Crítica Cultural*, no. 31 (2005).

———. "Cultural Peripheries: Latin America and Postmodernist De-centering." *Boundary 2* 20, no. 3 (1999): 156–61.

———. *Cultural Residues: Chile in Transition*. Translated by Alan West-Durán and Theodore Quester. Minneapolis: University of Minnesota Press, 2004.

———. *La estratificación de los márgenes: Sobre arte, cultura y políticas*. Santiago, Chile: Francisco Zegers, 1989.

———. "Globalización académica, estudios culturales y crítica latinoamericana." In Mato, *Estudios latinoamericanos*, 185–99.

———. *La insubordinación de los signos: Cambio político, transformaciones culturales y poéticas de la crisis*. Santiago, Chile: Cuarto Propio, 1994. Translated by Alice A. Nelson and Silvia Tandeciarz as *The Insubordination of Signs: Political Change, Cultural Transformation, and the Poetics of Crisis* (Durham, N.C.: Duke University Press, 2004).

———. "Intersectando Latinoamérica con el latinoamericanismo: Discurso académico y crítica cultural." In Castro Gómez and Mendieta, *Teorías sin disciplina*,. www.ensayistas.org/critica/teoria/castro/richard.htm.

———. "The Language of Criticism: How to Speak Difference?" Translated by Alessandro Fornazzari. *Nepantla: Views from the South* 1, no. 1 (2000): 255–62.

———. *Masculino/femenino: Prácticas de la diferencia y cultura democrática*. Santiago, Chile: Francisco Zegers, 1993.

———, ed. *Políticas y estéticas de la memoria*. Santiago, Chile: Cuarto Propio, 2000.

———. "The Reconfiguration of Post-Dictatorship Critical Thought." Translated by John Kraniauskas. *Journal of Latin American Cultural Studies* 9, no. 3 (2000): 273–81.

———. "Signos culturales y mediaciones académicas." In González Stephan, *Cultura y tercer mundo*, 82–97.

Riches, David. "The Phenomenon of Violence." In *The Anthropology of Violence*, 1–27. Oxford: Blackwell, 1986.

Ríos, Alicia, ed. "Homenaje a Ángel Rama." *Estudios* 10–11, nos. 22–23 (August 2003–June 2004).

———. "Traditions and Fractures in Latin American Cultural Studies." In Sarto, Ríos, and Trigo, *Latin American Cultural Studies Reader*, 15–34.

Ríos, Alicia, Ana del Sarto, and Abril Trigo, eds. "Los estudios culturales latinoamericanos hacia el siglo XXI." Special issue, *Revista Iberoamericana* 69, no. 203 (2003).

Rivera Cusicanqui, Silvia, and Rossana Barragán. *Debates post coloniales: Una introducción a los estudios de la subalternidad*. Translated by Raquel Gutiérrez et al. La Paz: Historias/Aruwiri/SEPHIS, 1997.

Roa Bastos, Augusto. "La narrativa paraguaya en el contexto de la narrativa hispanoamericana actual." In *Augusto Roa Bastos y la producción cultural americana*, edited by Saúl Sosnowski, 129–31. Buenos Aires: Flor, 1986.

———. *Yo, el Supremo*. Buenos Aires: Siglo XXI, 1974.

Robertson, Roland. *Globalization: Social Theory and Global Culture*. London: Sage, 1992.

———. "Glocalization: Time-Space and Homogeneity-Heterogeneity." In *Global Modernities*, edited by Mike Featherstone, Scott Lash, and Roland Robertson, 25–44. London: Sage, 1995.

Rodríguez, Ileana, ed. *Convergencia de tiempos: Estudios subalternos/contextos latinoamericanos estado, cultura, subalternidad*. Amsterdam: Rodopi, 2001.

———. "Heterogeneidad y multiculturalismo: ¿Discusión cultural o discusión legal?" *Revista Iberoamericana* 66, no. 193 (2000): 851–61.

———, ed. *The Latin American Subaltern Studies Reader*. Durham, N.C.: Duke University Press, 2001.

———. "Reading Subalterns Across Texts, Disciplines, and Theories: From Representation to Recognition." In *The Latin American Subaltern Studies Reader*, 1–33.

Rodríguez Juliá, Edgardo. *Cortijo's Wake/El entierro de Cortijo*. Bilingual edition. Translated by Juan Flores. Durham, N.C.: Duke University Press, 2004.

Rodríguez-Nuñez, Víctor. "Caliban, ¿antropófago? La identidad cultural latinoamericana de Oswald de Andrade a Roberto Fernández Retamar." In Oswald de Andrade, *Obra incompleta*, ed. Jorge Schwartz, 1095–1109. Paris: Archivos, forthcoming.

Rodó, José Enrique. *Ariel*. Mexico City: Miguel Ángel Porrúa, 1968.

Rofel, Lisa. *Other Modernities: Gendered Yearnings in China after Socialism*. Berkeley: University of California Press, 1998.

Rojas, Ricardo. *Eurindia: Ensayo de estética fundado en la experiencia histórica de las culturas americanas*. Buenos Aires: Librería "La Facultad" de J. Roldán, 1924.

Roncagliolo, Rafael. "Trade Integration and Communication Networks in Latin America." *Canadian Journal of Communication* 20, no. 3 (1995). www.cjc-online.ca/viewarticle.php?id=305&layout=html.

Rorty, Richard. *Objectivity, Relativism and Truth*. Cambridge: Cambridge University Press, 1991.

Rosaldo, Renato. Foreword to Canclini, *Hybrid Cultures*, xi–xviii.

Rosenzweig, Franz. *The Star of Redemption*. Translated by William W. Hallo. New York: Holt, Rinehart, and Winston, 1971.

Rossi, Paolo. *Logic and the Art of Memory: The Quest for a Universal Language*. Translated by Stephen Clucas. Chicago: University of Chicago Press, 2000.

Rotker, Susana. *Ciudadanías del miedo*. Caracas: Nueva Sociedad, 2001.

Rouse, Roger. "Migration and the Politics of Family Life: Divergent Projects and Rhetorical Strategies in a Mexican Migrant Community." *Diasporai* 1, no. 1 (1991): 8–23.

Rowe, John Carlos. "Post-Nationalism, Globalism, and the New American Studies." *Cultural Critique* 40 (1999): 11–28.

———, ed. *Post-Nationalist American Studies*. Berkeley: University of California Press, 2000.

Rowe, William. "Sobre la heterogeneidad de la letra en *Los ríos profundos*: Una crítica a la oposición polar escritura/oralidad." In *Heterogeneidad y literatura en el Perú*, edited by James Higgins, 223–51. Lima: Centro de Estudios Literarios Antonio Cornejo Polar, 2003.

Rowe, William, and Vivian Schelling. *Memory and Modernity: Popular Culture in Latin America*. London: Verso, 1991.

Rubin, Gayle S. "Thinking Sex: Notes on a Radical Theory of the Politics of Sexuality." In *The Lesbian and Gay Studies Reader*, edited by Henry Abelove, Michèle Aina Barale, and David Halperin, 3–44. New York: Routledge, 1993.

Rutter-Jensen, Chloe. *La heteronormatividad y sus discordias: Narrativas del afecto en Colombia*. Translated by Tiziana Laudato. Bogotá: Universidad de los Andes, 2009.

Said, Edward W. *Culture and Imperialism*. New York: Knopf, 1993.

———. *Orientalism*. New York: Pantheon, 1978.

———. *Out of Place: A Memoir*. New York: Knopf, 1999.

———. *The World, the Text, and the Critic*. Cambridge, Mass.: Harvard University Press, 1983.

Salas Astrain, Ricardo, ed. *Pensamiento crítico latinoamericano: Conceptos fundamentales*. 2 vols. Santiago, Chile: Ediciones Universidad Católica Silva Henríquez, 2005.

Salazar, Alonso. *No nacimos pa' semilla*. Bogotá: Corporación Región, CINEP, 1990.

Saldaña-Portillo, María Josefina. *The Revolutionary Imagination in the Americas and the Age of Development*. Durham, N.C.: Duke University Press, 2003.

Salessi, Jorge. *Médicos maleantes y maricas: Higiene, criminología y homosexualidad en la construcción de la nación argentina (Buenos Aires, 1871–1914)*. Rosario, Argentina: Beatriz Viterbo, 1995.

Sánchez, Rosaura, and Beatrice Pita. "Mapping Cultural/Political Debates in Latin American Studies." In *The Chicana/o Cultural Studies Reader*, edited by Angie Chabram-Dernersesian, 492–516. New York: Routledge, 2006.

Sánchez Prado, Ignacio M., ed. *América Latina en la "literatura mundial."* Pittsburgh, Pa.: Instituto Internacional de Literatura Iberoamericana, 2006.

———. *El canon y sus formas: La reinvención de Harold Bloom y sus lecturas hispanoamericanas*. Puebla, Mexico: Secretaría de Cultura, Gobierno del Estado de Puebla, 2002.

Sandoval, Chela. *Methodology of the Oppressed*. Minneapolis: University of Minnesota Press, 2000.

Sanjinés, Javier. "Outside In and Inside Out: Visualizing Society in Bolivia." In Rodríguez, *Latin American Subaltern Studies Reader*, 288–311.

Santiago, Silviano. "El *entrelugar* del discurso latinoamericano." In *Absurdo Brasil*, edited by Adriana Amante and Florencia Garramuño. Buenos Aires: Biblos, 2000.

———. *Uma literatura nos trópicos: Ensaios sobre dependencia cultural*. São Paulo: Perspectiva, 1978.

———. "The Wily Homosexual (First—And Necessarily Hasty—Notes)." In *Queer Globalizations: Citizenship and the Afterlife of Colonialism*, edited by Arnaldo Cruz Malavé and Martin F. Manalansan IV, translated by Robert McKee Irwin and Arnaldo Cruz Malavé, 13–19. New York: New York University Press, 2002.

Sarlo, Beatriz. *Escenas de la vida posmoderna: Intelectuales, arte y videocultura en la Argentina*. Buenos Aires: Ariel, 1994.

———. "Los estudios culturales y la crítica literaria en la encrucijada valorativa." *Revista de Crítica Cultural*, no. 15 (1997): 32–38.

———. *El imperio de los sentimientos: Narraciones de circulación periódica en la Argentina, 1917–1927*. Buenos Aires: Catálogos, 1985.

———. *Una modernidad periférica: Buenos Aires, 1920 y 1930*. Buenos Aires: Nueva Visión, 1988.

———. "El relativismo absoluto o cómo el mercado y la sociología reflexionan sobre la estética." *Punto de Vista*, no. 48 (1994): 27–31.

———. *Tiempo pasado: Cultura de la memoria y giro subjetivo de una discusión*. Mexico City: Siglo XXI, 2005.

Sarmiento, Domingo Faustino. *Facundo, o, Civilización y barbarie*. 1845. Caracas: Biblioteca Ayacucho, 1977.

Sarto, Ana del. "Cultural Critique in Latin America or Latin-American Cultural Studies?" *Journal of Latin American Cultural Studies* 9, no. 3 (2000): 235–47.

———. "The 1980s: Foundations of Latin American Cultural Studies." In Sarto, Rios, and Trigo, *Latin American Cultural Studies Reader*, 153–81.

———. "La sociología y la crítica cultural en Santiago de Chile: Intermezzo dialógico: De límites e interinfluencias." In Mato, *Estudios y otras prácticas*, 99–110.

Sarto, Ana del, Alicia Ríos, and Abril Trigo, eds. *The Latin American Cultural Studies Reader*. Durham, N.C.: Duke University Press, 2004.

Saussure, Ferdinand de. *Course in General Linguistics*. Translated by Roy Harris. LaSalle, Ill.: Open Court, 1986.

Schechner, Richard. *Between Theater and Anthropology*. Philadelphia: University of Pennsylvania Press, 1985.

———. *Performance Studies: An Introduction*. London: Routledge, 2002.

Schiller, Friedrich. *On the Aesthetic Education of Man*. Translated by Reginald Snell. New Haven, Conn.: Yale University Press, 1954.

Schmitt, Carl. *The Concept of the Political*. Translated by George Schwab. New Brunswick, N.J.: Rutgers University Press, 1976.

Schwarz, Roberto. *Ao vencedor as batatas: Forma literaria e proceso social nos inícios do romance brasileiro*. São Paulo: Duas Cidades, 1992.

———. *Misplaced Ideas: Essays on Brazilian Culture*. Edited by John Gledson. London: Verso, 1992.

Scott, David. *Conscripts of Modernity: The Tragedy of Colonial Enlightenment*. Durham, N.C.: Duke University Press, 2005.

Scott, James C. *Domination and the Arts of Resistence: Hidden Transcripts*. New Haven, Conn.: Yale University Press, 1990.

———. *Weapons of the Weak: Everyday Forms of Peasant Resistance*. New Haven, Conn.: Yale University Press, 1985.

Scott, Joan. "Gender: A Useful Category of Historical Analysis." *American Historical Review* 91, no. 5 (1986): 1053–75.

Searle, John R. *Speech Acts: An Essay in the Philosophy of Language*. London: Cambridge University Press, 1969.

Sedgwick, Eve Kosofsky. *Between Men: English Literature and Male Homosocial Desire*. New York: Columbia University Press, 1985.

———. *Epistemology of the Closet*. Berkeley: University of California Press, 1990.

Seed, Patricia. "No Perfect World: Aboriginal Communities' Contemporary Resource Rights." In Rodríguez, *Latin American Subaltern Studies Reader*, 129–42.

Shafir, Gershon. *The Citizenship Debates: A Reader*. Minneapolis: University of Minnesota Press, 1998.

Shils, Edward. "The End of Ideology?" *Encounter* 5 (November 1955): 52–58.

Showalter, Elaine. "Feminist Criticism in the Wilderness." *Critical Inquiry* 8, no. 2 (Winter 1981): 179–205.

Sierra Madero, Abel. *La nación sexuada: Relaciones de género y sexo en Cuba (1830–1855)*. Havana: Editorial de Ciencias Sociales, 2002.

Smythe, Dallas W. "On the Audience Commodity and Its Work." In Durham and Kellner, *Media and Cultural Studies*, 230–56.

Sommer, Doris. *Cultural Agency in the Americas*. Durham, N.C.: Duke University Press, 2006.

———. *Foundational Fictions: The National Romances of Latin America*. Berkeley: University of California Press, 1991.

———. *Proceed with Caution When Engaged by Minority Writing in the Americas*. Cambridge, Mass.: Harvard University Press, 1999.

Sontag, Susan. *Against Interpretation, and Other Essays*. New York: Farrar, Straus & Giroux, 1966.

Sorel, Georges. *Reflections on Violence*. Edited by Jeremy Jennings. Cambridge: Cambridge University Press, 1999.

Spitta, Silvia. *Between Two Waters: Narratives of Transculturation in Latin America*. Houston: Rice University Press, 1995.

Spitzer, Leo. *Hotel Bolivia: The Culture of Memory in a Refuge from Nazism*. New York: Hill and Wang, 1998.

Spivak, Gayatri Chakravorty. "Can the Subaltern Speak?" In *Colonial Discourse and Postcolonial Theory: A Reader*, edited by Patrick Williams and Laura Chrisman, 66–111. New York: Columbia University Press, 1994.

———. *A Critique of Postcolonial Reason: Toward a History of the Vanishing Present*. Cambridge, Mass.: Harvard University Press, 1999.

———. "History." In *A Critique of Postcolonial Reason*, 198–311.

———. *The Spivak Reader: Selected Works of Gayatri Chakravorty Spivak*. Edited by Donna Landry and Gerald MacLean. New York: Routledge, 1996.

Stavans, Ilan. *The Hispanic Condition: Reflections on Culture and Identity in America*. New York: HarperCollins, 1995.

Stephenson, Marcia. "The Architectural Relationship Between Gender, Race, and the Bolivian State." In Rodríguez, *Latin American Subaltern Studies Reader*, 367–82.

Stern, Steve J. *Battling for Hearts and Minds: Memory Struggles in Pinochet's Chile, 1973–88*. Durham, N.C.: Duke University Press, 2006.

———. *Remembering Pinochet's Chile: On the Eve of London, 1998*. Durham, N.C.: Duke University Press, 2006.

———. *The Secret History of Gender: Women, Men, and Power in Late Colonial Mexico*. Chapel Hill: University of North Carolina Press, 1995.

Stoller, Robert J. *Presentations of Gender*. New Haven, Conn.: Yale University Press, 1985.

Sunkel, Guillermo, ed. *El consumo cultural en América Latina*. 2nd ed. Bogotá: Andrés Bello, 2006.

———. "Las matrices culturales y la representación de lo popular en los diarios populares de masas: Aspectos teóricos y fundamentos históricos." In *Razón y pasión en la prensa popular: Un estudio sobre cultura popular, cultura de masas y cultura política*. Santiago, Chile: ILET, 1986.

Süssekind, Flora. "Chorus, Contraries, Masses: The Tropicalist Experience and Brazil in the Late Sixties." In *Tropicália: A Revolution in Brazilian Culture,* edited by Carlos Basualdo, 31–56. São Paulo: Cosac Naify, 2005.

Szurmuk, Mónica. "Voces y susurros en la literatura de la postdictadura argentina: Reina Roffé y Sergio Chejfec." In Martínez Zalce, Gutiérrez de Velasco, and Domenella, *Femenino/masculino en las literaturas de América*, 79–97.

———. *Women in Argentina: Early Travel Narratives*. Gainesville: University Press of Florida, 2000.

Taussig, Michael T. *Defacement: Public Secrecy and the Labor of the Negative*. Stanford, Calif.: Stanford University Press, 1999.

———. *The Devil and Commodity Fetishism in South America*. Chapel Hill: University of North Carolina Press, 1980.

———. *The Magic of the State*. New York: Routledge, 1996.

———. *My Cocaine Museum*. Chicago: University of Chicago Press, 2004.

———. *Shamanism, Colonialism, and the Wild Man: A Study in Terror and Healing*. Chicago: University of Chicago Press, 1987.

Taylor, Diana. *The Archive and the Repertoire: Performing Cultural Memory in the Americas*. Durham, N.C.: Duke University Press, 2003.

Tenorio-Trillo, Mauricio. *Mexico at the World's Fairs: Crafting a Modern Nation*. Berkeley: University of California Press, 1996.

Terán, Oscar. *En busca de la ideología argentina*. Buenos Aires: Catálogos, 1986.

Thompson, E. P. *The Making of the English Working Class*. New York: Pantheon, 1964.

———. *The Poverty of Theory, and Other Essays*. New York: Monthly Review Press, 1978.

———. *Whigs and Hunters: The Origin of the Black Act*. New York: Pantheon, 1975.

Thompson, John B. *The Media and Modernity*. Stanford, Calif.: Stanford University Press, 1995.

Thurner, Mark. *From Two Republics to One Divided: Contradictions of Postcolonial Nationmaking in Andean Peru*. Durham: Duke University Press, 1997.

Tizón, Héctor. *La casa y el viento*. Buenos Aires: Legasa, 1984.

Todorov, Tzvetan. *L'homme dépaysé*. . Paris: Seuil, 1996.

———. *On Human Diversity: Nationalism, Racism, and Exoticism in French Thought*. Translated by Catherine Porter. Cambridge, Mass.: Harvard University Press, 1993.

Tomlinson, John. *Cultural Imperialism*. London: Pinter, 1991.

———. *Globalization and Culture*. Chicago: University of Chicago Press, 1999.

Toro, Alfonso de, and Fernando de Toro, eds. *El debate de la postcolonialidad en Latinoamérica: Una modernidad periférica o cambio de paradigma en el pensamiento latinoamericano*. Madrid: Iberoamericana; Frankfurt am Main: Vervuert, 1999.

Tovar y de Teresa, Rafael. *Modernización y política cultural: Una visión de la modernización de México*. Mexico City: Fondo de Cultura Económica, 1994.

Trevisan, João Silvério. *Devassos no paraíso*. São Paulo: Max Limonad, 1986.

Trigo, Abril. "General Introduction." In Sarto, Ríos, and Trigo, *Latin American Cultural Studies Reader*, 1–14.

———. *Memorias migrantes: Testimonios y ensayos sobre la diáspora uruguaya*. Rosario, Argentina: Beatriz Viterbo, 2003.

Turner, Victor. *The Anthropology of Performance*. New York: Performance Arts Journal Press, 1988.

———. *Dramas, Fields, and Metaphors: Symbolic Action in Human Society*. Ithaca, N.Y.: Cornell University Press, 1978.

———. *The Ritual Process: Structure and Anti-Structure*. London: Routledge & Kegan Paul, 1969.

Valenzuela Arce, José Manuel. *¡A la Brava Ese! Cholos, punks, chavos, banda*. Tijuana: Colegio de la Frontera Norte, 1988.

———, ed. *Los estudios culturales en México*. Mexico City: Fondo de Cultura Económica, 2003.

———. *Impecable y diamantina: La reconstrucción del discurso nacional*. Tijuana: Colegio de la Frontera Norte; Tlaquepaque: Instituto Tecnológico de Estudios Superiores del Occidente, 1999.

———. *Nuestros piensos: Culturas populares en la frontera México-Estados Unidos*. Mexico City: Consejo Nacional para la Cultura y las Artes, 1998.

Vargas Llosa, Mario. *El hablador*. Barcelona: Seix Barral, 1987.

Vasconcelos, José. *La raza cósmica*. 1925. Mexico City: Espasa Calpe, 1948.

Vattimo, Gianni, José M. Mardones, Iñaki Urdanibia, Manuel Fernández del Riesgo, Michel Maffesoli, Fernando Savater, Josetxo Beriain, and Patxi Lanceros. *En torno a la posmodernidad*. Barcelona: Anthropos, 1994.

Vázquez García, Francisco, and Andrés Moreno Mengíbar. *Sexo y razón: Una genealogía de la moral sexual en España (siglos XVI–XX)*. Madrid: Akal Universitaria, 1997.

Vera Cruz, Alonso de la. *De dominio infidelium et iusto bello: Texto bilingüe*. Translated by Roberto Heredia Correa. Mexico City: Universidad Nacional Autónoma de México, 2000.

Vidal, Hernán. "Postmodernism, Postleftism, and Neo-Avant-Gardism: The Case of Chile's *Revista de Crítica Cultural*." In Beverley, Aronna, and Oviedo, *Postmodernism Debate in Latin America*, 282–306.

———. "Restaurar lo político, imperativo de los estudios literarios y culturales latinoamericanistas." In Moraña, *Nuevas perspectivas desde/sobre América Latina*, 139–46.

Vieira, Else Ribeiro Pires. "Liberating Calibans: Readings of *Antropofagia* and Haroldo de Campos' Poetics of Transcreation." In *Post-Colonial Translation: Theory and Practice*, edited by Susan Bassnett and Harish Trivedi, 95–113. London: Routledge, 1999.

Viñas, David. *Cuerpo a cuerpo*. Mexico City: Siglo XXI, 1979.

Vinkler, Beth Joan. "The Anthropophagic Mother/Other: Appropriated Identities in Oswald de Andrade's 'Manifesto Antropófago.'" *Luso-Brasilian Review* 34, no. 1 (1997): 105–11.

Viveiros de Castro, Eduardo. Interview. *Revista Azougue: Saque/Dádiva*, special edition 2006–8, 23–36. http://blogs.cultura.gov.br/culturaepensamento/files/2010/10/revista-AZOUGUE-2006-2008.pdf.

Voekel, Pamela. *Alone Before God: The Religious Origins of Modernity in Mexico*. Durham, N.C.: Duke University Press, 2002.

Vološinov, Valentin Nikolaievich. *Marxism and the Philosophy of Language*. Translated by Ladislav Matejka and I. R. Titunik. Cambridge, Mass.: Harvard University Press, 1986.

Wallerstein, Immanuel. *The Modern World-System*. 3 vols. New York: Academic Press, 1974–89.

Walsh, Catherine, ed. *Estudios culturales latinoamericanos: Retos desde y sobre la región andina*. Quito: Universidad Andina Simón Bolivar/Abya-Yala, 2003.

———. *Pensamiento crítico y matriz (de)colonial: Reflexiones latinoamericanas*. Quito: Universidad Andina Simón Bolivar/Abya-Yala, 2005.

Warner, Michael, ed. *Fear of a Queer Planet: Queer Politics and Social Theory*. Minneapolis: University of Minnesota Press, 1993.

Weeks, Jeffrey. *Sexuality*. 2nd ed. New York: Routledge, 2003.

Weinberg, Liliana. "Ensayo y transculturación." *Cuadernos Americanos*, no. 96 (2002): 31–47.

Weisz, Gabriel. *El juego viviente: Indagación sobre las partes ocultas del objeto lúdico*. Mexico City: Siglo XXI, 1986.

West, Candace, and Don H. Zimmerman. "Doing Gender." *Gender and Society* 1, no. 2 (1987): 125–51.

White, Hayden. *Metahistory: The Historical Imagination in Nineteenth-Century Europe*. Baltimore: Johns Hopkins University Press, 1973.

Williams, Gareth. *The Other Side of the Popular: Neoliberalism and Subalternity in Latin America*. Durham, N.C.: Duke University Press, 2002.

Williams, Raymond. "Base and Superstructure in Marxist Cultural Theory." *New Left Review* 1, no. 82 (November–December 1973): 3–16.

———. *Culture and Society: Coleridge to Orwell*. London: Hogarth Press, 1982.

———. *Keywords: A Vocabulary of Culture and Society*. Oxford: Oxford University Press, 1983.

———. *Marxism and Literature*. Oxford: Oxford University Press, 1977.

World Bank. *Culture Counts: Financing, Resources, and the Economics of Culture in Sustainable Development: Proceedings of the Conference*. Washington, D.C., 1999.

Xavier, Ismail. *Allegories of Underdevelopment: Aesthetics and Politics in Modern Brazilian Cinema*. Minneapolis: University of Minnesota Press, 1997.

Yelvington, Kevin. "Dislocando la diáspora: La reacción al conflicto italo-etíope en el Caribe, 1935–1941." *Estudios Migratorios Latinoamericanos* 17, no. 52 (2003): 555–76.

Young, Iris Marion. *Inclusion and Democracy*. Oxford: Oxford University Press, 2000.

Young, James E. *At Memory's Edge: After-Images of the Holocaust in Contemporary Art and Architecture*. New Haven, Conn.: Yale University Press, 2002.

Young, Robert J. C. *Colonial Desire: Hybridity in Theory, Culture, and Race*. London: Routledge, 1995.

Yúdice, George. "Contrapunteo estadounidense/latinoamericano de los estudios culturales." In Mato, *Estudios y otras prácticas*, 339–52.

———. *The Expediency of Culture: Uses of Culture in the Global Era*. Durham, N.C.: Duke University Press, 2003.

———. "From Hybridity to Policy: For a Purposeful Cultural Studies." In García Canclini, *Consumers and Citizens*, ix–xxxviii.

———. "La industria de la música en el marco de la integración América Latina–Estados Unidos." In *Integración económica e industrias culturales en América Latina*, edited by Néstor García Canclini and Carlos Moneta, 115–61. Mexico City: Grijalbo, 1999.

Zalce Martínez, Graciela, Luzelena Gutiérrez de Velasco, and Ana Rosa Domenella, eds. *Femenino/masculino en las literaturas de América: Escrituras de contraste*. Mexico City: Aldus/Universidad Autónoma Metropolitana–Iztapalapa, 2005.

Zamora, Lois Parkinson, and Wendy B. Faris, eds. *Magical Realism: Theory, History, Community*. Durham, N.C.: Duke University Press, 1995.

Zanetti, Susana. "Algunas consideraciones sobre el canon literario latinoamericano." In Cella, *Dominios de la literatura*, 87–105.

Zea, Leopoldo. *El problema de la identidad latinoamericana*. Mexico City: UNAM, 1985.

Zevallos, Juan. "Baile, comida y música en la construcción de una identidad cultural subalterna andina en el exilio norteamericano." In Rodríguez, *Convergencia de tiempos*, 365–80.

Žižek, Slavoj. "Introduction: The Spectre of Ideology." In *Mapping Ideology*, 1–33. London: Verso, 1994.

———. *Looking Awry: An Introduction to Jacques Lacan through Popular Culture*. Cambridge, Mass.: MIT Press, 1991.

———. "Multiculturalism, or, The Cultural Logic of Multinational Capitalism." *New Left Review* 1, no. 225 (September–October 1997): 28–51.

———, ed. *Revolution at the Gates: A Selection of Writings from February to October 1917*, by V. I. Lenin. Verso: London, 2002.

———. *The Sublime Object of Ideology*. London: Verso, 1989.

Contributors

Editors

Robert McKee Irwin is chair of the Cultural Studies Graduate Group and professor of Spanish at the University of California–Davis.

Mónica Szurmuk is research professor at the National Council of Science and Technology of Argentina (CONICET).

Authors

Carlos Aguirre is professor of Latin American history at the University of Oregon.

Valeria Añón teaches Latin American literature and popular and mass culture at the Universidad de Buenos Aires.

Nara Araújo was a professor at the Universidad Autónoma Metropolitana in Mexico City until her death in 2009.

Marisa Belausteguigoitia is the director of the Programa Universitario de Estudios de Género at the Universidad Nacional Autónoma de México.

Rebecca E. Biron is professor of Latin American literature at Dartmouth College.

Ximena Briceño is a lecturer in Iberian and Latin American cultures at Stanford University.

Marta Cabrera directs the Master's Program in Cultural Studies at the Pontificia Universidad Javeriana in Bogotá.

Debra A. Castillo is Distinguished Professor of Comparative Literature and Latin American Studies at Cornell University.

Maricruz Castro Ricalde is professor of humanities at the Tecnológico de Monterrey, Toluca, Mexico.

Juan Pablo Dabove is associate professor in the Department of Spanish and Portuguese at the University of Colorado in Boulder.

Claudia Darrigrandi is assistant professor in the Liberal Arts College of Universidad Adolfo Ibáñez, and postdoctoral fellow at the Universidad de Chile/Universidad Adolfo Ibáñez.

Román de la Campa is the Edwin B. and Lenore R. Williams Professor of Romance Languages at the University of Pennsylvania.

Ana Rosa Domenella is professor and researcher at the Universidad Autónoma Metropolitana–Iztapalapa in Mexico City.

Patrick Dove is associate professor of Latin American literature and culture at the University of Indiana.

Saurabh Dube is professor of history at the Centro de Estudios de Asia y África at the Colegio de México in Mexico City.

Christopher Dunn is associate professor of Brazilian literary and cultural studies at Tulane University.

Sebastiaan Faber is professor of Hispanic Studies at Oberlin College.

Héctor Fernández L'Hoeste teaches Latin American literature and culture at Georgia State University in Atlanta.

Graciela de Garay is professor and researcher in the area of oral history at the Instituto Mora in Mexico City.

María Inés García Canal is professor and researcher at the Universidad Autónoma Metropolitana–Xochimilco in Mexico City.

Gabriel Giorgi is associate professor of Spanish and Portuguese at New York University.

Leila Gómez is associate professor in the Department of Spanish and Portuguese at the University of Colorado in Boulder.

Erin Graff Zivin is associate professor of Spanish and Portuguese and comparative literature at the University of Southern California.

Luzelena Gutiérrez de Velasco is research professor at the Colegio de México in Mexico City.

Carlos Jáuregui is associate professor of Latin American literature and anthropology at the University of Notre Dame.

Kate Jenckes is associate professor in the Department of Romance Languages and Literatures at the University of Michigan.

Emeshe Juhász-Mininberg is research associate in the program Cultura, Comunicación y Transformaciones Sociales, CIPOST-FACES at the Universidad Central de Venezuela.

Michael J. Lazzara is associate professor of Latin American literature at the University of California, Davis.

Horacio Legrás teaches Latin American literature at the University of California, Irvine.

Guadalupe López Bonilla is professor and researcher at the Universidad Autónoma de Baja California, Ensenada.

Sandra Lorenzano is dean of research and graduate studies at the Universidad del Claustro de Sor Juana in Mexico City.

Desirée A. Martín is associate professor of English at the University of California, Davis.

Jesús Martín Barbero is professor and researcher in the Facultad de Comunicación y Lenguaje of the Pontificia Universidad Javeriana in Bogotá.

Alejandro Monsiváis is dean of graduate studies at El Colegio de la Frontera Norte, Tijuana.

Graciela Montaldo is professor in the Department of Latin American and Iberian Cultures of Columbia University.

Hortensia Moreno is academic coodinator of the Programa Universitario de Estudios de Género at the Universidad Nacional Autónoma de México.

Carmen Pérez Fragoso is a researcher at the Universidad Autónoma de Baja California, Ensenada.

Juan Poblete is professor of Latin American literature at the University of California, Santa Cruz.

Antonio Prieto Stambaugh is professor of theater at Universidad Veracruzana.

Isabel Quintana is professor and researcher at the Universidad de Buenos Aires and the Consejo Nacional de Investigación Científica, Educativa y Tecnológica.

José Rabasa is professor emeritus of University of California, Berkely.

Silvana Rabinovich is a researcher at the Instituto de Investigaciones Filológicas at the Universidad Nacional Autónoma de México.

Eduardo Restrepo is professor in the Department of Cultural Studies at the Pontificia Universidad Javeriana.

Cristina Rivera Garza is professor of writing at the University of California, San Diego, and the author of several works of fiction, including *Nadie me verá llorar.*

Ileana Rodríguez is Distinguished Professor at the Ohio State University.

Victoria Ruétalo teaches cultural studies at the University of Alberta.

Claudia Sadowski-Smith is associate professor of U.S. literature at Arizona State University.

Ute Seydel is professor in the Departamento de Letras Alemanas at the Universidad Nacional Autónoma de México.

Nohemy Solórzano-Thompson is Associate Provost for Diversity and Global Learning at Westminster College, Salt Lake City..

Estelle Tarica is associate professor of Latin American literature and culture in the Department of Spanish and Portuguese at the University of California, Berkeley.

Marcela Valdata is professor and researcher at the Escuela de Posgrado of the Facultad de Humanidades y Artes, Universidad Nacional de Rosario, Argentina, and coordinator of the Departamento de Investigaciones of the Museo de la Memoria de Rosario.

Felipe Victoriano teaches at the Universidad Autónoma Metropolitana–Cuajimalpa in Mexico City.

Núria Vilanova is assistant professor of language and foreign studies at American University.

Silvio Waisbord is professor in the School of Media and Public Affairs at George Washington University.

Liliana Weinberg is researcher at the Centro de Estudios de América Latina, and professor at the Facultad de Filosofía y Letras, at the Universidad Nacional Autónoma de México.

Rosalía Winocur is professor and researcher in the Department of Education and Communications at the Universidad Autónoma Metropolitana–Xochimilco in Mexico City.

Ana Wortman is professor in the Department of Sociology and researcher of cultural studies at the Instituto Gino Germani, Universidad de Buenos Aires.

George Yúdice is professor in the Department of Modern Languages and Literatures at the University of Miami.

Index

www.ingramcontent.com/pod-product-compliance
Lightning Source LLC
Chambersburg PA
CBHW020452270326
41926CB00008B/570

* 9 7 8 0 8 1 3 0 6 0 8 7 3 *